Jewish Social Ethics

Other Works by David Novak

Law and Theology in Judaism I
Law and Theology in Judaism II
Suicide and Morality
The Image of the Non-Jew in Judaism
Halakhah in a Theological Dimension
Jewish Christian Dialogue:
        A Jewish Justification

JEWISH SOCIAL ETHICS

DAVID NOVAK

New York   Oxford
OXFORD UNIVERSITY PRESS
1992

Oxford University Press

Oxford   New York   Toronto
Delhi   Bombay   Calcutta   Madras   Karachi
Kuala Lumpur   Singapore   Hong Kong   Tokyo
Nairobi   Dar es Salaam   Cape Town
Melbourne   Auckland

and associated companies in
Berlin   Ibadan

Copyright © 1992 by David Novak

Published by Oxford University Press, Inc.
200 Madison Avenue, New York, New York 10016

Oxford is a registered trademark of Oxford University Press

Library of Congress Cataloging-in-Publication Data
Novak, David, 1941–
Jewish social ethics / David Novak.
p.   cm.   Includes bibliographical references and index.
ISBN 0-19-506924-2
1. Judaism and social problems.   2. Natural law.
3. Social ethics.   4. Ethics, Jewish.
5. Judaism — 20th century.   I. Title.
HN40.J5N68   1992   303.3′72′089924 — dc20   91-46041

2 4 6 8 9 7 5 3 1

Printed in the United States of America
on acid-free paper

To the faculty and students of
The Institute of Traditional Judaism

"Give me Yavneh and her sages"

Preface

It was quite an honor when Cynthia Read, my editor at Oxford University Press, pleased with the reception of my 1989 book *Jewish-Christian Dialogue: A Jewish Justification*, asked me to submit material for a new book. The eleven essays herein have been put together for that purpose. All of them have been published in the past eight years or so, and all of them deal with "Jewish social ethics" as I define that term in the introduction.

It has been gratifying to be able to assemble the essays in one volume, and even more gratifying to attempt a presentation of the most coherent and comprehensive statement of my theological ethics or political theology to date. Because of this intent, I have written an introduction to this collection in which I give an outline of my basic Jewish position on this overall subject. Furthermore, I have thoroughly revised each essay in order that each one may be a more current statement of what I think and, also, to be more consistent with the rest of the collection as a whole. Finally, I have tried, as much as possible, to provide cross references among the chapters in the notes.

The first three chapters deal with the idea of natural law in the context of Judaism. It is my conviction that this idea is indigenous to the normative Jewish tradition (even if the terms *physis* and *natura* are not), and that its location and explication do much to uncover the intelligibility of the tradition as it pertains to interhuman relationships. Moreover, this idea enables Jewish thinkers to speak with authenticity and cogency in cross-cultural ethical discourse in today's world. For this reason, I have entered the philosophical debate over natural law and have critically engaged current opinions about it held by both Jewish and non-Jewish thinkers. Accordingly, I have disagreed with Jewish thinkers like Leo Strauss, Marvin Fox, and José Faur, as well as a Christian thinker like John Courtney Murray, while agreeing with a secular thinker like Giorgio Del Vecchio and a Christian thinker like Paul Tillich — and I have done so from what seems to me a major strand of rabbinic doctrine.

Grateful acknowledgment is made to the *Jewish Law Annual* for permission to use a revised version of "Natural Law, Halakhah and the Covenant," which appeared in volume 7; to *Soundings* for permission to use a revised version of "Theonomous Ethics: A Defense and a Critique of Tillich," which appeared in volume 69; and to Wm. B. Eerdmans Publishing Company for permission to use a revised version of "John Courtney Murray, S.J.: A Jewish Appraisal," which appeared in the volume *John Courtney Murray and the American Civil Conversation*.

Chapters 4 and 5 deal with the issues of human embodiedness as raised by sexuality in general (which has become so much more of a political question now than it was before), and by the social significance of the AIDS epidemic. These chapters have come here in the book's sequence because I believe the question of sexuality, both generally and particularly at this point in our history, lies at the core of what we mean by life together with others in human society.

Grateful acknowledgment is made to the Center for Judaic Studies at the University of Denver for permission to use a revised version of "Some Aspects of Sex, Society and God in Judaism," which appeared in the volume *Contemporary Ethical Issues in the Jewish and Christian Traditions*; and to B'nai B'rith International for permission to use a revised version of "The Problem of AIDS in a Jewish Perspective," which appeared in the volume *Frontiers of Jewish Thought*.

Chapters 6 and 7 deal with environmental issues, especially as epitomized by the nuclear threat. These chapters have come here in the sequence of the book because I believe social thought today, more than ever before, is directly affected by our relationship with the whole ecosphere.

Grateful acknowledgment is made to the Simon Wiesenthal Center for permission to use a revised version of "Nuclear War and the Prohibition of Wanton Destruction," which appeared in the volume *Confronting Omnicide*; and to *Research in Philosophy and Technology* for permission to use a revised version of "Technology and Its Ultimate Threat: A Jewish Meditation," which appeared in volume 10.

Chapters 8, 9, and 10 deal with the three issues of most political significance in this book: criminal justice, the treatment of minorities, and the creation of wealth. In this sense, they have been the most ambitious (or, perhaps, most foolhardy) efforts by one, who by all accounts, is certainly a political amateur. Nevertheless, a "social" ethics, Jewish or otherwise, could hardly be expected to be taken seriously without some such discussion.

Grateful acknowledgment is made to the American Jewish Committee's Institute of Human Relations for permission to use a revised version of "Violence in Our Society: Some Jewish Insights," which it first published as a pamphlet; to *S'vara: A Journal of Philosophy and Judaism* for permission to use a large excerpt from *"Lex Talionis*: A Maimonidean Perspective on Scripture, Tradition and Reason," which appeared in volume 2; to the Program in Judaic Studies at Brown University for permission to use a revised version of "Non-Jews in a Jewish Polity: Subject or Sovereign?" which appeared in the Festschrift for Professor Marvin Fox; and to the Institute for Contemporary Studies for permission to use a revised version of "Economics and Justice:

A Jewish Example," which appeared in the volume *The Capitalist Spirit: Toward a Religious Ethic of Wealth Creation*.

The last chapter deals with the issue of being a faithful Jew participating in American public life. I have chosen it as the conclusion because it presents my own Jewish rationale for being a social ethicist in the state of which I am a citizen and where, therefore, my political views are most appropriately expressed. Grateful acknowledgment is made to Wm. B. Eerdmans Publishing Company for permission to use a revised version of "American Jews and America: The Mission of Israel Revisited," which appeared in the volume *Jews in Unsecular America*.

When I published my first book some eighteen years ago (*Law and Theology in Judaism* I), I thanked my wife, Melva, for the type of home she has made for our family, and I acknowledged our children Marianne and Jacob, who were then "too young to have offered any tangible help," and whom "I look[ed] forward to learning with." In this book I have even more reason to thank my wife again for our home and for the contributions of her thoughts on the issues I discuss. And our children, who are now adults, both enthusiastically involved in public life, have let me learn not only *with* them but *from* them as well. Our discussions of many of the points of this book have greatly enriched my own thinking. This has also been the case with what I have learned from my students in various academic, religious, and cultural settings.

I have gained many insights, both general and specific, from conversations with many friends and colleagues. In preparing this preface the following names are particularly vivid: Gerald Blidstein, Eugene Borowitz, James Childress, Marc Gellman, Mary Ann Glendon, Lenn Goodman, Bernard Jackson, Robert Jenson, George Lindbeck, Richard John Neuhaus, Peter Ochs, Kenneth Seeskin, Chaim Waxman, and George Weigel. My thanks to all of them and others.

This book is dedicated to the faculty and students of the Institute of Traditional Judaism in Mount Vernon, New York, with whom I have been deeply involved from the very beginning. At a time when monumental changes are taking place before our eyes in the world at large and in the Jewish religious world, the Institute has become the true locus of my spiritual and intellectual life as a Jew. For this I give thanks to God. And I make special dedicatory mention of two colleagues and friends who lead the Institute: the rector, the incomparable Talmudist, Professor David Weiss Halivni, and the visionary and indefatigable dean, Rabbi Ronald Price.

Charlottesville, Virginia   D. N.
January 1992

Contents

Jewish Social Ethics

Introduction

What Is Jewish Social Ethics and Why?

The term "Jewish social ethics" does not designate any specific category of thought delineated in classical Jewish literature. It cannot be located by any particular reference to the data of the Jewish past. Rather, it is a term I have borrowed to designate my own reading of the normative Jewish tradition in order to uncover some of its vast riches so they might enter into discussions of the important ethical issues concerning society in today's increasingly cross-cultural world. And although the independence of the normative Jewish tradition must be vigilantly maintained, its voice should not be silent in the discussions because those faithful to the tradition, for better or for worse, are participating more and more in the world and these discussions are having greater effect on the lives of everyone. To keep the voice of our tradition silent strongly suggests that the tradition has nothing to say about vital social questions. That, of course, defames its truth and, ultimately, the One whom the tradition acknowledges as its prime authority.[1]

My reading of the normative Jewish tradition is selective but responsible, for the tradition is where I live. I am not looking in *at* it as would a tourist passing by; I am looking out *from* it onto the larger world on its horizon. Even when I seem to venture away from it at times, speaking the often strange language of the larger world, it is the home to which I must ever return, and where I must regularly answer whether I have spoken the tradition's truth in the world.

My selection from the tradition is regulated by what I judge to be its most appropriate truths for the larger world in its quest for justice. Further, by entering some of the tradition's riches into the ethical discussions in this larger world, I am prepared to learn as well as teach because my reading of the tradition's sources is basically philosophical — and philosophy is an activity that can be done well only in an atmosphere of dialogue, that is, mutually informed and informing discourse.[2] Philosophically attuned theologians throughout Jewish history have affirmed Judaism's ultimate truth, not its exclusive truth.[3] We have been open to truth's other localities without surrendering or relativizing our own. Therefore, entering these discussions has ramifications for inter-Jewish dialogue too.

Finally, by entering some of the tradition's riches into the ethical discussion of the larger world, I am prepared to argue as well as teach and learn, for philosophy is also a dialectical activity, in which one must be prepared to defend a position against the misunderstandings of both outsiders and insiders. In this book there is considerable argument against alternative positions on the various issues I discuss: those contrary to general truth, those less appropriate than Judaism's singular truth, and interpretations of Judaism itself that are either inadequate to its sources or insufficient for their proper discussion in contemporary society.

Most traditionalist Jewish thinkers who are willing to enter the riches of the Jewish tradition into the contemporary ethical discussions have an unfortunate tendency to confuse what I call here Jewish social ethics with applied Jewish ethics, what the tradition calls *halakhah le-ma'aseh*. When ethical issues are raised, they assume that immediately practical answers are being sought for particular questions (*sh'elot*), and they take this as their cue to write what in effect are legal responsa (*teshuvot*). That is probably why so much of their attention has been confined to medical ethics: it is so much more case-oriented than other areas of contemporary ethics.

Now, if and when immediately practical answers are being sought for particular cases at hand (*ma'aseh*), then a responsum is surely required. In such instances traditional Jews can be governed only by the practical rules of Halakhah.[4] (In this book, the closest I come to responsum-type writing, in which I have been involved for many years, is in the chapter on AIDS.) However, the ethical issues being raised in contemporary discussions are most often more general questions of policy or attitude rather than particular cases calling for the application of specific rules. They are more philosophical questions of what is good and to be done than they are legal questions of what is lawful and ought to be done here and now.

Moreover, the method of responsa presupposes that both the questioner and the respondent are members of the same normative community, both regarding themselves as answerable to the same authority. But in the cross-cultural context of ethical (as opposed to strictly legal) discussions today, such a supposition, of course, cannot be made at all. And if it is made covertly, the exposure of the supposition makes the Jewish voice in ethical discussions lose much of its credibility, for what is being asked of Jewish tradition today, along with other normative traditions, is guidance, not governance. The normative Jewish tradition can authentically govern only in its own house. Conversely, the error of most liberal Jewish thinkers who enter cross-cultural ethical discussions is that the normative Jewish tradition governs nowhere for them. What governs nowhere cannot offer consistent guidance anywhere.

What is being called for in our contemporary ethical discussions is more the enunciation of underlying principles than any specification of immediately applicable rules. To confuse rules with principles is to commit a fundamental category error in ethics. Accordingly, the task of Jewish social ethics is not to deduce conclusions from the rules at hand but, rather, to perform the more imaginative intellectual task of attempting to gain insight into the principles that inform and guide the whole normative Jewish enterprise in dealing with political and social issues. But, nevertheless, Jewish social ethics is necessarily related to applied Jewish ethics, and it must always recognize its immediate authority for governing the actions of Jews. That must never be forgotten no matter how abstract the discussion at times becomes.

The relation of Jewish social ethics to the more explicit applied Jewish ethics is much easier to appreciate than the reverse relation. However, careful examination of the normative Jewish tradition indicates that ethical principles often have informed the formulation of halakhic rules and even the practical judgment of how they are to be applied. Furthermore, these principles can once again inform the formulation of new rules or, at least, the reformulation of the old ones. This is especially so in the ethical issues discussed in this book, for these issues, in one way or another, are questions of political policy or social attitude. Questions of political policy pertain to areas where the very political marginalization of the Jews made the normative Jewish tradition inoperative and thus cease to develop. Questions of social attitude, on the other hand, do pertain to areas where the social cohesion of the Jews still allowed the normative Jewish tradition to be largely operative and to develop. Nevertheless, the radically changed political (and economic) situation of the Jews has led to major recontextualizations of our social situation as well. Therefore, in both the areas of political policy and social attitude, major rethinking is called for. Unlike many of the aspects of the normative Jewish tradition pertaining to the relationship between Jews and God (inadequately called "ritual" by some), where there has been historical continuity between the development of Jewish life and the development of Jewish law, in most areas of political policy and even social attitude there has been a historical hiatus between the ongoing development of Jewish life and the arrested development of Jewish law.

The greater integration of Jews in the areas of political and social power in society at large, along with the new responsibilities attending to it, calls for a renewed process of ethical reflection in order to allow the normative tradition to realize its potential more fully and begin to operate in the world. This is certainly the case in the State of Israel, where as a nation Jews have at long last become politically sovereign again. But it is also the case, quite differently to be sure, in many Diaspora societies, especially in the United States, where the largest and most powerful community of Diaspora Jews is located, for here Jews, communally and individually, are very much part of the whole structure of political and social power.

Being a Jew now living in the United States and participating as a citizen in this society, I can more directly address political and social questions in the context of American life. Yet, even though I am not an Israeli citizen, I accept the Zionist assumption that Israel is a Jewish state, not just an Israeli one. Certain political and social questions raised by the establishment of a Jewish state in the land of Israel call for at least ethical reflection, if not the direct practical opinion, of all thoughtful Jews wherever they might happen to be living. Ethical reflection on these questions by a Diaspora Jew is certainly appropriate, even though directly practical opinion might very well be impertinent at times.

Ethical reflection attempts to discover the justification for and limits of political and social power. It attempts to find its true sources and its true ends. But without the informing function of ethics, the new entrance of the normative Jewish tradition into the larger world easily becomes just one more political or social factor to be contended with rather than a source of moral guidance to be sought. Without ethical reflection, which is an integral part of the Jewish tradition, the tradition simply becomes the special interest of traditional Jews most conspicuously identified with it. Instead of being the manifestation of transcendent judgment, both positively and negatively, the tradition becomes an instrument for the enhancement of political and social power for its own sake. And as for the ethical reflection of most liberal Jews, who do not have a commitment to the essential authority of the tradition, it becomes at the highest level a variety of one philosophical school or another, and at lower levels a mere reflection of more general cultural trends.

Although the normative Jewish tradition distinguishes between duties *to* God (*bayn adam la-Maqom*) and duties *to* fellow human beings (*bayn adam le-havero*), both sets of duties are considered as being *from* God. Furthermore, even duties to fellow human beings are considered as being duties to God as well.[5] Thus God is the source of both sets of duties and the direct object of those we now call "religious" and the indirect object of those we now call "moral." Accordingly, religion contains and grounds morality, but morality does not contain and ground religion. One can see this essential connection between the divine-human and interhuman realms in such Jewish institutions as the Sabbath and marriage (*qiddushin*). To use more authentically Jewish terminology, the covenant between God and Israel contains the covenants between the people of Israel themselves and their covenants with others, but not vice versa. Accordingly, Jewish ethics is essentially a theological ethics.

In this way, one can see Jewish social ethics as being a Jewish political and social theology. Indeed, one can see the most fruitful areas in which Jewish theology can now function as being the areas of political policy and social attitude, for one of the great criticisms of the modern enterprise of Jewish theology has been that its connection to the normative Jewish tradition seems either nonexistent or tenuous. A renewal among contemporary Jewish thinkers of the theological enterprise, one that concentrates its attention on political and social issues, would certainly be able to answer such charges of inauthenticity to a far greater extent than other types of Jewish theology, whose connection to the normative tradition is much weaker, for although it is not Halakhah per se, it is still clearly answerable to it and practically subordinate to its governance.

Modernity and Its Responsibilities

Jewish social ethics must be cognizant of the historical context in which it conducts its reflection; only in this way can it possibly understand what are its responsibilities. Indeed, morality, the subject matter of ethical reflection, might well be characterized as modes of responsibility, how we are to answer the various demands made upon us in the world we live in. I see the responsibilities of Jewish thinkers in social ethics as twofold.

The first responsibility, mentioned briefly at the outset of this introduction, is the responsibility to the tradition itself, the responsibility of the Jewish thinker to speak its truth. This, of course, assumes that the thinker, in our case the social thinker, believes that the normative Jewish tradition is a source of truth, indeed *the* prime source of truth in the world. What this means is that the thinker must accept the tradition as the tradition essentially accepts itself, that is, he or she must accept it as *Torah*. The tradition takes its basic norm to be response to God's voice in the event of revelation. Without this acceptance, even admitting the theological latitude the tradition has allowed in understanding the event of revelation, the thinker is always an outsider, at most a respectful tourist, looking in *at* the tradition but not looking out *from* it. To be authentic, the Jewish social thinker must minimally be a theologian who is at home in the classical sources of the normative Jewish tradition.[6] He or she must be a participant in the covenant, even seeing more universalistic issues in the covenantal matrix.

The second responsibility is to the Jewish people. There can be no Torah without the Jewish people.[7] Responsibility to one is responsibility to the other. They cannot be separated without distorting both. The responsibility to the Jewish people is of two kinds: vertical and horizontal. Vertically, there is the responsibility to the Jewish people with whom the thinker is connected by historical continuity. This means that the Torah is mediated by a process of transmission, that it is passed down *through* tradition. For this reason, the voice of the Torah is never heard by Jews outside the context of this traditional transmission (*masoret*). If the full import of this is taken seriously today — what is involved in the classic Jewish doctrine of the Oral Tradition (*Torah she-b'al peh*) — then there is a responsibility to understand the historical contexts of the various utterances of the Torah's truth. We have a responsibility to take and implement the new investigative procedures for uncovering history offered to us by the modern world.[8] Nevertheless, this does not lead to relativism or historicism, as many traditionalists still seem to fear, for a vertical responsibility to the historical continuity of the Jewish people as the covenanted people of God means that we regard history as the *medium* for the transmission of the Torah *to us*, not as Torah itself. Torah is the word of God, whereas history, like nature, is a created effect of that word. By designating the 613 commandments of Scripture (*Torah she-bi-khtav*) and a small number of ancient practices (*halakhot*) as essentially immutable, the normative tradition has designated certain elementary data as being capable of intact transmission. Thus the active process of imaginative human interpretation,

implementation, and even supplementation of the Torah is ultimately subordinate to the passive process of obedient acceptance (*qabbalah*) of the Torah as
the word of God.

Horizontally, there is a responsibility to the Jewish people with whom the
thinker lives and works here and now. One must identify with their present
concerns and then see them as at least entailing the ethical concerns of the
larger world. In the area of social ethics, one can see three modern Jewish
concerns that must be addressed responsibly by the thinker. And, of course,
any concern that calls for responsibility also offers the temptation of irresponsibility.

The first modern Jewish concern to be addressed is that of political and
social Emancipation. In most parts of the modern world Jews are surely more
active participants in larger political and social orders than the more passive
resident-aliens they were in pre-Emancipation times. In the State of Israel
Jews are participants in a political and social order of their own, for which
they can now claim political sovereignty—although that claim is tempered in
an age of increasing international dependence. What responsibility does the
concern of Emancipation bring, and with what irresponsibility does it tempt
us? Let us take the latter question first. Irresponsibility, alas, is frequently
more apparent.

The political and social reality of Emancipation has brought two kinds of
Jewish irresponsibility, of which the Jewish thinker must be aware in order to
overcome them. The first irresponsibility has been the uncritical acceptance of
Emancipation, especially by intellectuals enchanted by the Enlightenment,
which made Emancipation possible. The more radical intellectuals, from the
late eighteenth century on, have been so enchanted by the Enlightenment that
they have been willing to see Judaism as something totally past, something
totally overcome by progress: the eager rush of the present *away from* the
past *into* the attraction of its own projected future. For them, the overcoming
of Judaism has been a moral imperative. In many ways, this has been the
Jewish version of the blasphemy "God is dead," proclaimed by Hegel, Nietzsche, and others.[9] This radical irresponsibility has called for the spiritual and
cultural suicide of the Jewish people. The Jewish thinker must counter this
irresponsibility on general ethical as well as specifically theological grounds.
On theological grounds, he or she must reaffirm the primacy of God's perpetual covenant with the living people of Israel, that God is the Lord of history
both past and future. "I am the first and I am the last; besides Me there is no
god" (Isaiah 44:6). In this case, the thinker must acknowledge that progress as
the human projection of future history is not autonomous. On ethical
grounds, the Jewish social thinker must argue that the spiritual and cultural
suicide of any tradition is not conducive to any greater universal good, that
suicide of any kind is evil, and evil does not bring good as its result.

But even less radical Jewish intellectuals, from the eighteenth century on,
have been enchanted enough by the Enlightenment to think that Jewish tradition can still survive as a part of a larger universal whole. They have attempted
to argue that Jews are simply a group of individuals in a larger group of

individuals, or simply one nation among many. By a variety of devices, from the philosophically sophisticated to the jingoistic, less radical Jewish intellectuals have attempted to justify the continued existence of Jewish tradition by criteria more fundamental than it itself. Although not as immediately irresponsible as the more radical advocates of spiritual and cultural suicide, their enchantment is nonetheless ultimately irresponsible to the Jewish tradition. On theological grounds, it is irresponsible to the tradition because it changes the tradition's fundamental claim to be *the* source of truth (*torat emet*) into a claim to be simply a partial source of truth in terms of some other criterion of truth itself. On ethical grounds, it is inauthentic because it insists on Jewish particularism — be it "Jewish genius" or "Jewish peoplehood" — even when the universalistic criteria it accepts call for the transcendence of such particularism. Particularism of this kind, unlike the transcendence of the general world by the singularity of the Jewish covenant with God, can be presented only as ethnocentricity or chauvinism.

It was clear to most traditional Jews, from the earliest days of Emancipation, that even the less-radical enchanted subordination to the Enlightenment of liberals (who often looked to forms of individualism for justification) and the advocates of secular Jewish "culture" (who often looked to forms of collectivism for justification) was inauthentic to the independent continuity of Jewish tradition. However, their antithetical reaction to the modern Jewish radicalism they rightly feared and suspected was to deny the new political and social reality and assume that they would immediately recover the authenticity of the Jewish past, a past they often romanticized. Thus, whereas the radicals could proclaim with Schiller that the new age's "magic had bound together what the old tradition (*die Mode*) had kept so far apart," the traditionalist reaction was epitomized by the motto of the early nineteenth-century Hungarian rabbinical leader Moses Schreiber (*Hatam Sofer*), "the new is prohibited (*asur*) by the Torah."[10]

Such radical denial, although not irresponsible to the tradition itself (but only myopic about it, perhaps), has been irresponsible to the modern concern of the Jewish people with their political and social liberation. Because of radically new economic, political, and even social realities for the Jews in the world after the Emancipation, Jews are participants in a new, unprecedented order. Even the desire for withdrawal from this order, which has characterized again and again a large segment of traditional Jewry, is one that must be negotiated with this new political and social order. But to do this, antimodern Jews have had to reconstitute themselves as a political and social special interest group in modern secular societies. In exchange for what they see as the religiously authentic return to the insulation of the Jewish past, they have had to adopt basically secular political and social strategies for what they perceive as their collective survival. Accordingly, in their political and social dealings, and especially their intense economic dealings with the outside world, they have too often regarded the normative Jewish tradition as something to be protected *from* the modern world rather than as something to be brought *into* it. Therefore, they have essentially denied its governance and its guidance in major areas of their own lives. In this sense, they have been irresponsible to the concerns of the Jewish people here and now by living in the modern world, benefiting from it and simultaneously divorcing political policy and social attitude from being constituted by a more imaginative theological and ethical reflection on the tradition than they are willing to conduct. One cannot engage in authentic reflection in areas of life that are taken to be worthy only of manipulation.

In this area of modern Jewish concern, then, the responsibility of the Jewish social thinker is carefully to avoid the extremes of capitulation to the modern world on the one hand and the manipulation of it on the other. This must be done with all the resources of learning, reason, and experience he or she can muster. The truth is that despite the many problems and frustrations brought by political and social liberation, the overwhelming majority of Jews regard it as having brought them opportunities that they certainly have no desire to lose. Even the traditional Jews who romanticize the simple piety of pre-Emancipation ghetto Jewry demonstrate little or no concomitant desire to return to the greater economic and political vulnerability of pre-Emancipation times. Modernity does not seem to be reversible.[11] Our responsibility is to regard it as a challenge to our powers of critical judgment and our imaginative rereading of the normative Jewish tradition.

The second modern Jewish concern to be addressed is that of the Holocaust. The difference between the Jews who personally—that is, physically—survived the Nazi genocide and the Jews who were not directly exposed to it is one of degree, not of kind. The truth is that all living Jews are spiritual survivors of the Holocaust, that all of us today still live in its dark shadow. All of us are "the saved remnant [sh'erit] of the house of Israel" (Isaiah 46:3). Here again we must ask: What responsibility does our survivorship bring and with what irresponsibility does it tempt us?

The irresponsibility our survivorship tempts us with is to assume that being survivors forever dispenses us from any further moral responsibility. This is fundamentally to confuse being a victim with being a survivor. Only the dead or those who have no control of their lives are dispensed from moral responsibility because they have no true choices at all.[12] The fact is that when we were their victims, the Nazi murderers and their eager accomplices did not offer us any choices at all. In the past, conversely, our medieval Christian and Muslim conquerors frequently offered us the choice of conversion to their faith; our ancient pagan conquerors, the choice of being their slaves. These previous conquerors, cruel as they were, still assumed our essential humanity and our moral personality by calling for our choice—gruesome as it was. But the Nazi program of extermination, the "Final Solution" (Endlösung), assumed that its victims were subhuman (Untermenschen). No choice was offered, for they saw no human beings before them to make one. The only choice Jews had was to survive by escaping the clutches of their imminent murderers. As we know now, six million did not succeed in that choice.

Under these extraordinary circumstances, for which no Jew could be truly prepared, the choice was premoral, the raw biological inclination to live and not die. Because the choice was premoral, those who did not personally face it cannot exercise any moral judgment. To do so is to commit the sin of arrogant self-righteousness. We do not have the right to judge how any physical survivor of the Holocaust survived—indeed, to even raise the question to him or her.[13] It is the survivor's privilege to tell us or not. It is our duty to listen to what is said or not said.

Nevertheless, the truth is that we are no longer helpless victims. That is what our survivorship, both collectively and individually, most immediately means. Hence, our duty is to reassert happily our moral responsibility and accept eagerly the renewed moral responsibility brought by power and the availability again of real choices in the world. Yet we know what the psychological scars of victimhood remain long after physical danger has departed. We still have our nightmares. That can be expected. What ought not be accepted, however, is the attempt to formulate political policy and social attitude based on the psychological effects of victimhood, for that is not the confrontation with the real world as it exists here and now, the only situation that calls for our moral responsibility, a responsibility that can be exercised only in the present. Rather, it is the cynical cultivation of paranoia by some to enable their political power and social influence to escape any moral judgment, any ethical limitation. There is a fundamental difference between recognizing and being prepared for real danger (of which there is still plenty lurking for Jews) and essentially defining one's identity by danger itself.

In this area of modern Jewish concern, the responsibility of the Jewish thinker is to be acutely aware of the conditions that made the Nazi program of extermination morally possible for its perpetrators, that is, how they could convince themselves and their sympathizers they were doing good, not evil. This requires the Jewish thinker to accept fully the historical fact that although our people were the prime victims of the Holocaust, we were not the only victims. The thinker can thus anticipate the probability that other peoples as well as the Jewish people could be victims again of some future Holocaust. To regard Jews as the only victims is to assume that Jews are a separate species and genocide is not, therefore, a human issue. But, then, was that not the logic of our murderers?

Usually, attempts to condemn the Holocaust on moral grounds judge the Nazi perpetrators to be immoral. They surely committed the sin of murder on the most ghastly scale. Yet they were unlike ordinary murderers, who are aware they are violating a moral rule and rationalize their acts by some private notion of what is their own good. Rather, the Nazis made an ontological judgment before they exercised an actual moral choice. They judged that the Jews are not human beings at all, and that the Jews pose an impersonal, subhuman threat to those who truly are human beings. In their eyes, then, they were not committing an immoral act at all; rather, they were protecting their own survival and that of all humankind. Killing a subhuman danger to human life (Jews were often portrayed as infected and infecting vermin) is not something morally debatable. Moreover, this type of ontological judgment was exercised even before the Final Solution of "the Jewish problem" in the designation of many mentally incapacitated *Germans* as "life unworthy of life" (*Unwerteslebensleben*). Therefore, in ethical terms, the fundamental condition that made the Holocaust a moral possibility for the Nazis was an ontological judgment that they assumed they alone could make. They alone assumed the power and right to declare *who* is an object of moral concern and *what* is not. Personalization and depersonalization became, for them, arbitrary.

Based upon this observation and reflection, then, the responsibility of the surviving Jewish thinker is to look to the ontological foundations of Jewish ethics and law to insure that Jews themselves will not make similar misjudgments of truth and be led thereby to inauthentic moral choices of what is good and inauthentic legal rulings of what is lawful. Now, to many it may seem outrageous that I would even suggest that Jews are threatened with the same temptations as were those who devised our extermination. Yet I would remind such critics that in classical Jewish literature from the Bible on it was vigorously asserted that our suffering did not deprive us of our moral personality, that we are always more concerned with our own capacity to sin than with that of others, primarily because we can make only our own moral choices not theirs.[14] To others we can offer only guidance; to ourselves we must reiterate commandments and, optimally, their reasons as well. The responsibility of the Jewish thinker in the area of social ethics is to confirm the Jewish teaching that whenever a moral choice can be made, the person is essentially an active subject, not a passive victim. And it must explicate that the persons who are the objects of our moral choice are objects of our response, not the projections of our own will.

The third modern Jewish concern to be addressed is the reestablishment of Jewish national sovereignty brought about by the founding of the State of Israel and its growth as a Jewish society. This has profoundly affected every Jew in the world, whether an Israeli citizen or not. We cannot think of the contemporary Jewish situation for very long without our concern for the State of Israel being felt. Here again we must ask: What responsibility does our national restoration bring, and what irresponsibility does it tempt us with?

The irresponsibility our national restoration tempts us with is closely related to the irresponsibility our survivorship of the Holocaust tempts us with, that is, to define ourselves as essentially the victims of the crimes of others against us. The obverse of this outlook is to define ourselves as essentially the beneficiaries of the largesse of others. This irresponsibility is a temptation because of the historical juxtaposition of the end of the Holocaust in 1945 and the founding of the State of Israel in 1948. Many Jews have been tempted to see a direct causal connection between the two events and to draw a moral conclusion from it. The moral conclusion they frequently draw is that the State of Israel is our deserved recompense from the world for our great suffering and loss, to which the world was largely indifferent if not actually approving.

Such a conclusion is both historically untrue and morally irresponsible. It is historically untrue because it assumes that our political sovereignty is something others have given us rather than something we essentially regained by ourselves. Surely, Zionism has been the supreme modern Jewish effort to restore our political and social responsibility, to make Jews more active and less passive in the world. And the conclusion is morally irresponsible because it looks to the largesse of the world to give our sovereignty to us rather than to the commandment of God that we regain it and reconstitute it for ourselves.[15] This view, then, causes us to direct our attention away from the real responsibilities that come with political sovereignty. The responsibilities are basically twofold.

First, we are now responsible for reconstituting a Jewish society in the land of Israel that allows the principles of Jewish ethics truly to inform application of the rules of Jewish law. But, unhappily, what we have seen too much of is that those who are most steeped in the normative Jewish tradition regard the secular Jewish state and society only as manipulable instruments to protect their interests as political parties. We have often seen the most self-serving interpretations of Jewish law imaginable and the almost total absence of authentic Jewish ethical reflection. "Those who grab [*tofsay*] the Torah did not know Me" (Jeremiah 2:8). This has largely come about, it seems to me, because the religious establishments have adopted a siege mentality, seeing themselves as victims not of gentile enemies but of the vast majority of the Jewish people trying to eliminate them — at least culturally. They, even more than the secularists, have exacerbated divisions and suspicions among the Jewish people, acts that the tradition itself regards as evil.[16]

To be sure, there are secularist elements who do want to eliminate Jewish religion and create a secular Jewish culture. However, to make reaction to that threat (far weaker now than thirty or forty years ago) one's political and social *raison d'être* is to lose that transcendent perspective gained by Jewish theology — particularly Jewish political and social theology — and to become one self-serving political party and special interest group among many. "And their fear of Me has become the commandment of men learned by rote" (Isaiah 29:13). That is a major abdication of Jewish religious responsibility.

Second, we are responsible to reconstitute a Jewish society where there is the classical Jewish concern for the rights of non-Jews living amongst us to be fully protected. That can become a reality only when we thoroughly understand our duties to them. This is an area of immense responsibility and one in which we have had no practical experience since the most ancient periods of our history. Nevertheless, to abdicate this responsibility, not to rethink the status of the "sojourner" (*ger*) in our midst in the radical new political and social context in which we live, is to fall into the most dangerous of temptations: to equate ourselves with humankind per se and thus to depersonalize the non-Jews living in our state — and even outside it — however troublesome they often may be. Here again, the temptation is exacerbated by the assumption of the status of perpetual victimhood, the notion that there are no gradations in the outside world, that everyone "out there" wants us dead. That is historically untrue, for if the whole world really wanted us dead, we probably would be. It is morally irresponsible because it is prejudice, prejudging a situation simplistically; it violates the rational requirement to "be deliberate (*metunim*) in judgment."[17] And it is theologically irresponsible because it ignores the meaning of the commandment that we Jews sanctify the name of God in the world by our moral action.[18] Clearly, that means that there are elements in the outside world who can appreciate our message and, therefore, want us to live. Every gentile is not Amalek.

Jewish Social Ethics Philosophically Conceived

For any ethics to be complete — and Jewish social ethnics is certainly no exception — it has to deal with three basic questions: (1) Who are its subjects and objects? (2) What is to be done by them and for them? and (3) How is society to regulate the proper claims made by them and to them? The key concepts involved in these questions, respectively, are (1) the true; (2) the good; and (3) the lawful.

There are systems of ethics that attempt to limit their inquiry to less than the three basic questions and their key concepts. Being both a Jewish and a philosophical enterprise, Jewish social ethics must separate itself from their methods, however, on both factual and rational grounds. On factual grounds it must do so because it is evident that the normative Jewish tradition, out of which Jewish social ethics must come and back to which it must return, is very much concerned with the true, the good, and the lawful.[19] It is hoped that will be demonstrated to the reader through the detailed data from the tradition presented in this book. On rational grounds it must separate itself from the methods of the more limited ethics because the three key concepts are themselves so interrelated. It is hoped that will also be demonstrated to the reader by the methods I employ in this book to uncover the richness of the traditional data.

Most obviously, the tradition is concerned with what is lawful, with the proper claims made by the legal subjects and for the legal objects in the normative Jewish community. That is what the Halakhah is all about. In fact, the tradition regards law to be such an indispensable requirement of human life that it actually mandates Jews to accept the rule of other societies in areas of human economic and political interaction whenever Jewish society is normatively inoperative in these areas.[20] *Dura lex sed lex*: better some law than none at all. Anarchy is considered to be the most obvious threat to authentic human life in common. The epitome of evil is seen as being justified by the assertion "there is no law and there is no judge" (*layt din ve-layt dayyan*).[21] The first requirement of authentic human life in common is that there be order within it, even before it is determined just where such order comes from and what it should be striving for.

Yet to remain at this level alone is to engage in what we now call "legal positivism." Legal positivism is incomplete because it does not adequately deal with the question of what the law intends. That question cannot be eliminated because the intelligent operation of the law itself requires that we deal with three questions: (1) Why should we freely accept the law and obey it? (2) How is the law to be applied in novel situations, what we now call "hard cases"? and (3) What good is the ongoing formulation of the law to bring about?

At this point more than anywhere else, the viewpoint of natural law is appropriate in Jewish ethical reflection; I would even say necessary for its very cogency, for even though the covenant between God and Israel transcends nature, it still accepts nature as a limit (*peras*) and its own precondition.[22] Jews are human beings who have been elected through the covenant, but they are still human beings within the natural order of things.[23] Nature, constituted as the covenant's general background and horizon, is not overcome. Hence, it functions as a formal criterion of judgment *within* the covenant itself and its law.

The question of why we should accept the law and obey it can be asked only by morally free persons.[24] The question can be intelligently answered only by the judgment that the law is good for us as communal beings (*bonum commune*). That is, it is good for us as members of a community of morally free persons, even though it might at times be at variance with our individually conceived interests (*bonum sibi*). That surely assumes that we are communal beings before we are private, autonomous beings. Without that judgment of what is our common good, we can only be coerced into obeying the law. Law, then, would become essentially heteronomy, the rule of an alien force.

Coercion, of course, must at times be exercised in the conduct of social life. At times law must be experienced at least by some citizens as heteronomy. When one person or group of persons threatens the common good by actively denying the rights of others or the order of society as a whole, the survival of the common good requires nothing less than coercion. In such cases, rectification of the injustice to whomever is the good to be pursued by society as a whole in its judicial power.[25] But society as a community of morally free persons breaks down when coercion becomes the norm rather than a specific application if it, for coercion as the norm, always exercised by one group over another, is power for its own sake. And, as Hegel most astutely showed, neither slave nor master is free.[26] Hence, there is no common good between the coerced and the coercers. Each can seek only its own interest. Minimally, then, the interest of the coerced is to disobey with impunity, to seek escape, as Israel sought escape from Egypt. And the denial of the freedom of the coerced is malevolent because of the nature of denial, even if benefits come from it. Indeed, the Israelites sinned by fondly remembering how much better they ate in Egypt under Pharaoh than in the open wilderness with Moses.[27] So, if law is to be more than coercion, we must be concerned with why—that is, for the sake of what good—its subjects are to accept it and obey it.[28]

Moreover, when situations arise for which there are no real precedents, one cannot simply locate a single rule and deduce a conclusion from it in syllogistic fashion. Rather, one must judge what the *overall* purposes of the law are—what good it intends—and attempt to make a new combination of a number of old rules to decide adequately the new hard cases before us here and now.

Furthermore, Jewish law is never fully formulated. There have always been times when new decrees (*taqqanot*) have had to be issued. However, if new decrees are not to be the caprice of those having political power—which we have seen would undermine the moral authority of the law itself—then they have to be justified. Justification cannot be strictly legal. Even more than the legal judgment of new hard cases, the moral judgment involved in such legislation cannot be concluded simply by deduction.[29] Even more than legal judgment it must reflect on the overall purposes or goods of the Torah itself in order ultimately to participate in it and not compete against it. Without this, the normative continuity of the law begins to unravel.

Finally, Jewish social ethics must deal with the question of who the subjects and objects of the normative order are. This is more than a question of ethics per se. Here ethics has to look to ontology, to something even more basic than its general prescription for its ultimate validation, just as it has to look to law, to something less basic than its general prescription and more specific for its immediate practical applicability. In other words, what is good presupposes what is true, just as it entails what is lawful.

There have been various philosophical approaches, most impressively that of Kant, that see ethics as containing its own ontology rather than having to look for one above it.[30] Here it is assumed that the human subjects of ethics are necessarily acting beings. There is simply no way they can be the passive spectators of their own lives as they can be passive spectators of what is separate from their own lives. Because human subjects cannot be other than active, the task of ethics is to reflect on the structures of the activity, that is, what enables it to construct its own world in a rationally coherent manner. Ethics, then, is what governs rational self-control. However, is there not more to ethics than control? Is there not more to human reason than technology?

In the assertion of the essentially active nature of human subjects, there is much truth in the above-mentioned philosophical approaches, what some now call "prescriptivism." Much of the so-called is/ought dichotomy, namely, how does one move from description to prescription, assumes that we are looking *at* an external world as spectators before we are actors (what some call "moral agents") *in our own world*. The move here from what "is" to what "ought to be" is a quantum leap. However, a more insightful phenomenology of human existence would show that it is the other way around. That is, we constitute the active content of our own vital concerns before we constitute the passive *things* that lie away from them. Any "is" not included in a prior "ought" is itself a human abstraction. What we have lived through (*Erlebnis*) is prior to what we have passed by (*Erfahrung*).

Yet, to leave our ethical reflection at this level is to assume that we rationally constitute our own lives. Accordingly, just as the subjects of the normative order must be rational agents, so must its objects. However, that is inadequate to the legal tradition (certainly, but not exclusively, the Jewish legal tradition), which recognizes as human persons those who are not rational agents: the unborn, infants, the mentally retarded, psychotics, the senile, the comatose, and so on. It is also concerned with our nonrational relationships with our own bodies and others, with issues of sexuality and family. And it is concerned with the nonhuman realm as well, protecting the integrity of the natural order (the ecosphere) and protecting it from arbitrary human appropriation. So, if the legal tradition seems to assume a larger ontological order above it, ethics cannot dispense with that assumption without coming into more and more conflict with the legal tradition. In Judaism, this would cause ethics to lose its credibility for the normative Jewish community. The tradition's wisdom as well as it authority cannot be overlooked.

It should be more adequately assumed that *our* being as human persons — both as subjects and objects of the normative order — as well as the being of fellow nonhuman beings, is confronted before we have to act. In other words, it is there (*Dasein*) with us (*Mitsein*) in the world, and then we have to act for its sake rather than seeing it as our own projection. From this follows an ethics of responsibility — being answerable to what *presents itself to us* — rather than an ethics of basically self-reference, or the avoidance of primary responsibility by escaping into pure observation of those things we abstract from our active engagement in the world and our desire for it.[31]

In Judaism, the ontology needed for this type of reflection, which a complete ethics presupposes, is found in the theology of creation. The being that confronts us and calls us to act for its sake is presented by God's creative word and providentially sustained by it (*hashgahah*).[32] It is the continual object of God's concern. Accordingly, our tasks are neither autonomous nor heteronomous. They are not autonomous because we do not create being — ours or that of our primary environment — or the acts done for their sake. Being is received, and only afterward can we partially order it. And these tasks are not heteronomous either, for we are not being coerced by an alien power. We are, rather, being called by the Creator freely to affirm being along with him. That is our affirmation of truth. From that affirmation we accept our duty to sustain the being that is presented to us for our care. That is our responsibility to do what is good.[33] These tasks, then, are theonomous; they are what God has made for his glory that then becomes our own good.[34] Thus if the greatest commandment is to love God and along with him our fellow human creatures created in his image, then that is possible only responsively. First we have to experience God's perpetual creative love of us and for us.[35] And we can care for the rest of created being only whenever and wherever it confronts us, after we have experienced God's perpetual care of it and for it and then involve ourselves in this care as stewards.[36]

The Messianic Future

Finally, we have seen that ethics needs to see itself as validated by a higher order so as to be complete. When it attempts to construct itself out of the characteristics of its own rational subjects, it loses contact with the broader class of humanity, and the nonhuman environment beyond. It, furthermore, overestimates its own effective power in history, for it sees its task as being capable of being fulfilled by its agents themselves. By so doing, it grossly inflates their capacities and continually ignores their finitude, mortality, and fallibility. It fails to recognize how tentative moral action really is. In the normative Jewish tradition, however, it is recognized that many of our practical decisions are often doubtful (*safeq*), and what we have to do here and now might very well be shown to be wrong at the end of history.[37] In the Jewish imagination, it is Elijah, the forerunner of the Messiah and his herald, who will finally decide what is truly good, based on an insight that is superhuman.[38]

Without this hope for messianic redemption and the acceptance of the tentativeness of our actions before it finally comes, we are sorely tempted by the pseudomessianisms and utopianisms that regularly appear in history, indeed in this closing century more than ever before. These beliefs and ideologies tempt us with the promise of our own imminent redemption by the works of our own hands. They present themselves as our supreme moral task and locate that task in the larger context of history. They assume progress either by revolution or evolution. But these promises involve psychological, ethical, and theological illusions.

Psychologically, they involve illusions that inevitably lead to despair, for they promise what they cannot deliver and thereby dash the elation of those who have put their trust in them. We have all seen the cynicism of former believers in failed utopian idealogies, for whom the failure of progress has made the world a hell of absurdity. In Judaism, conversely, we can only desire a radically transformed future; we cannot ever precisely anticipate that it will actually be ours. "Oh, would it only be [*lulae*] that I could be sure to see the goodness of the Lord in the land of the living!" (Psalms 27:13).[39]

Ethically, these utopian promises inevitably involve the illusion that evil means can lead to good results. Confident of the outcome of history, the inevitable culmination of progress, and being convinced that they themselves can anticipate it and even bring it about, they tempt their believers to let the end justify almost any means to it. The believers' impatience causes them to forget that acts must be judged good or evil based on their character here and now, for we can never accurately predict their final results. The believers forget that we cannot judge the end of history, and that at the end of history we will be judged for what we did here and now. This temptation is one that ensnares secularist utopians for whom history had replaced God. But, more subtly perhaps, it also ensnares religious triumphalists, the pseudomessianists who think they can force the Messiah to come now.[40] It is a special temptation of certain forms of religious Zionism today. But in the normative Jewish tradition, ethical judgments are based on the assumption that the Messiah is not here, that moral action not be confused with eschatological longing. Indeed, the hope for a truly transcendent future helps keep the responsibilities of the present within their immanent bounds. At least here and now, a "messianic law" (*hilkhata le-meshihah*) is regarded as fantastic.[41] Authentic Jewish eschatology is an indictment of perfectionism.

And theologically, these pseudomessianic promises involve the illusion that history is in our hands, not God's. Even though the Torah is no longer in heaven but in our hands on earth to interpret as best we can, God has not turned over the final outcome of history to our devices.[42] We are not God's successors, only his junior partners at best. Pseudomessianism assumes that what we do is optimally good and can only get better. But Judaism's greater sobriety teaches us that frequently all we can do is the lesser evil.[43] This is our more modest task. The complete and final victory of the true, the good, and the lawful will have to come from another place.[44]

NOTES

1. Note: "And it says: *Which shall hear all these statutes [huqqim] and say: Surely this great community is a wise and understanding people.* [Deut. 4:6] Thus it states explicitly that even all the statutes [*huqqim*] will show to all the nations that they have been given with *wisdom and understanding.*" Maimonides, *Guide of the Perplexed,* 3.31, trans. S. Pines (Chicago, 1963), 524.

2. See Jürgen Habermas, *The Theory of Communicative Action: Reason and the Rationalization of Society,* trans. T. McCarthy (Boston, 1984), 107ff.

3. Note: "Accept the truth from whomever said it." Maimonides, *Commentary on the Mishnah,* 3 vols.: Shemonah Peraqim: introduction, ed. Kafih (Jerusalem, 1965), 2:247. See also, *Hilkhot Qiddush Ha-Hodesh,* 17.24; *Guide of the Perplexed,* 1.71; B. Pesahim 94b.

4. See B. Baba Batra 130b. Even though all research and reflection (*talmud*) is to lead ultimately to praxis (*ma'aseh*), all of it is not immediately practical. See B. Kiddushin 40b and R. Isaiah Ha-Levi Horowitz, *Shnay Luhot Ha-Berit: Torah She-Bi-Khtav* (Amsterdam, 1648), pt. 3, 82b–83a.

5. See M. Yoma 8.9; B. Yoma 87a; *Sifra*: Vayiqra re Lev. 5:21, ed. Weiss, 27d.

6. See Maimonides, *Hilkhot Yesoday Ha-Torah,* 4.13.

7. B. Kiddushin 66a; I Macc. 2:41.

8. See Paul Ricoeur, *Hermeneutics and the Human Sciences,* ed. and trans. J. B. Thompson (Cambridge and New York, 1981), 288ff.

9. See Hegel, *Faith and Knowledge,* trans. W. Cerf and H. S. Harris (Albany, 1977), 190–191; Nietzsche, *Thus Spoke Zarathustra,* prologue, 2–3, trans. T. Common in *The Philosophy of Nietzsche* (New York, 1927), 5–6.

10. Schiller, "An die Freude," *Schillers Werke,* 5 vols., ed. J. Mueller (Berlin, 1967), 1:64; *Responsa Hatam Sofer* (Pressburg, 1855–1864): Orah Hayyim, no. 28; Yoreh De'ah, no. 19; Even Ha'Ezer, pt. 2, no. 29.

11. See Charles Taylor, *Sources of the Self: The Making of the Modern Identity* (Cambridge, Mass., 1989), 495ff.

12. See Niddah 61b re Ps. 88:6; B. Baba Kama 28b re Deut. 22:26.

13. See M. Avot 2.4.

14. See Amos 3:1–2. This theme plays an especially important role in the liturgy. Although the liturgists were certainly aware that Jews have suffered at the hands of gentile persecutors, their primary concern, nevertheless, was with our own sins. Note a prominent passage from the atonement rites of Yom Kippur: "O' Lord, remember the love of Jerusalem; never forget the love of Zion. O' Lord, remember the day of Jerusalem's fall against the Edomites, who shouted: 'Destroy it, destroy it, to its very foundation!' [Ps. 137:7]. . . . O' do not punish us for the folly and for the sin that we

have committed." *High Holyday Prayerbook*, trans. P. Birnbaum (New York, 1960), 838. It was this approach, I believe, that prevented the Jewish people, even in their worst periods of persecution, from suffering the psychological, moral, and theological degeneration entailed by assuming an identity of victimhood.

15. See Num. 33:53; Nahmanides, *Notes on Maimonides' Sefer Ha-Mitsvot*, Addenda, pos. no. 4.

16. See B. Yevamot 14a re Deut. 14:1.

17. M. Avot 1.1.

18. See B. Baba Kama 113a–b.

19. Note: "Rabban Simon ben Gamliel said that the world is sustained [*qayyam*] on three things: law [*din*], truth [*emet*] and peace [*shalom*], as it says [Zech. 8:16] 'Truth and good judgment [*u-mishpat shalom*] you shall judge in your municipalities.'" M. Avot 1.18. For *shalom* as the highest human good, see, e.g., *Sifra*: Behuqotai re Lev. 26:6 and Isa. 45:7, ed. Weiss, 111a.

20. See M. Avot 3.2; B. Baba Batra 54b and parallels; B. Sanhedrin 39b re Ezek. 5:7 and 11:12.

21. See *Vayiqra Rabbah* 28.1.

22. For the notion of *peras* as natural limit, see Aristotle, *Metaphysics*, 1022a10.

23. See Hermann Cohen, *Religion of Reason out of the Sources of Judaism*, trans. S. Kaplan (New York, 1972), 115ff.

24. See Maimonides, *Hilkhot Teshuvah*, chap. 5.

25. In civil cases, the tendency of the Halakhah as it developed was to emphasize arbitration (*pesharah*), which is less coercive, over formal judicial proceedings (*din*), which are more coercive. See B. Sanhedrin 6b re Zech. 8:16 and II Sam. 8:15; Maimonides, *Hilkhot Sanhedrin*, 22.4–6.

26. See *Phenomenology of Spirit*, secs. 178ff., trans. A. V. Miller (Oxford, 1977), 111ff.

27. See Num. 11:5.

28. The covenantal obligation to accept the authority of the Law is absolute (see T. Demai 2.4–5; Bekhorot 30b), but the commitment actually to do *all* the commandments can be only partial, considering sinful human nature. See Eccl. 7:20; Nahmanides, *Commentary on the Torah*: Deut. 27:26.

29. See, e.g., B. Kiddushin 74a and Rashi, s.v. "shuda de-dayyanay."

30. See Kant, *Groundwork of the Metaphysic of Morals*, trans. H. J. Paton (New York, 1964), preface, 59.

31. See Emmanuel Levinas, *Transcendence et Intelligiblité* (Geneva, 1984), 12–15, and from a very different philosophical perspective, L. E. Goodman, *On Justice: An Essay in Jewish Philosophy* (New Haven, 1991), 10, 30–32.

32. See Maimonides, *Guide of the Perplexed,* 3.17.

33. Note that in the order of the creation of the world, first there is God's creative word: "Let there be light" (Gen. 1:3). Second there is its real or true effect: "and there was light." Third there is God's judgment of it to be good: "And God saw that the light is good" (1:4). So in the order of the creation of man (*adam*), first there is God's creative word: "Let us make man in our image according to our likeness" (1:26). Second there is its real or true effect: "And man became a living being" (2:7). Third there is the designation of what is good for man to do: "It is not good for man (*adam*) to be alone . . . therefore, let a man (*ish*) leave his father and his mother and cleave to his wife and they shall become one flesh" (2:18, 24).

34. M. Avot 6.11 re Isa. 43:7, and M. Makkot 3.16 re Is. 42:21.

35. See *Sifra*: Qedoshim, ed. Weiss, 89b, and Y. Nedarim 9.3/41c re Gen. 5:1.

36. Gen. 2:8–9, 15. See Nahmanides, *Commentary on the Torah, ad locum.*

37. See, e.g., Bekhorot 24a re Hos. 10:12.

38. See, e.g., M. Eduyot 8.7; Menahot 45a.

39. See B. Berakhot 4a.

40. See B. Sanhedrin 97b re Isa. 30:18.

41. See Zevahim 45a and Tos., s.v. "hilkhata."

42. See B. Berakhot 34b re Isa. 64:3. Cf. B. Baba Metsia 59b re Deut. 30:12, which, however, applies only during the penultimate, normal course of history.

43. See, e.g., B. Kiddushin 21b–22a re Deut. 21:11; B. Baba Batra 89b.

44. See *Esther Rabbah* 8.6 re Est. 4:14; also, *Beresheet Rabbah* 68.8 re Gen. 28:11.

1

Natural Law, Halakhah, and the Covenant

Natural Law or Legal Positivism

Philosophers of law, certainly in modern times, can be divided into two main groups: legal positivists and natural law theorists. In essence, the difference between the two groups can be seen in their understanding of the relation of authority and right within a legal system. For legal positivists, authority is prior to right, that is, a legal system is grounded in the power of *the* political authority to make laws, which then determine what is right and what is wrong. For natural law theorists, right is prior to authority, that is, *a* political authority is ordained to make laws because such power is conceived to be right. For both schools of thought, legal authority is a manifestation of political power. For both, "right" means "that which is allowed" and "wrong" means "that which is not allowed." The point of difference, then, is whether there is a transpolitical validation for political power manifest as legal authority. Legal positivists would say that society itself (either collectively or in the person of its sovereign) is the *terminus a quo* and the *terminus ad quem* of its own authority. Natural law theorists would say that the political power qua legal authority of a society is derivative from something else and contained by it — traditionally called "nature."[1]

Into which school of thought a modern philosopher of law fits can be ascertained by looking at his or her answer to the challenge made by an outstanding contemporary legal philosopher, Ronald Dworkin, that one constitute rights as "the one feature that distinguishes law from ordered brutality."[2] A legal positivist would say that this distinction lies in *how* a legal system is ordered. If a legal system's commands are norms, that is, clearly defined rules consistent with an overall normative structure, then there is a sufficient distinction between these prescriptions and the arbitrary, erratic commands associated with "ordered brutality."[3] Natural law theorists would say that this distinction lies in the purpose, the *why*, of a legal system. If a legal system's prescriptions are rational norms, that is, ordered toward objective human goods qua ends, which themselves transcend the system, then there is a sufficient distinction between these prescriptions and the commands associated with "ordered brutality," commands that serve no end other than the exercise of political power as an end in itself.[4]

In times such as these, when rival political claims are so pronounced and have such staggering global consequences, it is easy to see why philosophy of law is of such current intellectual interest. Aside from the fact that Jewish theologians have always been interested in perennial philosophical problems (and, indeed, the philosophical problem of legal positivism versus natural law theory can be traced back to the time of Socrates, at least), and aside from the fact that Jews are part of the current international scene, there are two more particular historical factors that make this issue the point of considerable discussion among contemporary Jewish thinkers. These two factors are the most overriding events of modern Jewish history: the Holocaust and the establishment of the State of Israel. Both of these events call for discussion by Jews of the differences between legal positivism and natural law theory as a pressing practical need and not just as a speculative pastime (*pilpula b'alma*).

In the Holocaust Jews were the most cruelly ravaged victims of the most ordered brutality in history. They were victims not just of random acts of violence but of a system legally structured and aimed at their annihilation. The immediate Jewish reaction of "never again!" leads either consciously or unconsciously, I believe, to a concern with defining for all humanity the difference between law, which Judaism has always affirmed as being international in scope, and ordered brutality as an aberrational imitation of legal order. However, if Jews are interested in law on an international level, they cannot avoid asking the same philosophical questions about their own system of law, Halakhah. One cannot speak to the conscience of humanity without simultaneously speaking to his or her own conscience.[5] These philosophical questions, as we have just seen, concern the relation of right and authority.

The establishment of the State of Israel has given the Jewish people for the first time in over two thousand years sovereign political power. The political issues that concern the State of Israel, and along with it the overwhelming number of Jews throughout the world who have accepted Zionism as integral to their Judaism, practically involve the philosophical question of the relation of right and authority. Thus, for example, how Halakhah is used to determine a legal approach to non-Jews living under Israeli rule will probably be decided differently depending on whether the particular halakhist is an advocate of legal positivism or natural law theory.[6]

One can see an antinomy between legal positivism and natural law theory, and the Jewish theologian must bear it in mind in his or her attempt to define the essential character of Halakhah. The antinomy is as follows:

Natural law is a body of norms, rationally apprehended, universally applicable, independent of the promulgation of any authority.	Positive law is a body of norms, given for application in a particular society (and whomever it controls), dependent on promulgation by a particular authority.

It is clear that the natural law theorist can resolve this antinomy, that is, incorporate the two extremes into one coherent position, whereas the legal positivist cannot. Traditionally, natural law theorists have resolved the antinomy by asserting that positive law is the historical specification of the general principles of natural law, that is, whereas right is in principle changeless, authority is the temporal application of right by *an* authority conscious of both the general principles of natural law and the particular circumstances of a historical society.[7] Legal positivists, on the other hand, regard the natural law position as little more than an illusion, not required by the cogent operation of any system of positive law.[8] Like all positivists, they define a finite range of meaning and simply dismiss any issues outside that finite range as meaningless "pseudoquestions." However, as in all suppressions of perennial human concerns — and certainly natural law is such a perennial human concern — the suppressed keeps returning and raising its questions over and over again. Positivism does not seem to understand that rational response to hard questions requires that they be answered not dismissed, that our criteria of meaning strive to be adequate to truth rather than continually reducing truth to our range of meaning.

It seems that this position of legal positivism is the one that Jewish theologians would adopt in their essential characterization of Halakhah, for one can easily translate the positivist position into the following proposition:

> Halakhah is a body of norms, given for application among the Jewish people (and whomever they control), promulgated by God and subsequently by the Rabbis authorized by God in the revealed sources: the Written Torah and the Oral Torah.[9]

It seems that the adoption of a natural law position would require the authority of God's will as the prime authority of the halakhic system to be subordinated to a higher order of right. This seems to go directly against the transcendent theocentricity of Judaism, and hence it is not difficult to see why many Jewish theologians have willingly included themselves in the positivist school and have rejected the claim that Halakhah can be essentially characterized using natural law theory.

In this chapter, I propose that natural law theory is necessary for an adequate essential characterization of Halakhah. I will specifically argue against the claims of two contemporary Jewish theologians, Marvin Fox and José Faur, who have rejected natural law theory in their discussions of the character of Halakhah. I will also argue against the assertion of the late Jewish philosopher Leo Strauss (d. 1973) that there is no idea of nature in the Hebrew Bible (and, by extension, in normative Judaism per se). In developing my proposal, I will present the idea of covenant as one that correlates natural law and positive aspects of Halakhah in such a way as to avoid the attempt of positivists to deny natural law claims altogether, and the attempt of some natural law theorists to assume that an acceptance of natural law necessarily requires that all positive laws, in our case the *mitsvot*, be subordinated to it.

Marvin Fox: Law as Commandment

One of the most consistent advocates of legal positivism in contemporary Jewish thought is the American Orthodox theologian Marvin Fox. In a number of papers devoted to the legal philosophy of Maimonides, he has argued against other Jewish thinkers (one gets the impression that he is arguing in particular against Jewish neo-Kantians who follow Hermann Cohen) who have maintained that Maimonides is a natural law theorist. In presenting what he considers Maimonides' true position, Fox has generalized that Judaism itself is antithetical to any natural law position. "In Judaism there is no natural law doctrine, and, in principle, there cannot be. . . ."[10] Commenting on the famous passage in B. Yoma 67b that if the laws prohibiting idolatry, sexual immorality, murder, robbery, and blasphemy had not been written in the Torah "reason would have required that they be written" (*din hu she-yikatevu*), Fox writes, "What is asserted is only that, having been commanded to avoid these prohibited acts, we can now see after the fact, that these prohibitions are useful and desirable."[11] He goes on to say, "Seen this way, we can say of them that though they are not rational, in the sense of being demonstrable, they are reasonable in the sense that we can give good reasons for them."[12] Finally, he notes, "Just as the commandments are reasonable without being rationally demonstrable, so are they in accord with man's nature without being natural."[13]

Elsewhere I have criticized the positivist interpretation of Maimonides advocated by Fox and others.[14] It would take us too far afield to repeat those criticisms here. Let me, therefore, confine myself to Fox's rejection of a natural law position within Judaism per se. I would suggest that Fox's position is untenable on three grounds: (1) the theological sources he ignores; (2) the classical sources he interprets; and (3) the philosophical questions he does not discuss.

In denying a place for natural law theory in Judaism, Fox has ignored evidence to the contrary in Saadyah, R. Judah Halevi, Nahmanides, and R. Joseph Albo.[15] Even Maimonides, who Fox goes to such great lengths to show rejected natural law theory in the area of morality, nevertheless speaks of laws that "reason persuades" (*hekhrea ha-da'at*) and to which "reason inclines" (*ha-da'at noteh*), even though he denies such prudential reasoning alone transcendent validity.[16] Now, one certainly has the option of arguing against the position of the five theologians cited above (let alone the position of someone as unorthodox as Hermann Cohen).[17] However, unless one is prepared to eliminate their thought from Judaism, one cannot, therefore, say, "In Judaism there is no natural law doctrine."

In the much-quoted rabbinic source Fox explicates, one could well contend that what is rational before the fact can indeed be logically separated from what is only perceived as useful and desirable after the fact. One could say, taking an example of what the Rabbis clearly considered a nonrational commandment, that having been commanded to refrain from eating pork, I can subsequently consider this act to be "useful" (it reduced the amount of saturated fat in my diet, thus lessening the buildup of cholesterol in my blood vessels)[18] and "desirable" (it helps curb my gluttony).[19] These subsequent explanations are not rational in the sense that I could not have invented the exact prohibition by being aware of its "uses" and "benefits" before my actual obedience of the commandment, "and the pig . . . from its flesh you shall not eat" (Leviticus 11:7–8). However, this is the case because the needs fulfilled by ordinary eating do not lead one directly to the conclusion that eating pork will contradict them. Refraining from pork, then, introduces one to a level of cultural experience that is not universal. Thus the meaning of this experience can be inferred only *ex post facto*, that is, after the commandment has already been fulfilled.

Nevertheless, this type of explanation will not suffice when dealing with the first category of commandments with which the celebrated rabbinic source deals. First of all, they are all prohibitions dealing with what the Rabbis considered ordinary, universal experience. Let us take the most indisputable of these prohibitions, the prohibition of murder (*shefikhut damim*). Does not our experience of society and our need for society indicate to us *in advance* of any promulgated prohibition that murder is the most fundamentally antisocial act, that the permission of murder would destroy social intercourse? In other words, this commandment does not introduce us to a new experience whose meaning is only subsequently inferred; rather, it itself is inferred from an experience the Rabbis considered to be universal. Thus Maimonides, Fox's prime example of an anti-natural-law Jewish theologian, writes about the prohibition of murder, "Even though there are transgressions more serious than murder, none of them involves the destruction of society [*yishuvo shel olam*], as does murder."[20] The difference, then, between these two types of commandments, which the Rabbis so clearly separated, is that in the nonrational commandments the phenomenological sequence is (1) the commandment, (2) the experience, and (3) the inference of secondary meaning. In the rational commandments, conversely, the phenomenological sequence is (1) the experience, (2) the inference of primary meaning, and (3) the commandment, whose reason is the continued duration of that which the experience showed to be good. In our example of the prohibition of murder, the phenomenological sequence is as follows: (1) the experience of human society; (2) the inference from this experience that human society is a good that is required for satisfactory human life; and (3) that acts that counteract this good and prevent its duration in any situation are wrong and thus not to be done. The fact that a prohibition like that of murder is also a divine commandment indicates that it has a covenantal meaning *over and above* its ordinary human meaning.[21] The nonrational commandments, on the other hand, have only covenantal meaning, at least for us in this world.

It is clear, then, that explanations after the fact apply to only nonrational commandments. To give an explanation after the fact when dealing with a rational commandment such as the prohibition of murder, when there is a perfectly obvious reason or primary meaning for it, is to give a *rationalization*. A rationalization is the substitution of a secondary meaning or effect when a primary meaning or cause is available.[22] This is theoretically intolerable because it is a distortion of what we know to be true. In the case of the nonrational commandments, conversely, such as the prohibition of eating pork, we admit that the primary meaning, reason, or cause is unknown to us. Hence any secondary meaning we infer subsequent to our acceptance and observance of the prohibition is clearly only secondary and does not in any way masquerade as the primary meaning. Thus Fox's attempt to see the category of commandments universally practiced as having meaning only after the fact is untenable precisely because it ignores the clear distinction between the two types of commandments made by the Rabbis. Because some of the commandments have only secondary meanings known to us does not necessitate our looking at all the commandments this way. By making a serious confusion between "reasons" for these commandments and "rationalizations" for them, Fox has misinterpreted the famous rabbinic passage whose main point is that at least some of the commandments have reasons clearly evident even *before* the actual promulgation of the law. By not recognizing this distinction, I think, Fox has seriously underestimated this aspect of the "reasons for the commandments" (*ta'amay ha-mitsvot*) tradition in Judaism.

Fox's characterization of Halakhah as only positive law does not answer two basic philosophical questions: (1) Why did God command the people of Israel?, and (2) Why did the people of Israel accept God's commandments? Now the first question can be considered unanswerable in the sense of "My thoughts are not your thoughts" (Isaiah 55:8), although the kabbalists, especially, devoted considerable effort to formulating an answer to it.[23] Nevertheless, this question is one more for metaphysics than philosophy of law. Therefore, let us deal with the second question. It is especially pertinent in our day when the majority of the Jewish people do not seem to consider themselves obligated by divine commandments.

It seems that there are three possible answers to why the people of Israel accepted God's commandments: (1) fear of immediate negative consequences if they did not, (2) total caprice, and (3) faith in God's goodness. These alternatives are treated in several important aggadic sources. Indeed, such questions cannot be the subject of strictly halakhic answers because they deal with the foundations of the whole halakhic system itself.

Concerning acceptance of the Torah because of fear of immediate negative consequences if it were to be refused, we read the following:

"And they stood at the foot [*be-tahtit*] of the mountain" [Exodus 19:17]. R. Avdimi bar Hama bar Hasa said that this teaches us that the Holy-One-blessed-be-he turned the mountain over them like a tub and said to them that if you accept the Torah, it will be well and good [*mutav*]; if not, this will be your grave. R. Aha bar Jacob said that this constitutes a great indictment [*mod'a rabba*] of the Torah.[24]

According to Rashi, this means that such acceptance of the Torah out of fear of immediate death implies compulsion (*ones*).[25] Rabbenu Tam says that such divine compulsion implies lack of a sufficiently free human response (*b'al korham*).[26] Both commentators, no doubt, had in mind the halakhic rule that "one is not liable for acts done under compulsion" (*ones Rahamana patrayh*).[27] Indeed, the term *moda'a* ("indictment") is a halakhic term used to denote the nullification of a contract because it was made under coercion.[28]

Concerning acceptance of the Torah capriciously, the continuation of the Talmud's discussion above notes that a certain nonbeliever accused the Jews of being an impetuous people (*ama peziza*) because they accepted the Torah without first inquiring about its contents and judging whether or not to accept them.[29] The Babylonian sage Rava answered him that this is a sign of Jewish perfection. About this Rashi notes, "Because of our love [*me'ahavah*] we relied on God that he would not burden us with anything we could not stand."[30] This answer states that there is a fundamental difference between a capricious and a loving response.

A loving response to God's revelation provides an adequate reason for the acceptance of the Torah by the people of Israel. This is brought out by the following midrash:

"I am the lord your God who brought you out of the land of Egypt. . . ." [Exodus 20:2] . . . So did the All-Present One [*Ha-Maqom*] bring Israel out of Egypt, split the sea for them. . . . He said to them, "May I rule over you?" They said, "Yes, yes!"[31]

Later this same midrashic text continues:

He said to them, "Am I he whose kingship you accepted yourself in Egypt?" They said to him, "Yes." [He said to them] "As you have accepted my kingship upon yourself, so accept my decrees [*gezerotay*] too."[32]

In the Talmud text we examined earlier, the same sage, Rava, who answered the nonbeliever's accusation of Jewish impetuousness with the retort that the Jewish response to revelation was one of love, answered that in the days of Ahasuerus the Jews willingly upheld what had been forced upon them at Sinai.[33] As Rabbenu Tam interpreted this answer, "They accepted willingly [*me-da'atam*] because of the love of the miracle," namely, the deliverance from the extermination plot of Haman recorded in the book of Esther.[34]

It is the understanding of this reason for Jewish acceptance of the Torah, a motif having considerable development in the Aggadah and later theological writing, that enables one to see how the giving and the acceptance of the Torah is so helpful for our insight. The point underlying this whole discussion is that the Jews experienced God as good and thus judged it right to respond to his commandments. Before they responded to his specific commandments, they responded to his presence in Egypt. In accepting God's offer of liberation, they judged freedom to be good and, therefore, rejected Pharaoh's enslavement of them as wrong.[35] In other words, their response to God's presence presupposed that they had general criteria of good and evil, thus judging what acts are right and what acts are wrong. This is what made their response rational and not capricious. Their response to God's presence involved their admission that God's knowledge of their needs was greater than Pharaoh's and even greater than their own, and they were willing to accept the commandments of such a loving and knowing God even before understanding their meaning in detail. "And God saw the Israelites and God knew" (Exodus 2:25).[36]

Finally, the famous legend that describes God's offering the Torah to all the nations of the world, and its acceptance by Israel alone, implies prior standards of right and wrong that enable the Jewish people to accept the Torah rationally. The interesting thing about this legend, in all its versions, is that the nations of the world reject the Torah because they cannot accept the prohibitions of murder, sexual immorality, and robbery.[37] Why are they not told about the Sabbath or the dietary and clothing restrictions, which are themselves unique to the Mosaic Torah? The legend answers that the former, more universal, prohibitions are some of the Noahide laws incumbent upon all humankind, laws that the nations have already thrown off.[38] If, then, they cannot uphold these seven laws, how can they uphold the 613 commandments of the Mosaic Torah? It should be recalled that these three prohibitions are most of the ones that the Talmud text from B. Yoma 67b, brought by Fox, stated, "Had they not been written, reason would have required that they be written." Therefore, one can see how the Rabbis regarded these prohibitions as the necessary rational preconditions required by the free acceptance of the Torah based on cognitive criteria. The point made by Fox and other Jewish positivists is that all standards of right and wrong are *a posteriori*, that is, subsequent to the promulgation of the specific commandments of the Torah. The aggadic passages we have been examining seem to assume otherwise. They seem to assume that at least some standards of right and wrong are *a priori*, that is, they are presupposed by the promulgation of the specific commandments of the Torah.

Leo Strauss: Philosophy and Law

On the question of whether or not there is any natural law doctrine in Judaism, there is at least specific agreement between Fox and the German-then-American Jewish philosopher Leo Strauss. Both answer the question in the negative. Thus Strauss wrote in his major work on natural law:

> The idea of natural right must be unknown as long as the idea of nature is unknown. . . . The Old Testament, whose basic premise may be said to be the implicit rejection of philosophy, does not know "nature." The Hebrew term for "nature" is unknown to the Hebrew Bible. It goes without saying that "heaven and earth," for example, is not the same thing as "nature."[39]

Fox quotes this same statement with approval.[40]

One could even assume, to a certain extent, that Fox is the mirror image of Strauss.[41] That is, whereas Fox argues against natural law in Judaism in order to maximally emphasize the superiority of revelation over reason, Strauss seems to argue against natural law in Judaism in order to maximally emphasize the superiority of reason over revelation.[42] I now propose to show why Strauss is wrong about the Hebrew Bible (and, by extension, about Judaism per se) on factual grounds and, more important, on conceptual grounds.

It is true that the Hebrew word for "nature," *teva*, is not used in postbiblical or even in postrabbinic Hebrew. It does, of course, show the introduction into Jewish nomenclature of a term deriving from the Arabic *tabi'a*, which is itself a translation of the Greek *physis* (as is the Latin *natura*, too).[43] Nevertheless, in what might well be his most important statement on religion and philosophy, Strauss argues for philosophy's unique ability to transcend "a particular or contingent event" (like that of revelation).[44] Hence, he cannot be taken to limit his understanding of philosophy, which is the means to the discovery of nature's truth, to its *particular* enunciation by the ancient Greeks. If that were so, philosophy would have no more theoretical value than scriptural revelation, by Strauss's own criteria, that is. But Strauss indicates that "Philosophy is the quest for . . . 'first things,'"[45] that is, nature. Therefore, philosophy's proper object must be defined, not simply named. Strauss, to be sure, does define nature, following Plato and Aristotle:

> The purport of the discovery of nature cannot be grasped if one understands by nature "the totality of phenomena." For the discovery of nature consists precisely in the splitting-up of that totality into phenomena which are natural and phenomena which are not natural: "nature" is a term of distinction.[46]

Nature is thus to be seen as an intelligible order to be discovered by the intellect. It encompasses less than "the totality of phenomena," which are capable of being experienced. Being a term of distinction, "nature" functions as a transcendent criterion of judgment. In regard to moral questions, it is used to distinguish between "good and bad," and in the more specifically legal sense, to judge between "right and wrong" or "innocence and guilt."

However, if this is how the idea of nature functions in moral judgment, then Strauss has missed its functional (if not terminological) equivalent in the Hebrew Bible. That functional equivalent is the idea expressed in the word *mishpat*, which is the hypostatization of the verb *shafot*, "to judge" or "judging." *Mishpat* denotes (1) "judgment" (the act of judging), or (2) "verdict" (the result of judging), or (3) "rule" (the specific criterion of judging), or

(4) "justice" (the general criterion of judging).[47] In its first appearance in Scripture it means *justice*. That is in Abraham's dialogue with God concerning God's proposal to destroy the cities of Sodom and Gomorrah because of the wickedness of their inhabitants.

In this narrative God informs Abraham of how he plans to judge the cities so that Abraham "might command his children and household after him to keep the ways [*derekh*] of the Lord to do righteousness [*tsedaqah*] and justice [*mishpat*]" (Genesis 18:19). Although one could certainly interpret "righteousness" and "justice" as two separate things, one could also interpret them, with at least as much plausibility, as "righteous judgment" or *correct justice*, as in the verse "They shall judge the people justly [*mishpat tsedeq*]" (Deuteronomy 16:18).[48] The question is: How is Abraham to learn what he is authoritatively to teach thereafter? He is not just to reiterate precepts; he is to teach a "way," a *method* of acting in general.[49] Now, if Abraham did not have a prior notion of justice, he could only follow God's example. But, as the text dramatically shows, he did not follow it before questioning its very intelligibility: "Shall the Judge [*ha-shofet*] of the whole earth not do justice [*mishpat*]?!" (Genesis 18: 25). Thus it seems that Abraham already had some idea of what justice is to be; hence the basis of his question.[50] The basis of his question seems to be that correct judgment, *by definition*, requires making a consistent distinction between the innocent (*tsadiqim*) and the guilty (*resha'im*).[51] If God chooses to be a judge, and expects morally cogent imitation by his human creatures, his judging must be just.

The idea of *mishpat* as what might be termed "created order" is found in a number of places in the Hebrew Bible, and it is invoked for clearly normative reasons.[52] It also functions the same way in rabbinic teaching. Let it be recalled that the "rational commandments" are seen as the scriptural *mishpatim*.[53] Moreover, for the Rabbis, this idea of created order was expressed in such terms as *nivra ha'olam* ("as the world was created") and *beriyyato shel olam* ("the created structure of the world"), and these terms are invoked for normative reasons.[54] All these terms function as general moral principles, distinct from specific moral rules.[55]

The theological problem that now faces this line of argument, however, is that it seems to subject God, as it were, to a standard of judgment that transcends him. As such, it seems to deny that "I am the first and I am the last, and there is no God other than Me" (Isaiah 44:6). A natural law doctrine seems to subordinate God to some*thing* higher. Fox, especially, is quite aware of this problem. Denial of the doctrine of natural law altogether seems to him the only way out of it.[56]

The opponents of the doctrine of natural law in Judaism, for whatever philosophical reason, seem to accept the definition of natural law proposed by Cicero, a definition consistent with Stoic philosophy and having its roots in Plato. Cicero writes:

> Therefore, since there is nothing better than reason, and since it exists both in man and God, the first common possession of man and God is reason

[*prima homini cum deo rationis societas*]. But those who have reason in common must also have right reason in common. And since right reason is Law, we must believe that men have Law in common with gods. . . . Hence we must now conceive of this whole universe as one commonwealth [*una civitas communis*] of which both gods and men are members.[57]

In this definition of natural law, both God and humankind are included in a whole called *nature*, a whole that subsumes them and governs them.

However, if one adopts a more modest and limited definition of natural law, understanding it as the body of elementary norms without which a society of interpersonal communion would not be possible, then one can see these norms being presupposed by the Torah in its attempt to create the supreme example of such communion in a covenanted community. Although this natural order is the minimal *form* of such communion, personal-historical relationship with God and Israel is its maximal *substance*. The formal structure is the background, not the ground, of this reality; its *conditio sine qua non*, not its *conditio per quam*. In Platonic-Stoic metaphysics, conversely, form and substance are ultimately one.[58]

In this regard, the more modest natural law theory of the twentieth-century Italian neo-Kantian philosopher of law Giorgio Del Vecchio might be helpful. He writes:

Moreover, even when we distinguish . . . the various types of equality, there remains always the consideration that they have nothing to do with justice except in so far as they refer to subjects or persons; an equality or proportion of things . . . is not, properly speaking, either just or unjust. Only by beginning with the value of the person, and considering in some way its identity in different individuals, can one arrive at the basis of the concept of justice, which . . . is essentially a coordination and intersubjective relation.[59]

Del Vecchio clearly and persuasively puts forth a theory of natural law that does not subsume the norms of interpersonal relationship under some impersonal, eternal, and substantial cosmic order. Rather, he presents these norms as formal requirements of any genuine field of interpersonal relationships. In this formalism he is very much indebted to Kant. I think by seeing the relevance of this formalism for our understanding of the covenant and Halakhah, we can successfully avoid the type of natural law theory that many have seen as being incompatible with Judaism.[60]

In Kantian formalism, the data of experience, its "matter," manifest themselves singularly. The structure of experience, its "form," manifests itself conceptually, that is, by general categories.[61] However, because conceptual form structures perceptual matter, this does not mean that form has any substantial priority over matter. It is simply an intellectual precondition for matter's intelligibility. This is why Kant (as opposed to many later idealists) insisted on positing the *Ding an sich*, that is, that the particularities that experience intends themselves ontologically transcend our general categories of understanding.[62] What neo-Kantians like Del Vecchio have done is to apply Kant's formalism to the area of our social experience and its law, whereas Kant himself seemed to have limited his theory of experience to experience of sense data. (In his moral theory autonomous humans qua *homo noumenon* seems to create their own social experience.)[63] In other words, the Kantian formalism of someone like Del Vecchio saves the social meaning of natural law theory from being reduced to Platonic-Stoic metaphysics, which is so incompatible with the Jewish doctrines of creation and covenant.[64]

José Faur: Covenantal Law

The contemporary Sephardic theologian José Faur, like Fox and Strauss, rejects the idea of natural law as "totally foreign to Jewish thought."[65] However, unlike Fox and Strauss, he does see a necessary precondition to the acceptance of the commandments of the Torah. This precondition is the covenant, which Faur contrasts with the classical philosophical idea of nature, as the foundation of law.

> The effect of this conception of religion is the establishment of a bilateral pact, a *berit*, between God and man which both parties freely agree to maintain a relationship between themselves. Thus conceived, religion for Judaism is a relationship between God and man, the sole ground of which is the free and mutual election of God and man.[66]

In dealing with Faur's theory I propose three questions: (1) Are covenant and natural law in truth mutually exclusive ideas? (2) Is the *berit* in truth a "bilateral pact"? and (3) Is the human choice of God the same as God's choice of humans?

I certainly agree with Faur that the authority of the Torah's law could be understood more primarily on the basis of covenant than on the basis of divine will alone (heteronomy) or divine wisdom in nature alone (natural law). Covenant also involves these two other factors in a way that they, either separately or alone, do not involve covenant.[67]

But minimal natural law must not be excluded from one's understanding of the covenant. Indeed, it seems that Faur's covenantal theology requires natural law theory even more evidently than Fox's legal positivism, for Faur is basically taking the philosophical idea of social contract and placing it in a theological context. (As for Strauss, he does not deny natural law; he denies only its locus in Judaism.) Now, historically speaking, social contract theorists have themselves been proponents of natural law theory, some in a wider and some in a narrower sense. All of them posit some "state of nature" as the background of the social contract. One can see this in the theories of Hobbes, Locke, Rousseau, and most recently, John Rawls (whose theory is admittedly indebted to Kantian formalism).[68] Furthermore, two perennial philosophical questions must be dealt with in any cogent social contract theory: (1) Why do the parties choose to enter into the social contract? and (2) What enables the contract to endure?

In the context of the covenant the first question breaks into two subquestions: (1a) Why does God choose to covenant with humans? and (1b) Why do humans choose to covenant with God? As we saw before, the first subquestion might well be unanswerable, although the kabbalists did speculate about it. The second subquestion, however, must be answered because if it is not, then the ancient charge of Jewish capriciousness in entering the covenant is true.[69] If this is the case, then how can people who stood at Mount Sinai be considered to be bound by a totally irrational, blind choice — much less their descendents? Rational choice presupposes intelligent judgment (*nihil volitum nisi praecognitum*).[70] Therefore, it seems to me that the best reason for the choice of the Jewish people to enter into the covenant with God, as we saw before, was their judgment that God's knowledge of their needs and his concern for them was sufficient reason for them to choose to accept his authority, to accept his laws as continually binding obligations, for the keeping of these laws itself is man's active participation in this same divine concern first manifest in Egypt. "And it will be right [*tsedaqah*] for us when we observe and do this commandment before the Lord our God as he was commanded us" (Deuteronomy 6:25).[71] In order for the people to know that God's commandments are right for them, they obviously have to possess some knowledge of what is right in general. This precondition is simply unavoidable.

The second question, namely, what enables the contract to endure, also involves natural law theory, for a contract presupposes the norm that promises are to be kept (*pacta sunt servanda*).[72] Without this presupposition, a contract would have no duration and would be, therefore, meaningless. This natural law precondition seems to be an integral part of the convenantal theory in Scripture. Israel is frequently (and rightly) accused by the prophets of being unfaithful to the covenant, that is, of not keeping to its word. "Instead you have broken faith [*begadatem*] with me, as a woman breaks faith with a paramour, O' house of Israel . . ." (Jeremiah 3:20). And this unfaithfulness is the same as breaking a covenant between two persons. "Thus says the Lord, for three sins of Tyre, for four I will not forgive . . . for they did not remember the covenant [*berit*] of brothers" (Amos 1:9). If the covenant is the foundation of the Law, as Faur rightly maintains, then covenantal faithfulness cannot be commanded by the Law inasmuch as it is already presupposed by the Law itself.[73]

Before we can analyze the covenant as that which cogently correlates natural law and positive aspects of Halakhah, I must seriously question Faur's definition of the covenant between God and Israel as a "bilateral pact." It is bilateral, of course, in the sense that both God and Israel are bound by it. However, it is not bilateral in terms of its initiation or its enduring authority. In a bilateral pact, a social contract, both parties enter the agreement as legal equals and the requirements of the contract are based on *their* mutual authority to obligate themselves and each other. In the *berit*, on the other hand, God initiates the covenant as sovereign, the goals of the covenant are set down by

God, and the authority of the covenantal requirements is the will of God alone when there is human resistance to it.[74] This does not mean that humans cannot freely accept or reject the covenant. If they could not do that, they would not be morally responsible for it. The covenant and its commandments make no sense without this presupposition, as Maimonides most persuasively argued.[75] In constituting what is involved in this freedom to accept or reject the covenant and its norms, we have seen that natural law theory cannot be avoided. However, there is an essential difference between freedom of response and freedom of initiation. This is a crucial point overlooked by Faur.

This leads us into our last question about Faur's position, namely, is human choice of God the same as God's choice of humans? It seems, viewed from the scriptural and rabbinic sources of Jewish theology, that God's choice is fundamentally different from human choice. Covenantal theory must be seen in the context of creation theory.[76] Creation theory always emphasizes the absolute freedom of God. There are no causes for his creative acts and, therefore, there is no necessity for them. "For He spoke and it came to be" (Psalms 33:9). Just as nothing required God to create the world, nothing required God to make a covenant with Israel. His was always the option not to make the covenant, or to make one with some other people. When the Israelites assume God is obligated to tolerate anything they do out of necessity, the prophet reminds them, "To Me O' Israelites you are just like the Ethiopians" (Amos 9:7). Thus from God's perspective the covenant is like a contract in that *a party cannot be bound unless he or she chooses to be bound by obligating himself or herself.*[77]

The choice of humans, however, seems to be much more limited in that it is only the freedom to respond or not. The prime obligation already exists; humans in no way create it or even cocreate it. (Cocreation pertains only to secondary obligation, as we shall see in the next section.) It is this point that makes the *berit* for humans unlike a contract. In a contract, one in essence obligates oneself in general *beforehand*, and then participates with the contractual partner in the creation of mutual obligations *thereafter*. In the *berit*, conversely, humans are called by God to respond to a relationship that God has already initiated and structured.[78] In a contract, written or tacit, there is always the assumption that the agreement is initiated in mutual freedom and maintained in mutual freedom. Thus, it is always assumed that the contractual partners have other good options both before initiation of the contract and after its expiration.[79] But in the *berit*, these other options are only God's; for humans, the covenant is coeval with life. "To love the Lord your God and to listen to his voice and to cleave unto him: that is your life and the length of your days. . . ." (Deuteronomy 30:20). "If these statutes pass away from before me, says the Lord, so also will the seed of Israel cease to be a nation before me all the days" (Jeremiah 31:35).[80] Humans can accept the covenant or reject it, but cannot escape it because the covenant is the most immediately normative aspect of God's everlasting presence. "The corrupt one [*naval*] says in his heart 'there is no God' [*ayn Elohim*]. . . . God looks down from heaven on all humankind . . ." (Psalms 54:2–3).[81] "Where can I go away from your

spirit, and where can I flee from your presence?" (Psalms 139:7). But whereas
humans are obligated to enter the covenant, God alone binds himself to it
with no prior obligation. "This is my covenant with them, says the Lord . . .
from this time forth and forever" (Isaiah 59:21).

In this sense, then, the covenant is like natural law in that it is unavoidable.
Accordingly, just as the fact of human sociality makes such norms as the
prohibition of murder necessary, so does the covenant make the prohibition
of adopting the religious practices of the gentiles (Leviticus 18:3) necessary.
Without the former, society disintegrates; without the latter, the covenantal
community disintegrates.[82]

This inescapable element of the covenant, which is God's everlasting commitment to Israel, is what makes the covenant binding transgenerationally.
However, according to Faur's definition of the *berit* as a contract, why are the
descendents of the Israelites who stood at Sinai and on the plains of Moab
morally bound by a covenant accepted by their ancestors? It seems to be a
rational norm, one certainly accepted by the Halakhah, that personal obligation requires consent.[83] Faur states that "the nation of Israel of the future
participates in the pact by their solidarity with Israel of Sinai-Moab."[84] That is
well and good if future Jews *themselves* choose this solidarity, but what if
they do not? (In an age of such widespread Jewish secularity this is more than
just an academic question.) Does that mean that they are not, therefore,
bound by the covenant? Although such people might very well believe just
that and act accordingly, the Halakhah itself refuses to accept this in that it
rules that "even when he sins, a Jew is still a Jew."[85] This applies even to one
who becomes an apostate (*mumar*). Thus, the explanation of why the covenant
is binding on all generations of Jews is that God never stops offering it to
them.[86] It is divine offering, not human acceptance, that creates the obligation.
This seems to be the meaning of the well-known rabbinic doctrine that all
Jews were present at Sinai for the giving of the Torah.[87] In this context human
agreement is confirmation after the fact. Surely, this is the only cogent position Jewish traditionalists can assert in an age when the majority of Jews do
not regard themselves bound by the covenant and its law in any consistent
way.

The Human Side of the Covenant

We have seen heretofore that the covenant presupposes natural law and human freedom of choice, that is, human freedom to respond or not to God's
covenant, based on rational judgment. It does not, however, presuppose human freedom of will, that is, the freedom either to initiate the covenant or to
terminate it. Both decisions are God's alone. Indeed, both are based on grace:
"For the mountains will depart and the hills will be moved, but My kindness
will not depart from you and My covenant of peace will not be moved, says
the Lord who loves you" (Isaiah 54:10).

Nevertheless, the Halakhah and its development seem to manifest a role for human freedom over and above the choice to respond or not to what God has commanded. In this sense, the covenant seems to call forth not only a human response but, moreover, human initiative, even autonomy of sorts. This greater human freedom within the covenant is best seen in the role assigned to human implementation of the covenant. The Torah states, "According to the instruction [*torah*] which they will instruct you and the verdict [*mishpat*] they will render shall you act; you shall not depart from the ruling they will declare to you . . ." (Deuteronomy 17:11). According to the *prima facie* meaning (*peshat*) of the text, this verse is authorizing judicial application of the norms of the Written Torah by the duly constituted authorities of the Jewish people. Surely, the Law itself requires judicial authority to be operative. But this verse was used by the Rabbis to justify rabbinic innovation, that is, the rabbinic creation of positive law.[88] The Law itself, strictly speaking, does not require any such innovations, and this was the ancient Sadducee position. Nonetheless, the covenant does require these innovations lest new areas of Jewish experience (for example, Hanukkah as a response to the Hasmonean restoration of the Temple) be constituted outside its context and compete with it.[89] This freedom of innovation is broader than the freedom of choice presupposed by the covenant and its revealed law.

This power of human innovation entails the limitation of revelation to make room for this essentially human contribution to the covenant. Thus, the rabbinic doctrine that although the Torah is "from Heaven" (*min ha-shamayim*), it is no longer "in Heaven" (*lo ba-shamayim hi*), which means that its interpretation and application are now a human responsibility, performs this function of limitation.[90] The Written Torah as the repository of the direct divine revelation is now limited to the five books of the Mosaic Torah to which no new normative revelation can be added.[91] Indeed, even the prophetic books and the Hagiographia function only as either illustrations of the norms of the Mosaic Torah or as admonitions to be faithful to them. In themselves these latter two-thirds of Scripture are not normative.[92] Rabbinic law, although seen as authorized by scriptural law (*Oraita*) is, however, essentially different in that human beings now have the power of initiation of law and repeal of law. In rabbinic law the humanly appointed authorities can make either positive enactments (*taqqanot*) or restrictions (*gezerot*), and they have the power to repeal this legislation (*bittul*) — at least in principle.[93] In fact, the greater bulk of the halakhic system is not *from* direct scriptural revelation but from human reason, ultimately operating *for* the sake of the covenant.[94]

In considering the covenant in its aspect of divine revelation, we saw how natural law and positive factors are correlated. The so-called nonrational commandments are indeed experienced as *jus divinum positivum*. However, even if they do not seem to have rational grounds, they do have rational conditions. Without them human assent to this law would be nothing more than caprice itself, having no binding moral force. Furthermore, if the hallmark of natural law is that its norms are part of an intelligible order, then the assumption that divine positive law too has its reasons (*ta'amay ha-mitsvot*) is the point these two types of law have in common.[95] Both are aspects of the Torah as God's cosmic law. Their point of difference is that the norms of natural law, by virtue of their very generality, are more easily known, whereas the norms of the divine positive law, by virtue of their greater specific obscurity, are assumed to be intelligible even if that intelligibility is only partially perceived by us.

In considering the covenant in its aspect of human institutions (*mitsvot de-rabbanan*), we can see how natural law and positive factors are again correlated, for the interpretation of the divine law and, even more, the legislation of the Rabbis, requires natural law factors in order to be rationally convincing. Thus a number of important rabbinic institutions were justified on the basis of their being "for the benefit of society" (*mipnay tiqqun ha'olam*).[96] Here we see the natural law principle of the common good, namely, that which enhances the life of the human community.[97] The common good, moreover, can be served only when the dignity of the individual members of the community is mandated. Accordingly, the enhancement of human dignity (*kevod ha-beriyot*) finds important applications in rabbinic interpretations of scriptural law, and even more so in independent rabbinic legislation.[98] The covenantal element in this type of legislation is that the relationship with God is considered to be the highest human good. Therefore, the composition of the liturgy is seen as a positive human contribution to the covenant.[99] On the other hand, negatively speaking, any compromise with idolatry, even if in the interest of human goodwill, is to be rejected as countercovenantal, that is, contrary to the highest human good.[100]

Positive rabbinic law, precisely because it is humanly ordained, involves natural law factors in its very initiation, in the setting forth of its grounds. In divinely revealed positive law, natural factors are immediately present only in the conditions for human response to the commandments of God. However, even here, we assume that the reasons for the divine decrees are far better than those we see more readily in humanly instituted law because of the greater wisdom of God. Indeed, part of the messianic hope is that we will fully understand God's law so that it will immediately persuade us and require no external coercion. At this time we will fully and immediately understand the law of God in all its manifestations. "It will not be like the covenant which I made with their fathers on the day I forced them [*hehiziqi be-yadam*] to leave Egypt. . . . For this is the covenant which I will make with the house of Israel after these days, says the Lord: I will place my Torah in their innermost parts and I will write it upon their hearts; I will be for them God and they will be for me a people" (Jeremiah 31:31–32).[101]

NOTES

1. This discussion comes out as early as Plato's contraposition of the views of Thrasymachus and Socrates. Thus when Thrasymachus states, "The right [*dikaion*] for subjects [*tois archomenois*] is that which is to the rulers' advantage [*ksympheron*] and whoever deviates from it they call a lawbreaker and unjust" (*Republic*, 2 vols., 338E,

trans. P. Shorey [Cambridge, Mass., 1937], 1:48–49), Socrates asks, "Do you not hold that it is right to obey those in authority [*mentoi tois archousi*]?" (ibid., 339C, Shorey, 1:50–51). In other words, Socrates argues that political authority can function only because those following it have judged it (however inadequately) to be right. (See *Theatetus*, 177D; *Gorgias*, 483C.) This distinction comes out in modern times in Leo Strauss's polemic against Hans Kelsen. Whereas Kelsen wrote, "Vollends sinnlos ist die Behauptung, dass in der Despoten herrsche . . . stellt doch auch der despotisch regierte Staat irgendeine Ordnung menschlichen Verhalten dar. . . . Diese Ordnung ist eben die Rechtsordnung" (*Algemeine Staatslehre* [Berlin, 1925], 335, quoted in Strauss's *Natural Right and History* [Chicago, 1953], 4 n. 2), Strauss wrote contrarily, "To reject natural right is tantamount to saying that all right is positive right, and this means that what is right is determined exclusively by the legislators and the courts of various countries. Now it is obviously meaningful, and sometimes even necessary, to speak of 'unjust' laws or 'unjust' decisions. In passing such judgments we imply that there is a standard of right and wrong independent of positive right and higher than positive right . . ." (ibid., 2). See *infra*, 234f.

2. *Taking Rights Seriously* (Cambridge, Mass., 1978), 205.

3. See Hans Kelsen, *The Pure Theory of Law*, trans. M. Knight (Berkeley, 1970), 44ff.

4. See Thomas Aquinas, *Summa Theologiae*, 2-1, q. 90, a. 1 and a. 2; also, my teacher Germain G. Grisez, "The First Principle of Practical Reason," *Natural Law Forum* 10 (1965):168–201.

5. For the necessary personal involvement in all moral questions, see R. M. Hare, *Freedom and Reason* (New York, 1963), 73.

6. See *infra*, 187ff.

7. See Aquinas, *Summa Theologiae*, q. 91, a. 3.

8. See Kelsen, *Pure Theory of Law*, 217ff.

9. See M. Elon, *The Principles of Jewish Law* (Jerusalem, 1975), 10.

10. "Maimonides and Aquinas on Natural Law," *Dinē Israel* 3 (1972):v. Also see Fox's prolegomenon to A. Cohen, *The Teachings of Maimonides* (New York, 1968), xii–xlii; "On the Rational Commandments in Saadia's Philosophy: A Reexamination," in *Modern Jewish Ethics*, ed. M. Fox (Columbus, Ohio, 1975), 174ff.; *Interpreting Maimonides: Studies in Methodology, Metaphysics, and Moral Philosophy* (Chicago, 1990), pt. 2, passim. For other rejections of natural law in Judaism generally along similar lines, see M. Kadushin, *Worship and Ethics: A Study in Rabbinic Judaism* (Evanston, Ill., 1964), 39ff.; E. E. Urbach, *Ḥazal: Emunot Ve-De'ot* (Jerusalem, 1971), 283ff.; Y. Leibowitz, *Yahadut, Am Yehudi U-Medinat Yisrael* (Jerusalem, 1976), 26–27.

11. Fox, "Maimonides and Aquinas," viii. See the parallel to B. Yoma 67b in *Sifra*: Aharay Mot, ed. Weiss, 86a.

12. Fox, "Maimonides and Aquinas," xxvi.

13. Ibid., xxvii.

14. *The Image of the Non-Jew in Judaism: An Historical and Constructive Study of the Noahide Laws* (New York and Toronto, 1983), chap. 10. For another critique of Fox on the specific question of natural law, which explicitly agrees with mine *mutatis mutandis*, see M. P. Levine, "The Role of Reason in the Ethics of Maimonides," *Journal of Religious Ethics* 14 (1986):279ff., esp. 290–294; "Maimonides: A Natural Law Theorist?" *Vera Lex* 10 (1990):11–15, 26, esp. 26 n. 3. Also, for a critique of Fox's view of Maimonides on this point that influenced my own, see D. Hartman, *Maimonides: Torah and Philosophic Quest* (Philadelphia, 1976), 260–261 n. 38.

15. See Saadyah, *Emunot Ve-de'ot*, 9.2; Halevi, *Kuzari*, 1.48; Nahmanides, *Commentary on the Torah*: Gen. 6:2 and Deut. 6:20; Albo, *Iqqarim*, 1.5.

16. See Maimonides, *Hilkhot Melakhim*, 8.11 and 9.1; also *Hilkhot Yesoday Ha-Torah*, 5.7; *Hilkhot Gezelah*, 4.16; *Shemonah Peraqim*, chap. 6; *Commentary on the Mishnah*: Peah, 1.1.

17. See, e.g., *Religion of Reason out of the Sources of Judaism*, trans. S. Kaplan (New York, 1972), 123ff.

18. See Maimonides, *Moreh Nevukhim*, 3.48; *Hilkhot De'ot*, 3.3 re M. Avot 2.2; *Hilkhot Ma'akhalot Asurot*, 17.29–31. Cf. *Sifra*: Qedoshim, ed. Weiss, 93b, and David Novak, *Law and Theology in Judaism*, 2 vols. (New York, 1976), 2:38ff.

19. See Nahmanides, *Commentary on the Torah*: Lev. 19:2.

20. *Hilkhot Retsihah*, 4.9. See B. Ta'anit 23a. Cf. Aristotle, *Nicomachean Ethics*, 1155a1ff.; *Politics*, 1263a1ff.

21. See Emil Fackenheim, *Quest for Past and Future* (Bloomington, Ind., 1968), 208ff.

22. See Plato, *Euthyphro*, 10A–E.

23. See Gershom Scholem, *Kabbalah and Its Symbolism*, trans. R. Manheim (New York, 1969), 115–117.

24. B. Shabbat 88a. See B. Avodah Zarah 3a re Gen. 1:31.

25. Rashi, s.v. "moda'a rabba."

26. Tos., s.v. 'moda'a rabba." See also B. Yevamot 48a, Tos., s.v. "ella."

27. Baba Kama 28b re Deut. 22:26.

28. See Baba Batra 39b–40a and Rashbam, s.v. "ve-khen" and Tos., s.v. "meha'ah."

29. The Talmud text interprets Exod. 24:7 to mean that they agreed to perform the commandments before understanding their specific meanings.

30. Shabbat 88b, s.v. "de-saginan."

31. *Mekhilta*: Yitro, ed. Horovitz-Rabin, 219.

32. Ibid., 222. See M. Berakhot 2.2.

33. B. Shabbat 88a re Esther 9:27. Re rabbinic debate over whether future generations, who accepted the Torah voluntarily, were not actually more meritorious than the "generation of the wilderness," upon whom it was forced, see M. Sanhedrin 10.3; T. Sanhedrin 13.10–11; Y. Sanhedrin 10.4/29c; B. Sanhedrin 110b re Ps. 50:5; also Y. Shevi'it 6.1/36a re Neh. 10:1. Cf. B. Avodah Zarah 3a and parallels.

34. Tos., s.v. "moda'a rabba."

35. Later on, of course, some of them had a change of heart. See Num. 11:4–5. For the notion that they were rejecting moral responsibility, see B. Yoma 75a and Rashi, s.v. "hanakh."

36. See Novak, *Law and Theology in Judaism*, 2:22.

37. *Sifre*: Ve-z'ot Ha-Berakhah, no. 343, ed. Finkelstein, 395–397, and B. Avodah Zarah 2b re Deut. 33:2.

38. See Novak, *The Image of the Non-Jew in Judaism*, chap. 9.

39. *Natural Right and History*, 81.

40. *Interpreting Maimonides*, 126.

41. See, e.g., ibid., 150–151, 225.

42. Note: ". . . a philosopher . . . refuses assent to anything which is not evident to him, and revelation is for him not more than an unevident, unproven possibility." "The Mutual Influence of Theology and Philosophy," *Independent Journal of Philosophy* 3 (1979):113. (The original version of this essay was published in *Iyyun: Hebrew Philosophical Quarterly* 5 [1954]:110–126.)

43. See José Faur, *Iyunim Be-Mishneh Torah Le-Ha-Rambam* (Jerusalem, 1978), 64–65. For modern philosophical problems with the concept of "nature," see *infra*, 70ff., 141ff.

44. "The Mutual Influence of Theology and Philosophy, " 111.

45. *Natural Right and History*, 82.

46. Ibid.

47. For *mishpat* (a) qua "judgment," see, e.g., Lev. 19:5, Isaiah 28:6; (b) qua "verdict," see, e.g., Deut. 17:9, Jer. 4:12; (c) qua "rule," see, e.g., Exod. 21:1, Ps. 119:102; (d) qua "justice," see, e.g., Deut. 32:4, Isaiah 1:27. Also, *mishpat* can mean a "characteristic," e.g., Gen. 40:13, Jud. 13:12. See *infra*, 163f. Strauss only wanted, it seems, to understand *mishpat* in this philosophically weakest sense. See his "Progress or Return? The Contemporary Crisis in Western Civilization," *Modern Judaism* (1981), 1:4.

48. LXX translates *tsedaqah u-mishpat* as *dikaiosynen kai krisin*, "righteousness and judgment," which seems to mean general benevolence *and* specific punishment of wrongdoers. A modern commentator, A. S. Hartom, in his *Commentary on Genesis* (Tel Aviv, 1972), *ad locum*, interprets *tsedaqah* as the positive command to practice benevolence to others, and *mishpat* as the negative command to avoid harming others (p. 70). However, virtually all of the other commentators, ancient, medieval, and modern, see *tsedaqah u-mishpat* as one concept. For a homiletical use of *tsedaqah u-mishpat* as different concepts, see *Beresheet Rabbah*, 49.4, ed. Theodor-Albeck, 2: 502.

49. For the use of *derekh* as a "method" more general than specific rules (*mitsvot*), see *Sifre*: Devarim, no. 49 re Deut. 11:22, ed. Finkelstein, 114.

50. In the same sense, God can question Cain about the murder of Abel (Gen. 4: 9), based on the assumption that Cain already has some idea of what justice is to be (see ibid., 4:7).

51. See infra, 168f.

52. See, e.g., Jer. 8:7; Amos 3:3–6; Job 28:23–28 and 38:1ff.

53. *Sifra*: Aharay Mot, 86a; B. Yoma 67b.

54. M. Gittin 4.4; B. Yevamot 61b. See *infra*, 84f.

55. See John Finnis, *Natural Law and Natural Rights* (Oxford, 1980), 63–64, for the distinction between moral principles and moral rules.

56. See, e.g., *Interpreting Maimonides*, 141.

57. *De Legibus*, trans. C. W. Keynes (Cambridge, Mass., 1928), 320–323. For Plato's notion that the gods are subject to higher law or forms, see *Timaeus*, 29A–C; also, David Novak, *Suicide and Morality* (New York, 1975), 33–35. Cf. Aristotle, *Metaphysics*, 1015a15.

58. See David Novak, *Jewish-Christian Dialogue: A Jewish Justification* (New York, 1989), 152–154, where an answer to the "Euthyphro" problem (viz., if God is subject to a standard, then the standard is greater than God) is proposed from a covenantal perspective.

59. *Justice: An Historical and Philosophical Essay*, trans. Lady Guthrie (Edinburgh, 1952), 87 n. 3. See Aristotle, *Politics*, 1282b5ff. Even such a supposed legal positivist as H. L. A. Hart acknowledges a certain minimal natural law, in content not too different from what I am advocating here as a theological context. See *The Concept of Law* (New York, 1961), 188–189; also Novak, *The Image of the Non-Jew in Judaism*, 345–346.

60. This adoption of Kantian formalism regarding law per se does not, for me, entail adopting Kantian autonomy as the ultimate ground of law. See *Jewish-Christian Dialogue*, 135–137, 148–151.

61. *Critique of Pure Reason*, B34.

62. Ibid., B164, A249.

63. Ibid., B575ff.

64. See T. Bowman, *Hebrew Thought Compared with Greek*, trans. J. L. Moreau (New York and London, 1970), 172ff.

65. "Understanding the Covenant," *Tradition* 9 (1968):41. Faur also writes, "It is pertinent to add that the term and notion 'nature' are absent in the entire Biblical and rabbinical literature, and they are introduced into Jewish thought and vocabulary in the Arabic period" (ibid.). For Faur's sustained critique of Jewish natural law theory, see his *Iyunim Be-Mishneh Torah Le-Ha-Rambam*, 61ff. Cf. my later revered teacher Boaz Cohen. *Jewish and Roman Law* (New York, 1966), 2 vols., 2:28 n. 97; also Moshe Silberg, *Ba'in K'Ehad* (Jerusalem, 1981), 166.

66. "Understanding the Covenant," 42. See Otto Gierke, *Natural Law and the Theory of Society*, trans. E. Barker (Boston, 1957), 108–109; also S. Federbush, *Mishpat Ha-Melukhah Be-Yisrael*, 2d rev. ed. (Jerusalem, 1973), 33.

67. See David Novak, "The End of the Law: The Difference between Judaism and Christianity," *Taproot* (forthcoming).

68. See C. J. Friedrich, *The Philosophy of Law in Historical Perspective*, 2d rev. ed. (Chicago, 1963), 88–91, 101–103, 127. For Rawls's Kantianism, see his *A Theory of Justice* (Cambridge, Mass., 1971), 179ff., 251–257.

69. B. Shabbat 88a.

70. See Thomas Aquinas, *Summa Theologiae*, 2-1, q. 9, a. 1; q. 13, a. 1.

71. For *tsedaqah* as "right" rather than "merit," see Gen. 18:19 and B. Yoma 38b; also Nahmanides, *Commentary on the Torah*: Gen. 15:6 (contra LXX; I Macc. 2:52; *Targumim* and Romans 4:3).

72. See Charles Fried, *Contract as Promise: A Theory of Contractural Obligation* (Cambridge, Mass., 1981), 8–13.

73. For the notion that the Torah itself presupposes obligation, see, e.g., B. Kiddushin 13b and Rashi, s.v. "de-l'av" and Tos., s.v. "malveh." In the same logical sense, belief in the existence of God cannot be commanded by divine law because such a belief is itself presupposed by the acceptance of that very law. See David Novak, *Law and Theology in Judaism*, 2 vols. (New York, 1974), 1:138ff.

74. Thus the Hebrew word *berit* is rendered by LXX (e.g., Exod. 24:7) *diathēkē* in the sense of the Latin *testamentum*, rather than *synthēkē* in the sense of the Latin *pactio*. See W. F. Arndt and F. W. Gingrich, *A Greek-English Lexicon of the New Testament* (Chicago, 1957), 182. This also is the sense of *diathēkē* in rabbinic nomenclature. See, e.g., M. Baba Batra 8.6; *Bemidbar Rabbah*, 2.7; Y. Sanhedrin 2.6/20c. See Philo, *De Mutatione Nominum*, 5.52–53; my late revered teacher Abraham J. Heschel, *The Prophets* (Philadelphia, 1962), 229–230; Novak, *Law and Theology in Judaism*, 2:18ff.

75. *Hilkhot Teshuvah*, 5.1–4. For the difference between the ancient idea of freedom of choice (*liberum arbitrium*) and the modern idea of freedom of the will (*Willensfreiheit*), see Hannah Arendt, *The Life of the Mind: Willing*, 2 vols. (New York, 1978), 2:28–29.

76. See Jon D. Levenson, *Creation and the Persistence of Evil: The Jewish Drama of Divine Omnipotence* (San Francisco, 1988), 131ff.

77. Re God's binding himself to covenantal norms, not just the enforcement of covenantal sanctions, see Y. Rosh Hashanah 1.3/57a-b re Lev. 22:9; B. Berakhot 6a re I Chron. 17:21; also see David Novak, *Halakhah in a Theological Dimension* (Chico, Calif., 1985), chap. 9.

78. Re the historical background of *berit*, see D. R. Hillers, *Covenant: The History of a Biblical Idea* (Baltimore, 1969), 49.

79. Thus Socrates, who conceives of man's relation to a historical community as founded on tacit agreement (*homologia*) and contract (*synthēkē*), presents the policy of Athens in these words, "Anyone who is not pleased with us may take his property and go wherever he pleases. And none of us prevents or prohibits any of you to take his property and go away whenever he wants . . ." (*Crito*, 51D, trans. H. N. Fowler [Cambridge, Mass., 1914], 180–181). This rejection of a real possibility to do otherwise with impunity rather than remain an Athenian citizen convinces Socrates that he is morally bound to obey the laws of Athens (see ibid., 52D–E). See Strauss, *Natural Right and History*, 119. The *berit*, on the other hand, does not allow any such "check-out" clause. See L. E. Goodman, *On Justice: An Essay in Jewish Philosophy* (New Haven, 1991), 13–14, 41–42.

80. See B. Pesahim 68b.

81. The *naval* is not one who is a "fool" (as in the Vulgate's rendition of *naval* as *insipiens*) but, rather, one who acts with morally culpable, self-willed blindness to the provident and judging presence of God (see Isa. 40:27–31). Being a *naval* is to lack *yir'at Elohim* ("the fear of God"—see Gen. 20:11; Ps. 111:10; Prov. 1:7), which is a moral characteristic. See Job 2:9–10.

82. See *Encyclopedia Talmudit*, 17:305ff., s.v. "huqqot ha-goyyim."

83. See R. Isaac Abrabanel, *Commentary on the Torah*: Nitsavim, no. 1 re M. Eruvin 7.11; B. Ketubot 11a. Abrabanel argues that the acceptance of the covenant by ancestors thereby bound their descendents into perpetual slavery (*me-din avdut*). Aside from the irrelevance of this exposition today, when slavery is regarded as morally repugnant by *consensus gentium*, even children's involvement in parental obligation or responsibility is seen as contingent on their own choice. See, e.g., B. Berakhot 7a re Exod. 20:5. For the noncontractual character of the *berit*, see R. Isaiah Halevi Horowitz, *Shenay Luhot Ha-Berit*: B'Assarah Ma'amarot (Amsterdam, 1648), pt. 1, 31b–32a.

84. "Understanding the Covenant," 42. For the notion of the original power of a community to bind individuals perpetually, even transgenerationally, see R. Solomon ibn Adret, *Responsa Rashba Attributed to Nahmanides* (Warsaw, 1883), nos. 280 and 285 (end).

85. See B. Sanhedrin 44a re Josh. 7:11; T. Demai 2.4; Bekhorot 30b; *Tur*: Yoreh De'ah, 266 (end) and Karo, *Bet Yosef, ad locum*. See also B. Shabbat 87a and Tos., s.v. "ummah;" B. Yevamot 62a and Tos., s.v., "Ha-Torah." Cf. *Mekhilta*: Bo, ed. Horovitz-Rabin, 53 and Zevahim 22b re Exod. 12:43.

86. See B. Shevu'ot 29a–b and Tos., s.v. "ki," and *Hiddushay Ha-Ramban, ad locum*, ed. Lichtenstein (Jerusalem, 1976), 132–133; Maimonides, *Hilkhot Shevu'ot*, 6.8–9. Many statements about the obligation to obey divine law seem to imply that acceptance of this law creates the obligation to obey it (see, e.g., B. Shabbat 88a; B. Avodah Zarah 2b). However, we have seen that such is not the case. (Re the primordial character of the covenant, see Niddah 30b and R. Hanokh Zundel, *Ets Yosef ad locum* in *Ayn Ya'aqov*; cf. Plato, *Meno*, 81Cff.) Perhaps such statements, which imply acceptance as a ground of the Law rather than a subjective condition for its observance, can be illuminated by Maimonides' solution to the conflict between the law that a man can divorce his wife only of his own free choice (M. Yevamot 14.1) and the law that enables the Jewish court and even its agents to force him to do so against his choice in certain cases (M. Gittin 9.8; M. Arakhin 5.6; M. Ketubot 7.1ff). Is not the use of such judicial force invalid coercion (*me'ones*)? Maimonides writes, "We do not say that one

is coerced unless he is forced and pressured to do something for which he is not commanded in the Torah . . . but when he is overcome by passion (*she-toqfo yitsro ha-ra*) . . . his own bad character (*be-da'ato ha-ra'a*) coerced him. . . . [H]e really wants to perform all the commandments and to separate himself from sin, but his passions overcame him" (*Hilkhot Gerushin*, 2.10). In other words, we assume that if fully cognizant, one would have internalized the divine law *as if it were their own free choice*. See M. Avot 2.4; also *Bemidbar Rabbah*, 2.16 re Ezek. 20:32–33; B. Kiddushin 50a.

87. *Tanhuma*: Nitsavim (end), ed. Buber, 25b and Y. Nedarim 1.3/37d re Deut. 29:14. See *Sifre*: Devarim, no 33, ed. Finkelstein, 59 re Deut. 6:6; *Responsa Ribash* (Constantinople, 1507), no. 511.

88. B. Berakhot 20b; B. Shabbat 23a.

89. See Novak, *Law and Theology in Judaism*, 2:129–132.

90. M. Sanhedrin 10.1; B. Baba Metsia 59b re Deut. 30:12. See Temurah 16a.

91. The commandment "You shall not add [*lo tosifu*] onto the word [*davar*] which I command you" (Deut. 4:2) was interpreted by the Rabbis using *davar* in its specific rather than its general sense (cf. Isaiah 40:8), viz., new details cannot be introduced into the commandments accepted as *d'Oraita*. See *Sifre*: Devarim, no. 82. However, by freeing the general sense of *davar* from this restriction, rabbinic exegesis justified all the rabbinic additions to the corpus of the Law as a whole.

92. See B. Baba Kama 2b; also Chaim Tchernowitz, *Toldot Ha-Halakhah*, 2d rev. ed., 4 vols. (New York, 1945), 1:19.

93. M. Eduyot 1.5; Maimonides, *Hilkhot Mamrim*, 2.2–7.

94. It was Maimonides, more than any other halakhist, who emphasized the human contribution to the covenant and its law, but without eliminating its ground in revelation. See *Sefer ha-Mitsvot*, shoresh 1–2; also David Novak, "Maimonides and the Science of the Law," *Jewish Law Association Studies* 6 (1990):94–134. For a modern attempt to eliminate the ground in revelation, cf. Haim H. Cohn, "Secularization of Divine Law," in his *Jewish Law in Ancient and Modern Israel* (New York, 1971), chap. 1.

95. See Isaak Heinemann, *Ta'amay Ha-Mitsvot Be-Sifrut Yisrael* 2 vols. (Jerusalem, 1959), 1:29; Novak, *Law and Theology in Judaism*, 1:136–138.

96. M. Gittin 4.2ff.

97. See Aristotle, *Nicomachean Ethics*, 1129b15; *Politics*, 1252a1; Thomas Aquinas, *Summa Theologiae*, 2-1, q. 90, a. 2; *infra*, 98, n. 1.

98. See B. Berakhot 19b; Y. Kilayim 9.1/32a. For the idea of *imago Dei* as a more sufficient ground for human dignity than either rationality or political freedom, see Novak, *Halakhah in a Theological Dimension*, 96ff.

99. B. Berakhot 28b–29a; Maimonides, *Hilkhot Tefillah*, 1.1–2.

100. See M. Gittin 5.8; Y. Demai 4.3/24a; Y. Gittin 5.9/47c; Y. Avodah Zarah 1.3/39c. Cf. B. Avodah Zarah Ba re Exod. 34:15.

101. See Menahot 45a for the notion that all obscurity regarding the *mitsvot* will be removed during the days of the Messiah by Elijah.

2

Theonomous Ethics:
A Defense and a Critique
of Tillich

The Quest for Theonomy

In modern times ethical systems have often been characterized as either "autonomous" or "heteronomous," although the distinction itself is surely ancient.[1] This dichotomy is useful for purposes of description (metaethics), but it entails serious problems. Neither autonomy nor heteronomy alone seems to be adequate to deal with important moral questions that the modern world presents, or with the equally important moral questions bequeathed to us by tradition. Because autonomy and heteronomy per se are mutually exclusive, their respective strengths can be combined and their respective weaknesses eliminated only if they are seen as rooted in a law (*nomos*) constituted prior to them both. Indeed, they have been uprooted from their original ground, and this is the reason for the antinomy between them with which modern ethical thought has been so preoccupied. In other words, the identification and constitution of their ground must relativize them both.

This is precisely what Paul Tillich (d. 1965) attempts in his characterization of Christian ethics as "theonomous." Tillich sees it as the only solution to the antinomy between autonomy and heteronomy. He states that "the polarity of structure and depth produces a conflict between autonomous and heteronomous reason under the conditions of existence. Out of this conflict arises the quest for theonomy. . . ."[2]

In this chapter I shall attempt to do the following: (1) analyze the respective strengths and weaknesses of autonomy and heteronomy; (2) present and elaborate on Tillich's metaphysical concept of theonomy; (3) present the critique of this concept by the analytic philosopher William Frankena; (4) defend Tillich against Frankena's charges; (5) show how Tillich's concept of theonomy pertains to Judaism as well as to Christianity; and (6) criticize Tillich's suggestion that there is natural law without determinate precepts.

Autonomy and Heteronomy

Autonomous ethics recognizes the self as the ultimate moral authority. It holds that the only commands having moral validity are those that the self issues to itself. Minimally, autonomy means independence. The mode of society that autonomy posits is that created by *contract*—that is, morally valid social standards are those that are or can be agreed upon by equally independent selves as authoritative for all.[3] Heteronomous ethics, on the other hand, recognizes the self as being part of a larger structure and having to conform to commands not of its own making but to those of an external authority. Minimally, heteronomy means dependence. The mode of society that heteronomy posits is one having preexistent hierarchy—that is, morally valid social standards are ones that assign to a person his or her rightful *status* in a society, a status existing prior to one's individual entrance into it.[4]

The most cogent philosophical defense of heteronomy was made by Plato:

> Now the phrase "master of himself" [*kreittō hauton*] is an absurdity, is it not? For he who is master of himself would also be subject to himself, and he who is subject to himself would be master . . . the same person [*ho autos*]. . . . But the intended meaning of this way of speaking appears to me to be that the soul of a man within him [*ti en auto*] has a better part and a worse part, and the expression of "self-mastery" means the control of the worse by the naturally better part [*to beltion physei*].[5]

For Plato, the "naturally better part" is the rational self (*nous*).[6] And, so far, even an advocate of autonomy like Kant would agree—that is, the noumenal self (reason) should rule over the phenomenal self (the body as we are aware of it).[7] However, Plato assumes that the rational self is the discursive self (*to logistikon*), and discourse can be developed only by those who are naturally (philosophically) superior, working together as a ruling class.[8] This means that there must be a society wherein this discursive power is nurtured and extended. Because discursive ability is by no means equal, nor can it ever be, this society (*politeia*) is necessarily hierarchal.[9] Authority is in those having more philosophical ability, and they rule over those who have less or none at all. The philosophical guardians function the way God functions in the life and vocation of Plato's teacher, Socrates.[10] In other words, the hierarchy in society reflects the hierarchy in nature itself.

The problem with this philosophically constituted heteronomy, as with cruder varieties of heteronomy, is that responsibility for the true needs of those being ruled is in no way ascertainable, inasmuch as these needs are known only by the philosophical *cognoscenti*. What is known by all, however, is that the society is functioning for the immediate benefit of those who have authority in it. The vast majority of the members of such a heteronomous society experience self-alienation. In the second half of the twentieth century, in which Hitler and Stalin (both of whom considered themselves theoreticians) still have many imitators, it is understandable why heteronomy is now so immediately and intensely suspect.[11]

The most cogent philosophical defense of autonomy comes from Kant:

> Reason thus relates every maxim of the will, considered as making universal law, to every other will and also to every action towards oneself; it does so . . . but from the Idea of the dignity [*Würde*] of a rational being who obeys no law other than that which he at the same time enacts himself. . . . [It is] the law-making [*Gesetzgebung*] which determines all value [*Werth*] . . . the word "reverence" [*Achtung*] is therefore the ground of the dignity of human nature and of every rational nature.[12]

In Kant's view, great philosophical ability is not required to formulate ethical maxims as categorical imperatives.[13] There is an elementary equality among all rational participants in Kant's ideal democracy, which he calls a "kingdom of ends" (*Reich der Zwecke*). It is a society whose primary *raison d'être* is human dignity; no one is treated merely as a means.[14] Considering the horrors that have been perpetrated with special intensity in this century by hierarchical societies, it is not hard to understand why the idea of autonomy should have such renewed appeal. Why, for instance, the most influential book of political philosophy in recent years should be John Rawls's *Theory of Justice*, a work written under heavy Kantian influence.[15]

But there are a number of problems with autonomy. Essentially, it disregards dependence in human affairs. Persons are dependent on a number of forces beyond their making and often beyond their control.[16] Autonomy seems to entail that humans act as if the physical environment were made for their own use. Autonomy does not seem to be of any help in developing an ecological morality; many see it indeed as the cause of the ecological crisis in the industrialized world.[17]

Further, by limiting moral equality to "rational" persons, autonomy provides no moral criterion for dealing with those taken as physically human but who are either nonrational (for example, infants or the comatose) or irrational (for example, psychotics or the senile). Do these beings exist merely for the use of rational persons, as in this questionable view the physical environment itself does, or do they have an inherent human dignity? If, as has been traditionally assumed, they do, then that human dignity cannot be constituted on autonomous grounds.[18]

Still further, autonomy seems to underestimate the essential role of hierarchy in the socially necessary division of labor, for real (that is, arithmetic, "I-equal-you") equality is primarily operative in the secondary realm of retributive justice ("all are equal before the bar of justice"). The greatest equality that can be admitted, however, in the more primary realms of economics and politics is the proportional equality of distributive justice, namely, each should receive according to the value of his or her contribution to the welfare of society as a whole.[19]

Still further, autonomy seems to underestimate the role of tradition in human experience, that society is in many respects like a family into which one is involuntarily born (*Gemeinschaft*) rather than like a corporation one chooses to buy into (*Gesellschaft*), and that much of the structure we find so necessary for social cohesion and continuity is based on the authority of precedent, both legal and social.[20] The best example is the traditional nature of language, the most essential characteristic of human society.[21] (Since the heyday of Logical Positivism, I know of no philosophical attempts to construct a "rational language" *de novo*).[22]

Finally, and this is the most serious problem for Tillich or for any theologian, by positing the self as its own authority, autonomy makes the self morally — and therefore most importantly — the ground of its own being, that is, God.[23]

It is to these inadequacies of both autonomy and heteronomy, each taken separately, that Tillich presents theonomy as the solution.

Theonomy

In presenting theonomy as the solution to the inadequacies of both heteronomy and autonomy, Tillich regards autonomy as the first breakoff from primordial theonomous unity and heteronomy as its subsequent opposite. This is because the *nomos* of all three is reason. Thus reason is first self-sufficient and divine (*cogitatio*), then a subject (*cogito*), then an object (*cogitatum*). He writes, "Heteronomy imposes a strange [*heteros*] law [*nomos*] on one or all the functions of reason. . . . It represents at the same time, an element in reason itself, namely, the depth of reason."[24] In other words, autonomous reason itself is its own ground, which means that it thereby cuts itself off from any ground in being that transcends it. Here Tillich polemicizes against Hegel for attempting "to reestablish theonomy with autonomous means," that is, positing an "other" only to draw it back into the self at a higher level of its evolution.[25] (The same could be said against Husserl's constitution of the *cogitatum/noēma* as the intentional correlate of the *cogito/noēsis* qua "transcendental ego."[26]) Heteronomy, then, continually reminds autonomy of its transcendent ground (as opposed to itself being "transcendental," as in Idealism).[27]

Tillich emphasizes that only theonomy can be the ground for authentic community among humans, for autonomy, by regarding itself as its own ground and order, posits other selves after its own self-constitution, and, in consequence, does not respond to the presence of other persons (*Mitsein*) already there (*Dasein*).[28] Response presupposes the prior presence of the other, a priority autonomy in its egocentricity cannot apprehend. Conversely, heteronomy regards the self and other both as being grounded in institutions. Accordingly, it is impersonal because structure, not personal presence, is the priority here. Thus Tillich points out:

> Communal reason does not accept communal forms dictated by sacred ecclesiastical or political authorities, nor does it surrender human relations to their growth and decay through will to power and libido; it relates them to the ultimate and universal community, the community of love, transforming the will to power by creativity and the libido by *agape*. In very general terms, this is the meaning of theonomy.[29]

For Tillich, the human person is estranged from his or her essential being. Thus the impetus for morality is the desire for reunion with one's essential self, which (following Augustine, especially) is desire for reunion with God, the ground of being in general and the ground and *telos* of human existence in particular.[30] This desire for reunion is the *leitmotif* of human existence.

> The reason for the unconditional character of the moral imperative is that it puts our essential being as a demand against us. The moral imperative is not a strange law, imposed on us, but it is the law of our own being. In the moral imperative we ourselves, in our essential being, are put against ourselves, in our actual being.[31]

And because God in loving us manifests himself as personal (*impersonal love* being a contradiction in terms), human love is essentially responsive. This being so, the ground of love cannot be approached simply by human initiative (autonomy) because it would then not be responsive. One can respond only to one who reveals himself or herself (as in Heidegger's *alētheia*).[32] And the ground of love cannot present itself as wholly other (heteronomy) because it could not thereby elicit a loving response. As Tillich succinctly put it, "We cannot be obedient to the commands of a stranger even if he is God."[33] Finally, this response necessarily entails open human community because God is not the projection of one ego or a collective ego (Durkheim's "totemic principle").[34] He is the creator. God reveals himself to a community of persons — and the ultimate hope is that all persons will be finally included in it (redemption).

Frankena's Critique of Theonomy

Tillich's philosophical method and style are those of the architectonic metaphysics of the nineteenth-century German philosophers. He treats ethics with the same sweep with which he treats other areas of philosophy. This type of philosophy is much more for the sake of system (hence, Tillich's magnum opus is called *Systematic Theology*) than for the sake of solving specific problems. Tillich not only does not employ theonomy to show how it would make a difference in dealing with specific problems of normative ethics, but does not even seem to deal with some of the more general logical problems (meta-ethics) that theonomy surely presents.

Philosophers whose method and style are those of Anglo-American analytic philosophy are usually impatient with what seems to them to be the haziness of Tillich's type of philosophy. Thus William Frankena, greatly influenced by the early-twentieth-century British philosopher G. E. Moore, is impatient with Tillich's metaphysically based ethics.[35] He sees it as containing two logical problems. One, Frankena characterizes Tillich's concept of theonomy as positing "that certain theological propositions by themselves entail logical conclusions." He then proceeds to accuse Tillich of making a logical mistake:

> That this can be so has, however, often been categorically denied, even by some theologians. "No ought from an Is," "no ethical conclusions from non-ethical premises" — from Hume on this has been a familiar dictum, its neglect being generally castigated nowadays as "the naturalist fallacy."[36]

Two, Frankena then characterizes Tillich's concept of theonomy as essentially ethical (prescriptive) rather than theological per se (descriptive), and states that as such, it does not necessarily entail theological assertions.

> . . . morality by its very nature involves an attitude or supreme devotion to some cause or object, a state of what Tillich calls "ultimate concern"; but this is precisely what is meant by "religion" or by "religious faith;" hence morality is necessarily religious. . . . [b]ut let us grant this point; . . . it would only show that morality requires an agent to be ultimately devoted to an ideal, it would not show that this ideal depends for its justification on any religious belief of a theistic sort.[37]

So it seems that Frankena has backed Tillich into one of two logical conundrums: (1) either theology per se is descriptive and, therefore, does not entail ethics (prescription) at all; or (2) theology is essentially prescriptive and the assumption of its necessity is based on an invalid overextension of ethical premises. In either case, a theologically constituted ethics is a chimera. Theology is essentially independent of ethics, and ethics is essentially independent of theology. We are either back to the position of Euthyphro,[38] whose devotion to the gods led to an ethical dead end, or we are back to the position of Socrates, who used ethical criteria to determine the very existence or nonexistence of the gods.[39]

A defense of Tillich against these serious philosophical charges will have to show (1) that the is/ought dichotomy, so dear to Anglo-American philosophers, is a problem that a phenomenology of religio-ethical consciousness can adequately overcome;[40] and (2) that the admission that ethics leads to theology makes a necessary connection between the two, albeit in a teleological, not a deductive, way.

A Defense of Theonomy

Frankena's main case against Tillich is based on a point first put forth by Hume, that no descriptive statement ever entails a prescription. What-is does not necessarily lead to what-is-to-be (ought).

Hume's dichotomy is based on three assumptions: (1) that sense impressions are the only data of consciousness; (2) that desire, as a passion, is secondary, a reflection on those impressions directly impinging on human activity; (3) that theoretical reason is nothing but the discovery of the connections between passions and can at best direct them to their proper objects.[41]

Considering that practical reason is so far removed from the elementary data of consciousness, it is obvious why Hume calls it "the slave of the passions," which "can never pretend to any office than to serve and obey them."[42] Such a "slave" can hardly command its "master" to do anything. For Hume, there is hardly anything like moral obligation at all, morality being little more than a matter of taste. There is no real "ought."

Although Frankena begins with Hume, considering his obvious commitment to rational morality, it seems that he is coming from a position closer to that of Kant's, namely, that moral obligations arise from our interaction with other persons taken as autonomous beings like ourselves, rather than as the objects of sense, or the objects of calculation for the sake of our own pleasure. For Hume, practical reason is epiphenomenal; for Kant, it is noumenal—that is, intelligent and creative of its own laws. Accordingly, there is no phenomenal basis for rational morality for anyone in this tradition.

Tillich regards this dichotomy as highly artificial. What he wants is a morality with both Kant's sense of obligation and Hume's sense of the primacy of experience. He writes: "Values demand to be actualized in existence and through existence. The question arises: How is this possible, if there is no ontological participation of values in existence, but an unbridgeable gap between them?"[43] Indeed, Tillich insightfully shows that as social science emerged in the nineteenth century, following the lead of the natural sciences, more and more of the realm of "values" was being claimed by empirical psychology, sociology, and anthropology in their attempts to be as close to biological determinism as possible. This important cultural fact has made the formal ethics of neo-Kantianism (for example, as delineated by Nicolai Hartmann) and analytic philosophy (for example, as delineated by G. E. Moore and those who followed him) of less and less relevance to those having real power in dealing with the concrete problems of modern society and culture. This whole approach, then, surely cannot be adopted by any faith community that although "not of the world," is nonetheless "in the world" and intends to remain there.

After this crucial observation, Tillich begins a remarkable reconstitution of human existence, taking desire to be its prime datum, and seeing reason as the insight into the natural hierarchy of desire that makes it known to the will. Thus, contrary to Hume, he regards desire as being fundamentally desire-for-the-presence-of-other-persons (Buber's "thou") and not simply a reaction to pleasant sensations.[44] Desire, therefore, entails love as a personal response to those whom we desire and who desire us for ourselves. Love, then, is primary action, not secondary reaction, which is impersonal and thus abstracted from existence. We are engaged in the world by the primary process of this desire before we abstract "impressions" from it as spectators. Indeed, as Aristotle pointed out, we could not even be spectators at all without the ever-present desire of curiosity.[45] We desire the world before we examine it. And, contrary to Kant, Tillich does not regard desire's essential intention to be pleasure, that is, selfish passion.[46] If properly understood, desire does indeed entail the structure of morality.

What might be called Tillich's phenomenology of desire (*epithymia* in Greek; *libido* in Latin) is quite lucidly presented.

> Certainly there is *epithymia* in every *eros*. But *eros* transcends *epithymia*. It strives for a union with that which is a bearer of values because of the values it embodies. . . . [T]his *eros* is united with *epithymia* if *epithymia* is the desire for vital self-fulfillment and not for the pleasure resulting from this union.[47]

For Tillich, love is an ontological state, which humans immediately experience through desire. Desire's intentionality is suppressed if it is merely taken as the drive for pleasure (Freud's *Lustprinzip*), pleasure being its subjective accompaniment of love, not its ontological ground and end.[48]

The primacy of personal desire is our consciousness ("I desire to love and be loved in return"), much more immediately (that is, intensely) than our experience of external objects, shows also more immediately its intentionality. Desire is always desire-for and desire-to. Thus desire aims at its object and entails the ordering of activity toward that end. In its process three types of love emerge in apodictic succession.

> The *eros* quality of love is in a polar way related to what could be called the *philia* quality of love. While *eros* represents the transpersonal pole, *philia* represents the personal pole. . . .
>
> . . . in the holy community the *agape* quality of love cuts into the *libido*, *eros*, and *philia* qualities and elevates them beyond the ambiguities of their self-centeredness.[49]

Thus desire's ultimate fulfillment is in *agape*, which Tillich explains as alone being unconditional and absolute.

It seems to me that Tillich's triad of *philia*, *eros*, and *agape* as the *desiderata* of *epithymia* corresponds to the triad of autonomy, heteronomy, and theonomy as the manifestations of reason. Tillich states, "*Philia* is the movement of the equal toward union with the equal."[50] Autonomy, for Tillich, closely following Kant, is the rational self legislating for itself and for other rational selves in an ideal society of equality. Autonomous egalitarianism has been rightfully accused, however, of lacking the intensity that obtains in the attraction of those who are different. In other words, the leveling sobriety of *philia* produces too much similarity (Heidegger's "das Man").[51] (One should remember, for instance, the infatuation of many Americans for royalty and the attempts in American history to elevate certain families to quasi-royal status.) Heteronomy, on the other hand, succeeds only, as Plato insightfully noted, when there is an erotic connection between the ruler and the ruled.[52]

Heteronomy's danger is, however, that the *eros* of the lower for the higher is never reciprocated, that those at the top want to be loved much more than they want to love. (One should consider, for instance, Hitler's ultimate contempt for the German people—who certainly had an erotic attachment to him—after they failed to fulfill his dreams of conquest.[53])

Finally, human *agape* involves the intensity of *eros* with the justice that is inherent in authentic *philia*. Like theonomy, it does so with a prior unity that continues to transcend and limit them both. Moreover, human *agape* is only, at best, a weak imitation of divine *agape*. As Tillich puts it, "One's love of God is of the nature of *eros*. It involves elevation from the lower to the higher, from lower goods to the *summum bonum*."[54] The necessarily erotic element in even the highest human love prevents the human person from identifying himself or herself with the ground of his or her being.

The fact that love is to reunite, without loss of identity of the reunited persons, entails the constitution of justice.

> . . . love as a whole if it does not include justice is chaotic self-surrender, destroying him who loves as well as him who accepts such love. Love is the desire for reunion of the separated. It presupposes that there is something to be reunited, something relatively independent that stands upon itself. . . . Without this justice there is nothing to unite.[55]

For this reason, justice includes the equality characteristic of autonomy with the authority characteristic of heteronomy. And justice is rooted in God who judges (heteronomously) with equal justice for his human creatures (who are relatively autonomous when compared with the rest of creation). As Abraham said, "It is obscene [*halilah*] of you that the judge [*ha-shofet*] of all the earth not do justice [*mishpat*]!" (Genesis 18:25).

In showing how Tillich's ontology of love entails an ethic of justice, we can now see how he overcomes the is/ought dichotomy that Frankena, typical of so many modern ethicians, attempts to use against him, for, in taking desire as the fundament of human consciousness and uncovering its inherent intentionality (desire-for/desire-to), the very utterance "I desire you/I desire to come close to you" is something that simultaneously contains both an "is" and an "ought." In ontological terms, it is like saying *cupio ergo sum*. It is both a statement of fact and a statement of value. It is both a statement of what-is and a statement of what-is-to-be. The only sure sign of the inauthenticity of desire is if it is only uttered and not acted upon. Action is always morally relevant. Thus "amoral desire" is a contradiction in terms once desire has had an adequate phenomeno-logical constitution. Desire is never amorphous.

In following Hume's theory of the emotions (which lies at the heart of the is/ought dichotomy), Frankena has failed to see how Tillich, coming from a very different theory of the emotions, has a very different view of action and moral obligation. Furthermore, he wrongly assumes that theologians like Tillich deduce ethics from theology, whereas in fact Tillich develops a philosophical anthropology whose full intentionality leads to theology. Ethics stands between this anthropology and theology in Tillich's system.

Tillich also cannot be accused of another is/ought error, namely, the deduction of existence ("is") from thought ("ought"): "If I think it, then necessarily it must be." This error, of course, was most successfully exposed by Kant in his rejection of the proofs of the existence of God (especially those of Descartes and Leibniz.[56] In other words, one cannot deduce transcendence (being) from immanence (thought). Here Tillich's acceptance of the classical theological (but not philosophical) doctrine of revelation helps him avoid what Kant would surely have considered an invalid extension of pure reason. Tillich emphasizes that the ground of being is not the necessary conclusion from a set of universally valid premises.[57] Being personal, its manifestation is not necessary but free. It presents itself only when it presents itself, namely, "I will be there when I will be there" (*ehyeh asher ehyeh* — Exodus 3:13).[58]

One can see how Tillich incorporates virtually all the traditional distinctions between reason and revelation: "Revelation is the manifestation of the mystery of being for the cognitive function of human reason. It mediates knowledge — a knowledge, however, which can be received only in a revelatory situation, through ecstasy and miracle."[59] Revelation is neither the premise nor the conclusion of reason in its ordinary processes of ratiocination. Thus Tillich emphasizes:

> Revelation is the manifestation of the depth of reason and the ground of being. It points to the mystery of existence and to our ultimate concern. It is independent of what science and history say about the conditions in which it appears; and it cannot make science and history dependent on itself. No conflict between different dimensions of reality is possible. Reason receives revelation in ecstasy and miracles; but reason is not destroyed by revelation, just as revelation is not emptied by reason.[60]

Just as autonomy cannot lead to theonomy in any necessary (and thus predictable) way, so reason cannot necessarily lead to revelation. It can only prepare "hearers of the word," in Karl Rahner's terms.[61]

It is evident that Tillich's teleology of human desire is heavily influenced by the Augustinian tradition, where God is seen as the end of human *eros*, that is, *eros* that is conscious and freely directed to its own proper end. This teleology differs essentially from the Aristotelian-Thomistic tradition, where *eros* is characteristic of nature per se and, then, of the human being as a part thereof (and not even the most important part thereof).[62] In the Augustinian tradition revelation is much more of an integral requirement, inasmuch as teleology can be seen only from within human experience; there are no real prototypes in external nature, as there are most definitely for the Aristotelian-Thomistic tradition.[63] Hence, without revelation, that is, God as manifest and concerned (*agape*), it is hard to distinguish between God as the object of desire (*to orekton*, as Aristotle describes him),[64] and God as a project of human intellect, as, for example, Kant's designation of God as a postulate of pure practical reason.[65] In the Aristotelian-Thomistic tradition, conversely, universal natural teleology provides the needed externality to prevent God from being confused with a mere project of the human intellect.[66] However, it seems that the general Augustinian approach is more relevant to both biblical religion and the scientific paradigm of our present culture, for since Galileo science has not looked upon the cosmos as an entelechy, and in biblical religion God is certainly portrayed as being more in search of humans than humans are portrayed as being in search of God.[67]

The is/ought trap is one into which Tillich did not permit himself to fall, either in his ethics or in his metaphysics.

Frankena's second point against Tillich is that even if one accepts the notion of an ethics of aspiration,[68] namely, that some supreme object motivates and integrates all human action, this does not mean anything more than that ethics must include devotion to *an* ideal, but that ideal need not be God. In other words, he accuses Tillich of a fundamental category error: reducing religion to ethical idealism. Some more orthodox Christian theologians have made the same charge, but for very different reasons, of course.[69]

However, Frankena has missed the teleological relation Tillich has constituted between faith (one's state of being ultimately concerned) and morality (one's intentional action). Human aspiration, characterized as *eros*, is desire for the *summum bonum*. Thus it is more than being "devoted to an ideal" because any ideal simply will not do; only the ground of being—that than which nothing greater can be conceived, in Anselm's famous formulation.[70] In fact, ultimate concern (devotion) to anything less than the ground of being could be only idolatry: either the idolatry of self (autonomy) or the idolatry of something else (heteronomy).[71]

The logical connection between faith and morality is teleological, not deductive.[72] Because Tillich regards autonomy as ontologically prior to heteronomy, he is not asserting that one can have a morality only after acceptance of faith propositions (dogmas), a point that leads to absurdity, as a number of philosophers have correctly contended.[73]

Tillich's teleologically ordered process of aspiration renders Tillich's affinity to Aristotle important. Thus, in beginning his major work in ethics, Aristotle writes:

> Every craft and every endeavor [*methodos*], similarly every practical act [*praxis*] and every choice, seems to be directed [*ephiesthai*] toward some good [*agathou tinos*]. Hence, it has been well said that the Good [*t'agathon*] is that to which all things aim. . . . If, therefore, there is some end [*ti telos*] of practical acts which we freely desire [*boulometha*] for its own sake, then all others are for the sake of it.[74]

It is hard to tell, after seeing this definition in the background, just what Frankena means by an "ideal" in attacking Tillich's teleology. If he means that it is something-not-yet-real, then it is hard to see how it differs from what Aristotle calls a "wish" (*boulēsis*), that is, a fantasy, something not entailing any practical choice at all and, hence, not of any serious ethical import.[75] If, on the other hand, he means an end, then, for Aristotle, the end of human striving is contemplation, which is a state of supreme human activity. And, contemplation's proper object is God, who is *ens realissimum*.[76] Although Tillich is certainly not a strict Aristotelian (being closer to Plato in relating ethics and metaphysics, and closer to Augustine in limiting teleology to human existence), he is like Aristotle in insisting that the end of human desire is not the fantastic projection of human wishing. For him, the teleology of human striving is the desire for reunion with the ground of being, which is infinite, "the first and the last" (Isaiah 44:6). Ontology is the basis, not the project, of ethics. Hence, to see ethics as the *conditio sine qua non* of faith is not to make it a necessary consequence of faith, nor to make it the ground of faith (*conditio per quam*) in any logically necessary (deductive) way. Tillich emphasizes that

> one can say that love as an emotion is the anticipation of the reunion which takes place in every love-relation. . . . This means that the emotional element in love does not precede the others ontologically but that the ontologically founded movement to the other one expresses itself in emotional ways. Love is a passion . . . a consequence of the objective situation.[77]

I think Tillich's use of the word "consequence" here is descriptive rather than denotive of logical necessity in the formal sense.

One can, perhaps, see another Tillichian triad in the relation of being (the topic of ontology), emotion (the topic of psychology), and morality (the topic of ethics). The sequence of their relation is twofold. Subjectively viewed, the priority of emotion to morality explains Tillich's treatment of the great commandment of love. As he queries, "If love is emotional, how can it be demanded? Emotions cannot be demanded."[78] This is, of course, an old question. Kant, for example, asked it and concluded, following his metaphysic of morals, that rational—that is, morally obligatory—love cannot be "pathologi-cal," namely, affective rather than active.[79] But Tillich is saying something altogether different. He is saying that acts of love must have an emotional background, that feeling must lead into action and cannot be overlooked without action's becoming "behavioral" rather than "existential."[80] And for emotion to have this power, it must be as transparent as possible to its ontological source. Objectively, then, morality is prior to emotion and ontology is prior to them both. (One can see from this why some psychotherapists who are convinced that human emotion is more than Freud made of it without ontology and that it is certainly more than Behaviorism's designation of it as epiphenomenal have found in Tillich an important philosophical justification for their therapeutic approach.[81])

Theonomy and Jewish Ethics

Tillich might best be characterized as a Christian philosopher of religion, or a Christian philosophical theologian. As such, he did not deal with the specific problems of ethics per se, nor did he deal very often with Judaism, except for allusions made *en passant*.[82] However, he did provide important rationales for traditional moral precepts, and some of these rationales can be used to explicate the precepts that Judaism and Christianity, especially, share in common patrimony (the "Judeo-Christian ethic").[83] The precepts have a long and multifaceted discussion in the history of Judaism. This can be seen quite vividly in Tillich's treatment of the Fifth Commandment of the Decalogue, "Honor your father and your mother" (Exodus 20:12; Deuteronomy 5: 16).

In a remarkable, although oblique, polemic against Freud, Tillich writes:

> Religious symbols are double-edged. They are directed toward the infinite which they symbolize and toward the finite through which they symbolize it. . . . For instance, if God is symbolized as "Father," he is brought down to the human relationship of father and child. But at the same time this human relationship is consecrated into a pattern of the divine-human relationship. If "Father" is employed as a symbol for God, fatherhood is seen in its theonomous, sacramental depth.[84]

Here Tillich is turning on its head Freud's famous designation of God (where Freud closely follows Feuerbach's anthropology) as the projection onto the cosmos of the figure of the protecting father of childhood, a protecting power who is still desired by adults, even after the earthly father is either dead or discovered to have all the limitations of other mortals.[85] What Tillich is saying is that Freud has begged the essential question, namely, what it is that makes the father of flesh and blood the object of such reverence. Tillich's answer is that our childhood dependence on our father is itself symbolic, that is, an intentionality and a participation in the ontological dependence of the finite on the infinite. Because this childhood experience is the first revelation of this ontological truth, it provides us with the symbolic language to express this truth even after childhood has forever passed away.

Because the critique of Freud is oblique, Tillich does not argue that his interpretation of the religious commandment of filial piety is more convincing than Freud's. However, after having examined his dialectic of theonomy, autonomy, and heteronomy, we can, I think, elaborate on Tillich's particular point here. And this can be best done by looking at how Freud himself attempted to provide a solution to the problem of the religious sense of dependence, which he considered to be "the universal obsessional neurosis."[86] Freud wrote about those who he believed "have been sensibly brought up," namely, given a nonreligious childhood environment (the kind in which he himself reared his own six children),[87] as follows:

They will, it is true, find themselves in a difficult situation. They will have to admit to themselves the full extent of their helplessness and their insignificance in the machinery of the universe; they can no longer be the centre of creation, no longer the object of tender care on the part of the beneficent Providence. . . . But surely infantilism is destined to be surmounted. Men cannot remain children forever; they must go into "hostile life". . . . [T]he sole purpose of my book [*Future of an Illusion*] is to point out the necessity for this forward step.[88]

Here we can bring all of Tillich's points against absolute autonomy and those we can adduce to supplement them. It is not that humans are simply "helpless" and "insignificant" in the "machinery of the universe." This language and conceptuality come straight out of Freud's mechanistic, alienated view of nature. It is more accurate to view nature as an organism *in which* humans participate, *upon which* they are dependent, and *from which* they are also independent. Dependence is something we can never transcend ("progress from"), as Freud's belief in progress suggests. Because the relation between humans and nature is biologically conditioned, the relationship between child and parent is the situation that makes this biological condition psychologically evident. The child is biologically dependent on the parent, but by the time he or she becomes aware of this dependence (emotionally and then intellectually), the child has already achieved a degree of independence.

Here we see the tension between parental heteronomy and filial autonomy, which has become the hallmark of adolescence in our culture. The resolution of this tension is not the total victory of autonomy, which could mean only the total annihilation of the past as a mode of transcendence. Nor is it the total victory of heteronomy, which would make the past the only normative source. Rather, the solution is theonomy—a realization that our dependence upon the ground of being, the object of our ultimate concern (which we cannot separate from our own father in childhood), includes both autonomy and heteronomy. Being prior to them both, the ground of being harmonizes them and integrates them in a person's existence so their tension becomes creative rather than destructive (neurotic). The parent-child relationship is the most intense symbol we have of this theonomous dependence—which is our true self, not an alien and threatening force—because it manifests most intensely the relation between ontology, biology, and psychology in human existence. That is why it is unique and irreplaceable.

This understanding of the symbolic nature of the parent-child relationship enables one to see it in true perspective. The relationship has unique privileges, and it is not arbitrary. In Tillich's nomenclature it is not merely a "sign"; it is a *symbol*, that which points to and participates in a higher reality.[89] On the other hand, its limits must be enforced whenever it attempts to eclipse its source and become the object of ultimate concern.

This is an accurate and profound description of the way classical Jewish ethics has treated this relationship. It becomes particularly evident when we look at the following text from the Talmud:

Is it possible for one to have to listen to his father and his mother who told him to transgress one of the commandments of the Torah? Scripture states, "A man shall fear his mother and his father and keep My Sabbaths" [Leviticus 19:2] — all of you are obligated [*hayyavim*] to honor Me.[90]

It is clear from this text that the honoring of parents has a special place in Jewish religious life. In fact, when this conflict between the will of parents and the will of God does not present itself, the honoring of parents is compared to the honoring of God himself.[91] The Talmud records, with approval, a number of examples of the great lengths some of the ancient Rabbis went to keep this commandment superlatively.[92] Nevertheless, if parents attempt to put themselves in the place of God in the eyes of their children, when, as a medieval exegete put it, "the first father" is impersonated by "the last father," then the symbolic justification for the obedience due parents is lost and the primacy of the authority of God must be affirmed — now at their expense.[93] Later Jewish ethicians, however, still aware of the symbolic importance of parenthood even when particular parents abuse its sanctity, debated whether the children of such parents were still obligated to honor their evil parents. Even the ethicians who did insist upon the honoring of such parents assumed, nevertheless, that such honoring could not include compliance with parental commands to break the law of God.[94]

The same symbolic nature applies to the commandment to keep the Sabbath, which is juxtaposed to the commandment of filial piety in both versions of the Decalogue, as well as in the passage in Leviticus with which the Talmud text quoted above dealt. Although the invalid parental command mentioned above is taken by many to be a command by the parent to the child to desecrate the Sabbath at the parents' will or whim, even the Sabbath itself is symbolic. As another passage in the Talmud puts it, "It is not the Sabbath we fear, but Him who commanded us to keep it."[95] Furthermore, for the Rabbis (as well as for Jesus of Nazareth), "the Sabbath was made for man, not man for the Sabbath."[96] In other words, there is a hierarchy of symbols, and the symbolic participation of human life in the ground of being was judged to have priority over that of the Sabbath. The only absolute prohibition is that of idolatry, precisely because idolatry is totally nonsymbolic; it is the most radical human attempt possible to displace the infinite by a finite entity, to obliterate the only authentic object of our ultimate concern.[97] When directly confronted by idolatry, both Judaism and Christianity have insisted upon martyrdom (from *martyrein*, "to witness"), namely, death becomes the only affirmation of God possible; it is the only symbol left for the human person to express existentially his or her ultimate concern.[98]

Tillich on Natural Law: A Critique

Tillich's concept of theonomy has some important affinities to natural law theory. For example, Thomas Aquinas regards "natural law," that is, those humanly kept precepts that take precedence over merely human-instituted precepts ("positive law") as being "a share of the eternal law" (*participatio legis aeternae*).[99] Furthermore, Aquinas insists upon "divine law" (*supra legem naturalem et humanum*) over and above natural law per se because "man is ordained to an end of eternal happiness which exceeds man's natural ability."[100] Earlier, Maimonides had insisted that without a normative relationship with God, one could be a "sage" (*hakham*) but never "godly" (*hasid*)—that is, never a participant in the transcendent-eternal realm.[101]

In discussing theonomy Tillich states:

> The law is not strange to man. It is natural law. It represents his true nature from which he is estranged. Every valid ethical commandment is an expression of man's essential relation to himself, to others, and to the universe. This alone makes it obligatory and its denial self-destructive. This alone accounts for the unconditional form of the moral imperative, however conditioned the contents may be.[102]

In this last point Tillich seems to hold that natural law/theonomy makes moral precepts obligatory but that natural law itself has no immutable precepts. Moreover, revelation "transcend[s] the rational norm without destroying it"; it gives reason "another dimension."[103]

The question is, what sort of reason—here, what sort of moral reason—is given this "other dimension"? Could any kind of moral reason, producing any kind of moral precept, be given this "other dimension"? Is revelation/theonomy an empty form that can be fitted onto any content at all? If so, then religion could be used as a justification for any political or social system that has the power to enforce its morality—that is, to be taken as obligatory (even Kantian autonomous ethics is enforced by conscience).[104] Surely Tillich's own experience in Wilhelmine Germany (and in Nazi Germany) taught him how easily political regimes can involve *Gott mit uns* to give their authority a theonomous aura.[105] The ancient prophets of Israel (the first "Protestants") protested the pretensions of kings and priests. As Jeremiah typically protested, "Me they forsook, and My Torah they did not keep!" (Jeremiah 16:11).[106]

Is everything equally symbolic of the ground of being? Or is every historically evolved symbol equally transparent to the ground of being? Surely, there is a determinate hierarchy of symbols. Surely, some symbols are more transparent than others. Indeed, many of the problems that dogmatic theology has posed in its own context are questions about the priority of symbols in potentially chaotic situations where priorities must be affirmed. We have seen how in Jewish tradition a hierarchy of symbols was constituted: the Sabbath is prior to filial piety, human life is prior to the Sabbath, and martyrdom in the face of idolatry is prior to human life.

And surely Tillich himself would distinguish between martyrdom and suicide, which are phenomenally identical but phenomenologically (that is, in meaning) diametrically opposed.[107] Suicide is ultimately egocentric; martyr-dom is wholly theocentric. Note what Tillich writes about suicide:

> . . . that the moral imperative is unconditional because it expresses man's essential being. . . . But one could ask: Why should one affirm one's essential being rather than destroy one's self? The answer to this must be that the person becomes aware of his infinite value or, ontologically expressed, of his belonging to the transcendent union of unambiguous life which is the Divine life; this awareness occurs under the impact of the Spiritual Presence.[108]

Here Tillich both affirms the unconditional nature of the prohibition of sui-cide and illustrates its ultimate justification. Suicide is not an act of the self but an unsuccessful (even if physically successful) attempt to be released from "the dimension of the ultimate and unconditional."[109] For this reason, Tillich could not justify any suicide under any circumstances. And other ethical con-clusions can be drawn by close analogy—for example, the prohibitions of murder and wanton destruction.[110]

To return to the language and conceptuality of natural law, human nature (which Tillich repeatedly affirms) requires that certain acts be done and certain acts be avoided for the sake of its own fulfillment. It requires laws. But to say that theonomy is formally necessary but substantially contingent leads to no law at all. It is an abstraction admitting of any or no concretization. That is why "situation ethics," with its emphasis on love as the only immutable norm, can produce any ethical maxim short of overt sadism (and even sadism usually rationalizes itself erotically).[111] Tillich's insistence on the ontology of love should lead one way from any such sentimental (that is, purely emotional) view of love. Love has a structure and a limit, which for Tillich, entails justice.

This does not mean that historical and even individual contingency is not to be taken seriously. Otherwise, natural law would be taken not only as necessary but also as sufficient. But natural law requires positive law and even individual conscience.[112] Furthermore, many natural law theorists today are quite appreciative of modern advances in the social sciences, and admit that many claims for precepts as "natural law" in the past were overstated.[113] Many of these precepts are either positive law or they are religious statutes, valid only within a particular historical context. Roman Catholic moral teaching until quite recently often overextended the reach of natural law. So Tillich's statement about "conditional contents" may have been polemical hyperbole and not fully consistent with his philosophically developed ethics. The follow-ing seems to me to be more consistently Tillichian:

> Natural laws are based on the rational structure of man and society, therefore, they are unconditionally [sic] valid, although the positive laws of social groups may contradict them. If the concept of natural law is applied universally to nature, it designates the structural determinateness of things and events. . . . The law of nature does not remove the reactions of self-centered *Gestalten*, but it determines the limits they cannot trespass.[114]

This later statement is more likely than the earlier one about "conditioned contents" to allow Tillich's concept of theonomy to be a fruitful hermeneutical criterion within the structured ethical systems of both Christianity and Judaism.

NOTES

1. See Plato, *Laws*, 716C; also *Cratylus*, 386A and *Theatetus*, 152A; Cicero, *De Republica*, 3.22.

2. Paul Tillich, *Systematic Theology* 3 vols. (Chicago, 1951), 1:83.

3. For the definitive contemporary statement on this whole subject, see John Rawls, *A Theory of Justice* (Cambridge, Mass., 1971), esp. 11ff.; also Charles Fried, *Contract as Promise* (Cambridge, Mass., 1981), esp. 13–16.

4. See Aristotle, *Politics*, 1254a15.

5. *Republic*, 2 vols., 431A, trans. P. Shorey (Cambridge, Mass., 1930), 1:358–359. See Aristotle, *Magna Moralia*, 1213^a7; cf. *Metaphysics*, 1072^b15ff.

6. *Republic*, 490B.

7. For Kant, the noumenal self is an "end-in-itself" (*Zweck an sich selbst*), and the phenomenal self is subservient to it as a "means" (*bloss als Mittel*). *Grundlegung zur Metaphysik der Sitten* in *Kants Werke*, Prussian Academy ed. (Berlin, 1968), 4:428. See *Groundwork of the Metaphysic of Morals*, trans. H. J. Paton (New York, 1964), chap. 2; also *Critique of Judgment*, trans. J. H. Bernard (New York, 1951), sec. 84. In the same way, Plato asserts that the lower faculties of the soul/society "serve" (*doulein*) the higher ones. See *Republic*, 444B.

8. *Republic*, 441A.

9. Ibid., 433A–B; 494A.

10. See Plato, *Apology*, 31D; also David Novak, *Suicide and Morality* (New York, 1975), 29ff.

11. See Karl Popper, *The Open Society and Its Enemies*, 2 vols. (Princeton, 1950), 1:86ff.

12. *Groundwork of the Metaphysic of Morals*, 102, 103 = *Grundlegung*, 4:434, 436.

13. See Kant, *Critique of Practical Reason*, trans. L. W. Beck (Indianapolis, 1956), pt. 2.

14. *Groundwork of the Metaphysic of Morals*, 102ff.

15. See *A Theory of Justice*, 251ff., 563ff.

16. For a current theologian's emphasis on the general dependency inherent in human existence (admittedly quite influenced by Schleiermacher), see James M. Gustafson, *Ethics from a Theocentric Perspective* 2 vols. (Chicago, 1981), esp. 1:176–177. See also *supra*, 35. For a critique of autonomy on the basis of its own claims, see David Novak, *Jewish-Christian Dialogue: A Jewish Justification* (New York, 1989), 148–151.

17. See Karl Jaspers, *The Future of Mankind*, trans. E. B. Ashton (Chicago, 1961), passim; also *infra*, 135ff.

18. See David Novak, *Law and Theology in Judaism* 2 vols. (New York, 1976), 2: 108ff.; *Halakhah in a Theological Dimension* (Chico, Calif., 1985), 94ff.

19. See Aristotle, *Nicomachean Ethics*, 1131a12ff. Also, see *infra*, 206ff.

20. The *Gemeinschaft/Gesellschaft* distinction was made by Ferdinand Tönnies in his *Community and Society*, trans. C. F. Loomis (New York, 1963). For a critique of

autonomous culture's unsuccessful attempt to transcend history, see Alasdair MacIntyre, *After Virtue* (Notre Dame, 1981), 35ff.; Jeffrey Stout, *The Flight from Authority* (Notre Dame, 1981), 72ff.

21. See Aristotle, *Politics*, 1253a10–15.

22. See J. Harnack, *Wittgenstein and Modern Philosophy*, trans. M. Cranston (Garden City, N.Y., 1965), 54ff.

23. It should be remembered that for Kant the subjective ground of morality is the rational person as an end-in-himself or herself (see *supra*, n. 7). God, on the other hand, is only a postulate of pure practical reason (see *Critique of Practical Reason*, 128ff.). For subsequent theorists in this tradition, God is either eclipsed or regarded as a threat to human independence qua autonomy. See, e.g., J. Rachels, "God and Human Attitudes," in *Divine Commands and Morality*, ed. P. Helm (New York, 1981), 34–38.

24. *Systematic Theology*, 1:84.

25. Ibid., 1:86.

26. See Edmund Husserl, *Cartesian Meditations*, sec. 41, trans. D. Cairns (The Hague, 1960), 83–88.

27. See Kant, *Critique of Pure Reason*, B352, B561–562.

28. I have used Heidegger's terms as coined in *Being and Time*, but I reject his constitution of them. See David Novak, "Buber's Critique of Heidegger," *Modern Judaism* 5 (1985): 129–131. Re the priority of the "other one" in ethics, see Emmanuel Levinas, *Existence and Existents*, trans. A. Lingis (The Hague, 1978), 94–96.

29. *Systematic Theology*, 1:149.

30. See Augustine, *Soliloquies*, 1.7.

31. Tillich, *Theology of Culture* (New York, 1959), 136.

32. Martin Heidegger, *Being and Time*, sec. 44, trans. J. Macquarrie and E. Robinson (New York and Evanston, 1962).

33. *Theology of Culture*, 136.

34. See Émile Durkheim, *The Elementary Forms of the Religious Life*, trans. J. W. Swain (New York, 1965), 236–237.

35. See G. E. Moore, *Principia Ethica* (Cambridge, 1903), 110ff.

36. William K. Frankena, "Is Morality Dependent on Religion?" in *Divine Commands and Morality*, ed. P. Helm (New York, 1981), 18.

37. Ibid., 28–29. For a critique of Frankena, see Stout, *The Flight from Authority*, 179ff.

38. See *Euthyphro*, 15C.

39. See *Apology*, 29Bff.; also *Republic*, 377Cff. Cf. Novak, *Jewish-Christian Dialogue*, 151–154.

40. Along these lines, see G. E. M. Anscombe, "Modern Moral Philosophy," in *The Is-Ought Question*, ed. W. D. Hudson (London, 1969), 175–195.

41. See Hume, *A Treatise of Human Nature*, ed. L. A. Selby-Bigge (Oxford, 1888), I.1.1, 4; II.3.3, 9; III.1.1.

42. Ibid., II.3.3, pp. 414–415.

43. Tillich, *Love, Power, and Justice* (Oxford, 1954), 74.

44. See Martin Buber, *I and Thou*, trans. W. Kaufmann (New York, 1970), 94–95. For Tillich's appreciation of Buber, see *Theology of Culture*, 188ff.

45. See Aristotle, *Metaphysics*, 980a22–30.

46. See Kant, *Critique of Practical Reason*, 20ff.

47. *Love, Power, and Justice*, 30.

48. See Plato, *Philebus*, 60Dff.; Aristotle, *Nicomachean Ethics*, 1172b30ff. Also see *infra*, 96f.

49. *Love, Power, and Justice*, 31, 116.

50. *Systematic Theology*, 1:280. See Aristotle, *Nicomachean Ethics*, 1158b12ff.

51. See Heidegger, *Being and Time*, sec. 27.

52. See Plato, *Republic*, 402D, where the philosophical leader is "most lovable" (*erasmiōtaton*) but feels only "pity" (*eleos*) for those beneath him. See Novak, *Suicide and Morality*, 21ff.

53. See William L. Shirer, *The Rise and Fall of the Third Reich* (New York, 1959), 1432–1433.

54. *Systematic Theology*, 1:282. Here Tillich is arguing against the views of the Swedish Lutheran theologian Anders Nygren, viz., that *eros* is essentially pagan and *agape* essentially Christian. Cf. *Eros and Agape*, trans. P. S. Watson (Chicago, 1982), 49–52, 160ff.

55. *Love, Power, and Justice*, 68–69.

56. See Kant, *Critique of Pure Reason*, B630.

57. *Systematic Theology*, 1:205. See David Novak, "Are Philosophical Proofs of the Existence of God Theologically Meaningful?" in *God in the Teachings of Conservative Judaism*, ed. S. Siegel and E. B. Gertel (New York, 1983), 188–200.

58. Note the translation of Martin Buber and Franz Rosenzweig, *Die Fünf Bücher der Weisung* (Olten, 1954), 158: "Ich werde dasein, als der ich dasein werde . . . ICH BIN DA. . . ." See also Buber, *Zu einer neuen Verdeutschung der Schrift* (Olten, 1954); Rosenzweig, *Kleinere Schriften* (Berlin, 1937), 185ff.; David Novak, *Law and Theology in Judaism*, 2 vols. (New York, 1974), 1:147–149.

59. *Systematic Theology*, 1:117–118.

60. Ibid., 1:129.

61. See Karl Rahner, *Theological Investigations*, trans. C. Ernse, 20 vols. (Baltimore, 1974), 6:78–81; also Novak, *Law and Theology in Judaism*, 2:15ff., and *The Image of the Non-Jew in Judaism: An Historical and Constructive Study of the Noahide Laws* (New York and Toronto, 1983), 410–413.

62. See Aristotle, *Physics*, 193b12–20; Maimonides, *Guide of the Perplexed*, 1.69; Thomas Aquinas, *Summa Theologiae*, 1, q. 44, a. 4, and *Summa Contra Gentiles*, III, chaps. 21ff.

63. See esp. Augustine, *Confessione*, 7.10; Étienne Gilson, *Reason and Revelation in the Middle Ages* (New York, 1938), 16ff.; also David Novak, "The Origin and Meaning of *Credere ut Intelligam* in Augustinian Theology," *Journal of Religious Studies* 6–7 (1978–1979):38–45.

64. Aristotle, *Metaphysics*, 1072a25. Re the importance of *orexis* in Aristotle's thought, see Martha C. Nussbaum, *The Fragility of Goodness: Luck and Ethics in Greek Tragedy and Philosophy* (Cambridge and New York, 1986), 273ff., 7n.

65. Kant, *Critique of Practical Reason*, 128ff.; cf. *Critique of Pure Reason*, B669ff.

66. See Thomas Aquinas, *Summa Contra Gentiles*, I, chap. 1, and *Summa Theologiae*, 1, q. 2, a. 1, for the rejection of Anselm's approach. For Tillich's basic sympathy with its theology (but not its philosophical appropriation as a "proof"), see *Systematic Theology*, 1:208. In this sympathy he comes quite close to his old theological rival Karl Barth. See Barth, *Fides Quarens Intellectum*, trans. I. W. Robertson (London, 1960), 74–75; also David Novak, "Before Revelation: The Rabbis, Paul, and Karl Barth," *Journal of Religion* 71 (1991):63ff.

67. Re Galileo's rejection of teleology in physics, see "The Assayer" in *Discoveries and Opinions of Galileo*, trans. S. Drake (Garden City, N.Y., 1957), 262–263. For the notion of changing scientific paradigms, see Thomas S. Kuhn, *The Structure of Scientific Revolutions* (Chicago, 1962), 91ff. For the problem of a "natural" law ethics when "nature" is quite differently conceived now that it was by Aristotle et al., see Leo

Strauss, *Natural Right and History* (Chicago, 1953), 8; MacIntyre, *After Virtue*, 152; Jürgen Habermas, *Communication and the Evolution of Society*, trans. T. McCarthy (Boston, 1979), 201. Also see *infra*, 141ff. For the idea of God seeking man more than man seeking God, see my late revered teacher Abraham Joshua Heschel, *God in Search of Man* (New York, 1955), 136ff.

68. See H. B. Veatch, *Rational Man: A Modern Interpretation of Aristotelian Ethics* (Bloomington, Ind., 1962), 47ff.

69. Along these lines, see Karl Barth, *Church Dogmatics* I/1: *The Doctrine of the Word of God*, trans. G. W. Bromiley and T. F. Torrance (Edinburgh, 1936), 156. Even Reinhold Niebuhr, who was much more sympathetic to Tillich's position than was Barth, nevertheless voiced similar criticism. See his "Biblical Thought and Ontological Speculation," in *The Theology of Paul Tillich*, ed. C. W. Kegley and R. W. Bretall (New York, 1952), 218. That Tillich himself was quite sensitive to this criticism can be seen from the preface to *Systematic Theology*, 3 vols. (Chicago, 1957), 2:viii.

70. See *Proslogion*, chap. 2. Re desire for God as the *summum bonum*, see Aquinas, *Summa Contra Gentiles*, I, chaps. 37–38, 40–41.

71. See *Systematic Theology*, 1:13.

72. For distinctions between logical and causal necessity and teleology, see Aristotle, *Prior Analytics*, 24b20; *Posterior Analytics*, 94b35; *Physics*, 198b1–10; *Nicomachean Ethics*, 1094b12; Aquinas, *Summa Theologiae*, 1, q. 82, a. 1 and a. 2.

73. See Frankena, "Is Morality Logically Dependent on Religion?" 20; also Peter Geach, "The Moral Law and the Law of God," in *Divine Commands and Morality*, ed. P. Helm (New York, 1981), 167.

74. Aristotle, *Nicomachean Ethics*, 1094a1, 20 (my translation). See also my teacher Germain G. Grisez, "The First Principle of Practical Reason," *Natural Law Forum* 10 (1965):168–201.

75. See *Nicomachean Ethics*, 1113a15–20.

76. See ibid., 1177b30–1178a1. G. E. Moore was correct, it seems to me, when he noted that contemplation (*theoria*) is, for Aristotle, "the only thing good in itself," (*Principia Ethica*, 176). For Plato, conversely, the highest good is that which is "good for itself and for its results." The "results" (*ap' autou*) refer to society; the "for itself" (*di' hauto*) refers to contemplation. See *Republic*, 358A, 516C; Novak, *Suicide and Morality*, 22ff.

77. *Love, Power, and Justice*, 26–27.

78. Ibid., 4.

79. See Kant, *Critique of Practical Reason*, 85–86.

80. See *Systematic Theology* 3 vols. (Chicago, 1963), 3:272ff., and *Theology of Culture*, 142.

81. See Rollo May, *Love and Will* (New York, 1969), 244–245.

82. See, however, A. H. Friedlander, "Tillich and Jewish Thought" in *The Thought of Paul Tillich*, ed. J. L. Adams et al. (San Francisco, 1985), 175–196; also Bernard Martin, *The Existential Theology of Paul Tillich* (New York, 1963), passim. Special mention should be made of Tillich's moving speech against the persecution of the Jews of Germany at Madison Square Garden in New York City on November 21, 1938 (less than two weeks after the pogrom of *Kristallnacht* on November 9), where he reaffirmed the common ties between Jews and Christians and between Judaism and Christianity. See his "The Meaning of Anti-Semitism," *Radical Religion* 41 (1939):34–36.

83. See Tillich's "Is there a Judaeo-Christian Tradition?" *Judaism* 1 (1952):106–110. Cf. Arthur A. Cohen, *The Myth of the Judeo-Christian Tradition* (New York, 1970).

84. *Systematic Theology*, 1:240–241. See *Theology of Culture*, 140.

85. Freud, *The Future of an Illusion*, trans. W. D. Robson-Scott, rev. J. Strachey (Garden City, N.Y., 1961), 34–35.

86. Ibid., 69ff.

87. See Ernest Jones, *The Life and Work of Sigmund Freud* (New York, 1953), 1: 140ff.

88. *The Future of an Illusion*, 81.

89. See *Systematic Theology*, 1:239–240.

90. B. Yevamot 5b. See Novak, *Law and Theology in Judaism*, 2:47ff., for a full discussion of filial piety in Judaism.

91. B. Kiddushin 30b.

92. B. Kiddushin 31a; Y. Peah 1.1/15c.

93. Nahmanides, *Commentary on the Torah*: Exod. 20:12.

94. See Novak, *Law and Theology in Judaism*, 2:72–75.

95. B. Yevamot 6a-b; also B. Shabbat 97b and *infra*, 151f.

96. B. Yoma 85b re Exod. 31:14. Cf. Mark 2:27.

97. See *Systematic Theology*, 1:13; cf. 1:148. See Emil L. Fackenheim, *Encounters Between Judaism and Modern Philosophy* (New York, 1973), 188ff.

98. See B. Sanhedrin 74a; II Maccabees, chap. 7; Augustine, *De Civitate Dei*, 8.27 and 1.20ff.

99. *Summa Theologiae*, 1-2, q. 91, a. 2, trans. in *Basic Writings of Saint Thomas Aquinas*, ed. A. C. Pegis, 2 vols. (New York, 1945), 2:750; Latin text, *Summa Theologiae*, ed P. Caramello (Rome, 1962).

100. *Summa Theologiae*, 1-2, q. 91, a. 4, p. 753.

101. *Hilkhot Melakhim*, 8.10. See Novak, *The Image of the Non-Jew in Judaism*, 276ff.

102. *Love, Power, and Justice*, 76–77.

103. Ibid., 83. See *Systematic Theology*, 3:252, 267.

104. See Kant, *Critique of Practical Reason*, 101–102.

105. See Tillich's *On the Boundary: An Autobiographical Sketch* (New York, 1966), 21ff., 40ff., 94ff.

106. Note the rabbinic interpretation of this verse: "R. Hiyyah bar Ba said that if they had only forsaken Me but kept My Torah, I [God] would have overlooked that . . . for if they had only forsaken Me and kept My Torah, the leaven in it would have brought them back to me. R. Honeh said that one should study the Torah even not for its proper end, because even when it is not being studied for its proper end, one should eventually come to study it for its own proper end [*li-shmah*]." Y. Hagigah 1.7/76c; cf. B. Nazir 23b.

107. See Novak, *Suicide and Morality*, 57–59; also Novak, *Law and Theology in Judaism*, 1:83–84.

108. *Systematic Theology*, 3:159.

109. Ibid., 2:76.

110. See Ludwig Wittgenstein, *Notebooks 1914–1916*, 2d ed., trans. G. E. M. Anscombe (Chicago, 1974), 91e.

111. See Joseph Fletcher, *Situation Ethics: The New Morality* (Philadelphia, 1966), 95–96. Cf. Germain Grisez, *Abortion* (New York, 1970), 291ff.

112. See Aquinas, *Summa Theologiae*, 1-2, q. 19, a. 5 and a. 6; 1-2, q. 95, a. 2; 1, q. 79, a. 13.

113. See ibid., 1-2, q. 94, a. 5, where Aquinas distinguishes between unchangeable first principles of natural law and changeable secondary principles. See also A. Battaglia, *Toward a Reformulation of Natural Law* (New York, 1981), esp. 110ff.

114. *Systematic Theology*, 1:186.

3

John Courtney Murray, S.J.: A Jewish Appraisal

John Courtney Murray as Philosophical Model

I did not have the privilege of knowing the late Father John Courtney Murray (d. 1967) personally, but nevertheless he played an important role in my intellectual development. I read his book *We Hold These Truths* one year after its initial publication, just after I was graduated from the University of Chicago in 1961, and just before I was to enter the Jewish Theological Seminary of America in New York to begin my studies for rabbinical ordination. That was a point of crucial transition in my life.

The University of Chicago in the late 1950s and early 1960s was still very much under the influence of the Aristotelian educational philosophy of its legendary former chancellor, Robert Maynard Hutchins. In that supportive atmosphere I discovered the tradition of natural law. This tradition, it seemed to me then, presented the bridge I very much needed to interrelate my Jewish faith and my commitment to reason. All other intellectual traditions to which I had been exposed seemed to affirm faith but deny reason, affirm reason but deny faith, or deny both faith and reason. The tradition of natural law, though, asserted that there is an intelligible order in the universe, and that by proper inquiry a human intelligence could discover his or her consistent place in that universal order.

Recognition of an intelligibility beyond mere human invention also entailed, at least for most of those who considered themselves to be the perpetuators of the natural law tradition, the further recognition that the universal intelligible order is ultimately dependent upon God. Of course, this recognition alone could not constitute the far more intense content of Jewish faith (or Christian or Muslim faith), but it could at least make the connection between faith and reason possible. At that time and for a time afterward, it seemed to provide me with what was intellectually necessary, although never what was spiritually sufficient. Even then, however, I was left with this gnawing question: If natural law as a bridge between faith and reason is appealing in theory, can it still have any practical significance in our society, which was where I was to live and work at my vocation?

During that transitional summer of 1961, when this question was very much on my mind, I discovered Murray's work. It was an important discovery because Murray as a Catholic had virtually the same problem I as a Jew had. And he, being older and wiser than I, seemed to be far ahead of me in dealing with it.

Both Catholicism and Judaism were regarded as outside the mainstream of American thought, indeed outside the mainstream of modern Western thought altogether. In the eyes of many, intelligent Catholics and intelligent Jews were faced with one of two options: either to opt for the integrity of their own faith tradition and thus remove themselves from present intellectual discourse, or to opt for the present realm and thus bracket their faith tradition, if not leave it altogether. The latter step, of course, is the one taken by many of the best and the brightest. The intellectual landscape then was filled with former Catholic and former Jewish (and former Protestant, especially Evangelical) believers, as it is now. But Murray, in sharp contrast to both of these options, suggested a third way, which, culturally at least, was more radical than both of them. It is boldly expressed in the passage from his book that to this day is still quite vivid in my mind.

> [A] Catholic . . . knows that the principles of Catholic faith and morality stand superior to, and in control of, the whole order of civil life. The question is sometimes raised, whether Catholicism is compatible with American democracy. The question is invalid as well as impertinent; for the manner of its position inverts the order of values. It must, of course, be turned round to read, whether American democracy is compatible with Catholicism.[1]

One must remember, furthermore, that the book in which these lines were written was published in 1960, the very year when, for the first time in U.S. history, a Catholic candidate for president, John F. Kennedy, had a real chance to win.

In the American Catholic community at the time there was an understandable attempt to show how thoroughly American Catholicism really is. This attempt, of course, was largely polemical in intent. It was formulated and argued in order to counter strongly the aspersions that had long been cast on the consistent patriotism of all Catholic Americans, aspersions coming from certain Protestant circles and drawing upon the whole history of anti-Catholicism in this country.

On the other hand, there were elements in the American Catholic community who were highly suspicious of the easy marriage between their God and this new American version of Caesar. They were drawing upon an older type of European Catholic suspicion about the whole American democratic proposition, this *novus ordo seclorum*, especially its pluralism, which would never afford their church the place of political or even cultural preeminence it still enjoyed in some older European societies. For them, anything but an explicitly pragmatic *modus vivendi* with the United States would surely prove to be dangerous to their faith before long. Murray's voice, then, provided a way out of this impasse for Catholics and, by analogy, for other religious believers as well.[2]

At the time I first read Murray, virtually all the rabbinical statements I had read or heard that dealt with the role of Judaism in the United States were of two kinds. On the one hand, the statements of the more liberal rabbis were almost always attempts to show how thoroughly American Judaism really is. The conclusion that could be drawn from their statements was, however (whether or not consciously intended by these liberal rabbis), that Judaism had done a fine job in providing historical precedent for American democracy, and that the United States should be grateful for these past services. Nevertheless, since the contribution had already been made, American thought could suffice on its own — even for Jews.

On the other hand, the statements of the more traditional rabbis usually were an attempt to show how subtly dangerous American culture and thought really are to the survival of Jewish faith and observance. To be sure, these rabbis were grateful that Jews were not being murdered and persecuted in the United States as they had been in the countries most of them had personally fled, like Czarist Russia or, most recently then, Nazi Germany. However, anything more than an explicitly pragmatic *modus vivendi* would surely prove to be dangerous to traditional Jewish life before long. And unlike the more liberal rabbinical statements about Judaism and the United States, whose assimilationist conclusions were mostly implicit and perhaps even unconscious, these more traditional rabbis were quite explicit in drawing their own conclusions (as they were, indeed, about everything else they taught). As one who was exposed to their teaching during his impressionable adolescence, I can attest that nothing was left to the imagination or powers of inference of those who sat at their feet.

The parallels between the American Catholic and the American Jewish situation in the mid-twentieth century are indeed striking. (The fact, moreover, that both communities then were still composed of mostly immigrants or their children explains the further similarity: like most more recent arrivals here, many Catholics and Jews were either too enchanted or too frightened by this radically new society to be quite rational about it.) Nevertheless, despite these similarities, there was an important difference (at least for me). No one in the American Jewish community was offering the alternative John Courtney Murray was offering in the American Catholic community.

As time went on, it became increasingly evident to me that the reason the Murray project (as it has now come to be called) was not finding an analogue in the American Jewish community was not because of the very fundamental differences between Judaism and Catholicism, for, although Murray was a distinguished Catholic theologian, his political thought was not formulated with the Christological or ecclesiological doctrines of Christianity in general or Roman Catholicism in particular—doctrines that make the differences between Judaism and any form of Christianity *toto caelo*. Murray's political thought was formulated with the doctrines of the natural law tradition. And as he himself insisted about this tradition's independence:

> It is sometimes said that one cannot accept the doctrine of natural law unless one has antecedently accepted "its Roman Catholic presuppositions." This, of course, is quite wrong. The doctrine of natural law has no Roman Catholic presuppositions. Its only presupposition is threefold: that man is intelligent; that reality is intelligible; and that reality, as grasped by intelligence, imposes on the will the obligation that it be obeyed in its demands for action or abstention.[3]

The reason for the absence of a Jewish project like the Murray project was not because of what differentiates Judaism from Catholicism or Catholicism from Judaism. Rather, it was that Jewish natural law theory was mostly unknown to Jews themselves, let alone to non-Jews. And this is not because of any intellectual inferiority of Judaism in comparison to Catholicism. Rather, it is because Judaism's presence in the intellectual discourse of the non-Jewish world is much newer than that of Catholicism, even though it is the older faith. Surely, this has been so for the past fifteen hundred years. But, because of the new pluralistic cultural climate that has slowly been developing in the United States, the voice of Judaism—and not just the voice of dejudaized Jews—is being actively sought, especially in the area of public moral discourse. Hence, I gradually resolved (beginning with my graduate work at Georgetown University with the Thomistic philosophers Germain Grisez and the late Heinrich Rommen) to expose Jewish natural law theory to my fellow Jews and then beyond.[4] The task has not been easy. There are still many in both worlds who are incredulous about the whole project. But I must thank John Courtney Murray for providing me with a powerful intellectual model. And although Murray was a Catholic theologian, he was relevant to my project because he was a philosopher as well.

The Philosophical Problem of Natural Law

So far I have tried to show the desirability of an appropriation of the natural law tradition for a Jewish or Christian believer who is also convinced that there is a connection between faith and reason as two independent but mutually related spheres of human activity in the world. There still remains, however, the question of the current plausibility of this tradition, let alone the question of its truth. Even the plausibility of the assertions of the natural law tradition requires more than just the type of historical research that uncovers a history of Catholic or Jewish (or Protestant or Muslim) recognition and development of it. Natural law as *law* has always proclaimed itself to be normative, not just descriptive. Although history certainly plays a role in any normative system, history alone, as the record of the past, cannot make a primary normative claim on the present. Even when history functions normatively, it does so only because present criteria have been constituted that indicate why those who are present ought to listen to voices from the past.[5] That is why the problem of law — natural law or any other kind — is a philosophical problem before it is a historical one. To deal with this philosophical problem comprehensively would require far more space than the confines of this chapter; therefore, I shall concentrate on Thomistic natural law theory as it is found in Murray's *We Hold These Truths*.

In speaking of the premises of natural law, Murray states:

> [I]t supposes a metaphysic of nature, especially the idea that nature is a teleological concept, that the "form" of a thing is its "final cause," the goal of its beginning; in this case, that there is a natural inclination in man to become what in nature and destination he is — to achieve the fullness of his own being. . . . [I]t supposes a natural theology, asserting that there is a God, who is eternal Reason *Nous*, at the summit of the order of being. . . .[6]

Clearly, he is affirming Thomistic natural law theory in a most explicitly Aristotelian way. However, here is where a number of astute philosophical commentators, even some who are themselves wholly sympathetic with the project of natural law in the contemporary world, have found a major obstacle. That major obstacle is Aristotelian metaphysics.

The very term *metaphysic(s)* admits of several meanings as it is first used to designate Aristotle's chief work on ontology. *Meta* means "that which follows," and it can signify nothing more profound than the literary fact that Aristotle's work on ontology follows his chief work on natural science in his *ouvre*; hence, it is *meta ta physika*. Although this is certainly so, the term has also been seen as having conceptual significance. It can also mean that ontology, for Aristotle, is that which goes beyond what is physical, moving from the physical up to that which is beyond it, as a cause is beyond its effect by being its ground.[7] Both cause and effect are related in a hierarchal order: Nature (*physis*, now more widely conceived than the sum of *ta physika* — "physical entities"). Metaphysics constitutes those first principles (*archai*) the full functionality of physics calls for.[8] And, even though in the ontological order, metaphysics precedes physics, in the epistemological order, that is, the way we learn these truths, physics precedes metaphysics. Metaphysics is the expansion of physics to what must be finally seen as its epistemological conclusion, or to what must be originally seen as its ontological foundation. That ontological foundation, as Murray correctly represented it, is teleological.

Physical teleology, the type that leads directly up into metaphysical teleology, is normative in the Aristotelian system because it is primarily seen in astrophysics. Aristotelian astrophysics deals with a higher form of entity, one that is both superior in intelligibility and superior in intelligence. The very matter of the heavens is different in kind from earthly matter. As such, and only as such, can the heavenly bodies function as exemplars for the lower human intelligences. Human intelligences can view these bodies only from afar, from the earth, and yet they desire to be like them as much as is possible for their limited intelligence. The summit of the intelligent and intelligible heavenly realm is God. God is so intelligible that everything else in nature is intelligible in relation to him in a descending order. God is so intelligent that he (actually, "it" is the more appropriate pronoun to be used for this intransitive God) is interested in nothing but himself. Thus in their striving to order their lives intelligently, humans are to look to those higher beings that are already functioning with this desired excellence. Being intelligible, these higher beings can be the objects of human intelligence. Being intelligent, they can be exemplary for human intelligence as subject.[9]

What Galileo and Newton did to make this system lose its key physical point of reference was to show that heavenly matter like earthly matter is only intelligible, not intelligent. As such, it thereby loses its exemplary status, leaving the human being as the only intelligent being whom we can identify in ordinary experience or in any valid abstraction from it. Thus the whole system requires acceptance of a physical paradigm that has been consistently inoperative in physical science since the Renaissance. Final causes are simply no longer part of the world of discourse in physics, and it is physics that still largely determines the parameters of discourse for all the other natural sciences. Without physics, there is no meta-physics in the Aristotelian sense. One of the obvious facts of modernity (and postmodernity, where many believe our culture is now located) is not that metaphysics has died (as only the Logical Positivists once thought) but that metaphysics has never again been able to display the same self-confident hegemony it once displayed when Aristotle was *the Philosopher.*

One can see an admission of the fundamental impediment to the philosophical reintroduction of traditional Aristotelianism, however desirable that might be, in the work of the contemporary philosopher, Alasdair MacIntyre. MacIntyre himself not only is sympathetic with the comprehensiveness of Aristotelianism but even attempts to reintroduce Thomistic Aristotelianism into current philosophical discourse. Nevertheless, he is certainly aware that he can do so only through a method radically different from that of traditional Thomists like Murray. Hence, MacIntyre admits that

> what is clear is that the Aristotelian scheme provides a link between science and the type of ultimate explanation provided by rational theology and that this kind of link, although far from absent in the science of Galileo and Newton, has disappeared in nineteenth- and twentieth-century science.[10]

However, even in Galileo and Newton, the link between the two is not a teleological one.

One sees this post-Renaissance lack of any similar relation between metaphysics and ethics in the work of all the major modern philosophers. Thus, for example, even though Kant could devise a "metaphysic of morals," that metaphysic is not presented as an ontology, a science of being that underlies both physical and moral reality.[11] And even though Whitehead did devise such a metaphysics as an ontology, it seems to function only as a ground for physical reality. Whitehead himself did not use his ontology to ground any kind of ethical system, and it is doubtful that his contemporary disciples could do so following from his metaphysics alone.[12] As for Heidegger's ontology, it should be recalled that he never constituted being per se (*Sein*) but only being-as-manifest-in-human-consciousness (*Dasein*). In other words, his phenomenology never led into the ontology he himself originally promised in his magnum opus, *Being and Time*.[13] And Heidegger, like Whitehead, also did not ground anything like an ethical system.

Now some neo-Aristotelians, both Thomistic and non-Thomistic, have attempted to get themselves out of this impasse by asserting that the teleology of human life, upon which Aristotelian ethics is based, does not need the kind of ontological grounding that traditional, pre-Galilean and pre-Newtonian physics-cum-metaphysics formerly provided.[14] Nevertheless, none of the neo-Aristotelians of whom I am aware is able to recapture Aristotle's sense of humankind's natural teleology being ultimately located in the realizable human *aspiration* to be like the higher, superterrestrial intelligences, for that presupposes the by now irretrievable Aristotelian astrophysics. Accordingly, even they are able to constitute nature only as a *conditio sine qua non* — a limit — not as a *conditio per quam* — the ultimately attractive end/final cause.[15] In short, they can do no more than modern natural rights theorists, who conceive nature in minimal rather than maximal terms.[16] They cannot, therefore, locate essential human motivation to *be better* in nature precisely because humankind can no longer recognize any *higher* (that is, exemplary) nature — at least "naturally."

Without this ontological grounding, or at least some other ontological grounding, it is hard to see how this can lead to anything more than Kantianism. In Kantianism we do see teleology, but the only *telos* turns out to be human reason itself as it constructs its own universe *by and for* itself. The human actor, then, in this system actually projects his or her own ends based on self-knowledge as a first cause: the maker of a world rather than a participant in one already there. The human being as an end-in-itself is a self-constituting, autonomous being. This, then, is the basis of the nineteenth-century distinction between the so-called cultural disciplines (*Geisteswissenschaften*) and the natural sciences (*Naturwissenschaften*) — that is, between the realm of values and purposes and the realm of mechanical causes.[17] Purposes clearly transcend nature taken as anything other than human nature. And, surely, the mid-twentieth-century attempt to see even the natural sciences as being cultural constructions moves even further away from the ancient and medieval attempt to see nature as normative.[18]

All of this is essentially different from Aristotelianism, certainly from that of the Thomistic variety. Here human reason can effectively order natural inclination to do good only because the seeker of the goods and the goods being sought are already present to each other in a larger reality: nature. That is why these goods are capable of being achieved by the human actor, for he or she knows himself or herself in essentially the same way he or she knows the rest of nature. Thus neither human nor nonhuman nature is a *de novo* construction or projection of *homo faber*. Murray himself emphasizes this distinction when he writes:

> Reason does not create its own laws, any more than man creates himself. Man has the laws of his nature given to him, as nature itself is given . . . and so his reason reflects a higher reason; therein consists its rightness and its power to oblige. . . . [I]t appoints an order of nature—an order of beings, each of which carries in its very nature also its end and purposes. . . .[19]

Whether or not one agrees with Murray's particularly Thomistic presentation of the relation between human reason and what lies beyond it, one can generally agree with him that human reason cannot sustain itself without being located in a larger context of some kind. The question is: What is that larger context if Aristotelian metaphysical nature can no longer preform that comprehensive function?[20]

The Theological Problem of Natural Law

There are also theological problems facing Murray and other traditional Thomists in their natural law theory. The usual problem raised against them (and their counterparts in Judaism and Islam) comes from fideists. They argue that humans are simply unable to perceive clearly what is good for themselves in any unambiguous sense. It is only through revelation pointing to salvation by God alone that humans can hope for any true fulfillment at all. This problem is best known when raised by Protestants heavily influenced by Luther. Nevertheless, this type of problem, *mutatis mutandis*, is raised by Jewish and Muslim fideists against those who are the equivalents of the Thomists in their own respective traditions.[21]

Theologians who also affirm the reality of natural law have an answer to this sort of challenge to the validity of their position. Murray himself expresses it quite cogently.

> The Christian call is to transcend nature, notably to transcend what is noblest in nature, the faculty of reason. But it is not a call to escape from nature, or to dismantle nature's own structure. . . . In so far as they touch the moral life, the energies of grace . . . quicken to new and fuller life the dynamics of nature, which are resident in reason. Were it otherwise, grace would not be supernatural but only miraculous.[22]

Here again, it is not only Christianity that sees itself as the divinely given means for transcending the limitations of nature. The difference between Judaism and Christianity (and Islam) is just what the content of this divine grace is. The formal theological problem of nature and grace is virtually the same in the respective faith traditions, even if the real differences as to what this grace consists of are *toto caelo*. Jews and Christians (and Muslims) have enough resources in their respective traditions at least effectively to counter if not actually refute the antirational fideism also present in these same traditions.

The more difficult theological problem does not come from the outside, from those who deny the legitimacy of any theological affirmation of natural law. It comes, rather, from the inside. The question here is: If teleological metaphysics and its natural theology can no longer cogently ground natural law by connecting it to God, what can reestablish that grounding connection? Metaphysics and theology are no longer part of the same order. And if metaphysics is the only link between ethics (pertaining to what is between humans) and theology (pertaining to what is between humans and God), we seem to be left with three alternatives.

First, believers from the respective faith traditions can confine *their* ethics to the specific content of *their* own revelations. All ethics, then, can be divine positive law only as interpreted and applied by the authority structures in each of the traditions. Ethics in this view is possible only when it has a direct theological grounding. It follows from this, of course, that ethics thereby ceases to be an area in which adherents of the different faith traditions can intelligently interact with each other, let alone with American society as a whole, where theology—anybody's theology—has no such immediate authority. And those who persist in talking this kind of theological language in public discourse are rightly suspected of being religious imperialists who are attempting to force *their* religious ethics down *everyone else's* throat.[23] This objection comes from the adherents of the other religious traditions in our pluralistic society just as fast and just as vehemently as it does from avowed secularists. (This should offer some small comfort to the secularists who worry that more religion in public discourse will lead to some kind of official state religion.)

Second, one can accept the kind of spiritual schizophrenia, which I described at the beginning of his chapter, by which one simply separates his or her religious thinking and acting from his or her thinking and acting in regard to everything not directly involving God. This, of course, leaves one's religion an ever-shrinking role in one's life as the secular world claims more and more of one's time and energy, intellectual as well as physical.[24]

Finally, one can adopt a Kantian-type approach and argue for an ethical metaphysics rather than a metaphysical ethics of the Aristotelian type. This approach is attractive to philosophers because it can produce at least a minimal natural law theory—something most ably shown of late by the influential philosopher John Rawls.[25] The question is, though, whether such philosophical attractiveness can still be integrated with religious faith.

This approach, when more strictly Kantian, is based on the idea that humans are the autonomous creators of a universal morality (*causa noumenon*). We have seen above why on Aristotelian grounds alone a Thomist like Murray rejects this approach philosophically. However, its rejection on theological grounds by a Jewish or Christian believer (and Murray was a Catholic before he was an Aristotelian) must be even stronger, for any connection between ethics and God as either *archē* or *telos* of the moral life is ruled out by this approach in principle. It can accept only human transcendence; God at best becomes a postulate. I do not see how any Jewish or Christian believer, however much he or she might want to constitute a natural law theory, can possibly accept with any kind of theological consistency an approach to ethics whose very ground is that the human being is the measure of all things.[26]

When this approach, on the other hand, might be termed neo-Kantian rather than strictly Kantian, it is based on the idea that a finite number of humanly sought values or goods are simply given and that practical reason can determine an ordered relationship with them—a rational ethical system. However, for this approach, the human relationship with God is either irrelevant or only one good among others. But, surely no Jewish or Christian believer can with any theological integrity accept an approach (let alone actually devise it) where God is neither *origo* of nor *summum bonum* for what humans are to do with their lives.[27]

The revival of natural law can be only a cogent option, however, if these extremes can be successfully avoided. Without that it cannot be more than nostalgia. I have tried to show that the metaphysically constituted theology of Aristotelian Thomism proposed by Murray cannot effect this revival (nor can a Kantian or even most neo-Kantian approaches). In other words, I agree with Murray's overall project; I do not agree with the way he attempts to argue for it at this point in history.

A Philosophical Alternative

The assumption, held by traditional Thomists like Murray, is that there is a definable human nature to which everyone can refer without prior allegiance to any religious tradition, and from which natural law precepts can be derived. However, this assumption is philosophically unconvincing at the present time. It is unconvincing because it invokes a correspondence theory of truth when there is no longer any commonly accepted object of correspondence. If "truth is the agreement of thinking with reality" (*veritas est adaequatio intellectus ad rem*), the statement only has a noetic function when there is some agreement about which "reality" is the criterion of what is true as opposed to false thinking about "it.' Only when this is the case does truth follow being (*veritas sequitur esse rerum*). Only when there is a common acceptance of a "nature" can "natural" law be rationally persuasive.

When that is not the case, however, what if one takes natural law as it has been affirmed by Jews and Christians (and Muslims) as being *part of their* traditional teaching about and to the world at large, rather than an independent tradition of its own? Here, it is clear, a different theory of truth is called for.

Within the covenantal community of faith itself a correspondence theory of truth is still valid. The community acknowledges a body of normative revelation from God. It itself is the criterion of what is true as opposed to what is false thinking about it. Thus one could say that truth is the agreement of thinking with the word of God (*veritas est adaequatio intellectus ad verbum Dei*). The word of God as the criterion of truth cannot be established on the basis of any external criterion and still retain the absolute primacy the religious traditions claim for it. Thus Jews praise God as the giver of *torat emet*, which means "the doctrine of truth," the corollary of which is that nothing else can be true if it is inconsistent with it.[28] That is why Judaism and Christianity call their unique truths *mysteries*.[29] They are inaccessible to outside judgment or appropriation.

Despite the necessity for a correspondence theory of truth in the internal discourse of the covenantal community, the community also has something to say beyond its own borders. Here a correspondence theory of truth, at least at this point in history, cannot be employed for the reasons we have already seen. That is why the Thomistic version of natural law as presented by a theologian like Murray cannot have enough plausibility to be convincing in social discourse outside the Catholic world in which it has been traditionally developed. (And even there its theory is hardly *philosophia perennis* anymore.) *Jus naturale* will have to give way to *jus gentium*, namely, not what the community accepts as a priori universal truth but only what it itself constitutes as generally normative in and for the world beyond the immediate pale of its own adherents.[30] Here one will have to appeal to historically evident data rather than to the type of metaphysics Murray suggested.

This broader teaching about the world is one that contains the minimal constituents of the fuller revelation proclaimed by Judaism and Christianity, respectively. This point comes out in the works of both Maimonides and Aquinas, each basing himself on earlier sources in his own religious tradition.[31] If one now removes their addition of an Aristotelian metaphysics of nature from both of their formulations of earlier Jewish and Christian tradition, one now needs a coherence theory of truth to talk about this teaching in the world beyond the faith communities. This world is the secular world as it has been with us since the dawn of modernity.

A coherence theory of truth says that one explanation of a problematic situation is better than another if it offers a more coherent reconstitution of its elements, thereby leading to a more comprehensive solution of it. Actually, there are three possible explanations. One explanation reconstitutes some aspects of the problem. A second explanation reconstitutes more of the aspects of the problem. A third explanation reconstitutes even more of the aspects of the problem but requires the acceptance of more new assumptions than the second explanation. Based on the coherence theory of truth, the explanation that reconstitutes the most aspects of the problem with the fewest assumptions is the best explanation now available for our use. Truth, then, is to be found in the second explanation. The first explanation is less plausible because it has not gotten as strong a handle on the situation as the second explanation has. The third explanation, conversely, is less plausible because it has gotten too strong a hold on the situation. For it, the situation is an expendable example of its own preconceived idea. The situation has fallen too far behind it. This latter solution is usually seen as being insuperably vulnerable to the refutation known as Occam's razor. The second explanation avoids the pitfalls of the two extremes. Nevertheless, even here, truth is not something eternal because every explanation is inherently surmountable at some later time.[32] It is a pragmatic theory of truth because truth is judged by the criterion of temporal value, not that of everlasting being.[33]

This is precisely how the broader teachings of the religious traditions, which pertain to the world beyond their respective covenants, can speak to, in, and about that world with more persuasiveness than Murray's type of natural law theory, for being partially in the same world as the adherents of secularist traditions, they are faced with certain common problematic situations. These situations call for normative answers. Furthermore, there is now the recognition that all our positions are tradition-bound, that there is no nature standing over and above the traditions that can be invoked here as a transcendent criterion of truth, one to which the true answer must ultimately correspond. Therefore, it becomes the case that either we find certain common substantive overlappings between traditions, or one tradition has to show that it has the better resources for dealing with a problem facing all the traditions, religious or secular, represented in that society at that time. Alasdair MacIntyre shows quite astutely how this latter case of interaction between traditions takes place.

> Yet the achievement of the understanding of one tradition by the adherents of another . . . in certainly rare but crucial types of cases . . . may lead to a judgment that by the standards of one's own tradition the standpoint of another tradition offers superior resources for understanding the problems and issues which confront one's own tradition.[34]

This is where Jewish-Christian dialogue, which has long been an important component in my own experience and theological reflection, plays a key role in the process of dialogue between religious communities and the secular world.[35] In the old Aristotelian model, the one accepted by premodern theologians like Maimonides and Aquinas (and Muslims like Avicenna), metaphysics supplied the medium needed for that dialogue.[36] Following this model, these religious thinkers thought they could reach beyond their immediate religious traditions and speak *both* to each other *and* even to that which was not specifically religious at all ("the philosophers") in the *same* way. That medium, as we have seen, is no longer available.

Following the model of the overlapping of traditions I have tried to present briefly here, Jews and Christians must first be able to talk to each other *before* they can talk to the secular world, which is further removed from both of them. Discourse must begin with those whose traditions overlap most. It can then proceed to those whose traditions overlap less. Surely, no two religious traditions have overlapped more than Judaism and Christianity.[37]

At points of mutually identifiable overlap, discourse can still, to a certain extent, be structured by a correspondence theory of truth. In the case of Jews and Christians before us, the common acceptance of the Hebrew Bible as the word of God, as preserved in its present text, provides the needed transcendent object by which discourse can be judged true or false depending on its correspondence or lack of correspondence with the text as the basic normative datum. Now, in fact, Jews and Christians have disagreed about more in the Hebrew Bible than they have agreed. For example, one community says that the Sabbath is perpetually binding on all members of the covenant; the other says that "the Son of man is the lord of the Sabbath."[38] Nevertheless, on the doctrinal level there remains essential agreement about God as creator and revealer, and the still unredeemed condition of this world; on the practical level there remains agreement about the sanctity of human life, the integrity of the family, and the right to a variety of individual and cooperative achievements. This is the Judeo-Christian tradition, one shared by both communities without at all compromising their respective covenants with God.

With the secular world there is much less commonality because there is much less of substance held in common. Therefore, here is where a coherence theory of truth is what Jews and Christians, largely in concert, will have to employ in their discourse with the secular world. At this point they also come closest to the issues of the natural law project, if not theory, of a Thomistic thinker like Murray.

This theory will work quite well when dealing with an issue like ecology.[39] Virtually everyone is now agreed that the modern technological relationship between humans and their nonhuman surroundings is becoming more and more unacceptable for both physical and spiritual reasons. There are some — even some theologians — who blame the problem of technology on the biblical teaching about humans having dominion over the earth (à la Genesis 1:26).[40] The fact is, however, that biblical teaching in its normative thrust (which is the most immediate aspect of that teaching) structures, guides, and limits the human relationship with the environment, while not reducing humans to the level of all other nonspiritual parts of that environment. That is done by an elaborate system of norms of responsibility: responsibility *to* God, *with* one another, and *for* the world. What Jews and Christians have to do in regard to this common problem, a problem recognized by secularists as keenly as by themselves, is to constitute a more coherent solution than that which secularists can provide out of their traditions. And here "more coherent" does not mean "final" or "unfalsifiable." A coherence theory of truth cannot make any such absolute claims for any conclusion reached by it. This is only one important example. Here I can only obliquely suggest the possibility of constituting a better solution, not what the content of that solution is actually to be or how it is specifically to be argued.

Affirming Divine Creative Wisdom

I have tried to show in this chapter that the universal truth a Thomist like Murray assumed to be the correspondence with nature as a transcendent object cannot be constituted, for it requires a transcendence of traditions that is simply untenable for both philosophical and theological reasons. Surely, this does not mean, however, that transcendence cannot be affirmed and a correspondence theory of truth never employed. Both are indeed possible, but they are possible plurally, not singularly. Each tradition constitutes its *own* relationship with its *own* respective transcendent object. Judaism and Christianity each constitute their respective transcendent objects as the word of God. There are some areas of substantive overlap; there are more and deeper areas where there is none. In the case of the secular world, there is even much less overlapping with Judaism or Christianity. But when there is overlapping between the secular and religious worlds, it is almost always at the point where the two religious traditions themselves overlap. Thus, there are only more specific truths and more general truths. Other than some basic logical truths, universal truth in theology or even philosophy will have to wait for the final redemption of the world.[41] In the meantime, rationalities function within their respective traditions, a point Alasdair MacIntyre has helped us to understand better.

Yet, it seems reason has the best chance of surviving and persisting in traditions like Judaism and Christianity, in which the tradition itself is grounded in the affirmation of a divine creative wisdom who governs the whole universe, albeit known only by created minds in very small, often disjunctive ways, for reason does not seem to be capable of surviving and persisting in an otherwise absurd universe and in an otherwise meaningless process of history. Even when Judaism and Christianity become antirational, which they too often do, their respective traditions provide the means for correcting this error from out of their very sources. In other words, reason needs faith as much as faith needs reason. (It is *intellectus quarens fidem* as much as *fides quarens intellectum*.) Hence, despite our fundamental philosophical differences over metaphysics and natural law, let alone our even more fundamental religious differences, I am nevertheless convinced that the late John Courtney Murray and I, as both believers and thinkers, could agree on this last point. In light of that agreement, and considering how many in the world would surely disagree with us, our differences do not seem overwhelming after all.

NOTES

1. *We Hold These Truths: Catholic Reflections on the American Proposition* (New York, 1960), ix–x. Also see *infra*, 232.

2. For a thorough discussion of this whole situation in American Catholic thought, as well as a thorough analysis of Murray's role in it, see George S. Weigel, *Tranquillitas Ordinis: The Present Failure and Future Promise of American Catholic Thought on War and Peace* (New York, 1987), 107ff.

3. *We Hold These Truths*, 109.

4. For my main work on this whole subject, see *The Image of the Non-Jew in Judaism: An Historical and Constructive Study of the Noahide Laws* (New York and Toronto, 1983).

5. See *infra*, 188f.

6. *We Hold These Truths*, 327–328.

7. See J. Ritter and K. Gruender, *Historisches Wörterbuch der Philosophie*, 7 vols. (Basel, 1980), 5:1186, 1197.

8. See Aristotle, *Metaphysics*, 981b25–30.

9. See Aristotle, *Nichomachean Ethics*, 1141a34ff.; *Metaphysics*, 1026a20ff.

10. *Whose Justice? Which Rationality?* (Notre Dame, 1988), 101. Also see his *After Virtue* (Notre Dame, 1981), 152.

11. See Kant, *Groundwork of the Metaphysic of Morals*, trans. H. J. Paton (New York, 1964), 94.

12. See A. N. Whitehead, *Process and Reality* (New York, 1929), 405.

13. See Martin Heidegger, *Being and Time*, trans. J. Macquarrie and E. Robinson (New York and Evanston, 1962), 32–35.

14. See, e.g., H. B. Veatch, *Rational Man: A Modern Interpretation of Aristotle's Ethics* (Bloomington, Ind., 1962), 76 and passim; P. T. Geach, *The Virtues* (Cambridge, 1977), 9–19; J. Finnis, *Natural Law and Natural Rights* (Oxford, 1980), 52–53. See *infra*, 141f.

15. For Aristotle, "necessity" (*to anangkaion*) is that without which something could not possibly be (*Metaphysics*, 1015a20ff.). A final cause (*telos*) is necessary, but not everything necessary is a *telos* (ibid., 1072b10). Similarly, every *telos* is a "limit" (*peras*), but not every limit is a *telos* (ibid., 1022a14). The neo-Aristotelians are able to constitute nature only in the minimal sense of *to anangkaion* and *peras*, not as a hierarchal *telos*, as did Aristotle, a hierarchal *telos* maximally culminating in nature's God. Aristotle maintains that God as *the* ultimate *telos* is that for whose sake (*hou heneka*) everything acts (ibid., 994b10). It is this ultimately *attractive* sense of hierarchal nature that the neo-Aristotelians cannot retrieve.

16. See *infra*, 139.

17. See the neo-Kantian philosopher Ernst Cassirer's *The Logic of the Humanities*, trans. C. S. Howe (New Haven, 1961), 117ff.

18. See Thomas S. Kuhn, *The Structure of Scientific Revolutions* (Chicago, 1962), esp. the introduction. For the modern problem of ascribing normativity to nature, see Sidney Hook, "The Ethics of Suicide," *International Journal of Ethics* 37 (1927):179; David Novak, *Suicide and Morality* (New York, 1975), 45ff. Re ethics presupposing ontology, see *supra*, 16f.; *infra*, 235.

19. *We Hold These Truths*, 330.

20. The current inappropriateness of Aristotelian teleology in either philosophy or theology does not mean that therefore all teleology need be abandoned. For its continued theological use, see *supra*, 54ff.

21. See *supra*, 25ff. For an example of traditional Lutheran-Protestant opposition to natural law, see Helmut Thielecke, *Theological Ethics*, 2 vols., trans. J. W. Doberstein (Grand Rapids, Mich., 1979), 1:383ff.

22. *We Hold These Truths*, 298.

23. See David Novak, "Bioethics and the Contemporary Jewish Community," *Hastings Center Report* 20, Special Supplement (1990):14–17.

24. See *infra*, 225f.

25. See *A Theory of Justice* (Cambridge, Mass., 1971), passim.

26. See Kant, *Critique of Pure Reason* B819; *Critique of Practical Reason*, trans. L. W. Beck (Indianapolis, 1956), 234ff.; Rawls, *A Theory of Justice*, 252ff.

27. For an insightful critique of these Kantian-type natural law theories, including the neo-Kantian versions (whether so named by their authors or not) adopted by some religiously committed philosophers, see R. Hittinger, "Varieties of Minimalist Natural

Law Theory," *American Journal of Jurisprudence* 34 (1989):155ff. For my own *quali-fied* theological use of a certain type of neo-Kantian philosophy of law, see *supra*, 32f.

28. For Jews, the truth of the Torah is the truth of God's own revelation. Thus the Y. Sanhedrin 1.1/18a notes that "the seal of God is truth [*emet*]." A homily that follows this dictum sees it based on Isaiah 44:6: "I am the first and I am the last and besides Me there is no god." Hence, the Torah is Truth per se, to which all that is true must correspond; that is why *emet* essentially means "being faithful": the consistency of God's word to those to whom it is addressed (see, e.g., Psalms 111:8), and the requirement of consistency from those to whom that word is addressed (see, e.g., Psalms 15:2). In rabbinic theology the Torah is the *hagia sophia*, with which God creatively orders the world. See *Beresheet Rabbah*, beg. re Prov. 8:30.

29. For rabbinic emphasis on the Oral Tradition as being more mysterious and, therefore, holier than even the Written Torah, see *Shemot Rabbah* 46.1 re Hos. 8:12; *Tanhuma*: Ki Tissa, printed ed., 34; also, B. Gittin 60b re Exod. 34:27.

30. For the complex relations between the concepts of *jus gentium* and *jus naturale* as used in Roman law, see A. P. d'Entreves, *Natural Law: An Historical Survey* (New York, 1965), 17–32. For some Roman legal thinkers (e.g., Ulpian), *jus naturale* is based on a simple empirical observation of what is common to all animals, humans included. In this view, then, *jus gentium* stands above *jus naturale* as intellect stands above instinct. But, for other Roman legal thinkers, largely influenced by Stoic philoso-phy, *jus naturale* stands above *jus gentium* as a higher intellect stands above a lower intellect, it being the criterion of *quod semper aequum ac bonum est*. In the Muslim, Jewish, and Christian natural law tradition, which accepted the second view and dis-carded the first, the vague Stoic idea of nature was replaced by the more precise Aristotelian idea of nature when the Aristotelian corpus came to be translated into Arabic, then Hebrew, and then Latin in the twelfth and thirteenth centuries. Neverthe-less, because one cannot go back to the Aristotelian idea (nor, *a fortiori*, to the Stoic idea) of nature, it seems that the relation between *jus gentium* and *jus naturale* of Ulpian et al. comes closer to the modern emphasis of the more empirical meaning of "nature" and the greater emphasis on historical reality (of which *jus gentium* has always been explicitly seen as a part). The human desire for *quod semper aequum ac bonum est*, it seems, must be sought in the revelations proclaimed in and by the covenantal traditions. Of course, this contemporary understanding of *jus gentium* must carefully disassociate it from its imperialist origins in Roman jurisprudence. See Novak, *The Image of the Non-Jew in Judaism*, 13–14; David Novak, *Jewish-Christian Dialogue: A Jewish Justification* (New York, 1989), 115–117.

31. Thus Maimonides sees the minimal seven Noahide laws, laws that the Rabbis considered binding on all humankind, as included in the larger and the deeper Mosaic Torah. See *Hilkhot Melakhim*, 9.1; *Guide of the Perplexed*, 2.40; also B. Sanhedrin 59a. Aquinas, *mutatis mutandis*, makes the same point regarding the relation between natural law and revealed law. See *Summa Theologiae*, 1-2, q. 94, a. 4, ad 1. For a classical Protestant statement consistent with this general line, see John Calvin, *Insti-tutes of the Christian Religion*, 2.7.10; 4.20.16.

32. See Karl Popper, *Popper Selections*, ed. D. Miller (Princeton, 1985), 133ff., 179.

33. For Judaism and Christianity (and Islam), on the other hand, the word of God functions as the criterion of everlasting truth to which everything that is true must correspond. "The grass withers, the flower fades; but the word of our God endures forever [*l'olam*]" (Isaiah 40:8). Nevertheless, this does not mean that there is no em-ployment of the coherence theory of truth in theological reasoning. Theological prob-

lems frequently require the same problem-solving techniques that we have seen operating according to the coherence theory. Such is often the case when the desired correspondence is neither apparent nor direct. Indeed, the greater gap between reader and text, entailed when critical historical scholarship is used by theologians, makes this situation of less apparentness and directness more prevalent now than it was before this method of scholarship became unavoidable in our culture. Even here, however, the correspondence theory is not replaced. Theological reasoning must always include an ongoing hermeneutic of commonly accepted revelation whose truth transcends whatever particular theological problem is now being attempted to be solved and the community of discourse now attempting to solve it, for the attempted solution of any such problem must be conducted with revelation in the background and redemption in the foreground. In relation to the former, it must always see itself as originally derivative; in relation to the latter, it must always see itself as ultimately tentative. For use of the coherence theory in theology, see David Novak, "The Role of Dogma in Judaism," *Theology Today* 45 (1988):54ff.

34. *Whose Justice? Which Rationality?*, 370.

35. See Novak, *Jewish-Christian Dialogue*, esp. 114ff.

36. See H. A. Wolfson, *Spinoza* (Cambridge, Mass., 1934), 10–11.

37. See Ludwig Wittgenstein, *Philosophical Investigations*, 2d ed., trans. G. E. M. Anscombe (New York, 1967), secs. 66–67 (pp. 31–32).

38. Matthew 12:8. Cf. Maimonides, *Sefer Ha-Mitsvot*, pos. nos. 154 and 155.

39. See *infra*, 118ff.

40. See G. Kaufman, *Theology for a Nuclear Age* (Philadelphia, 1985), 31.

41. Ultimately, this *lex divina* is seen by each covenantal community as being universal law; but it cannot be considered intelligible either immediately (*ratio quoad nos*) or even by inference (*ratio per se*) without historical revelation. See Job 38:1ff.; B. Pesahim 68b, and Niddah 73a re Habbakuk 3:6.

4

Some Aspects of Sex, Society, and God in Judaism

The Thesis about the Relation of Sex, Society, and God

In this chapter I propose a thesis about the relation of sex, society, and God in Judaism, and then I pose two questions that arise directly out of this thesis. In exploring how the questions are dealt with in Jewish tradition, I hope that helpful insights will emerge, for the questions call for rational reflection on the part of all moral and religious persons. The thesis I propose: Judaism teaches that the human person is essentially (1) a sexual being; (2) a social being; and (3) the image of God. From this thesis I now ask two questions: (1) What is the relation between human sexuality and human sociality? and (2) How are human sexuality and human sociality related to God?

Human Sexuality

The first part of the thesis stated that the human person is an essentially sexual being. This is brought out in the following Mishnah:

> One who was half-slave and half-free is to serve his master one day and himself the other—in the opinion of the School of Hillel. The School of Shammai said to them . . . he may not marry a slave woman because he is already half-free; and he may not marry a free woman because he is still half-slave. Shall he do nothing [*yibbatel*]?! Was not the world created [*nivra ha'olam*] for procreation? For Scripture states, "He did not create it as a void, but formed it for dwelling" [Isaiah 45:18]. . . . And the School of Hillel reversed themselves to rule according to the opinion of the School of Shammai.[1]

The case here seems to involve a slave owned by two partners after only one of them emancipated him.[2] The solution to the sexual dilemma of the slave in the above-quoted text is that he be fully emancipated and that he sign a note for his emancipation price. By being emancipated, he then became a full member of the community.[3]

Concerning this text, my late revered teacher Professor Boaz Cohen wrote:

> The phrase *nibra' ha'olam* [the world was created] is the nearest the rabbis came to the term *Natura*, which literally means to be born. Since the Beth Shammai invoke natural law as their reason, they cite Isa. 45:18, and not Gen. 1:28 which lays down the religious law from which the slave was exempt.[4]

Sex is considered a natural right precisely because its legitimacy is based on a recognition of the normative order of creation rather than on a specific precept. This also comes out in a later talmudic treatment of the dispute between the School of Hillel and the School of Shammai concerning how one fulfills the commandment "Be fruitful and multiply" (Genesis 1:28, 9:1). The Shammaites require that one have at least two sons; the Hillelites require that one have a son and a daughter, as Scripture states, "Male and female He created them" (Genesis 5:2). The Talmud states that the reasoning of the Hillelites is based on "the creation of the world" (*me-briyyato shel olam*).[5] This is important because the seeming admonition "Be fruitful and multiply" is taken as a recognition of the normative order of creation rather than as a specific prescription. The scriptural text, then, confirms the norm rather than establishing it *de novo*.

It should be emphasized, too, that this text does not deal with specifically Jewish sexuality but, rather, with human sexuality. The theory behind it is a reflection on the essential character of human life. The question here is that a legal difficulty has prevented a human being from exercising his or her sexuality. Sexuality is rooted in the natural order created by God. Although the Law itself is also a creation of God, legal difficulties come from the social order created by humans.[6] Here the Halakhah is indicating that the social order may not obliterate the created natural order, that society is to fulfill created human needs, not deny them. This is why celibacy is so roundly condemned.[7] Along the same lines, the Rabbis went to unusual lengths to alleviate the plight of the *agunah*, a woman who, because it is uncertain whether her husband is dead, is unable to live with any other man as his wife.[8] Moreover, in the Aggadah, the denial of sexuality is considered destructive of human life.[9] Human sexuality is not to be suppressed but channeled.[10]

Human Sociality

The indispensability of sociality in human life is seen, for example, in the legal plight of the *mamzer*. According to scriptural law, as traditionally expounded, a person born of an adulterous or an incestuous union "may not enter the congregation of the Lord" (Deuteronomy 23:3), which precludes marriage with any fully pedigreed member of the community.[11] The problem of *mamzers* is social, not sexual. They may marry virtually any member of the community who is less than fully pedigreed — and there seem to have been many of them in talmudic times.[12] The *mamzers'* frustration is the social stigma they carry, a stigma that prevents full participation in society and that is perpetuated in their descendants. The following Mishnah shows a solution to this problem: "R. Tarfon says that *mamzerim* are able to be cleared [*lee-taher*]. How so? Let a [male] *mamzer* marry a female slave [*shifha*] and the offspring will then have the status of a slave [*eved*]. Let the offspring be emancipated and have the status of a freeman [*ben horeen*]."[13]

The ingenious legal solution of R. Tarfon is accepted as valid by later authorities.[14] Also, there was a tendency among the Rabbis not to delve very carefully into family pedigree.[15] Furthermore, the offspring of a union between a Jewish woman, even a married one, and either a gentile or a slave was not a *mamzer*.[16] This may well have been an attempt to remove any social stigma from rape victims and their offspring.[17] Finally, an aggadic text reports a complaint against the Jewish legal authorities who have it in their power to alleviate the social stigma of the *mamzer* totally and yet do not act as boldly as they could.[18] All of this reflects the notion that no innocent person is to be denied fulfillment of his or her sociality. The plight of Honi Ha-Me'agel, the rabbinic forerunner of Rip Van Winkle, as expressed in aggadic language, shows the motivating idea behind the attempts to remove legal barriers to full sociality. Honi says, "Either fellowship [*haveruta*] or death."[19] Even a criminal sentenced to death, and thereby permanently severed from human society (even denied burial in a regular cemetery), is allowed to repent of his crime publicly so as not to lose the fellowship of the world-to-come.[20]

The Socialization of Sexuality

We have seen how both sexuality and sociality are considered to be natural needs that society as an institution is to help fulfill. Accordingly, they assume the status of "natural rights," namely, society's recognition that the fulfillment of the needs of its human participants is its authentic task.[21] However, because sociality is the immediate source of society's *raison d'être* and its guiding goal, society in its law and institutions channels sexuality in socially acceptable directions, thereby limiting its intentional range. As Maimonides succinctly put it, "What is natural is left to nature, but measures are taken against excess."[22]

The following legal exegesis shows this social process of sexual limitation at work. Commenting on the scriptural verse "And a man shall leave his father and mother and cleave to his wife and they shall be one flesh" (Genesis 2:24), R. Akibah states:

> "His father" means his father's wife; "his mother" literally means his mother; "he shall cleave" means not with a male; "with his wife" means not with his

neighbor's wife. "And they shall be one flesh" means with those whom he is capable of becoming one flesh, thus excluding an animal or beast with whom he cannot become one flesh.[23]

This text is the basis of the elimination of incestuous, homosexual, and nonhuman objects from socially legitimate sexuality. The socialization of sexuality is the constitution of the family. The family, then, is the institution that directs natural sexuality toward personalistic goals. As Hegel insightfully noted, the family is "a *natural* ethical community" and "the *immediate* being of the ethical order."[24] That is, it relates the biological order to the larger society. Both the attempt to solve the sexual problem of the person half-slave and half-free and the attempt to solve the social problem of the *mamzer* involve removing the legal barriers to their living in a normal family/social situation.

In their aggadic speculations about human sexuality, the Rabbis see its primordial manifestation as incestuous. Incest is seen as the natural human state, which is overcome only in the interest of sociality. Note the following rabbinic text:

> Scripture states, "If a man takes his sister, the daughter of his father, or the daughter of his mother, and she sees his nakedness, it is a reproach" [*hesed*— Leviticus 20:17]. R. Avin said that one should not say that Cain's marrying his own sister and Abel's marrying his own sister are a reproach. Rather, "I [God] said that the world is built by kindness [*hesed*—Psalms 89:3]."[25]

Here in the passage from Leviticus we see the word *hesed*, which usually means "kindness," used in its opposite sense of "reproach."[26] The text plays on this disparate double meaning and states that what is now a reproach was at the dawn of humanity a social necessity, namely, the outward extension of the human race, beginning with siblings. Thus, in a parallel text we read:

> If you say, "Why did not Adam marry his own daughter?" The answer is, in order that Cain might marry his sister so that "the world be built by kindness" [Psalms 89:3].[27]

These discussions are based on the older legend that Cain and Abel were each born with a twin sister, which explains how Scripture can all of a sudden say, "And Cain knew his wife" (Genesis 4:17).[28] The assumption behind all of these discussions seems to be that sibling incest at a very primitive level might well be motivated by a desire to build a world—a society—a motive considered good.[29]

The same aggadic reasoning comes out in this discussion of the incest between Lot and his daughters:

> R. Yohanan said that what does Scripture mean when it states, "The ways of the Lord are straight, and the righteous walk in them, but the wicked stumble in them" [Hosea 14:10]? . . . [F]or example, this refers to Lot and his two

daughters. They, whose intent was good [le-shem mitsvah] are "the righteous [who] walk in them." He, whose intent was evil [le-shem averah], is "the wicked [who] stumble in them."[30]

It will be recalled from the scriptural story of Lot and his daughters that they justify their incest by stating, "There is no man on earth to come upon us according to the way of all the earth. Come, let us give our father wine to drink, and we will lie with him, and we will then continue life from our father" (u-nehayeh me'avinu zara—Genesis 19:31). But about Lot it is stated, "he was unaware (ve-lo yada) when she lay down and when she rose up" (Genesis 19: 32, 35). Thus, Lot acted out of immediate physical desire, unaware of the personal identities of the objects of his desire, much less justifying it by any human purpose.[31] It is this socialization that effects the sublimation of sexuality's most immediate objects.[32]

Philo of Alexandria, the first-century Hellenistic Jewish sage, sees the rationale for the prohibition of incest as follows:

> Why hamper the fellow-feeling (koinōnias] and intercommunion of humans with other humans [pros tous allous anthrōpous] by compressing within the narrow space of each separate house the great and goodly plant which might extend and spread itself over continents and islands and the whole inhabited world [oikoumenen]? For marriages with outsiders [othneious] create new kinships.
> On this principle he [Moses] prohibits many other unions. . . .[33]

Philo is advocating that each generation break out of the consanguineous circle of the immediate family when marrying.

The Halakhah recognizes the universal ban of incest.[34] It also eliminates a loophole in Jewish law that would, in effect, allow de facto incest, for according to the law a convert is "born again" (ke-qatan she-nolad dami). If this juridical notion is carried to its furthest logical conclusion, a convert could even marry his own mother (who had also converted to Judaism, she also being "born again"). De jure, they are no longer consanguineously related. Nevertheless, direct incest of this type was prohibited so that the converts might not say, "We have come from a higher level of sanctity to a lower one."[35] Incest is considered to be radically disruptive of society because it introduces regressive sexuality rather than sublimation. Thus, the ninth-century theologian R. Saadyah Gaon sees the prohibition of incest as required by the integrity of the familial relationship. In presenting his rationale for the commandment of filial piety, he writes:

> . . . in order that men might not become like the beasts with the result that no one would know his father so as to show him reverence in return for having raised him. . . . A further reason was that a human being might know the rest of his relations . . . and show them whatever tenderness he was capable of.[36]

The rationale for the prohibition of homosexuality is closely connected to the prohibition of incest. Homosexuality is considered to be counterfamilial and, also, counterprocreative. Its intentionality is purely sensual.[37]

In the Aggadah, heterosexuality is seen as rooted in the essentially bisexual nature of human beings. "R. Jeremiah ben Eleazar said that the first man has two faces [*du partzuf panim*] . . . as it is written, 'Male and female He created them [Genesis 5:2].'"[38] This theme appears in a number of rabbinic texts. Another aggadic text expresses it as follows: "R. Eliezer said that they were created as a hermaphrodite (*androgynos*). . . . R. Samuel said that He created him with two faces, front and back, and split him and sawed him in two."[39] This notion of the original bisexuality of man, which has been confirmed by modern embryology, was prevalent in the ancient world.[40] Its most famous enunciation was by Plato.[41] The idea here is that a man's experience of himself as lacking his "missing other half" is the source of heterosexual desire.[42] Thus homosexuality is considered a regression in that it does not seek its true "other." Only the successful consummation of this desire for the human other leads to the recognizable family unit and the possibility of procreation.

The biblical idea that true humanness is rooted in the indispensable connection between man and woman was profoundly seen by the Protestant theologian Karl Barth (d. 1968), who wrote:

> The real perversion takes place, the original decadence and disintegration begins, when man will not see his partner of the opposite sex and therefore the primal form of fellow-man (*die Urgestalt des Mitmenschen*) . . . but trying to be human in himself sovereign man or woman. . . . For in this supposed discovery of the genuinely human man and woman give themselves up to the worship of a false god.[43]

Sexuality, then, presents a dialectic between self-possession and relatedness. In Barth's words, "Male and female being is the prototype of all I and Thou, of all individuality in which man [*Mensch*] and man differ from and yet belong to one another."[44] When human beings attempt to construct their autonomous self-sufficiency collectively, *hetero*sexuality asserts their fundamental differentiation as separate bodies. And when human beings attempt to construct their autonomous self-sufficiency individually, hetero*sexuality* asserts their fundamental relatedness to the other side of their humanness.

Another aggadic text interprets homosexuality per se as a fundamental human error.

> Bar Kappara said to R. Judah the Prince, "What does 'abomination' [*to'evah*—in the prohibition of homosexuality in Leviticus 20:13] mean?" . . . R. Judah the Prince said God meant 'abomination' means 'something in which you err [*to'eh attah*].[45]

Homosexuality is based on a fundamental lie. There can be no good (the object of ethics) that is not based on truth (the object of ontology).[46] In a homosexual relationship between men, one of them assumes a female role; in a homosexual relationship between two women, one of them assumes a male role. Furthermore, even the masculine man in a male homosexual relationship is not relating to a real woman but, rather, to his male alter ego. Even the feminine woman in a female homosexual relationship is not relating to a real man but, rather, to her female alter ego. And even if each participant in a male homosexual relationship asserts he is wholly masculine to the other, and even if each participant in a female homosexual asserts she is wholly feminine to the other, this celebration of absolute masculinity or absolute femininity belies the very biological truth of the essentially intersexual relatedness attested by the fact that the sexual organs and the organs of procreation are the same.

Homosexuality is considered inconsistent with authentic human sociality, that is, it is considered inconsistent with human nature.[47] In the Aggadah it is seen as part of the overall degradation of human life and society in Sodom: "And they called to Lot and they said to him, 'Where are the men who came to you; bring them out to us that we might know them [ve-ned'ah otam]'" (Genesis 19:5). In one rabbinic source the last phrase is interpreted to mean "that we might have intercourse with them [u-neshamesh imehon]."[48] The point is made elsewhere too.[49] Obviously, the aggadists took the verb "to know" [yado'a] in the sense of "carnal knowledge" as in "And the man knew [yada] Eve his wife and she conceived" (Genesis 4:1). Because Scripture designated the Sodomites as "exceedingly wicked and sinful unto the Lord" (Genesis 13:13), homosexual rape is seen as one of their foremost sins.[50] The Rabbis were clearly aware of the prevalence of homosexuality in the Greco-Roman world. Various halakhic rulings reflect this awareness.[51] Indeed, their ostensible reflections about the sins of Sodom probably had a more contemporary situation in mind.[52] Furthermore, the concern of this aggadic source with homosexual rape might very well be the Rabbis' reflection about the presence of sadistic elements in many homosexual acts, a view found in the Halakhah.[53] However, even fully consensual homosexuality is forbidden. Female homosexuality, too, is considered by the rabbis as "lewdness" (peritsuta b'alma) because there is no explicit scriptural prohibition of it, as there is of male homosexuality.[54]

The Rabbis were especially critical of any society that would formally legitimize homosexual unions, undoubtedly because they are considered to be fundamentally antisocial in that they are a burlesque of heterosexual family life. Thus, an aggadic text reads:

R. Hiyya taught why is "I am the Lord" repeated twice [Leviticus 18:3 and 4]?—I am he who punished the generation of the Flood and Sodom and Egypt; I will in the future punish whoever does according to their deeds. The generation of the Flood was blotted out from the world because they were steeped in immorality [shetufin be-zenut]. . . . R. Huna said in the name of R. Yose that the generation of the Flood was blotted out from the world only because they wrote marriage contracts [gomasiyot] for male unions and for female unions.[55]

The Rabbis seem to be making a distinction between a society in which homosexuality is prevalent and one in which there is an official sanction and recognition of it. This text might well be based on a report that the Roman emperor Nero went so far as to write a marriage contract for one of his favorite male lovers.[56] Perhaps even in the Greco-Roman world, where individual homosexuality was quite common, Nero's elevating a homosexual relationship to the level of a "marriage" was considered shocking and a sign of extreme social decadence. It is something more serious than individual decadence because of its public moral approval.

The prohibition of bestiality was also used by the Rabbis to speculate about the development of human sexuality. The Rabbis seemed to have recognized that at the level of what psychoanalysts call "primary process," bestiality, or at least the motif of bestiality, is a human possibility. Thus, when Scripture states about animals, "He [God] brought them unto man to see what he would call them" (Genesis 2:19), an aggadist speculated as follows:

> R. Eleazar said that why did Scripture state [that is, the first man's words], "This time it is bone from my bone and flesh from my flesh" [Genesis 2: 23]? — It teaches that Adam had sexual relations with every animal and beast, but he was not satisfied [*ve-lo nitqarerah da'ato*] until he had sexual relations with Eve.[57]

Eve satisfied him because with her he could once again — following the motif of primordial bisexuality — "become one flesh." Furthermore, it is emphasized that with Eve alone could Adam speak.[58] Whereas speech is not required by sexuality, it is required by sociality.[59] Thus heterosexuality between human partners is a restriction of biological primary process by human sociality. Satisfaction in the personal sense is even more social than it is physical.

The Socialization of Sexuality and the Status of Women

The socialization of human sexuality in Judaism can be seen in the way the legal status of women in the marital relationship developed into one of true mutuality, for if one reflects on heterosexuality as a physical phenomenon, it clearly requires male initiation and suggests male dominance. This is assumed by the Halakhah where marriage and divorce are initiated by the man.[60] Reflecting on this legal fact, the Talmud records the following aggadic speculation:

> R. Simon says that why did the Torah state, "When a man takes [a woman]" [Deuteronomy 24:1], but does not state, "When a woman takes a man"? This is because it is the way [*darko*] of a man to go after a woman, but it is not the way of a woman to go after a man. It is like one who lost something. Who goes after whom? The owner [*ba'al*] of the lost article goes after the lost article.[61]

Thus at this level, we see that the desire for the primordial bisexual union, which we discussed before, is *initially* male.

Nevertheless, the Talmud notes that in a key rabbinic text, the woman, not the man, is made the subject of the initiation of marriage.[62] From this, among other texts, it is inferred that a woman may not be married against her will, that is, be acquired like chattel.[63] Furthermore, even though according to scriptural law a female child may be married off by her father without her consent, and even rabbinic law had to accept the validity of such a marriage as valid *ex post facto*, this practice was subsequently prohibited *ab initio*, that is, a father is to wait until his daughter is mature enough to say, "It is he whom I want."[64] The following aggadic texts shows how the lack of mutual consent in marriage was seen as socially disadvantageous:

> A Roman lady asked R. Yose bar Halafta, "Everyone agrees that God created the world in six days. From the sixth day on what has he been doing?" . . . R. Berakhyah said . . . he said to her that He arranges marriages in his world. . . . She said that she could make a thousand such marriages in one day . . . so she brought a thousand male slaves and a thousand female slaves and paired them off. . . . However, when night came, fighting broke out among them.[65]

The point that emerges from this is that slavery, that is, the subjugation of one human person by another, is inimical to human fulfillment, including human sexual fulfillment. One can see the entire development of Jewish matrimonial law as the steady emancipation of women from anything even resembling slavery.[66]

Along these same lines, even though according to scriptural law only a man could divorce his wife, rabbinic law subsequently enabled a woman to sue for divorce based on certain objective conditions that make true marital mutuality impossible.[67] Moreover, in rabbinic law a woman is to be provided with a marriage contract (*ketubah*), which stipulates that in the event of a divorce (or the death of her husband) she is to be paid a considerable sum of money. The reason for this is given as being "so that she not be easy [*qalah*] to be sent away."[68] Later authorities ruled that under any circumstances a woman could not be divorced against her will.[69] Thus the mutuality that was eventually recognized as being required at the initiation of marriage was finally required at its termination as well.[70] Also, as early as the first century C.E., Rabban Yohanan ben Zakkai eliminated the ordeal of the woman suspected of adultery (*sotah*). He argued that it presupposed mutual standards of virtue, something that could no longer be assumed.[71] And as late as the sixteenth century, R. Moses Isserles made male unfaithfulness grounds for divorce, just as female unfaithfulness had always been the grounds for divorce in the past.[72]

The social requirement of true mutuality can be achieved only in monogamy. The introduction of monogamy as the only acceptable heterosexual union in Judaism ultimately required the elimination of concubinage as well as polygamy (polyandry never having been permitted).[73] It should be noted that concubinage and polygamy were taken for granted in Scripture as perfectly acceptable practices.[74]

It was Maimonides in the twelfth century who banned concubinage. He gave a historical context to the ruling as follows:

> Before the giving of the Torah it was that a man would meet a woman in the marketplace and, if they mutually agreed, then he would give her her price, having relations with her along the way, and would then go on his way. Such a woman is what is called a *qedeshah*. When the Torah was given, the *qedeshah* was outlawed . . . therefore, anyone who has relations with a woman for purposes of fornication [*le-shem zenut*] without marriage [*be-lo qiddushin*] is to be lashed according to scriptural law because he has had relations with a *qedeshah*.[75]

Maimonides' scriptural proof-text is "There shall not be any *qedeshah* among the daughters of Israel, nor any *qadesh* among the sons of Israel" (Deuteronomy 23:18). Even though one might think that *qedeshah/qadesh*, coming as they do from the root *qadosh* ("sacred"), refer only to prostitutes (female or male) connected with pagan shrines, Maimonides makes no distinction between "sacred" and "secular" prostitution.[76] As one of the commentators on Maimonides notes, his reference concerning pre-Torah conditions is the story of Judah and Tamar recorded in Genesis 38.[77] There, Tamar, posing as a prostitute in a clearly noncultic setting, is called a *qedeshah* (38:21). The term is used there interchangeably with the term *zonah* (38:15), an ordinary prostitute. In other words, anything less than a full wife is, for Maimonides, in essence a prostitute, and the Torah outlawed *all* prostitution.

Now a number of subsequent halakhists, although in basic sympathy with Maimonides' high moral standards and aspirations for the Jewish people, nevertheless argued that concubinage, as distinct from full marriage, is permitted by both Scripture and the Talmud.[78] It seems, then, that Maimonides was making an explicit innovation in Jewish law, something he did in other areas as well.[79] He might very well have been repulsed by the use of women as concubines (and as prostitutes) in the upper-class Muslim circles in which he worked as a physician. Indeed, the concubine is in essence woman as sexual object alone.[80]

It was the eleventh-century German halakhist Rabbenu Gershom of Mainz who banned polygamy. Here, too, there is clearly no explicit precedent in either Scripture or the Talmud. Indeed, we do not even have the original text of this ban, much less Rabbenu Gershom's reasoning for it.[81] Nevertheless, one can see its effect at least as being one more step in the process of making true mutuality in the personal relationship of marriage a social reality. It is interesting to note the following aggadic speculation concerning the first polygamous marriage recorded in Scripture, namely, that of Lamech and his two wives Ada and Zillah (Genesis 4:19):

R. Azariah said in the name of R. Judah that this was what the men of the generation of the Flood were doing. One would take two wives, one for procreation and one for sex [le-tashmish]. The one for procreation would be sitting like a widow during her lifetime; the one for sex would be given a sterilizing potion to drink, and she would sit before him like a prostitute.[82]

The important thing to note about this speculation is that neither woman is treated as a person. Both are used by the man. Now, of course, one could say that this speculation only concerns the generation of the Flood. However, it should be recalled that polygamy is often described in Scripture as a cause of human unhappiness.[83] Indeed, in Scripture the first marriage between Eve and Adam, which according to the Aggadah God himself celebrated, was monogamous.[84] In any polygamous marriage the man is necessarily divided in his heterosexual affection, whereas the woman becomes a particular functionary rather than a whole person relating to another whole person. It is only in a monogamous union that in effect *both* the man and the woman are exclusively sanctified to each other.[85]

Sexuality and God

In classical Jewish teaching all aspects of human life are ultimately related to God. Therefore, we should now examine how the human person as a sexual/ social being is the image of God.

At the beginning of the talmudic tractate *Kiddushin*, which primarily deals with Jewish marriage, the Palestinian version records the following statement:

For we learn that the gentiles do not have religious marriage [qiddushin], so how can they possibly have religious divorce [gerushin]? R. Judah ben Pazzi and R. Hanin said in the name of R. Honeh, elder of Sepphoris, that either they do not have religious divorce or they divorce each other.[86]

Undoubtedly basing his discussion of Jewish marriage law on this text, Maimonides begins as follows:

Before the giving of the Torah a man would meet a woman in the marketplace. If they mutually agreed he would marry her, then he would bring her into his house and would have sexual relations with her privately and she would become his wife. When the Torah was given, Israel was commanded that if a man marry a woman, he would take her [yiqah otah] initially in the presence of two witnesses and afterward she would become his wife, as Scripture states, "When a man takes a woman and comes to her" [Deuteronomy 24:1].[87]

Now, at first glance these texts seem to indicate that the Torah removed an original mutuality from the initiation of marriage. Nevertheless, the subsequent factor of the woman's required consent clearly indicates that even when marriage is a state initiated by the man, it surely requires mutuality to be valid.[88] Therefore, one must see the point being made that Jewish marriage is more than a civil contract; rather, it is a covenant rooted in the covenant between God and his people Israel. This explains why Maimonides emphasizes the presence of witnesses. Obviously, the initiation of pre-Toraitic marriage, taking place as it does "in the marketplace," is also a public matter. However, whereas this marriage is *consummated as a private sexual matter* between the man and the woman, Jewish marriage is consummated as a public nonsexual matter.[89] The witnesses represent the minimal presence of the sacred community, and as such, they do not simply confirm a legal fact but actually constitute its essential meaning.[90] Indeed, in order for the liturgical rite of marriage to be fully celebrated (with the full invocation of God's name), a minimum quorum of ten is required.[91]

The presence of God in Jewish marriage is the subject of profound aggadic speculation, as for example:

> He [R. Simlai] said to them [his students] that originally Adam was created "from the dust of the earth" [Genesis 2:7], and Eve was created from the man. After Adam they [men and women] were created "in Our image after Our likeness" [Genesis 1:26]. It is impossible for man to live without woman; it is impossible for woman to live without man; and it is impossible for both to live without God's presence [*Shekhinah*].[92]

This idea is further reflected in the talmudic statement that "there are three partners in the formation of a human being: God and the father and the mother."[93] In other words, God is present in Jewish marriage and its fruits.

We have seen how human sexuality and human sociality are correlated in marriage. The idea of marriage as a sacred covenant correlates this relation with the status of the human person as the image of God. Now we must ask: Does this acknowledgment of marriage as a sacred covenant add anything significantly new? Or, is the sacred dimension simply the deification of society as a whole greater than the mere sum of its individual parts, as Émile Durkheim, one of the founders of modern sociology, so consistently and powerfully argued.[94]

In answering this question, I call attention to the analogy between marriage as the male-female relationship and God's relationship with his people Israel, so often made in Scripture and the rabbinic writings. The analogy is based on the idea of faithfulness (*emunah*), which is to be the foundation of both relationships.

> And it shall come to pass on that day, the Lord says, that you will call me "my husband" [*ishi*] and you will no longer call Me "my master" [*ba'ali*]. . . . And I will make a covenant [*berit*] with them on that day. . . . [A]nd I will betroth you unto to Me forever, and I will betroth you unto me rightly and with justice and with kindness and with compassion. And I will betroth you unto Me in faithfulness [*b'emunah*], and you will know the Lord. (Hosea 2:18–21)

And this second thing you do to cover the altar of the Lord with weeping and
wailing. . . . And you say, "why?" — Because the Lord witnesses between you
and the wife of your youth against whom you have been unfaithful [*baga-
data*], and she is your companion, your covenanted wife [*eshet beritekha*].[95]
(Malachi 2:13–14)

In rabbinic literature the most outstanding example of this line of thought is
the interpretation of Song of Songs, which uses the image of a male-female
love relationship to express God's love for the people of Israel allegorically.[96]

This analogy is usually explained as being a comparison of God's love for
his people with the relationship of a man and a woman in a loving marriage.[97]
But I find such an interpretation to be wide open to the critiques of religion
made by Ludwig Feuerbach and Sigmund Freud, namely, that religion projects onto an idealized realm what is a purely human reality.[98] It seems to me
to be more accurate and theologically more cogent to explain the analogy the
other way around, namely, it is a comparison of male-female love with God's
love of his people. In other words, God's love is the primary reality in which
human love becomes a participation. This can mean one of two things.

For the kabbalists, male-female union is a symbolic participation in the
union of the male-female aspects of the Godhead itself. As the *Zohar* puts it:

Come and see that the desire of a male for a female and the desire of a female
for a male and their union [*v'itdavquta*] produces a soul . . . and this early
desire is included in heavenly desire [*be-t'euvtah de-l'ela*].[99]

The problem with this line of interpretation is that it is, as is all kabbalistic
theology, a compromise with strict monotheism—a point made by Jewish
traditional critics of Kabbalah.[100] Furthermore, by making human sexuality
only a symbol of a truly divine reality, it eclipses the factor of finite human
embodiment, which seems to be such an essential factor in this human reality.
As such, it can be seen as countersexual.[101] Finally, it is a serious departure
from the essential aspect of divine love emphasized in Scripture and the rabbinic writings, namely, love as an act of God's self-transcendence, his recognition of a truly nondivine *other*. In Kabbalah, all divine love is essentially a
self-enclosed love *into which* creatures are ultimately incorporated.

I would rather emphasize that sexual love in the sacred covenant of marriage is a participation in a higher relationship, that of God's everlasting love
for his people. At its best, it reflects that everlasting love. Deutero-Isaiah
perhaps best expressed this foundation of all covenantal love when he wrote:

. . . with everlasting kindness I have loved you, says the Lord your redeemer.
. . . For the mountains will depart and the hills be moved, but my covenant
of peace will not be moved, says the Lord who loves you.[102] (Isaiah 54:8–10)

This connection comes out more clearly if we consider the phenomenology
of sexual love. It is mistaken, it seems to me, to consider the essence of sexual

love to be pleasure, although it is certainly a *sine qua non* of it, for in all other bodily pleasures, such as eating, drinking, bathing, we seek a heightened sense of awareness of our own bodies. Our pleasure is essentially a taking-in, that is, our desire is to make our world around us an extension of our own bodies. In heterosexual love, on the other hand, we seek ecstasy, which comes from two Greek words, *ex histēmi*, meaning "to stand out." In other words, our sexuality intends transcendence. Eros seeks spirit.[103] It seems that in true eros we seek *to go beyond our bodies through them*. For a moment we experience a going beyond the body, which is ordinarily the limit of the soul.[104] Nevertheless, sexual love in itself lasts only for a moment before the body, the ever-present, finite, mortal vessel, claims the soul once again. This is pointed out in the following aggadah:

David said before God, "My father Jesse did not intend to sire me, but intended only his own pleasure. You know that this is so because after the parents satisfied themselves, he turned his face away and she turned her face away and You joined the drops."[105]

Eros is not a function of the body but, rather, the eroticized body ultimately intends that which is beyond limit, that which is beyond death. As embodied souls,[106] we can experience this only by moving through the body beyond it. It cannot be done through any ascetic shortcuts; we cannot pretend to be angels when we are only flesh and blood.[107] And this is why the periodic monthly separation (*niddah*) enjoined by Halakhah on husband and wife at the time of the menses is seen as a cultivation of eros that is more than bodily.[108] Indeed, even the most banal love lyrics sung today almost inevitably long for "undying love." The intention of what is everlasting seems to be essential to even the most crudely expressed sexual desire.

In Judaism such desire is seen as being grounded in God's everlasting love for his people. This grounding alone enables sexual love to be an expression of creative energy and the ultimate antithesis of all narcissism.[109] This comes out in the rabbinic interpretation of the most erotic of all Scripture, Song of Songs. In conclusion let me cite one outstanding example. Scripture states, "For love is strong as death [*azah ke-mavet*]; jealousy is harsh as the grave; its flashes are fiery flashes, the very torch of God" (Canticles 8:6). From the text it seems as though "death" is used as a superlative, namely, it is the strongest thing we experience, beyond which we know nothing. Love is considered equally strong and equally final. However, the Rabbis seem to want to make love stronger than death. Thus, they revocalized the word *ke-mavet* ("like death") and read it as *ke-mot*, "it is like." It is like what?

For love is strong as [*ke-mot*] the love which God has for you, as Scripture states, "I have loved you, says the Lord" [Malachi 1:2]. "Jealousy is harsh as the grave"—this refers to the times they made Him jealous with their idolatry [*avodah zarah*], as it says, "They made Him jealous with strange gods" [*zarim*—Deuteronomy 32:16]. . . . Another interpretation: "For love is strong as death"—this is the love of a man for his wife, as it says, "experience life with a woman you love" [Ecclesiastes 9:9]. . . . "Its flashes are fiery flashes, the very torch of God"—R. Berakhyah said it is like the heavenly fire which does not consume the water nor does the water extinguish it.[110]

In Judaism human sexuality, socialized and sanctified in the covenant of marriage, becomes the way two mortal creatures together existentially affirm God's love, which alone never dies.

NOTES

1. M. Gittin 4.5 and M. Eduyot 1.13. See B. Gittin 43b; Y. Gittin 4.5/46a; Maimonides, *Hilkhot Avadim*, 7.7. But cf. M. Kiddushin 4.3; B. Kiddushin 75ª; R. Vidal of Tolosa, *Maggid Mishneh* on Maimonides, *Hilkhot Isuray Bi'ah* 15.21; *Tur*: Even Ha'Ezer, 4 (end). Also see B. Gittin 41b, Tos., s.v. "kofin" re ibid., 38b, which suggests that this is permitted because of *mitsvah de-rabbim*, which can well be seen as a rabbinic term for the common good (see B. Berakhot 47b; B. Baba Batra 13a and Tos., s.v. "shene'emar;" B. Shabbat 4a and Tos., s.v. "ve-khi"). See *supra*, 38; *infra*, 165f.

2. B. Gittin 42a.

3. See B. Shabbat 135b and B. Berakhot 47b. This full integration into the community was seen as entailing a limitation of the licentiousness formerly enjoyed by the slave. See B. Gittin 12b; B. Baba Metsia 19a and Rashi, s.v. "zekhut;" Maimonides, *Hilkhot Avadim*, 5.2 and 6.1; *Vayiqra Rabbah* 8.1.

4. *Jewish and Roman Law*, 2 vols. (New York, 1966), 1:28 n. 97.

5. B. Yevamot 61b–62a.

6. See Maimonides, *Moreh Nevukhim*, 1.65 and 2.40. Re the human source of legal difficulties, see T. Sotah 14.9; B. Sanhedrin 88b.

7. M. Yevamot 6.6 and B. Yevamot 63b. For the fulfilling status of female sexuality, see B. Sanhedrin 22b re Isa. 54:5.

8. See M. Yevamot 16.7; M. Eduyot 6.1 and 8.5; B. Gittin 3a and parallels; also B. Kiddushin 7a and parallels; David Novak, *Law and Theology in Judaism*, 2 vols. (New York, 1974), 1:31ff.; David Novak, *Halakhah in a Theological Dimension* (Chico, Calif., 1985), 29ff.

9. B. Yoma 69b and B. Sanhedrin 64a. Cf. B. Sotah 47a and B. Kiddushin 81b. See D. M. Feldman, *Birth Control in Jewish Law* (New York, 1968), 88. The celibacy of the first-century C.E. sage Ben Azzai is considered his personal peculiarity. See B. Yevamot 63b; cf., however, Maimonides, *Hilkhot Ishut*, 15.3. For Ben Azzai's unhappy end, see B. Hagigah 14b. Also see *Tanhuma*: Aharay Mot, ed. Buber, 31b–32a, for the notion of celibacy as arrogance. The dangers of denying sexuality are brought out by the ancient Greek dramatist Euripides, who in his play *Hippolytus* has Aphrodite say, "Hippolytus, alone among the inhabitants of Troezen, calls me the most pernicious of the heavenly powers; he abhors the bed of love; marriage he renounces. . . . But Hippolytus has insulted me and shall suffer for it." *Euripides: Three Plays*, trans. P. Vellacott (Baltimore, 1953), 28. Cf. Sigmund Freud, *The Origin and Development of Psychoanalysis* (Chicago, 1955), 67–68.

10. For rabbinic recognition of sublimation, see B. Shabbat 156a.

11. M. Yevamot 4.13; M. Kiddushin 3.12.

12. See M. Kiddushin 4.1ff. For a discussion of this whole ethical problem of *mamzerut*, see Novak, *Halakhah in a Theological Dimension*, 11ff.

13. M. Kiddushin 3.13. Upon manumission a gentile slave became a full Jew. See B. Berakhot 47b.

14. B. Kiddushin 69a.

15. Ibid., 71a.

16. B. Yevamot 45b and parallels.

17. See, e.g., M. Ketubot 2.5 and B. Ketubot 23a; Isserles, *Darkhay Mosheh* on *Tur*: Even Ha'Ezer, 7, n. 13.

18. *Vayiqra Rabbah* 32.7. See B. Berkakhot 7a re Exod. 34:7 and Deut. 24:16. Cf. B. Gittin 33a and Tos., s.v. "v'afqa'inu." For attempts to play down pedigree, see, e.g., B. Horayot 3.8 and Y. Horayot 3.5/48c; B. Nazir 23b re Prov. 18:1; M. Yadayim 4.4.

19. B. Ta'anit 23a. For separation from the discursive community as a cause of depression, see Menahot 29b. For sympathy for those separated from the community because of disease, see B. Mo'ed Qatan 5a; *infra*, 108.

20. M. Sanhedrin 6.2 and B. Sanhedrin 47a.

21. See R. Joseph Albo, *Iqqarim*, 1.5.

22. *Guide of the Perplexed*, 3.49, trans. S. Pines (Chicago, 1963), 611.

23. B. Sanhedrin 58a. Freud saw this verse as describing the normal course of psychosexual development. See "The Most Prevalent Form of Degradation in Erotic Life" (1912) in *Collected Papers*, 5 vols., trans. J. Strachey (London, 1950–1952), 4: 205–206.

24. *Phenomenology of Spirit*, no. 450, trans. A. V. Miller (Oxford, 1977), 268. So, also, Aristotle argues against the suggested abolition of the family (at least for the ruling guardians) in Plato's *Republic* (463Dff.) by asserting that without first having an allegiance to one's own biological family, one would not be able to form enduring allegiances to the larger civil community of which it is part (*Politics*, 1262a5ff.). Certainly, part of that familial allegiance is one's desire to continue the family through his or her procreation. Thus it is quite interesting to note the suggestion of Martha C. Nussbaum in *The Fragility of Goodness: Luck and Ethics in Greek Tragedy and Philosophy* (Cambridge and New York, 1986), 370–371, that Aristotle's emphasis of the political necessity of the family (contra Plato) is related to his heterosexuality. See, also, Harry V. Jaffa, *Homosexuality and the Natural Law* (Claremont, Calif., 1991), esp. 25–37.

25. Y. Yevamot 11.1/11d. Cf. Y. Sanhedrin 5.1/22c. For "seeing" as a euphemism for possession, see B. Pesahim 5b re Exod. 13:7.

26. See Rashbam, *Commentary on the Torah*: Lev. 20:17.

27. B. Sanhedrin 58b.

28. *Beresheet Rabbah* 22.1. Re the question of the Rabbis supplying missing data about biblical characters, see B. Baba Batra 91[a].

29. For a certain tolerance of quasi-incest, see B. Yevamot 62b–63a; B. Sanhedrin 76b re Isa. 58:7.

30. B. Horayot 10b re Hos. 14:10.

31. See B. Nazir 23b re Prov. 18:1 and Tos., s.v. "le-ta'avah."

32. See B. Yoma 69b.

33. *De Specialibus Legibus*, 3.25–26, in *Philo*, 9 vols., trans. F. H. Colson (Cambridge, Mass., 1937), 7:488–489. Cf. Augustine, *De Civitate Dei*, 15.16.

34. See Maimonides, *Hilkhot Melakhim*, 9.5.

35. B. Yevamot 22a. See Maimonides, *Hilkhot Isuray Bi'ah*, 14.12.

36. *Book of Beliefs and Opinions*, 3.2, trans. S. Rosenblatt (New Haven, 1948), 141. See Nahmanides, *Commentary on the Torah*: Gen. 2:24.

37. See Maimonides, *Moreh Nevukhim*, 3.49; *supra*, 000. Cf. Aristotle, *Nicomachean Ethics*, 1174b30ff. Much of the discussion here concerning incest, homosexuality, and so on is taken from my book, *The Image of the Non-Jew in Judaism: An Historical and Constructive Study of the Noahide Laws* (New York and Toronto, 1983), chap. 6.

38. B. Eruvin 18a. See B. Berakhot 61b re Ps. 139:5; B. Megillah 9a; B. Ketubot 8a; B. Sanhedrin 38b; Louis Ginzberg, *Legends of the Jews*, 7 vols. (Philadelphia, 1925), 5:88–89 n. 42.

39. *Midrash Tehillim*, 139.5, ed. Buber, 265a. See *Beresheet Rabbah* 8.1; Ginzberg, *Legends*, 5:90 n. 48.

40. See K. L. Moore, *The Developing Human*, 2d ed. (Philadelphia, 1977), 228ff.

41. *Symposium*, 191D–192B.

42. See *Zohar*: Qedoshim, 3:81a–b re Job 23:13.

43. *Church Dogmatics*, auth. Eng. trans. (Edinburgh, 1961), III/4:166. Re the priority of "the other" (*l'autre*) in ethics, see Emmanuel Levinas, *Existence and Existents*, trans. A. Lingis (The Hague, 1978), 94–96.

44. *Church Dogmatics*, III/4:150. See also Barth's *Ethics*, ed. D. Braun and trans. G. W. Bromiley (New York, 1981), 181. Some of this material is from my article, "Before Revelation: The Rabbis, Paul and Karl Barth," *Journal of Religion* 71 (1991): 59–60.

45. B. Nedarim 51a. See also B. Sanhedrin 82a re Mal. 2:11; Y. Berakhot 9.2/13c re Jer. 25:30.

46. See *supra*, n. 24.

47. See *infra*, 106ff.

48. *Targum Pseudo-Jonathan, ad locum.*

49. See *Beresheet Rabbah* 50.5; *Tanhuma*: Va-yere, printed ed., no. 12; Josephus, *Antiquities*, 1.200.

50. T. Sanhedrin 13.8. See *Mekhilta*: Be-Shalah, ed. Horovitz-Rabin, 177; Y. Kiddushin 1.7/61a re II Chron. 24:24.

51. See, e.g., M. Avodah Zarah 2.1 and T. Avodah Zarah 3.2. Cf. M. Kiddushin 4.14; B. Kiddushin 82a; Y. Kiddushin 4.11/66c; also Karo, *Shulhan Arukh*: Even Ha'Ezer, 24.1.

52. See B. Gitten 57b. Thus, e.g., when the Rabbis mentioned Edom, they were referring to Rome; see *Vayiqra Rabbah* 13.5.

53. See M. Sanhedrin 8.7.

54. B. Yevamot 76a; B. Sanhedrin 65a, Rashi, s.v. "gena'an;" Maimonides, *Commentary on the Mishnah*: Sanhedrin 7.4; *Hilkhot Isuray Bi'ah*, 21.8.

55. *Vayiqra Rabbah* 23.9 re *Sifra*: Aharay Mot (ed. Weiss), 86a. See B. Sanhedrin 54b re I Kings 14:24; Hullin 92a–b. Re the image of the generation of the Flood as a paradigm of future divine punishment, see M. Baba Metsia 4.2.

56. Suetonius, *Lives of the Caesars*, 4.28.

57. B. Yevamot 63a.

58. See *Beresheet Rabbah* 18.4; David Novak, *Law and Theology in Judaism*, 2 vols. (New York, 1976), 2:13–14.

59. See Aristotle, *Politics*, 1253a10. For attempts to qualify the rabbinic maxim "Do not engage in much discourse with a woman, even one's own wife" (M. Avot 1.5), see *Avot de-Rabbi Nathan* A, chap. 7, ed. Schechter, 18a (cf. B, chap. 15; B. Hagigah 5b re Amos 4:13); B. Eruvin 53b.

60. B. Kiddushin 5b; Y. Kiddushin 1.1/58c; B. Gittin 88b.

61. B. Kiddushin 2b. See *Beresheet Rabbah* 17.8. For the use of the noun *derekh* as a euphemism for sexual intercourse, see Gen. 19:31 and Prov. 30:19.

62. M. Kiddushin 1.1.

63. B. Kiddushin 2b. See B. Gittin 85b.

64. B. Kiddushin 41a. Cf. ibid. 3b re Deut. 22:16.

65. *Bemidbar Rabbah* 3.4. See *Vayiqra Rabbah* 8.1, ed. M. Margulies (Jerusalem, 1953), 1:166 n. 4; Novak, *Law and Theology in Judaism*, 2 vols., 1:5–9.

66. See Novak, *Law and Theology in Judaism*, 2:140–142. Indeed, the fourteenth-century Provençal exegete R. Menahem Meiri noted that if Scripture had explicated the originally involuntary initiation of marriage and divorce, "there would not be any daughter left to Abraham our father!" *Bet Ha-Behirah*: Kiddushin, ed. A. Sofer (Jerusalem, 1963), 8 (cf. B. Ketubot 72b), viz., no woman would want to remain a Jewess.

67. M. Ketubot 5.6 and B. Ketubot 77a. See Novak, *Law and Theology in Judaism*, 1:31–33.

68. B. Baba Kama 89a. See B. Ketubot 11a and 57a.

69. Isserles, note on *Shulhan Arukh*: Even Ha'Ezer, 119.6.

70. For the essential analogy between divorce and marriage, see B. Kiddushin 5a and parallels.

71. M. Sotah 9.9 re Hos. 4:14 and B. Sotah 47b re Num. 5:31; Y. Sotah 9.9/24a.

72. Note on *Shulhan Arukh*: Even Ha'Ezer, 154.1. Cf. M. Sotah 6.1; B. Gittin 46a.

73. See B. Kiddushin 2b and Tos., s.v. "d'asur." Cf. B. Me'ilah 18a–b, Tos., s.v. "ayn" and "v'omer;" Y. Kiddushin 3.1/63c.

74. See, e.g., Cant. 6:8.

75. *Hilkhot Ishut*, 1.4 à la *Sifre*: Devarim, no. 260, ed. Finkelstein, 283; *Sifra*: Qedoshim, ed. Weiss, 90d; T. Kiddushin 1.4 re Lev. 20:14. See B. Sanhedrin 82a re Mal. 2:11 and Maimonides, *Moreh Nevukhim*, 3.49, trans. Pines, 603.

76. See J. Reider, *Deuteronomy with Commentary* (Philadelphia, 1948), 217.

77. R. Vidal of Tolosa, *Maggid Mishneh* on Maimonides. *Hilkhot Ishut*, 1.4.

78. See note of R. Abraham ben David of Posquières (Rabad) on Maimonides, *Hilkhot Ishut*, 1.4; Nahmanides, *Responsa Ha-Ramban*, ed. C. B. Chavel (Jerusalem, 1975), no. 105; R. Solomon ibn Adret, *Responsa Ha-Rashba* (Jerusalem, 1960), 4, no. 314.

79. See Novak, *Law and Theology in Judaism*, 2:121–122.

80. See B. Sanhedrin 21a re II Sam. 5:13; Y. Ketubot 5.2/29d. Most concubines were captives taken in war. The Talmud considers the scriptural permission to take a war bride (Deut. 21:10–14) as a compromise with lust (see B. Kiddushin 21b–22a and B. Sanhedrin 59a). Indeed, the initial contact of the Jewish soldier with such a woman was premarital, i.e., her status was that of a concubine. See Maimonides, *Hilkhot Melakhim*, 8.5–6; also B. Kiddushin 22a, Tos. s.v. "she-lo" (cf. Rashi, s.v. "she-lo"); Y. Makkot 2.6/31d.

81. See Feldman, *Birth Control in Jewish Law*, 38ff.

82. *Beresheet Rabbah* 23.2, ed. Theodor-Albeck, 1:222–223.

83. See, e.g., Gen. 16:5; 21:10; 30:15; also M. Sanhedrin 2.4 re Deut. 17:17 and B. Sanhedrin 21b re I Kings 11:4.

84. *Beresheet Rabbah* 18.3 re Gen. 2:22.

85. See B. Kiddushin 4b, Tos., s.v. "haykha" and 7a.

86. Y. Kiddushin 1.1/58c. Cf. Y. Baba Batra 8.1/15d–16a; Josephus, *Antiquities*, 15.259.

87. *Hilkhot Ishut*, 1.1. Cf. *Hilkhot Melakhim*, 9.8.

88. *Hilkhot Ishut*, 4.1. See B. Yevamot 110a and B. Baba Batra 48b.

89. Thus the original scriptural permission to initiate marriage by a publicly evident (although not seen—B. Gittin 81b) act of sexual intercourse (M. Kiddushin 1.1; T. Kiddushin 1.3; *Sifre*: Devarim, no. 268; Y. Kiddushin 1.1/58b) was later removed in the interest of public propriety. See B. Kiddushin 12b; also B. Ketubot 56a and Maimonides, *Hilkhot Ishut*, 10.2.

90. This point was brilliantly expounded by S. Atlas, *Netivim Be-Mishpat Ha'Ivri* (New York, 1978), 246–247; also see Novak, *Halakhah in a Theological Dimension*, 34–36.

91. B. Ketubot 7b.

92. Y. Berakhot 9.1/12d.

93. Niddah 31b; B. Kiddushin 30b; Y. Kiddushin 1.7/61b.

94. See his *Elementary Forms of the Religious Life*, trans. J. W. Swain (New York, 1965), 236–237. For a theological critique of the equation of society and transcendence, see Novak, *Law and Theology in Judaism*, 2:19–20.

95. See B. Gittin 90b; Novak, *Law and Theology in Judaism*, 1:12–14.

96. See *Shir Ha-Shirim Rabbah* 1.11; also my late revered teacher Saul Lieberman, appendix to G. Scholem, *Jewish Gnosticism and Merkabah Mysticism* (New York, 1960), 118ff.

97. See, e.g., R. Gordis, *The Song of Songs and Lamentations*, rev. ed. (New York, 1974), 1–3.

98. See Feuerbach, *The Essence of Christianity*, trans. M. Evans (London, 1893), secs. 643–644; Freud, *The Future of an Illusion*, trans. W. D. Robson-Scott (Garden City, N.Y., 1964), 48ff.; *supra*, 57f.

99. *Zohar*: Lekh Lekha, 1:85b. See also *The Holy Letter*, chap. 2, trans. S. J. Cohen (New York, 1970), 48–49, 58–59.

100. See R. Isaac bar Sheshet Parfat, *Responsa Ha-Ribash* (Constantinople, 1574), no. 159.

101. Thus an important scholar of Jewish mysticism, R. J. Z. Werblowsky writes, "The Jewish kabbalist . . . performed his marital duties with mystico-theurgic intentions, but realized that he was not allowed to give himself up either to his partner or to his passion. Transformed, in theory, into a sacramental act, the 'holy union' of husband and wife was in practice an ascetic exercise which admitted of no genuine relationship between the partners because the kabbalist had to identify with the mystical intention of the act and not with its actuality." *Joseph Karo: Lawyer and Mystic* (Oxford, 1962), 137.

102. See Isa. 40:6–8; Job 19:25–26; also I Sam. 13:15 and M. Avot 5.16.

103. Thus the late-nineteenth-century English poet Robert Bridges wrote in his poem "Eros":

> Why hast thou nothing in thy face?
> Thou idol of the human race,
> Thou tyrant of the human heart,
> The flower of lovely youth thou art;
> Yea, and thou standest in thy youth
> An image of eternal Truth. . . .

Seven Centuries of Verse, 2d rev. ed., ed. A. J. M. Smith (New York, 1957), 543–544.

104. For the inconceivability of unembodied human life, see *Vayiqra Rabbah* 4.5.

For embodiment as a limit, see Maimonides, *Hilkhot Yesoday Ha-Torah*, 1.7; *Moreh Nevukhim*, 1.49.

105. *Vayiqra Rabbah* 14.5, ed. Margulies, 2:308.

106. See Maurice Merleau-Ponty, *Phenomenology of Perception*, trans. C. Smith (London, 1962), 148ff.

107. See B. Kiddushin 54a and parallels; *Shir Ha-Shirim Rabbah* 8.13 re Num. 19: 14.

108. See R. Moses Cordovero, *Tomer Devorah*, chap. 9. Cf. Plato, *Symposium*, 202E.

109. Freud writes, "But towards the outer world at any rate the ego seems to keep itself clearly outlined and delimited. There is only one state of mind in which it fails to do this. . . . At its height the state of being in love threatens to obliterate the boundaries between the ego and object." (*Civilization and Its Discontents*, trans. J. Riviere [Garden City, N.Y., 1958], 3.) He then goes on, "Originally the ego includes everything, later it detaches from itself the external world. The ego feeling we are aware of now is thus only a shrunken vestige of a far more extensive feeling—a feeling which embraced the universe and expressed an inseparable connection of the ego with the external world" (p. 6). For Freud, sexual love is the experience of the strongest pleasure. Even more than other pleasures it is a *taking-in* of the external world, a narcissistic reduction of sorts. But the phenomenology of sexual love seems to indicate that it is essentially the intention of the *other*, irreducible to the embodied ego or any of its functions. As such, sexual love is transcendent in essence; it is not enclosed in an immediately human (and, for Freud, individual) circle. In other words, there is an essential difference between sexual love and all other "pleasures." The difference between sexual love and all other pleasures is generic, not just specific, as it is for Freud.

110. *Shiur Ha-Shirim Rabbah* 8.6. It might be useful to compare this ancient Jewish statement about the essence of love with a modern one. In his 1927 novel *The Bridge of San Luis Rey* (2d ed. [New York, 1955], 148), Thornton Wilder concludes with these words: "But soon we shall die and all memory . . . will have left, and we ourselves shall be loved for a while and forgotten. But the love will have been enough; all those impulses of love return to the love that made them. Even memory is not necessary for love. There is a land of the living and a land of the dead and the bridge is love, the only survival, the only meaning." If love, as Wilder seems to be saying, is a *state of being* (as we would say today, "I am in love"), then it is conceivable that it can transcend individual persons and individual memories. But if love is an act, then it is only a person who can consciously *do* it. If, then, we can love with an undying love, it is only because we have been loved by God.

5

The Problem of AIDS in
a Jewish Perspective

Current Public Concern with AIDS

Since the discovery, about ten years ago, of the growing health problem of acquired immune deficiency syndrome (AIDS), public concern with this new phenomenon has increased significantly. In fact, public discussion of it has far outstripped discussion of any other health problem in our society. The media are constantly filled with everything from personal testimonies by and about AIDS sufferers and their loved ones to predictions by various experts on the future course of the problem and how we might best cope with it. Indeed, interest in the problem is so widespread, and fear about it so rampant, that the surgeon general of the United States prepared a booklet about AIDS and how to avoid contracting it. The booklet was sent to every American household.

If AIDS were just a health problem per se, that is, simply a physical disease (actually, it is the result of a virus that weakens the natural immune system of the body to such an extent that there is no effective defense against any infection that might attack the body), the degree of public concern we have seen heretofore might well be out of proportion to the actual physical danger at hand. Despite the growing number of patients dying as the result of AIDS-related diseases, their number is smaller than the number of patients who die as the result of cancer, heart disease, and other more familiar fatal maladies. Moreover, despite warnings by some experts—warnings disputed by other experts—that the general population is at an increasing risk, male homosexuals and intravenous drug users are still the highest risk groups.[1] Therefore, there must be something about this malady that inspires more than just the fear of imminent physical contagion in the general population, the overwhelming number of whom do not fall into the two highest risk groups just noted. For most of us, then, AIDS has created more of a spiritual problem, in truth, than a physical one. As such, any human approach to this problem — certainly any religious approach, which must deal with concerns of both body and soul — will be inadequate if it deals with the AIDS problem only as it would with any other epidemic or threatened epidemic. Indeed, it seems that the very phenomenology of AIDS involves religious questions in a more immediate way than any other modern health problem. And because so much of the population has been so thoroughly secularized, certainly in terms of attitudes toward health and disease, the especially religious phenomenology of AIDS is something for which they have been ill prepared by our culture.

The religious phenomenology of AIDS becomes evident in three spiritual issues AIDS inevitably raises. First, AIDS seems to question the prevailing hedonism of our culture, for before the appearance of AIDS, it was far easier to argue that our bodies are simply there to be used for our pleasure, that there are no bodily impediments per se, that we can do with our bodies whatever we will. The availability of antibiotic drugs (that have supposedly cured the old venereal diseases like syphilis and gonorrhea), birth control drugs and devices, and legalized hygienic abortion certainly had made the arguments for a "sexual revolution" more compelling, although the dangers of the drug aspect of this overall *hedonistic revolution* were becoming increasingly evident even before AIDS came on the scene. But AIDS has now demonstrated that the promiscuity that generally characterizes those at greatest risk of contracting it (including more and more heterosexuals) is physically dangerous. In other words, the old warnings about the physical consequences of hedonistic promiscuity ("You'll get a terrible disease if you do that!") suddenly have a new truth about them. AIDS has now shown us that the body is not just the tool of the soul's willful capacity but that it has an inherent integrity of its own that must be respected for the sake of the good of the whole human person. And it has shown that the human will is only part of a larger created nature and that the will's pretensions to omnipotence, pretensions supremely manifest in hedonism, are mortally dangerous on the most immediate physical level.[2] Furthermore, it is important to add, at this point, that our lack of preparation for the AIDS crisis because of our hedonism is in essence akin to our lack of preparation for the whole ecological crisis because of our uncritical faith in technology.[3] In both cases, human pretensions of omnipotence are being directly challenged by the biological order of nature, which is beyond our control.

Second, AIDS seems to raise what was thought by most moderns to be an ancient superstition long behind us, namely, the whole issue of God's punishment of sin through physical maladies. Yet, as anyone with either therapeutic or pastoral experience well knows, the first question most often raised even today, even by many "nonreligious" people, who have discovered serious disease in themselves is: "What did I do for God to do this to me?".[4] Now, in the case of most other diseases, whose epidemiology is totally external, one can attempt to reason with the patient by showing that the disease was contracted through no fault of his or her own. (Whether such "reasoning" is psycholog-

ically helpful to this type of patient is another question in and of itself.)
Nevertheless, in regard to AIDS, the patient most often does indeed know
just what he or she did that caused his or her body to be so receptive to the
AIDS virus and thereby set in motion the deadly syndrome.

This entails considerable guilt, for most of the people in our culture, however otherwise secularized they may be, still regard homosexual acts and the
use of narcotic drugs to be not only immoral but sinful, that is, they are acts
for which God will punish us. Therefore, the cultural message about AIDS
seems to be that it is caused not only by one's own acts but by one's immoral
or sinful acts. Indeed, one need no longer argue for the immorality of these
acts based on abstract philosophical or theological definitions; rather, one
can now actually point to concrete and seemingly inevitable consequences.
Arguments on behalf of AIDS sufferers that ignore these indisputable facts
can be regarded only as rationalizations motivated by pathological denials of
empirical reality.

Finally, the fact that children can be born with AIDS because of the acts
of their parents seems to raise the old fear that "God punishes the children for
the sins of the parents."[5] This fear also applies to those who have contracted
AIDS because of having been infused in one way or another with the bodily
fluids of someone who did contact AIDS because of his or her own acts. In
other words, we suffer not only for our own sins but for the sins of others
before us. This raises the whole question of "original sin," a doctrine most
Jews (at least most liberal Jews) are surprised if not shocked to learn that
Judaism affirms as does Christianity after it, albeit with some important differences.[6]

It is because of these considerations that a Jewish approach to the problem
of AIDS must incorporate both the immediately practical norms of Halakhah
and, also, some of the more theoretical reflections of Jewish theology about
disease in general, reflections that can be seen as informing the whole normative process of which Halakhah is always the most evident aspect.[7] For an
adequate Jewish discussion of AIDS must address not only the bodily needs
of those specifically afflicted with it but their spiritual needs and, indeed, the
spiritual needs of all those for whom the very social presence of AIDS has
raised some old religious questions in some surprisingly new ways.

Indiscriminate Treatment of the Sick

It must be emphasized at the very outset that for Traditional Judaism, male
homosexual acts are absolutely prohibited, both for Jews and non-Jews. (Female homosexual acts are also prohibited, but their prohibition is based on
quite different sources. Moreover, because female homosexuals are not a
high-risk AIDS group, we need not be concerned with them in this specific
context.)[8] According to one major authority in the Talmud, both Jewish and
non-Jewish males are proscribed from homosexual acts by the scriptural prohibition "You shall not lie with a man as with a woman; it is an abomination

[*to'evah hi*]" (Leviticus 18:22).[9] According to another authority, this verse specifically proscribes Jewish men only, non-Jewish men being so proscribed by the scriptural verse "a man . . . shall cleave to his wife [and they shall be one flesh]" (Genesis 2:24), which is interpreted to mean "but not with a male [*zakhar*]."[10] This latter interpretation, which is taken to be the normative one, entails the view that the Jewish proscription of such homosexual acts is a reaffirmation of a more general human proscription, whereas the former interpretation sees the Jewish proscription as being primary and the general human proscription as being derivative. The acceptance of this latter interpretation is important in emphasizing that for subsequent Jewish tradition, the proscription of male homosexual acts is neither something applying only to Jews nor something "Jewish" to be imposed on the general population by Jews or by the influence of Judaism. It can be addressed as a human issue per se. Therefore, Traditional Judaism can make common cause with other religious and ethical traditions that affirm the same human proscriptions, without any one of them subordinating its own moral authority to the other.[11]

The same type of moral presentation can be seen in the prohibition of acts that are clearly destructive of life and health, of which intravenous drug use is such an obvious example to everyone by now. Thus one of the main grounds given in the Talmud for this prohibition is the verse addressed to Noah and his sons (for the Rabbis, "sons of Noah" is a synonym for humankind per se), "Surely I shall hold you responsible for your own lifeblood" (Genesis 9:5).[12] Indeed, in a famous passage in the Talmud, where a rabbi being martyred is urged to shorten his suffering by hastening his own death while being burned at the stake, the rabbi refuses, arguing along general human lines that "it is best that He who gave life take it, but that a person not destroy himself."[13]

So we can now see that the majority of AIDS sufferers are considered to be in the category of sinners (including promiscuous heterosexuals), and it is irrelevant whether they be Jews or non-Jews. However, this should in no wise prevent full care being extended to AIDS patients, even though sympathy with their plight must never lead to approval for their way of life. This needs to be emphasized because I strongly suspect that there is a concerted attempt on the part of apologists for homosexuality (as well as for sexual license of any kind) to extend normal human sympathy for AIDS suffering in particular to a more general human sympathy for *everything* about those suffering from AIDS. In terms of Jewish teaching as well as ordinary human reason, such an extension of sympathy is totally misplaced. It is as misplaced as attempting to extend our normal human sympathy with smokers suffering from lung cancer to their practice of smoking cigarettes. Nevertheless, our obligation *to* AIDS patients must be internalized as sympathy *with* them for three reasons.

First, according to Jewish tradition, everyone is essentially a sinner. "There is no person [*adam*] on earth who is so righteous that he will do only good and not sin" (Ecclesiastes 7:20).[14] And even certain extraordinary scriptural personalities, who are seen by the Talmud as being themselves without sin, are still included in the mortality decreed for all humankind because of original sin.[15]

Second, the Talmud sees all human suffering as a means for intensifying our relationship with God. This turns out to mean that even if a person cannot discern specific sin in oneself when suffering, one is to act as if he or she were a sinner, namely, he or she must return to God (the Hebrew for "repentance" is *teshuvah*—"return").[16] Therefore, sin is so pervasively human that the difference between the righteous and the wicked is ultimately one of degree, not of kind. This does not, of course, excuse anyone's particular sin, but it does indicate that the self-righteous confidence that assumes its own security because it is not suffering at present as is someone else, that such self-righteous confidence is religiously abhorrent. As the atonement liturgy used on Yom Kippur succinctly puts it, "We are neither so arrogant nor so stubborn as to say before You O' Lord our God and God of our ancestors that we are righteous [*tsadiqim anahnu*] and have not sinned."[17]

Third, because we are all, therefore, subject to both disease and death due to our sins, we are in an existential position to *sympathize* with (literally "feel with" from the Greek *sympathein*, as in the German *Mitgefuehl*) those suffering from any disease, including AIDS. This is brought out in the rabbinic treatment of the scriptural norms concerning the disease *tsara'at* (wrongly translated "leprosy"; actually a far less fatal disease than what is for us *leprosy*, namely, Hansen's disease). According to the Rabbis, the reason that Scripture specifically singles out this disease for its concern is because it is the punishment for a number of antisocial vices, most especially slander.[18] The community is commanded to quarantine those suffering from this disease.[19] Now it seems that this is for the sake of the community, that it not become contaminated by contact with them, either physically or spiritually. "And the one who is afflicted with the disease [*ve-ha-tsarua*], his clothes shall be rent and his head disheveled, and he shall cover his upper lip and cry "Unclean! Unclean! [*tamē*]'" (Leviticus 13:45). However, the Rabbis emphasize that this is not done to humiliate the *tsara'at* sufferers but to give them the public opportunity to express their pain and anguish and to beseech others to "seek compassion [*rahamim*] for them."[20] *Compassion* is to be exercised both in prayer (beseeching God) and personal attention (beseeching humans). Both acts are the two parts of the overall commandment to attend to the needs of the sick (*biqur holim*).[21]

The treatment of those suffering from this disease is more for their sake than for the sake of the community in which they live. The community clearly has a responsibility for them, a responsibility involving both its physical and spiritual involvement. Furthermore, this concern is not limited to sufferers from the specific disease. In a parallel passage, the Talmud extends this procedure to those suffering from any other disease or misfortune as well.[22] Finally, once again emphasizing the general human problem involved in the AIDS problem, Jews are to be indiscriminate in terms of those who are the object of their medical attention, be they Jews or non-Jews.[23]

A serious problem does arise, however, when confronting the Talmud's rule that in the case of a "provocative sinner" (*mumar le-hakh'is*), one not only is not to help such a person but actually is not to save his or her life (*moridin ve-lo ma'alin*).[24] The question that must be honestly faced by all those who accept the authority of Jewish law, despite its obvious difficulty, is twofold: (1) whether the male homosexual or the drug user suffering from AIDS falls into this category, and (2) whether enforcement of the rule still applies under contemporary conditions.[25]

Regarding the first aspect, the provocative sinner is contrasted with the "sinner for appetite" (*mumar le-te'avon*). At first glance, it seems that because both active homosexuals and drug users apparently are motivated by "appetite," that their immediate gratification takes precedence over the observance of moral restraints. If this is the case, then the drastic action mandated by this Talmudic rule does not apply to them after all. However, the essential distinction between these two types of sinners is not seen to be the motivation behind their respective acts, that is, the former being motivated to rebel against the authority of God by violating what has been revealed in the Torah, and the latter being motivated by the desire for instant gratification. Rather, Maimonides interprets the difference between the two types of sinners to be whether the sin is habitual and willful or not.[26] If one sins habitually and willfully, then he or she is considered to be a *provocative* sinner. On the other hand, if one sins occasionally and with guilt, then he or she is considered to be a sinner *for appetite*. Actually, the term *appetite* is used here as an euphemism for weakness of will. The Talmudic way of describing such a person is that "he would not eat nonkosher food if kosher food were readily at hand."[27]

By this criterion, active homosexuals and drug users seem to fall into the category of provocative sinners. Their actions seem to be both habitual and willful. Furthermore, the recent attempt of some religious apologists for homosexuality to see active homosexuals as being under the influence of an avoidable compulsion (*ōnes*) and thus not morally culpable is rationally flawed,[28] for it confuses the state of homosexual desire (or desire for drugs, if one is to follow this same logic) with homosexual activity. The Torah prohibits only homosexual activity, not homosexual desire, which can hardly be the subject of conscious choice.[29] Of course, because the presence of such desire makes avoidance of proscribed homosexual acts quite difficult, one could argue for the moral counsel that someone who is continually experiencing it seek professional help in order to sublimate it or, optimally, to experience heterosexual desire.[30] To assume that homosexual activity is as consciously involuntary as homosexual feeling and desire is to classify all homosexuals as being deprived of free choice. But that is hardly compassion, for it denies them their moral personality, an essential part of their full human function.[31] It erroneously assumes that only heterosexuals can separate sexual desire and sexual activity.

The designation of homosexuality as provocative sin has profound implications for understanding its essence from a Jewish point of view, as well as its current manifestation in connection with AIDS.

Because of the growing epidemic among heterosexuals (especially in Africa and Asia), there has been a concerted effort to deny any essential connection between AIDS and homosexuality. In terms of a specific connection, this argument is correct. AIDS is transmitted by heterosexual acts, just as it is transmitted by homosexual acts. But the argument misses the general, deeper point: AIDS is mostly transmitted by sexually promiscuous persons, whose very socially irresponsible promiscuity leaves them open to a whole series of infections, most seriously, but not exclusively, AIDS. The fact is that male homosexuals as a group are probably the most sexually promiscuous segment of our society. Hence, one can see AIDS as a problem primarily for the sexually promiscuous—both homosexual and heterosexual, but especially for homosexuals.

The question is why homosexuals are so promiscuous. Is their promiscuity essential to their homosexuality? There is good reason to believe so precisely because homosexuality cannot be socially structured into a procreative familial relationship, which Judaism has certainly seen as the foundation of society. The family is as much human society's connection to created nature as it is created nature's connection to human society.[32] In consequence, homosexuality is ultimately answerable only to the fulfillment of its immediate desire. It cannot essentially limit itself because it itself is not answerable to any greater order in which it participates. That is why, it seems to me, the Rabbis considered homosexuality to be an epitome of sin.[33] If humans are to rule over sin (Genesis 4:7), that rule must begin with the control of their own bodies, with what the Rabbis termed "conquering one's libido" (ha-kovesh et yitsro).[34] This is why, it seems to me, habitual and committed homosexuals are considered to be motivated by more than "appetite." It is not that they have succumbed to appetite; rather, they have constituted their very identity in it.

However, despite the fact that according to traditional criteria, active homosexuals are provocative sinners, even provocative sinners are capable of repentance and repentance can thus be expected of them.[35] That still requires our respect; those deprived of free choice, on the other hand, can be the objects only of our pity. Our obligation then, to care for AIDS patients, even if their disease is the result of grave sin, must not only tend to their bodies but respect their souls. Even the soul of the sinner is of infinitely greater importance than his or her sin.[36]

Despite the fact that many AIDS patients do fall into the category of the provocative sinner, there are times when the sanctions entailed by sin are not enforced.[37] In the Middle Ages, it was questioned why all provocative sinners are not included in the category of those whose lives are not to be saved. In fact, it was noted that the rule itself seems to be inconsistent, for it actually includes certain persons guilty of relatively minor sins and excludes other persons guilty of much more grave sins. One exegete explained this seeming inconsistency by noting that the criterion of inclusion is not due to the inherent nature per se of the proscribed acts being performed but, rather, to the likely consequences the Rabbis thought would result from issuing such a harsh warning.[38] Thus if the Rabbis thought that a relatively minor offense was being treated too lightly by the people, and that the threat of such a severe punishment would have a sobering effect on them, they enacted such a harsh sanction. This is seen as being justified by the power given to contemporary rabbinical authorities to exercise judgments more severe than those actually mandated by statute, if and when they deemed a situation in public morality an emergency.[39] So this category is subject to a high degree of judicial discretion.

Furthermore, it seems that by the time of the Middle Ages, the category of those whose lives are not to be saved was almost exclusively confined to persons whose deeds actually endangered the lives and property of the entire community, most notably, informers (*mosrim*).[40] Along these lines, it seems that this type of reaction could conceivably apply to the AIDS patients who, despite their awareness of their highly contagious condition, still engage in sexual activity with unknowing partners. In the case of other AIDS patients, however, such sanctions, or even the threat of such sanctions, would be counterproductive. In modern times, this latter conclusion was powerfully formulated by the influential Israeli Talmudist and jurist R. Abraham Isaiah Karelitz (d. 1953), known as the Hazon Ish. He insisted that the purpose of all such rabbinic legislation is only to be constructive, a matter dependent on a judicial consideration of the times.[41]

The Question of Danger to Health Care Personnel

One of the moral problems that has arisen in connection with the AIDS crisis is the refusal of many health care personnel to treat AIDS patients at all. They argue that not only is AIDS highly contagious but the actual means of its contagion have by no means been ascertained. Without such definition, there is no real containment within predictable boundaries. Hence, the only sure way of not contracting the disease is to avoid any contact whatsoever with those who have AIDS. The question, then, is to what extent may the religiously based duty of self-preservation be invoked as prior to the religiously based duty to treat the sick, especially when one has unique skills for this through professional training.[42]

A truly adequate approach to this problem must begin with the question of what is the source of the obligation to treat the sick. This can be the only proper context for dealing with the more specific question of what is required of us in treating AIDS patients. In the classical Jewish sources there are two main theories concerning the source of the obligation to extend treatment to the sick: that of Maimonides (d. 1204), and that of Nahmanides (d. 1267).

In an early work, Maimonides argues that the obligation of the physician (*rofē*—which in our day can certainly be extended to all health care personnel) is derived from the fact that the scriptural law requiring that we return a lost article to this owner (Deuteronomy 22:2) is extended by the Talmud to include "returning his body to him," that is, saving his life.[43] In a later work, he reiterates the scriptural command, "You shall not stand idly by the blood of your neighbor" (Leviticus 19:16), which the Talmud connects with the previous interpretation of returning lost property (including a "lost" body) to its owner.[44] The latter verse is seen as being needed to teach the obligation to engage in such saving action even if it entails considerable effort and expense.

Even though Maimonides does not mention the actual duty of a physician in this later text, one can clearly extend the point made in it to include the physician. And, in regard to our problem of to what extent are health care personnel obligated to treat AIDS patients who do place them at some risk, the most important commentator on Maimonides, R. Joseph Karo (d. 1575), connects this text with an obscure rabbinic text that states that one is required to "expose himself to possible danger" (safeq sakkanah) when saving a human life.[45] Needless to say, the difference between "possible" danger and "definite" danger (sakkanah vad'ai) can be determined only on an ad hoc basis.

There are a number of problems with basing the duty to care for the sick on Maimonides' theory, and especially the duty to care for AIDS patients on it. First, the connection of the duty to extend oneself to someone in physical danger with the duty to expose oneself to possible danger is highly tenuous. Moreover, later commentators have great trouble altogether finding the rabbinic text that mandates exposure to possible danger. It is said to be from the Palestinian Talmud, but the great Talmudist R. Naftali Berlin (Netsiv, d. 1893) could find only a text there that deals with an individual's volunteering to risk his life for that of another.[46] Clearly, the permission and even the encouragement of a supererogatory act by a heroic individual cannot be the basis for a general norm requiring everyone in a similar situation to do so.[47]

Second, all of the Talmudic sources deal with situations where one happens to encounter other persons in dangerous situations. None of them deals with any obligation to choose and to remain in a health care profession and regularly treat all patients indiscriminately, for there such encounters are regular occurrences, not chance happenings. This is not to say that Maimonides himself, who was a distinguished physician, did not regard his profession of medicine to be a vocatio; from his biographical testimony we know that he did.[48] However, his theory of the obligation to extend medical care, indeed to choose to become a professional who regularly does so for better and for worse, does not seem to explain this obligation sufficiently.

To many students of Maimonides' writings, it has seemed quite odd that he did not quote or even paraphrase the well-known Talmud text that states, "It was taught in the School of R. Ishmael that from Scripture's words, 'he shall surely provide for his healing' [Exodus 21:19] is derived the permission for a physician to heal."[49] Perhaps Maimonides believed that the use of the term "permission" (reshut) indicated that such activity is only optional; therefore, the obligation to heal requires a stronger scriptural and Talmudic ground.[50] Nevertheless, Nahmanides (who was Maimonides' most cogent legal and theological critic) does quote this very text, and his exposition of it shows another theory, one that I believe is more adequate to the task at hand, both in terms of Jewish law and in terms of Jewish theology. The key difference between his theory and that of Maimonides is that he does not base the obligation to heal on an analogy between human life and human property, as does Maimonides.[51] Nahmanides writes:

The explanation of this Talmud text is that the physician might say, "Why do I need this trouble; perhaps I might make a mistake [*et'eh*] and the result be that I have killed lives through error [*bi-shegagah*]?"; therefore, the Torah authorizes him [*natnah lo reshut*] to heal. . . . [T]here are those who say that the physician is like a judge who is obligated to judge [*metsuveh la-doon*]. . . . And it makes sense . . . also that they should not say, "God wounds and He heals" since . . . human beings have become accustomed to medical treatment [*be-refu'ot . . . she-nahagu*]. . . . Here "permission" [*reshut*] means an obligation [*reshut de-mitsvah*] . . . which God has designated for him to do.[52]

Here "permission" is not taken in its usual sense of that which is optional but, rather, it is taken negatively, namely, that which is not prohibited.[53] It is an authorization to perform a commandment, one that one might think is for God alone to do.

Nahmanides' analogy between a physician and a judge lies at the heart of the theological point he is making here. In both professions, namely, those of healing and judging, the activity is regarded as essentially divine and human only by participation. Thus Scripture assures the judges that they should not be deterred by the fact that their efforts have only partial results in this world; indeed, it could not be otherwise because justice is essentially transcendent.[54] "You shall not fear any man for judgment is God's" (Deuteronomy 1:17).[55]

God is also designated by Scripture as a physician. "Every disease which I placed in Egypt I shall not place on you for I the Lord am your physician [*rof'ekha*]" (Exodus 15:26).[56] Just as, ideally, God should be the only judge, so, ideally, God should be the only physician.[57] However, it is the less than ideal conditions of human life on earth that require human judges and, for Nahmanides, especially require human physicians.[58] Nevertheless, these human physicians must always appreciate their essentially subordinate role in the true created order.[59]

Nahmanides' theory of the obligation to heal makes it not just an ordinary obligation but, rather, an act of *imitatio Dei*.[60] Indeed, what for the Rabbis are the two main attributes of God, that of judgment (*Elohim* qua *middat ha-din*) and that of compassion (*YHWH* qua *middat rahamim*), can be seen as the basis for the participatory status of judges and physicians: judges in the attribute of judgment; physicians (and all other "healers") in the attribute of compassion.[61]

In terms of the obligation to treat AIDS patients, this is a crucial point, for AIDS is a disease, which at least for the time being, allows its sufferers only to be treated, not cured. No one's life, now anyway, can be "saved." We can only *care for* these lives in the little time they have left. This requires greater effort; it also entails greater frustration because the ideology of modern medicine, like so much of the ideology of our technological civilization, is totally success oriented. We always want lasting results for our efforts, and here there are none. Yet Judaism obligates care, not just cure.[62] Here is where understanding our obligation as a divine commandment, one that is uniquely grounded in divine example, not just divine decree, alone makes sense of it, for it requires the infinite expenditure of compassion rather than the efficacy needed for finite results. That is why it cannot be an ordinary commandment, one simply based on divine decree.[63] This is important, too, for justifying treatment that only palliates (alleviating suffering as much as possible) rather than cures a disease, something that is clearly not the case at present with AIDS patients. In Maimonides' medical model, based as it is on the analogy of returning a lost piece of property, however, we are dealing with a case where a problem (a lost piece of property) is actually solved (it is returned to its owner). By contrast, Nahmanides' medical model explains only *care* of the sick, even when there can be no successful completion of a procedure.

The true results of our obedience to the commandments, the recompense for our exposure to toil and even danger in order to keep them, we are taught lies in a realm beyond our experience and certainly beyond our grasp.[64] Hence, we can care for the AIDS patients because their imminent mortality does not catch us unaware. The commandments are addressed to us as equally mortal persons; we would not need them if we were anything else.[65] And the commandments save us from ultimate despair, which in the case of treating AIDS patients is such a strong and ever-present temptation. It saves us from despair because we are involved through the commandments in the very life of God himself, in which life, not death, is the final victor.[66]

NOTES

1. Re the debate on this subject, see M. A. Fumento, "AIDS: Are Heterosexuals at Risk?" *Commentary* 84 (1987):21 ff.

2. Re hedonism and Judaism, see David Novak, *Halakhah in a Theological Dimension* (Chico, Calif., 1985), 80–81.

3. See *infra*, 135ff.

4. The persistence of this question alone explains the enormous popularity of Harold Kushner's book, *When Bad Things Happen to Good People* (New York, 1981). However, Rabbi Kushner's conclusion, viz., that these things *happen* rather than being *caused* by God (see esp. 113ff.) is hardly consistent with the emphasis of traditional Jewish theology that everything other than our own free response to God is indeed "in the hands of God" (see B. Berakhot 33a and parallels re Deut. 10:12), and, as we shall soon see in this chapter, according to that theology, none of us can claim to be "good people."

5. The disturbing message of this verse (Exod. 20:5 and 34:7; Num. 14:18; Deut. 5:9) already troubled the prophets (see Jer. 31:28; Ezek. 18:2ff.). The Talmud, in one comment, tries to qualify the message by stating that it applies only "when the children hang onto [i.e., willfully repeat] the deeds of their parents" (B. Berakhot 7a and B. Sanhedrin 27b). Nevertheless, the fact that children do suffer because of their parents' misdeeds is too apparent ever to be fully explained away. See, e.g., Y. Megillah 4.12/ 75d and esp. R. Samuel David Luzzatto (Shadal), *Commentary on the Torah*: Exod. 20:5; also Novak, *Halakhah in a Theological Dimension*, 11ff.

6. See Gen. 8:21; also Solomon Schechter, *Some Aspects of Rabbinic Theology*

(New York, 1936), 242ff., and Will Herberg, *Judaism and Modern Man* (New York, 1951), 74ff.

7. See David Novak, *Law and Theology in Judaism*, 2 vols. (New York, 1974–1976), 1:1ff.; 2:xiii ff.

8. See, e.g., B. Yebamot 76a; Maimonides, *Hilkhot Isuray Bi'ah*, 21.8; also David Novak, *The Image of the Non-Jew in Judaism: An Historical and Constructive Study of the Noahide Laws* (New York and Toronto, 1983), 213–215.

9. B. Sanhedrin 57b re Lev. 18:6. For a fuller discussion of the prohibition of homosexuality, see *supra*, 89ff.

10. Ibid., 58a.

11. See David Novak, *Jewish-Christian Dialogue: A Jewish Justification* (New York, 1989), introduction.

12. B. Baba Kama 91b.

13. B. Avodah Zarah 18a. See B. Berakhot 32b re Deut. 4:9, 15.

14. See B. Sanhedrin 46b.

15. B. Baba Batra 17a. See B. Yevamot 103b and parallels with Maharsha, *Hiddushay Aggadot, ad locum*; Wisdom of Solomon 2:24; Nahmanides, *Torat Ha'Adam*: Sha'ar Ha-Gemul, introduction, in *Kitvay Ramban*, 2 vols., ed. C. B. Chavel (Jerusalem, 1963), 2:12.

16. B. Berakhot 5a–b.

17. *The Authorized Daily Prayer Book*, ed. S. Singer (London, 1962), 353. See M. Sanhedrin 6.2; B. Shabbat 32b; Nahmanides, *Torat Ha'Adam*: Inyan Viduy, *Kitvay Ramban*, 2:47; *Shulhan Arukh*: Yoreh De'ah, 338.2.

18. See, e.g., T. Nega'im 6.7; Arakhin 15b re Lev. 14:2.

19. See Arakhin 16b re Lev. 13:46. However, it is important to note that the Rabbis regarded *tsara'at*'s contagion to be moral rather than physical. See, e.g., M. Nega'im 3.2; Maimonides, *Hilkhot Tum'at Tsara'at*, 9.8.

20. B. Mo'ed Qatan 5a. Cf. Maimonides, *Hilkhot Tum'at Tsara'at* 10.8.

21. See B. Nedarim 39b–40a.

22. B. Sotah 32b; *Shulhan Arukh*: Yoreh De'ah, 335.8.

23. See B. Gittin 61a.

24. B. Avodah Zarah 26b.

25. Theoretically, a rabbinic law (such as this one) can be repealed (see M. Eduyot 1.5); however, in actual practice, reexamination of the conditions required for the application of the law was the usual procedure for effecting change. See, e.g., M. Kiddushin 4.14; B. Kiddushin 82a; Karo, *Shulhan Arukh*: Even Ha'Ezer, 24.1 and Sirkes, *Bach* on *Tur*: Even Ha'Ezer, 24; also Karo, *Kesef Mishneh* on Maimonides, *Hilkhot Tefilah*, 11.1.

26. *Hilkhot Rotseah*, 4.10 and *Hilkhot Teshuvah*, 3.9 (see Karo, *Kesef Mishneh, ad locum*); also *Hilkhot Yesoday Ha-Torah*, 5.10.

27. Hullin 4a and parallels. For eating as a euphemism for sexual activity, see Semahot 7.8 and B. Kiddushin 21b–22a.

28. See H. J. Matt, "An Approach to Homosexuality," *Judaism* 27 (1978):16.

29. See Norman Lamm, "Judaism and the Modern Attitude to Homosexuality," *Encyclopedia Judaica Yearbook: 1974*, 194ff. For further background, see Samuel H. Dresner, "Homosexuality and the Order of Creation," *Judaism* 40 (1991):309–321.

30. See David Novak, "On Homosexuality," *SH'MA*, 11/201 (November 14, 1980), 3–5.

31. See Maimonides, *Hilkhot Teshuvah*, 4.1ff.

32. See *supra*, 87.

33. See *supra*, 90. For the authoritative view that all nonmarital sex is sinful, see *Sifre*: Devarim, no. 260 re Deut. 23:18; Maimonides, *Hilkhot Ishut*, 1.4 and R. Vidal of Tolosa, *Maggid Mishneh, ad locum*.

34. See M. Avot 4.1 re Prov. 16:32; B. Avodah Zarah 19a re Ps. 112:1; B. Sanhedrin 19b–20a.

35. See Maimonides, *Hilkhot Teshuvah*, 7.1ff.

36. For the refusal to equate the sinner with his or her sin, see B. Berakhot 10a re Ps. 104:35.

37. See B. Betsah 28b. For the whole problem of the administration of punishment in Jewish law, see M. Elon, *Ha-Mishpat Ha'Ivri*, 2 vols., 2d ed. (Jerusalem, 1978), 1: 421ff.

38. R. Joseph ibn Habib, *Nimuqay Yosef* on B. Avodah Zarah 26b, ed. Blau, 203 in the name of *Tosfot Ha-R'osh*. Also see *Tosfot Rabbenu Samson of Sens, ad locum*, ed. Blau, 82.

39. See B. Sanhedrin 46a; also Maimonides, *Hilkhot Sanhedrin*, 24.10.

40. See *Responsa Ha-R'osh*, ed. Venice (1552), 17.1.

41. *Hazon Ish*: Yoreh De'ah (B'nai B'rak, 1958), sec. 2, 7d. Cf. B. Gittin 33a, Tos., s.v. "v'afqa'inhu."

42. See *Sifra*: Behar re Lev. 25:36, ed. Weiss, 199c; B. Baba Metsia 62a.

43. *Commentary on the Mishnah*: Nedarim 4.4.

44. *Hilkhot Rotseah*, 1.14 elaborating on B. Sanhedrin 73a.

45. See Karo, *Kesef Mishneh* on Maimonides, *Hilkhot Rotseah*; also Karo, *Bet Yosef* on *Tur*: Hoshen Mishpat, 426 re Lev. 19:16 and M. Sanhedrin 4.5. Along similar lines, see B. Baba Metsia 30b re Exod. 18:20; R. Solomon Luria, *Yam Shel Shlomoh*: Baba Kama, 6.26 re B. Baba Kama 60b. Cf., however, R. David ibn Abi Zimra, *Responsa Ha-Radbaz*, 3, no. 627; R. Joshua Falk, *Me'irat Aynayim* on *Shulhan Arukh*: Hoshen Mishpat, 426.

46. *Ha'Ameq Sh'elah* on *She'iltot de-Rav Hai Gaon*: Shelah, end re Y. Terumot 8.4/46b. Viktor Aptowitzer argued in his "Unechte Jeruschalmizitate," *Monatschrift für Geschichte und Wissenschaft des Judenthums* 55 (1911):419ff., and in this point he has been followed by other modern critical Talmudists, that when a medieval source quotes the *Yersuhalmi* and we do not have this source in our Yerushalmi text, then the citation may very well be from a now lost rabbinic collection (*Qovetz Yerushalmi* or *Sefer Yerushalmi*). See also R. Zvi Hirsch Chajes' note on B. Megillah 12b, and *Imray Binah*, sec. 2 in *Kol Sifray Maharats Chajes* 2 vols. (B'nai B'rak, 1958), 2:891ff.

47. See J. Halberstam, "Supererogation in Jewish *Halakhah* and Islamic *Shari'a*," in *Studies in Islamic and Jewish Traditions*, ed. W. M. Brinner and S. D. Ricks (Atlanta, 1986), 85ff.

48. See my late revered teacher Abraham Joshua Heschel, *Maimonides: A Biography*, trans. J. Neugroschel (New York, 1982), 213ff.

49. B. Baba Kama 85a.

50. See, e.g., B. Berakhot 27b; Maimonides, *Hilkhot Tefillah*, 1.6. For the attempt to see *reshut* as designating a low level of obligation rather than a pure option, see M. Betsah 5.2 and B. Betsah 36b; B. Berakhot 26a, Tos., s.v. "ta'ah"; ibid., 27b, Tos., s.v. "halakhah." Regardless of which interpretation one accepts, however, the term *reshut* is not strong enough to ground the sense of *vocatio* needed for the practice of medicine as a profession.

51. For the pitfalls of using economic analogies when dealing with the protection of human persons, see R. Stith, "Toward Freedom from Value," *Jurist* 38 (1978): 48ff.

52. *Torat Ha'Adam*: Inyan Ha-Sakanah, *Kitvay Ramban*, 2:41–43. See, also, David Novak, *The Theology of Nahmanides: Systematically Presented* (forthcoming).

53. For *reshut* in this stronger sense, see esp. R. Joshua Falk, *Perishah* on *Tur*: Yoreh De'ah, 336 n. 4.

54. See M. Avot 2.16; *infra*, 163ff.

55. See B. Sanhedrin 6b.

56. For God's greater healing power than man's, see *Mekhilta*: Be-Shelah, ed. Horovitz-Rabin, 156.

57. For uneasiness with human authority in relation to divine authority, see Jud. 8:22–23; I Sam. 8:5ff.

58. See, e.g., Nahmanides, *Commentary on the Torah*: Lev. 26:11.

59. For a powerful theological statement against the prevailing medical absolutism of this secular age, see my late friend Paul Ramsey, *The Patient as Person* (New Haven, 1970), 115, 156–157.

60. See B. Shabbat 133b re Exod. 15:2; *Beresheet Rabbah* 8, end.

61. See A. Marmorstein, *The Old Rabbinic Doctrine of God*, 2 vols. (New York, 1968), 1:43ff.

62. See B. Yoma 85a; B. Yevamot 80a–b and Rashi, s.v. "mipnay sakkanah"; B. Shabbat 151b; B. Nedarim 39b (the retort of R. Aha bar Hanina); Sirkes, *Bach* on *Tur*: Hoshen Mishpat, 426 re the limitations of the Maimonidean model for medical treatment.

63. See B. Sotah 14a re Gen. 18:1; B. Baba Kama 99b–100a re Exod. 18:20.

64. B. Kiddushin 39b. See B. Berakhot 34b re Isa. 64:3.

65. See B. Kiddushin 54a; *Shir Ha-Shirim Rabbah*, 8.13 re Num. 19:14.

66. See B. Pesahim 68b.

6

Nuclear War and the Prohibition of Wanton Destruction

The Precedented and the Unprecedented

In regard to the question of whether it is permitted or forbidden to wage nuclear war, it seems that if an authentically Jewish answer is to be found, the place to look for it would be in the speculations of Aggadah more than in the precedents of Halakhah,[1] for according to virtually all the experts dealing with the question, nuclear war would alter human life and society in a totally unprecedented way; indeed, it might very well destroy all life on this planet. Halakhah is a system of precedent and rules derived from precedent. Even though the system itself is subtle enough to treat unusual, even bizarre, cases adequately, it is an axiom of the system that its general rules are formulated for what will usually obtain in human affairs, not for what might happen but never has.[2] If, as the experts maintain, nuclear war entails the probability of the end of the world as we know it, then it seems we should examine Jewish eschatology, which, although entailing some halakhic issues, is essentially an exercise in speculation about the "end of days" and how human expectations and hopes are to be formulated in relation to it. In an earlier study I engaged in such aggadic speculation about the scriptural and rabbinic descriptions of God's lordship over his creation and the correct meaning of his promise of created continuity made to Noah and his descendants, that is, to humankind, and what the loss of faith in that promise entails in terms of responsible human action.[3] Such speculation might indeed be one of the subjects that Maimonides regarded as ultimately more important than the more mundane analysis of what is usually forbidden and permitted (*he'asur ve-ha-muttar*).[4]

The Prohibition of Wanton Destruction

Nevertheless, there is one area of Halakhah that might provide some directly normative guidance to Jews agonizing over this very real question facing all of humankind, and that is what is usually called in English, the prohibition of "wanton destruction" (*bal tash'hit*).[5] In this chapter I shall analyze the various interpretations of the meaning of this prohibition in an attempt to derive at least some guidance for an authentically Jewish approach to the question of waging a nuclear war.

The prohibition of wanton destruction is found in a passage in the Pentateuch that presents a very clear prohibition and then connects it with a very unclear reason.

> When you lay siege to a city for many days, battling against it to capture it [*le-tofsah*], do not destroy [*lo tash'hit*] its trees wielding the ax against them, for [*ki*] from them you do eat and you may not cut them down. For [*ki*] are the trees of the field human to withdraw from before you in a siege?! (Deuteronomy 20:19)

From this specific prohibition is derived the general prohibition of destroying anything for no good reason. According to some halakhic authorities, this general prohibition is directly prescribed by the passage quoted above, and the specific case mentioned there is simply an example of a larger class of prohibited acts (*binyan av*).[6] According to at least one other halakhic authority, however, the scriptural prohibition is confined to the case at hand and the more general prohibition, mentioned frequently in the Talmud, is a decree of the Rabbis, which they associated with only this relevant scriptural passage (*asmakhta*).[7]

In the strict halakhic sense, this dispute seems to affect only the actual punishment administered to a person convicted of the crime of wanton destruction. If the crime is considered to be a scripturally prohibited offense, the punishment would be more severe.[8] But if, on the other hand, only the wanton destruction of fruit trees violates the explicit scriptural prohibition, then one convicted of any other act of wanton destruction is to receive only a somewhat lesser punishment.[9]

There is, however, another effect of this exegetical dispute, and that pertains to the reason given in the last part of the verse from Deuteronomy 20:19. If the prohibition of wanton destruction is directly scriptural, then the reason supplied in the last part of this verse grounds and thereby limits the entire prohibition. But if the prohibition of wanton destruction is rabbinic, with the specific exception of the destruction of fruit trees proscribed by Scripture explicitly, then the reason given in Scripture in connection with this proscription only applies to it alone and does not, therefore, ground and thereby limit the more general prohibition. Accordingly, one could supply a more all-encompassing and thereby more sufficient reason for it.[10]

The Reason for the Prohibition

The reason for the commandment given in Scripture is enigmatically worded, but most of the commentators seem to follow the Septuagint, which translates this second part of the verse as "perhaps [*mē*] the trees in the field are human [*anthrōpos*] to come from before you into the fortified place?!"[11] Thus Rashi (following *Targum Onqelos*) writes, "Perhaps the trees of the field are human to be punished with hunger and thirst like the people of the city [*k'anshav ha'ir*]; why do you destroy them [*lamah tash'hiteno*]?!"[12] This reasoning seems to entail an ethic of retribution, namely, you may not harm *what* has not harmed you, unlike those *who* have harmed you, *whom* you may indeed harm. Furthermore, according to this interpretation, it even entails an ethic of retribution by anticipation, namely, you may not harm what will not harm you *later*, unlike those who will harm you *later*, whom you may indeed harm *now*.[13] All of this is based on the fact that the earliest rabbinic sources place this commandment in the context of a permitted offensive war (*milhemet reshut*).[14] Thus, following this line of reasoning, the sixteenth-century Italian exegete R. Obadiah Sforno wrote in his commentary:

> For it is indeed so that the trees of the field are human to surrender themselves over [*li-msor et atsmah*] into your hands because of the force of the siege?! And inasmuch as this is not so, and that it is right [*ra'uy*] to harm the inhabitants of the city with weapons of war . . . to bring the city under siege, and this will not be accomplished [*she-lo tasig zeh*] by the destruction of the trees, hence it is not right [*ayn ra'uy*] to destroy them as it is right [*she-ra'uy*] that you destroy the human inhabitants of the city.[15]

In other words, this type of interpretation not only entails an ethic of retribution by anticipation (in today's military parlance, a "preemptive strike") but seems to entail placing a higher value on trees than on the lives of human beings, even if they happen to be one's enemies.

What emerges from this is an ethic of rather extreme utilitarianism, where all arguments must satisfy the demands of immediate self-interest in order to be valid. Thus Philo writes:

> On the contrary, it benefits [*ōphelei*] you by providing the victors with abundance both of necessities [*anangkaion*] and of the comforts which insure a life of luxury. For not only men but plants also pay tributes to their lords [*pherousi tois kyriois*] . . . and theirs are the more profitable [*tous ōphelimoterous*] since without them life is impossible.[16]

And Josephus follows the same line when he concludes that trees "were created for the service of men [*ep' ōpheleia . . . tōn anthrōpōn*]."[17]

This line of reasoning has proven to be quite consistent in its logic. In fact, it is able to solve the apparent contradiction between the commandment against wanton destruction in Deuteronomy 20:19 and the later commandment of the prophet Elisha to the kings of Israel and Judah: "You shall smite every fortified city and every choice city, and every good tree you shall fell and all of the sources of water you shall stop up and every good field you shall ruin with stones" (II Kings 3:19). Instead of trying to explain away the prophetic text that seems to contradict the text from the Pentateuch, the advocates of this line of reasoning, consistent with their utilitarianism (at least in this case), turn the commandment from Deuteronomy into a hypothetical imperative (to use Kant's helpful terminology and conceptuality) rather than a categorical imperative.[18] Thus the nineteenth-century Romanian exegete R. Meir Leibush Malbim writes:

> "Battling against it to capture it" [*le-tofsah*] — this is added because siege may be made against the city in order to destroy it and make it uninhabitable [*u-le-hashbitah*] as a city. Therefore, the explanation is that the intention [*ha-kavvanah*] should only be to capture the city that it be yours . . . but this consideration is eliminated [*l'afuqay*] if they want [*im rotsim*] to destroy the city as in the case of Moab. [II Kings 3:19].[19]

In other words, Malbim makes the efficacy of the earlier commandment contingent on prior human choice, namely, *if* you want only to capture a city, *then* do not wantonly destroy its fruit trees, but *if* you want to destroy a city, *then* you may do so, as exemplified by the commandment of Elisha regarding Moab.[20] Earlier, the fifteenth-century Turkish exegete R. Elijah Mizrahi argued, basing his opinion on the same rabbinic comment in the *Sifre* later used by Malbim, that the whole restriction was confined to an authorized offensive war, but "if it were a defensive war [*be-milhamah shel mitsvah*], the city is to be made uninhabitable and not to be captured intact."[21] One could, indeed, see this very same type of reasoning employed by the United States in the 1945 atomic bomb attack on Hiroshima, a major city of Japan, the nation that had attacked the U.S. fleet at Pearl Harbor, without direct provocation, in 1941.

Now, if one were to follow this whole line of reasoning to the logical conclusions I have attempted to draw from it heretofore, a case could still be made for judging the waging of nuclear war in our day to be immoral. For now, unlike 1945 when nuclear weapons were a monopoly of the United States, a number of nations (the number of which is growing frighteningly) do have nuclear weapons. Thus even if a nuclear-power nation were to wage nuclear war against a non-nuclear-power nation, considering the balance of power in the world of realpolitik today, it is inevitable that the non-nuclear-power nation would be allied with another nuclear-power nation, which would rise to its defense (or to avenge it). Weaker nations now invariably fall within the sphere of global influence and power of stronger nations. So it seems most likely that the initiation of nuclear hostilities in today's world would quickly trigger a worldwide conflagration, the results of which would soon prove to be disastrous for any and all nations. In other words, the qualification of the prohibition of wanton destruction, based on utilitarian considerations of immediate self-interest, would not apply in a situation where an act of nuclear aggression would result in ultimately suicidal consequences.[22] Surely, the logic of ordinary warfare, in which there is a clear and sustained difference in kind between the victors and the vanquished, no longer applies in a nuclear war. The advantage of delineating the utilitarian point of view in classical Jewish sources is that utilitarianism is the most minimal moral point of view possible and is seemingly the easiest to defend;[23] yet even on the grounds of this minimal moral point of view there is no good justification for waging a nuclear war in the world today.

Contra Utilitarianism

Although utilitarianism is an easy moral point of view to defend, it is based on an anthropocentricity that is rather atypical, considering Judaism's theocentricity and the human self-transcendence (which some would call altruism) it so frequently requires. Thus the nineteenth-century Italian exegete R. Samuel David Luzzatto criticized the whole utilitarian line of reasoning we have been examining, noting that in his opinion this commandment "was not given to teach human beings to make calculations [*heshbonot*] for their own benefit [*le-han'at atsmam*] but, on the contrary, it was given to strengthen in our hearts compassion [*ha-hemlah*] and graciousness and opposition to our own purposes [*ve-na-mitnagdut le-to'eletenu*]."[24]

Furthermore, the second part of the verse might not be a reason at all but, rather, the second part of the commandment itself by inference, namely, in your wartime panic do not look upon the fruit trees of your enemies as being themselves enemies. In other words, the full two-part commandment might very well be (a) Do not cut down the fruit trees of your enemies; *and* (b) do not regard them as you would your human enemy.[25] Thus the first part of the commandment proscribes action; the second part, attendant attitude. If so, then the sufficient reason for the commandment is not found in this verse at all.[26] Moreover, if the general norm against wanton destruction is actually rabbinic in origin, then we can avoid all the exegetical problems we have seen in looking at Deuteronomy 20:19 and immediately look for the sufficient reason elsewhere, a reason both evident to our intellect (*ratio quoad nos*) and one grounded in the objective moral order of creation itself (*ratio per se*).[27]

One could indeed argue that the very technology, especially the military technology that produces nuclear weapons, that has had to answer only to minimal utilitarian criteria of immediate use has had to answer only to itself, and thus not to a moral criterion transcendent enough to contain it and prevent its abuses. Indeed, historically, the very credibility of utilitarianism beginning in the nineteenth century seems to have been possible largely through the social successes of technology. Hence, technology can be contained only when an objective moral order stemming from an ontological order is affirmed, for technology is manifest as human power for its own sake alone. Technology per se is ultimately purposeless and, therefore, without limit.[28] Surely, our very recent experience of uncontrolled and perhaps uncontrollable technology has shown us in a far more vivid way than was available to the medieval

Jewish thinkers I have labeled "utilitarians" how morally deficient any utilitarianism is in preventing technological abuse of the created natural order.

The explicit appeal to an objective moral order to explain the prohibition of wanton destruction seems to have been made by the eleventh-century Spanish exegete R. Abraham ibn Ezra. He writes:

> For the trees of the field are humanlike [*u-kemohu*] because one is injuring [*hovel*] human beings [*nefesh*] by injuring the means of human life [*hayay nefesh*]. . . . You shall not destroy fruit trees, which are a source of life for humans [*hayyim le-ven adam*]. It is only permitted [*muttar*] to eat from them and it is forbidden [*asur*] for you to destroy them in order to lay siege against a city.[29]

The important point to note in this explanation is the emphasis on the priority of human life—all human life—even over considerations of military advantage. For Ibn Ezra, the destruction of the food-producing trees is no longer a hypothetical imperative contingent upon the fulfillment of a subjective aim; rather, it is a categorical imperative, namely, food-producing trees are not to be destroyed, even when their destruction would contribute to your own military advantage, because they are *necessary for human life in general*. The prohibition thus absolutely eliminates from the realm of the permitted what in the twentieth century came to be termed the "scorched earth policy." For Ibn Ezra, destruction of an enemy is not an end in itself, thereby justifying whatever means. Any destruction, even in wartime, must be both temporary and partial in order to be justifiable. Cutting down fruit trees, especially in an arid region like the Middle East, results in both permanent and widespread damage.[30]

Ibn Ezra's anti-utilitarian line of reasoning was picked up in the thirteenth century by the Spanish exegete, halakhist, and theologian Nahmanides. He writes:

> R. Abraham [ibn Ezra] explained it well . . . but the opinion of the Rabbis is that it is permitted to cut down fruit trees to build a siege. . . . [F]ruit trees are mentioned only to indicate that one should use a non-fruit tree first [*she'ilan sereq qodem*]. If so, then the explanation of this passage in their view is that the Torah prohibited [*she-hizhirah*] . . . cutting them down destructively [*derekh hash'hatah*] not for the sake of a siege, as is the practice of military expeditions [*ke-minhag ha-mahanot*]. . . . [A]s it is said in II Kings 3:19, "and every good tree you shall fell, etc." . . . and you shall not do this to destroy them, but you shall trust in the Lord that he will deliver them into your hand.[31]

Nahmanides allows an exception to this rule only in the case where fruit trees will be used for military purposes by your enemies against you there and then, even if that requires cutting trees down.[32] However, cutting them down may not be a matter of long-term strategy inasmuch as destruction for the sake of some remote goal might very well be, in truth, destruction for its own sake.

This would be directly contrary to faith in God as Creator and Deliverer. In other words, the long-term goal might be a rationalization for present nihilism. This type of pseudomoral reasoning was termed by the Rabbis "a transgression for the sake of a commandment" (*mitsvah ha-ba'ah b'averah*) which is, of course, an oxymoron.[33] The means must be consistent with the end; if not, the end cannot justify them.

Nahmanides' problem is how to deal with Ibn Ezra's seeming departure from the rabbinic interpretation of this commandment. For the line of utilitarian reasoning we saw from Philo to Malbim seems to arise directly out of the rulings of the Rabbis as halakhic sources. Thus the *Sifre* on Deuteronomy 20: 19 rules, "'to withdraw from before you in a siege': if they prevent you [*im m'akevekha*] by coming before you in a siege, then cut them down [*qatsatsehu*]."[34]

Justified versus Wanton Destruction

In dealing with the general prohibition of wanton destruction the Talmud teaches:

> R. Hiyya bar Avin said in the name of Samuel that if one lets blood and becomes chilled, a fire is made for him even during the summer. A teak chair was broken up for Samuel [for firewood]. . . . A footstool was broken up for Rabbah. Abaye said to Rabbah that this was a violation of the prohibition of wanton destruction [*bal tash'hit*]. He replied his own body is more important [*de-gufayh adif*].[35]

Now, this type of reasoning must be carefully delineated because it seems to be of the "slippery slope" variety, eventually justifying just about any destructive act on the basis of the most paltry subjective reason.

One can see another seeming example of this type of reasoning in the law pertaining to Sabbath desecration. There, according to the Mishnah, only constructive acts are considered within the category of the scripturally prohibited labors (*avot mel'akhah*).[36] However, the Talmud includes one who tore his clothes in anger in this category because he "assuaged his feelings of rage" (*de-k'avad nahat ruah le-yitsro*).[37] In Maimonides' words, "He is like one performing a constructive act [*ke-metaqen*]."[38]

However, there is a difference between the law of the Sabbath and the law of wanton destruction on this very point, and the contrast between them will better explain the law of wanton destruction. The Sabbath was given to place a limit on man qua *homo faber* in both a social and an individual sense. Objective constructive acts (even those that initially entail some destructive preparatory work), which the Rabbis discerned in the building of the Sanctuary by Moses and the Israelites, have tangible, socially beneficial results.[39] Subjective acts, such as acting out one's anger, only have an emotional effect. They lack any tangible social benefit. Nevertheless, both are forms of prohibited "labor," which interferes with the experience of the Sabbath as a full human celebration of the creative work of God. Regarding destruction, on the other hand, in order to be justified (and thus not "wanton"), it must have some immediate and tangible, socially beneficial result. But if the act does not have this social value, if it is to satisfy only some subjective emotional aim, then it is considered destruction for destruction's sake. Even Rabbah's burning a stool to keep himself warm was a socially justifiable act in that his bodily need could be the bodily need of anyone else in the same situation.

The fact that wanton destruction cannot be justified on subjective emotional grounds is brought out in the following Talmudic passage: "R. Huna tore silk garments in the presence of Rabbah, his son, saying, 'I am going to see whether he will become angry or not.' . . . And did he not violate the prohibition of wanton destruction?! No, because he tore them on the seams."[40] Now, the interpretation of this episode is that tearing the silk garments on the seams would enable them to be so easily repaired and restored to their original quality so as not to constitute destruction at all.[41] However, were this not the case, then R. Huna would have been in violation of the prohibition. What is important to note here is that the Talmud does not suggest that R. Huna would have been exonerated on the grounds that he was gaining some kind of emotional satisfaction by so testing his son's practice. That would have been an insufficient justification precisely because it is too subjective and too private. Furthermore, it is clear from the questions the Talmud raised about this bizarre incident, the Rabbis did not approve of R. Huna's conduct at all.

Indeed, this very unjustifiable destruction is considered to have idolatrous implications. Thus the sixteenth-century halakhist R. Joseph Karo connects the prohibition of wanton destruction as codified by Maimonides with a Talmudic text that follows the Talmudic text, which we examined earlier, that designated destruction out of anger as a positive violation of the Sabbath.[42] This Talmudic text reads:

> One who tears his clothes in anger, and who breaks his things in anger, and who scatters his money in anger, he should be considered as an idolator in your eyes. For such is the craftiness [*umanuto*] of the evil inclination [*yetser ha-ra*]: today it says to him, "Do such and such," tomorrow it says to him, "Do such and such," until it says to him, "Worship idols," and he goes and does so.[43]

It is important to note that Maimonides uses the language of this aggadic passage to warn of the seriousness of uncontrolled anger.[44]

What emerges from all of this is that idolatry is the very epitome of wanton destruction. If so, then the service of God the Creator is the essential opposite of this. "From the negative we infer the positive," as the Talmud puts it.[45] In our century it was Freud who most insightfully designated the human capacity for nihilation as the "death drive" (*Todestrieb*), contrasting *thanatos* (death) with his earlier reduction of all human thought and action to *eros* (sensual drive).[46] Unfortunately, although Freud was a Jew — and a proud one at that —

he was also an atheist, and being an atheist, he missed the theological truth that the drive for *thanatos* and the drive for idolatry (*avodah zarah*) are in essence the same.[47] This is what Nahmanides was trying to express in his attempt to harmonize the theological insight of Ibn Ezra with the precedents of Halakhah. For Nahmanides' own insight was that wanton destruction is performed precisely when faith in God's future saving action is lost.

If this is the case, then even destructive action performed in the ultimate interest of the state — even the Jewish state constituted by the Torah itself — cannot be justified,[48] for nationalism per se, where the life and activity of the political community are posited as ends in themselves requiring no further justification and admitting no transcendent source of criticism, is itself idolatry. Indeed, it is *the* idolatry of the twentieth century, a century that has witnessed more bloodshed and more wanton destruction than perhaps the whole history of humankind before it. As the victims of the greatest program of mass murder and destruction in human history, Jews should remember that the Holocaust was the ultimate example of wanton destruction, serving no constructive purpose even for the Nazi murderers themselves.[49]

It was the prophets of Israel who in God's name challenged the nationalist pretensions of the kings and the people of Israel in ancient days. Even though the Talmud sees the actual prophetic experience as ending with the downfall of the Second Temple in 70 c.e., it still recognizes some residue of prophetic insight left in the people of Israel and their historical experience.[50] Thus the prophetic critique of the ultimate nihilism of absolute ethnocentricity can still be spoken today — indeed, with some very current applications.

This critique of ethnocentricity and the nihilism it inevitably entails comes out in the treatment of this whole issue in the Bible commentary of the fifteenth-century Spanish exegete, theologian, and statesman Don Isaac Abrabanel. In commenting on Deuteronomy 20:19 he writes:

> This means that they should not cut down the fruit-producing trees that are in the city, like the practice of the warriors whose purpose [*she-magamatam*] is to destroy and annihilate everything, as it states in II Kings 3:19. . . . Therefore, it is not right [*ayn ra'uy*] to destroy them, for it is not good [*ayn ne'ot*] that man should destroy what benefits himself [*she-yo'ilehu*].[51]

It seems that Abrabanel means by "man" (*ha'adam*) what Ibn Ezra meant by it, namely, humankind in general, whose life and well-being depend on care and nurture of the created order of nature.

An earlier medieval source emphasized this objective and universal criterion by stating:

> The root of the commandment is known and that is to teach us to love the good and the purposeful [*ha-tov ve-ha-to'elet*] and to cleave to it, and from this the good will cleave to us and we will remove ourselves from everything destructive [*mi-kol davar hash'hatah*]. . . . It is not so with the wicked, the brothers of destructive demons [*maziqim*], who rejoice in the destruction of the world and who destroy themselves.[52]

Along these lines the fourteenth-century Provençal exegete and theologian Gersonides went so far as to emphasize that this commandment reflects God's providence (*hashgahah*) even over plants, proscribing the destruction of those that benefit others, especially.[53] It is the emphasis of an objective moral order, which is part of a universal order presided over by God's providence, that provides the ontological grounding for the altruism — the self-transcendence — that this commandment truly requires of us. The integrity of the moral realm involving fellow humans presupposes the integrity of the larger created realm of nature. One cannot work to improve the moral quality of human life and society without working to improve the quality of creation.[54] In our day the concern for nuclear disarmament and the concern for ecology complement each other and ultimately coalesce into the concern for God's creation itself.

We have seen earlier that the most utilitarian treatments of Deuteronomy 20:19 have treated the "scorched earth policy" of II Kings 3:19 as being on a par with the former, that is, one has the legitimate choice of either approach depending on how one — in this case, how one nation — judges its own immediate self-interest. However, in his comment on II Kings 3:19, Abrabanel, basing his thinking on a midrashic text, declares this to be an emergency measure for that time only, a prophetically revealed dispensation (*bi-dvar Ha-Shem le-fi sha'ah*).[55] Although his justification of this emergency measure as being due to the incorrigible corruption of the Moabites begs the question in this particular case, his isolation of it by this means does remove it from being a precedent for any such action at any other time. Thus the contradiction he rightly sees between these two scriptural norms is solved in the sense that the prohibition of absolute destruction is taken as the categorical imperative and the commandment of Elisha to the kings of Israel and Judah is taken as the lone exception *sui generis*. This is very much in line with the traditional rabbinic method of interpretation used in resolving seeming contradictions between the Pentateuch and the prophets.[56]

The Interdependence of Humans and Nature

It should be noted that following the line of interpretation developed from Ibn Ezra in the eleventh century to Luzzatto in the nineteenth century, the enigmatic reason presented in Deuteronomy 20:19 is a sufficient grounding not only for the specific prohibition of wanton destruction of fruit trees but also for the general prohibition of wanton destruction per se, for by comparing trees (*ets*) and humans (*adam*) it indicates that destruction of the environment and destruction of human society go hand in hand. Ultimately, even self-interest requires a transcendent frame of reference.

But on the other hand, if we follow Maimonides' interpretation that the general prohibition of wanton destruction is rabbinic, then we need not concern ourselves with the minute analysis of Deuteronomy 20:19b and its enigmas.[57] We can simply see this general prohibition as being based on the general scriptural affirmation of the sanctity of all created being, perhaps best expressed by the prophet, "He did not create it to be a wasteplace [*tohu*], but he formed it to be a dwelling [*la-shevet*]" (Isaiah 45:18).[58] Furthermore, this also precludes the problem we saw earlier in the comment of R. Elijah Mizrahi, namely, that the whole scriptural prohibition of wanton destruction applies only in an authorized offensive war (*milhemet reshut*), but that in a defensive war (*milhemet mitsvah*) wanton destruction not only is permitted but is actually its goal. If, however, the general commandment, with which we are concerned as a source of guidance about the waging of nuclear war, is rabbinic, then it does not really matter for our purposes whether or not the specific scriptural prohibition pertains only to an authorized offensive war (which could not be waged today by halakhic criteria).[59] Moreover, even in a defensive war the enemy is not to be destroyed unconditionally; peace terms are to be negotiated with everybody.[60] So, if we are not to destroy our enemies unconditionally, then we are not to destroy their environment unconditionally, based on the analogy of trees and humans in Deuteronomy 20:19b. This is certainly the case in a situation like the nuclear threat today, where our destruction of somebody else's environment would inevitably entail the destruction of our own environment. Indeed, even without the actual use of nuclear weapons, we have painfully seen from the ecological devastation wrought by Saddam Hussein and his Iraqi troops in the Persian Gulf in 1991 that Iraq itself did not escape its horrible effects.

Some Practical Considerations

After this analysis of the prohibition of wanton destruction, arguing for the line of interpretation that sees its rationale as being grounded in an objective moral order within a providential created order, I would like to draw some tentative practice points from it, which pertain to the question of nuclear war.

First, the evil of nuclear war, which cannot be justified by any of the usual criteria of temporary destruction for the sake of ultimate victory, is to be emphasized continually. Those who advocate otherwise are like the fools whom the Talmud said love their property more than their own lives.[61] Such fools, especially when they occupy positions of political, military, or economic power, are not only foolish, they are dangerous. Therefore, it seems to me that normative Jews, who live by the Torah's principles and precepts, should participate with those who work publicly to expose these dangerous delusions of nuclear victory.[62]

Second, it seems that multilateral, not unilateral, disarmament is what is required. Unilateral disarmament on the part of any side can only encourage others to engage in what military strategists call a "surgical strike." This would be like the situation noted earlier by Nahmanides: cutting down the fruit trees would enable the enemy to use them as offensive weapons of destruction. We must never forget that the disarmament of the Western nations after World War I led to a state of military impotence that encouraged Mussolini and Hitler to engage in such unlimited aggression, believing as they did that there would be no real opposition to it. Therefore, multilateral disarmament must be pursued to lessen the likelihood of nuclear aggression by any side.

Third, because war and aggression begin in the stubborn and arrogant pride of human beings, which the prophets and sages saw as the source of all sin,[63] normative Jews should endeavor in their individual lives and in their various societies to banish from their hearts all arrogance and hatred among themselves and toward others. And they should pray that God will purify our hearts and enable us to be a light to the nations, who in our day are groping in the darkness of the nuclear threat, which hangs over our heads like a terrible sword.

NOTES

1. For the notion that Aggadah can be directly normative when it does not contradict previously codified Halakhah, see R. Zvi Hirsch Chajes, *Darkhay Ha-Hora'ah*, sec. 2, *Kol Kitvay Maharats Chajes*, 2 vols. (Jerusalem, 1958), 1:251–252.

2. See B. Eruvin 63b and parallels; B. Sanhedrin 52b and Tos., s.v. "hilkhata"; Zevahim 45a; B. Yoma 13a, Tos., s.v. "halakhah"; also, Maimonides, *Moreh Nevukhim*, 3.34.

3. *Halakhah in a Theological Dimension* (Chico, Calif., 1985), chap. 7, "The Threat of Nuclear War."

4. *Hilkhot Yesoday Ha-Torah*, 4.13 re B. Sukkah 28a.

5. See *Encyclopedia Talmudit*, 3:335b–337b, s.v. "bal tash'hit."

6. See *Semag*, neg., no. 229; *Semaq*, no. 175. If one follows the line of reasoning that sees Deut. 20:19 as a general prohibition *exemplified* by the specific prohibition of cutting down fruit trees, then this is a case of "Scripture taking a contemporary example" (*dibber ha-katuv be-hoveh*), without its norm being limited to that specific example (*ba-meh matsinu*). See M. Baba Kama 5.7; *Sifra*: intro., 13 principles, no. 3; *Encyclopedia Talmudit*, 2:1ff., s.v. "binyan av."

7. Maimonides, *Hilkhot Melakhim*, 6.10; also *Sefer Ha-Hinukh*, no. 529. Nevertheless, in *Sefer Ha-Mitsvot*, neg., no. 57, Maimonides designates all wanton destruction (*kol hefsed*) as being in violation of the scriptural law.

8. See M. Makkot 3.1ff.

9. See R. Isaac Lampronti, *Pahad Yitshaq*, 10 vols., ed. Leghorn (1840), 4:119b, s.v. "makkat mardut."

10. For the notion that all rabbinic legislation has evident reasons (*ta'ama*), see B. Gittin 14a and Tos., s.v. "ke-hilkhata."

11. Ed. A. Rahlfs (Stuttgart, n.d.), 323.

12. *Commentary on the Torah*, ed. C. B. Chavel (Jerusalem, 1982), 563.

13. See M. Sanhedrin 8.5; also, *infra*, 179.

14. *Sifre*: Devarim, ed. Finkelstein, no. 238.

15. *Commentary on the Torah*, ed. Z. Gottlieb (Jerusalem, 1984), 339.

16. *De Specialibus Legibus*, 4.226, 228 in *Philo*, 9 vols., trans. F. H. Colson (Cambridge, Mass., 1930), 8:148–149.

17. *Antiquities*, 4.299 in *Josephus*, 9 vols., trans. H. St. John Thackeray (Cambridge, Mass., 1930), 4:620–621.

18. See *Groundwork of the Metaphysic of Morals*, trans. H. J. Paton (New York, 1964), 82ff.

19. *Commentary on the Torah* (Jerusalem, 1957), 4 vols., 2:760a, no. 126. Also see Rashbam, *Commentary on the Torah*: Deut. 20:19.

20. Cf. Maimonides, *Hilkhot Berakhot*, 11.2.

21. *Sefer Otsar Ha-Payrushim al Ha-Torah: Mizrahi* (New York, 1965): Deut. 20:19, 2:28b. For the difference between *milhemet reshut* and *milhemet mitsvah*, see *infra*, 191ff.

22. One should compare the conciliatory stand of Rabban Yohanan ben Zakkai, as recorded in B. Gittin 56b, with the endorsement of mass suicide for reasons of national pride made by the Zealot leader Eleazar ben Yair, as recorded by Josephus in *Bellum Judaicum*, 7.334–336. See also David Novak, *Law and Theology in Judaism* (New York, 1974), 2 vols., 1:83ff. For a similar type of moral reasoning, see Pope John XXIII, *Pacem in Terris*, Eng. trans. (Washington, 1963), 30.

23. For probably the most classic statement of utilitarianism, see Jeremy Bentham, *An Introduction to the Principles of Morals and Legislation* (London, 1823), chap. 1.

24. *Commentary on the Torah*, ed. P. Schlesinger (Tel Aviv, 1965: Deut. 20:19, p. 537. See also his comment on Exod. 22:20. Later on in his comment on Deut. 20:19 (pp. 538–539), however, in order to justify the command of Elisha in II Kings 3:19, Luzzatto provides an explanation that seems to contradict his critique of the utilitarian interpretation of Deut. 20:19. Nevertheless, he concludes (p. 539) with the suggestion that the reason for this norm is to show gratitude to anyone or anything that has benefited us. Indeed, gratitude per se cannot be justified on utilitarian grounds (see *Beresheet Rabbah* 96.5 re Gen. 47:29).

25. The conjunction *ki* in this verse probably functions as "a neutral interrogative . . . expecting a negative answer." Francis Brown, S. R. Driver, and C. A. Briggs, *A Hebrew and English Lexicon of the Old Testament* (Oxford, 1966), 472a. For a similar interpretation of a two-clause verse connected by the conjunction *ki*, note Exod. 22:20: "You shall not oppress the sojourner [*ger*] or persecute him, for [*ki*] you were sojourners [*gerim*] in the land of Egypt." Ibn Ezra interprets the second clause as being itself a command, viz., "*and* remember [*u-zekhor*] that [*ki*] you were like him [*kemohu*]." *Commentary on the Torah*, 3 vols., ed. A. Weiser (Jerusalem, 1977), 2:156. Here, too, the first part of the command prescribes action; the second part, an attendant attitude. For the argument that the second clause is an insufficient reason [*ta'am*] per se for the first, see Nahmanides' comment *ad locum*; cf. Rashi, *Commentary on the Torah, ad locum*, however.

26. The same line of reasoning is employed in the Talmud (B. Sanhedrin 21a) in explaining the fact that R. Simon (M. Sanhedrin 2.4 and B. Baba Metsia 115a) opines that even when reasons seem to be given for specific norms in the Torah itself, these seeming reasons are themselves norms (*darash ta'ama de-qra*), and the true and sufficient reasons are not revealed in the text but, if possible, inferred from it. See E. E. Urbach, *Hazal: Emunot Ve-De'ot* (Jerusalem, 1971), 328; *Halakhah: Meqoroteha Ve-Hitpatehutah* (Jerusalem, 1984), 106.

27. See Thomas Aquinas, *Summa Theologiae*, 1–2, q. 94, a. 2.

28. See Jacques Ellul, *The Technological System*, trans. J. Neugroschel (New York, 1980), 129, 256; *infra*, 135ff.

29. *Commentary on the Torah*, 3:272.

30. For an aggadic expression of the tragedy of cutting down a fruit tree, see *Pirqay de-Rabbi Eliezer*, chap. 34.

31. *Commentary on the Torah*, 2 vols., ed. C. B. Chavel (Jerusalem, 1963), 2:438. In his addenda to Maimonides' *Sefer Ha-Mitsvot*, pos., no. 6, Nahmanides designates

the prohibition of *bal tash'hit* as only prohibiting wanton destruction (*hash'hatah be-hinam*) during an invasion of Israel into enemy territory, but during the time of Israel's retreat from enemy territory, "all is permitted" (*kol zeh muttar*). It is worth noting that in his actual comment on Deut. 20:19 he does not mention this qualification. It seems to me that this is because he moved closer to the more categorical position of Ibn Ezra. (See also Maimonides, *Hilkhot Melakhim*, 6.8.) for Nahmanides' emphasis of the inherent integrity of the created natural order and the obligation to respect it, see his comment on Lev. 19:19; also David Novak, *The Theology of Nahmanides: Systematically Presented* (forthcoming).

32. *Commentary on the Torah*, 2:439. See also his comment on Num. 31:10.

33. See B. Sukkah 30a and parallels; P. Hallah 1.5/58a; LXX and *Targum Pseudo-Jonathan* on Deut. 16:20; also B. Sanhedrin 74a, *infra*, 167ff.

34. No. 203, ed. Finkelstein, 239.

35. B. Shabbat 129a; cf. B. Baba Kama 91b.

36. M. Shabbat 7.2.

37. M. Shabbat 13.1; B. Shabbat 105b.

38. *Hilkhot Shabbat*, 8.8 and 10.10.

39. See B. Shabbat 49b, 97b re Exod. 35:1; Y. Shabbat 7.2/9b; *Mekhilta*: Vayaq'-hel, ed. Horovitz-Rabin, 345. See *infra*, 148.

40. B. Kiddushin 32a.

41. See Rashi, *ad locum*, s.v. "be-fombay."

42. *Kesef Mishneh* on Maimonides, *Hilkhot Melakhim*, 6.10.

43. B. Shabbat 105b.

44. *Hilkhot De'ot*, 2.3.

45. B. Nedarim 11a.

46. See *Beyond the Pleasure Principle*, trans. J. Strachey (New York, 1959), 70ff.

47. See Psalms 115:2–8; *Mekhilta*: Yitro, ed. Horovitz-Rabiu, 223 and n. 8, *ad locum*.

48. See Shalom Spiegel, *Amos versus Amaziah* (New York: Jewish Theological Seminary of America, n.d.).

49. See William L. Shirer, *The Rise and Fall of the Third Reich* (New York, 1960), 1432–1434.

50. See B. Baba Batra 12a–b; B. Pesahim 66a.

51. *Commentary on the Torah*: Deut. 20:19 (Warsaw, 1862), p. 41b.

52. *Sefer Ha-Hinukh*, no. 529 (New York, 1966), 78b.

53. *Commentary on the Torah* on Deut. 20:19 (Venice, 1547), 129b, no. 5.

54. See Gen. 2:15; 8:22–9:8.

55. *Commentary on Former Prophets*: II Kings 3:19 (Jerusalem, 1955), 614. The midrashic text is *Tanhuma*: Pinhas, printed ed., no. 3. There the Midrash also indicates that in the campaign against Midian (Num. 25:17) the prescription of Deut. 20:19 did not apply. The reason given for this dispensation is self-defense. See B. Sanhedrin 72a re Exod. 22:2.

56. See, e.g., B. Yevamot 90b and Tos., s.v. "ve-li-gmar"; B. Sanhedrin 89b and Tos., s.v. "Eliyahu"; B. Kiddushin 43a re II Sam. 11:11 and Tos., s.v. "mored." See also comments of Gersonides and Abrabanel on II Sam. 1:15.

57. For Maimonides' overall attempt to limit the role of scriptural exegesis in halakhic reasoning, see David Novak, "Maimonides and the Science of the Law," *Jewish Law Association Studies* 6 (Atlanta, 1990)6:108ff.

58. See M. Gittin 4.5, cf. *supra*, 84f. See L. E. Goodman, *On Justice: An Essay in Jewish Philosophy* (New Haven, 1991), 39.

59. For the prerequisites of *milhemet reshut*, see B. Berakhot 3b–4a; B. Sanhedrin 16a–b re I Chron. 27:34; also Y. Sanhedrin 1.3/19b re II Sam. 24:19, II Chron. 3:1 and Deut 32:7; Y. Shabbat 2.6/5b re Num. 27:21; Maimonides, *Hilkhot Melakhim*, 5.1.

60. Y. Shevi'it 6.1/36c and Maimonides, *Hilkhot Melakhim*, 6.1, 5; B. Gittin 46a, Tos., s.v. "kayvan"; Nahmanides, *Commentary on the Torah*: Deut. 20:10; *infra*, 190ff.

61. B. Berakhot 61b re Deut. 6:5.

62. See B. Sanhedrin 108a–b; *Beresheet Rabbah* 30.7.

63. See M. Avot 3.1.

7

Technology and Its Ultimate Threat

Technology and Human Relationships

During the all-day service of Yom Kippur, the Day of Atonement, a significant section of the liturgy consists of a vivid reenactment of the rites of atonement that took place in the Second Temple in Jerusalem. In one of the most prominently practiced Jewish rites, that of the Ashkenazim (Jews of German and Central and East European origin), a concluding prayer is ascribed to the high priest: "For the people of Sharon he would say, 'May it be Thy will O' Lord our God and God of our ancestors that their homes shall not become their graves.'"[1] (According to scholars, Sharon was a valley subject to devastating flash floods, against which its residents were helpless.)[2] The source of this liturgical piece is the Palestinian Talmud, which elaborates on an earlier statement in the Mishnah that the high priest prayed a short prayer just after leaving the Holy-of-Holies, he being the only person allowed entrance into it, and only once annually, on Yom Kippur. The prayer was to be kept short lest the people assembled in the Temple fear that the high priest had died in the mysterious chamber.[3] In the original version of the prayer, according to the politically sophisticated rabbis of the Roman city of Caesarea, the high priest said, "And concerning Thy people Israel, may they not dominate one another [*yigbahu serarah*],"[4] in addition to his prayer for the hapless people of Sharon, who were constantly in such jeopardy. The prayer, then, consists of two distinct parts: (1) a call for deliverance from political tyranny; (2) a call for deliverance from physical cataclysm. The high priest, as both spiritual and political leader of his people,[5] at a moment of his own immediate relief from anxiety (lest he die in the Holy-of-Holies, or lest his atonement rites for Israel be rejected by God), was thus in a position to sympathize truly with those whose vicar he was.

Now, in that far-off time, anxiety about the political realm and anxiety about the physical realm, although generically connected, could still be specifically separated. In our day, however, the nuclear threat has specifically connected these two sources of anxiety. This closer connection between the political and physical realms is because of the predominance of technology in the modern world, a predominance whose epitome is the nuclear threat. Accordingly, radical thought is demanded of all who care about humankind and its earthly dwelling.[6]

Because care can certainly be expected from the theologians in the various religious traditions, nothing less than a radical reexamination of their respective traditions is called for. The reexamination, this *re-search*, can be of two kinds. One, it can have a more specifically practical thrust, that is, it can suggest a definite course of action to be taken in the interest of lessening or eliminating the nuclear threat for the sake of world peace. Or two, it can have a more reflective thrust, that is, it can mediate on the more general issues of life and death, the human relationship with the earth, and the human relationship with the works of human hands—which is the essential question of technology itself.

This chapter is a reflective reexamination. It does not presume to offer any specific, immediately practical suggestions. That would require a knowledge of the scientific, technological, and political issues involved in the nuclear threat, knowledge that is not within my own range of expertise or direct interest—although I by no means minimize their importance because of my own limitations. Rather, this essay is an attempt by a Jewish theologian to meditate on the essential question of technology itself. It is thus theoretical, not practical, although it could, I hope, *inform* practical discussions on the very pressing normative issues of deterrence, disarmament, and the like. However, that *information* of practical discussion could only be inferred *from* what I have to say here; it cannot be found explicitly *within* it. Therefore, this chapter is about technology whose epitome is the nuclear threat, not about the nuclear threat per se. Indeed, it seems to me that more reflection on the general question of technology might lead to new ways of thinking about and acting on the nuclear threat. But I am as yet unable to do that.

The ancient prayer presented at the beginning, like all significant petitionary prayers, deals with three essential relationships: (1) between God and humans; (2) among humans themselves; and (3) between humans and their world. One could make a convincing argument that the nuclear threat has radically changed all three of these essential relationships. If so, each must be reconstituted in order that a meditation in this area might be truly in the present and for the future, that it might address what is before us and what lies ahead of us.

This process of reconstitution involves a radical reexamination of our past. It must be a process of reinterpretation, a contemporary hermeneutic. The question is, Where is the process to begin? Where does the apodictic sequence start? This is the crucial methodological question because if Jewish theology is to say something to the world—in our case, the world dominated by technology—then it must understand that technology itself can be intelligently approached only on a level where it is most immediately experienced by all humankind who are facing it.

That level is neither the relationship among humans themselves nor the relationship between humans and God. It is not immediately on the level of the interhuman relationship because the nuclear threat as the epitome of technology is not human destructiveness of other humans per se but, rather, the threat of humankind's being destroyed by the technical environment of its own making. Human destructiveness of other humans has been with us since Cain and Abel; being literally destroyed by the works of our hands is the *novum*. Moreover, the level of intelligent approach is not the relationship between humans and God for two reasons. First, a large and significant segment of humankind is either indifferent to this relationship as it is understood in the West or willfully denies its existence altogether. Second, even for those of us who are neither indifferent nor denying, the nuclear threat seems to confirm vividly the Psalmist's utterance, "The heavens, the heavens are the Lord's, but the earth he has given to humankind" (Psalms 115:16).

It seems that the level of intelligent approach for a contemporary theologian is to examine how the nuclear threat has changed the relationship between humans and their environment, and then what traditional resources are available to us for rethinking that relationship. In light of this project, the traditional understandings of the interhuman relationship and the God-human relationship must be reexamined and choices made from among them.[7]

For a Jewish theologian especially (although Christian theologians are not exempt in that the Hebrew Bible is their "Old Testament"), the charge must be faced that the Hebraic doctrine of the all-powerful and authoritative God and the human person created in the image of this God is itself largely responsible for the stance toward the environment that has led to the threat of the destruction of humankind and its earthly dwelling. If this charge is true, then it is hard to see how anyone can still affirm the moral relevance (however generally understood) of a book and its tradition whose doctrine of the essence of humanness is now judged to be the source of death rather than its own proclamation that "it is a tree of life [*ets hayyim*] to those who hold fast to it" (Proverbs 3:18).[8]

Modern Technology

Let us now turn to the question of modern technology itself. Modern technology is concerned with the relationship between humans and the works of their hands. Nuclear bombs are such works, and their meaning in terms of human self-understanding can be determined only within this overall context. And although ancient technology and its role in antiquity are very different from modern technology and its role in our world, nevertheless, a fundamental distinction made by Aristotle is indispensable at the outset of any reflection on any technology at any time.

At the very beginning of the *Nicomachean Ethics*, when positing that the meaning of all human action is determined by the purpose it intends, Aristotle makes the following point: "Sometimes the activities [*energeiai*] are themselves the ends; othertimes the ends are certain products [*erga tina*] apart from the activities themselves. . . . [I]n the latter situation, the products are inherently [*pephyke*] superior to the activities which produced them."[9] Now, for Aristotle, the only truly fulfilling human life of *eudaimonia* (inadequately translated "happiness"; better translated "doing and being well") clearly involves the activities that are ends-in-themselves and that are coequal with human nature in the most serious sense. *Technē*, that is, the human making of tangible things, conversely, is not a eudaimonic activity precisely because there is a gap between the producer and the product.[10] Accordingly, although *technē* is necessary for human life, it is not coequal with it because the nonliving, nonconscious thing would become more valuable than the living, conscious human agent who made it. Essentially, they are disparate in that once production is complete, they are no longer related. In other words, for Aristotle — and here he is the quintessential ancient philosopher — *technē* is fundamentally paradoxical if elevated to an end-in-itself, namely, what is inherently inferior would be valued as superior. In this sense, Aristotle's designation of the paradoxical valuation of things over persons is somewhat comparable to the scriptural designation of the paradox of idolatry. "Their idols are silver and gold, the works of human hands. . . . [T]heir makers will become like them, all who trust in them" (Psalms 115:4, 8). One can and should today be even more emphatic about the nuclear weapons we have made. Are not silver and gold rather benign compared to plutonium?

However, with the growing modern emphasis of the human person as *homo faber* — what might be called "technical man" — the gap between the producer and his or her products was viewed in a new way. The transcendence of the product was now regarded as only temporary. Thus Hegel, almost paraphrasing Aristotle, describes the product of human work first as an "object" (*Gegenstand*) belonging to consciousness as a "purpose" (*Zweck*), and then as something *external* and *other*.[11] But he does not stop here, nor does he abruptly eliminate *technē* from activity essentially human, as did Aristotle. Rather, Hegel — and here he is the quintessential modern philosopher — sees *technē* as but one movement included in and transcended by (*aufgehoben*) the ongoing historical development of spirit/consciousness. "Consciousness [*das Bewusstsein*] stepping back from its product [*Werk*] is in fact the universal . . . against its product, which is that which is determined [*das Bestimmte*], transcends itself qua product and is itself the undetermined space, which does not find itself fulfilled by its product."[12]

Humankind as emerging consciousness at this moment is *homo faber*, who is capable of creating much more than things and, hence, is subordinate to them only for a moment in its history as consciousness. After the dialectical transcendence of this technical historical moment, consciousness is now free to deal with the higher, nontangible realms of morality, politics, religion, and, ultimately, philosophy.

Following in Hegel's footsteps, Marx stops the dialectic, however, at this productive, economic point, and he sees the subsequent realms of morality, politics, religion, and philosophy as being reducible to the realm of production, and basically illusions if regarded as truly transcending them.[13] Nevertheless, even for Marx, the human person is not subordinate to the works of human hands. And whereas Hegel employs a dialectic of transcendence to affirm human autonomy over things, Marx employs what I would call a dialectic of infinity, namely, the human person qua uniquely human life makes itself through the works of its hands. Yet the capacity for production is limitless. The maker, who is the human species-being (*Gattungswesen*), conscious of its own creative power, values itself over any finite product it happens to produce at any one time. In the human individual's identification with the total human collective, that individual is no longer subordinate to the alienation (*Entfremdung*) of being dominated by the surplus value of his or her own labor in the hands of someone else.[14] For that "someone else" has also been totally identified with the full human collective and thus ceases to be alienating. The master-slave dialectic has been at last overcome, in Marx's eyes. For Marx, then, *technē* returns to the rightful role of being a subordinate effect when *homo faber* becomes fully collectivized and is conscious of this collectivization as the *prima causa* of human life and its fabricated, social environment. The fundamental human problem here is not the works of human hands but that they are not controlled by the whole human collective in and for itself alone.

What we see in Hegel, and even more so in Marx, is a radical change of the four Aristotelian causal principles. For Aristotle, in making (*poiēsis*)—which includes human *technē*—the purpose (*telos*) is a preexistent entity that determines how it is viewed as an intelligible form (*eidos*) by a maker (*poioun*), who molds what is physically given.[15] For Hegel, and especially Marx, on the other hand, the maker himself or herself creates an intelligible form, and then molds what is given into a finished product (*der Werk/das Bestimmte*), to which he or she is essentially superior.[16]

However, there is one of these causal principles that does not seem to have changed at all from Aristotle to Marx, and that is the material principle. Although Aristotle had a specific term for it, *hylē*,[17] when presenting his concise theory of all four principles in concert, he basically describes it as "that from which something becomes" (*to ex hou ginetai*).[18] And it is precisely here where the nuclear threat belies Hegel's confidence in human transcendence and Marx's confidence in human infinity,[19] for it shows that humankind is neither transcendent nor infinite. It even belies Kant's moral confidence in the human person as "an end-in-itself" (*Zweck an sich selbst*) because, as Hannah Arendt insightfully pointed out, the end the human person is, is itself what it becomes through *homo faber*, its maker.[20] So how is "self-creation" any better or any safer than the self's creation of things? For Kant, the autonomous human person can be constituted as superior only to the human person as a sensuous being, who is still part of the phenomenal order. The antinomies between the collective and between the individual, and between the present and the future—which most directly concern *homo faber*—are left as unsolved "casuistical questions" by Kant. Is the human person an end-in-itself as an individual or as a species-being? The history of philosophy shows what Hegel and Marx and others did with Kant's unfinished philosophical agenda, and this seems to show that Kant stands with them, not above them. The same problem confronts them all.[21]

The nuclear threat shows itself to us as the transcendence of the work of our hands over and against us. That is why there is no "technical solution" to it, no simply "getting a handle on it," as Heidegger convincingly stated.[22] The works of our hands themselves, through the military persons or technicians who serve them and not even through the scientists who made them, these *things* are the threat, a threat that could very well be realized by human mistake, not even by human intent. And this is so universally, irrespective of the ideologies (capitalistic, socialistic, or whatever) of the societies involved in them. They now directly threaten the full human collective, and seem to be possessed by more and more members of that collective—that collective in which Marx and many other modern Utopians placed such absolute faith. They have transcended us, not we them. Moreover, that transcendence is not intelligible per se, and thus it is not benignly attractive, like Aristotle's *telos*. Modern technology asks for no justification and gives none.[23] Rather, we seem to be returning to the pre-Aristotelian (and, thus, prephilosophical) notion of *telos* as blind fate, an unintelligible, malignant temporal end to human life.[24] And whereas for the pre-Aristotelians, that unintelligible and unpredictable temporal end presented itself only as the terminus of the life of the human individual, it now shows itself as the terminus of the entire human species, if not even beyond that. Hans J. Morgenthau, not as the expert on the specifics of the nuclear threat that he surely was but, rather, as a philosopher presenting the essence of the issue, wrote over thirty years ago:

> It is a distinctive characteristic of our secular age that it has replaced the belief in the immortality of the human person with the attempt to assure the immortality of the world he leaves behind. . . . The significance of the possibility of nuclear death . . . destroys the meaning of immortality by making both society and history impossible.[25]

Finally, we cannot invoke a better technology to overcome our dilemma inasmuch as all technology from Aristotle, who minimized it, to Marx, who maximized it, has assumed that the material principle, which for humans can only be the earth, is a perpetual *datum*—something always there for whatever we want to do with it. Yet the nuclear threat has destroyed our conscious relationship with the very matter of our planet. The earth no longer shows itself to us as the irreducible substratum upon which we forever stand. Could anyone after 1945 simply write, "And the earth stands forever [*l'ad*]" as did the author of Ecclesiastes (1:4)? It seems that a nuclear holocaust will destroy not only human civilization but also the very earthly possibility that even a "saved remnant" of human civilization will ever regenerate itself.[26]

A Return to Nature: Modern Proposals

Even before the actual emergence of the nuclear threat to both civilization and the biosphere (to use Teilhard de Chardin's felicitous phrase[27]), there have been modern attempts to challenge the supremacy of technology by calling for a return to nature. This attempted return to nature has taken three main forms, it seems to me.

The first attempted return to nature is modern *natural rights* theory. This theory can be characterized by its minimal claims, a characterization consistent with modern science's assumption of the methodological primacy of Occam's razor.[28] Modern natural rights theory has been concerned with what is minimally indispensable for human society to persist, with such rights as the protection of human life, dignity, and property. Here the "nature" in "natural" (contrary to classical natural law theory, as we shall soon see) is not a substantial transcendent whole of which human social nature is a part. In the modern theory, nature is not a ground but only a limit, something human inventiveness must take into account but that is not or cannot be its source of norms. It is only a *conditio sine qua non*. Because of this minimal view of nature, this type of natural rights theory has been endorsed by some recent philosophers who would be the first to deny that they are part of the classical tradition of natural law at all.[29]

The weakness of this theory is that it presupposes more of the *status quo ante* than can be taken for granted today, certainly after the rise of the nuclear threat, and even after the purposeless destruction seen in the two world wars. Much of it never deals with the human capacity for nihilistic destruction, so manifestly evidenced in this century's first half alone. Along with the medievals (but, significantly, without their theological and metaphysical grounds), it seems to assume that there is an immanent *inclinatio naturalis* in human life to preserve itself both individually and collectively.[30] But, as Émile Durkheim showed, loss of social cohesion and purpose can often be the antecedent rather than the consequence of human self-destructiveness.[31] Even the immanent will to live is contingent on something that transcends it. Thus our postnuclear question is not what the social and political order is to be but, more radically, what can inspire us to preserve society and human life at all. This more radical question presupposes the very transcendence that modern natural rights theory either denies altogether or prudently brackets. Without this transcendence, however, it is hard to see how technology can be limited in any cogent way.

The second attempted return to nature I call, for want of a better term, "naturism." Naturism, by affirming the ecological dangers technology poses to the integrity and viability of the earth, thereby recognizes the unique gravity of the nuclear threat and that the technology that brought it about must be limited. However, its practical program has been simply to reject technology as much as is humanly possible today, and with whatever political and even physical means at its disposal. Theoretically, it seems to be based on the notion that humans are essentially sentient beings and they should be reintegrated back into sentient nature, back to the earth.[32] The means to this return have, of course, been quite varied. Thus naturism has taken such diverse forms as pacifism, conservationism, vegetarianism, nudism, and nature worship.

Nevertheless, the weakness of naturism is that it fails to realize that the violence it so abhors is not a technical invention, that it too is part of the sentient realm, that "the wolf shall dwell with the lamb" (Isaiah 11:6) is a prophetic hope, not a description of nature as it is here and now to be imitated. Indeed, sentient nature itself is morally neutral, offering no intelligible criterion for emphasizing peace and rejecting aggression. It is simply no normative standard. Today's "naturists" would be very hard pressed to argue why their peaceful view of nature is any truer than the aggressive view of nature advocated by the so-called Social Darwinists, whose ideology they no doubt abhor.[33] Finally, the romantic rather than rational outlook of naturism has led some of its proponents to employ the very violence that they see coming from technology against technology—a vicious circle indeed! As Plato astutely pointed out, the sentient realm cannot be normative precisely because it shows itself in paradoxes.[34]

Finally, the greatest philosophical attempt in modern times to reintegrate the human person back into a transcendent natural realm (similar to the project, if not the actual systems, of Aristotle and Spinoza) is that of A. N. Whitehead. For Whitehead, nature is conceived of as a developing process toward higher and higher levels of consciousness and freedom. The process is, moreover, open-ended and, therefore, infinitely progressive essentially. Within this system of nature, God functions as the "lure" for all lesser entities, namely, God, by virtue of having knowledge of all possibilities, provides tempting opportunities for each creative entity to develop further into higher and higher levels of actualization.[35] However, this God functions neither as first sufficient cause, as does Spinoza's *causa sui*, nor as the wholly determined end, as does Aristotle's *telos*.[36] And, this God does not function like the God of Scripture, who directly commands his people.

It is hard to see what this God could possibly forbid. He seems incapable of saying no in any radical sense, that is, a no not just for the sake of a yes coming quickly on its heels. There seems to be no limit to the creative thrust into the future by either God or man. Indeed, creativity seems to be God's only imitable attribute, or, more accurately, God seems to be part of a creativity whose name is *progress*. As Whitehead writes, "The novel hybrid feelings derived from God with the derivative sympathetic valuations are the foundations of progress."[37] Yet has not an uncritical, that is, unlimited, acceptance of the value of progress led to our present crisis of technology, not only with the nuclear threat but also with the whole ecological dilemma? Hence, technology must be limited by humans, and it can be so limited only when humans accept an intelligible moral standard that transcends their own inventiveness. The containment of technology surely requires such a transcendent no.[38] And in the moral sphere, such a no manifests itself as a prohibition, a "thou shalt not." For example, the first scriptural commandment, according to the rabbinic tradition, is a negative commandment, namely, "And the Lord

God commanded humans [*'al ha'adam*] . . . from the tree of knowledge of Good and Evil you shall not eat" (Genesis 2:16).[39]

A Return to Nature: The Classical Approach

The classical idea of nature regarded it as a transcendent realm in which humans could intelligently participate by looking to it as a normative standard. This realm, especially as it was constituted by Aristotle, was regarded as both intelligible and intelligent.[40] The apex of this intelligible/intelligent nature is God, who is thinking (*noēsis*) who thinks (*noēseōs*) thinking (*noēsis*).[41] Being intelligible, human intelligence can know it; being intelligent, human intelligence can imitate it. In other words, it transcends human consciousness as both object and as subject, but human consciousness cannot transcend it. That is why it is *the* normative standard. And this idea has had an enormous influence on subsequent thought, indeed on theology most of all. For example, Maimonides, who interpreted numerous scriptural passages figuratively when they conflicted with what he accepted as philosophically proven truth, interprets literally the Psalmist's words, "The heavens declare [*mesapprim*] the glory of God" (Psalms 19:2).[42]

This idea of nature was based on the assumption that the heavens are of a different and more perfectly indestructible matter than the earth, and that the circular motion of heavenly bodies is more perfectly perpetual than the linear, terminable motion found on earth, for this latter motion seems to involve constant exertion (*bia*) and eventual exhaustion, being weighted down as it is with the inertia of earthly matter.[43] In terms of the human relation to this higher realm, Aristotle saw truly human active well-being (*eudaimonia*) as being the theoretical life, whose object is the eternal heavens as they orbit around God as the Prime Attractive Mover. The theoretical life is preeminently eudaimonic precisely because it seems to remove the human agent from the physical exertion and exhaustion associated with *technē*, which is the constant battle with nonhuman forces on earth. The theoretical life, rather than the technical life, is seen as the only antidote to the violence and alienation that is so regressive and opposed to intellectual progress, progress determined by how much of the preexistent norm is discovered and understood. For Aristotle, it is the only opportunity for the human soul to become at least functionally divine.[44] The practical corollary regarding our nuclear threat, as I have outlined it, can be quickly drawn. In this view, nature humbles technology by showing itself as the ultimate attraction to the human intellect.

How much of this is plausible, let alone applicable, today, however? Since Galileo, we no longer regard heavenly matter and heavenly motion as different from or superior to earthly matter and earthly motion.[45] Since Newton, we regard the laws of gravity as applying universally. The resulting mechanization of physics led to the rejection of the idea of a cosmic organism both intelligible and intelligent.[46] Even if teleology is still a useful concept in describing certain phenomena of the biosphere, it is nonetheless difficult to ascribe an intelligence to these phenomena, let alone one that transcends human intelligence and can thus be normative for it.[47] Hence, Leo Strauss, one of the most vigorous, insightful, and learned opponents of mechanistic explanations of human affairs, was honest enough to admit at the very beginning of his now-classic study of the idea of natural law and the historical shift to the idea of natural right

> . . . that people were forced to accept a fundamental, typically modern, dualism of a non-teleological natural science and a teleological science of man. . . . An adequate solution to the problem of natural right cannot be found before this basic problem has been solved. Needless to say, the present lectures cannot deal with this problem.[48]

In other words, we are left, for the time being at least, with Kant's humanly limited teleology, namely, humankind as an end-in-itself,[49] and all the problems Kant's moral theory entails in terms of being integrated with the rest of human social life, as well as with the nonhuman realm. Indeed, as we have seen, Kantianism is particularly weak in providing limits for *homo faber*.

Strauss saw the problem as being the reconciliation of modern natural science with the idea of human virtue. However, even were this not an issue, there is a much more ancient moral problem facing classical teleology, for the culture that a life according to nature (*kata physin*), as opposed to a life contrary to nature (*para physin*), presupposes is itself a culture that is fundamentally morally suspect. Thus a moral critique of classical culture long predates a scientific critique of the cosmic teleology its greatest philosopher proclaimed.

The moral problem concerns the essential character of such a culture, a culture so profoundly committed to leisure (*scholē*). Here again we return to Aristotle, for he, to a large extent following his teacher Plato, saw leisure not as indolence but, rather, as a climate in which the technical response to bodily needs and their management is handled by one type of person, who is thus subordinate to another type of person. This latter type alone enjoys leisure, and by so doing, is alone freed by this service to engage in theoretical activity. "It seems that human active well-being is to be within the context of leisure [*en ta scholē*]. We exert ourselves [*ascholoumetha*] in order that we might be leisurely, just as we wage war in order that we might bring about peace."[50]

Moreover, this peaceful leisure requires slavery.[51] Now, it is true that in principle Aristotle is not defending slavery as a historical institution; for him, slavery is justified only when it is a case of those who are naturally (that is, intellectually) superior ruling those who are naturally inferior. Clearly, the historical accident of being captured in war, which was how most slaves became slaves in the ancient world, does not *ipso facto* mean that such hapless victims are naturally inferior to their captors.[52] However, when this was indeed the case, Aristotle regarded the slave as one whose very *raison d'être* lies in someone else, and that is not only necessary but desirable as well.[53]

Against all of this, it was Hegel — knowing Aristotelian philosophy so well —

who insightfully showed that the master is just as alienated from himself as is the slave, in fact more so, for the master winds up being more dependent on the slave than the slave is on him. The whole system of slavery entails the negation of "independent consciousness" (*selbständiges Bewusstsein*).[54] Thus, whereas historical slavery does not necessarily have Aristotle's philosophical justification for it, the principle of absolute dominance does, and hence there is a justification for an interalienation within society itself even without the legal institution of slavery per se. And, finally, it is based on the metaphysical dualism of the dominance of matter by consciousness, or of the body by the mind.[55] As Descartes and others have asserted, our mental relationship with our own bodies is the beginning of our extensive relationship with physical nature.[56]

The nuclear threat involves a fundamental interalienation among humans, namely, the belief that one human group knows what is best for itself and everyone else, so that everyone else must be subordinate to it. And the nuclear threat results from a fundamental alienation of the human person from earthly nature, the belief that this nature is essentially there as a human resource.[57] Therefore, it seems rather unlikely that the cultural matrix of beliefs that posits the dominance of one human group by another, and the dominance of earthly nature by humans, is going to be able to provide us with the radical guidance we need to contain technology, which in essence is the issue of dominating and being dominated. It seems we should look elsewhere for the radical guidance we so desperately need to overcome this vicious and mortally threatening syndrome.

The Sabbath and Its Law

It was the first-century Hellenistic Jewish theologian Philo of Alexandria who presented Judaism as transcending Greek philosophy, that is, both containing its truths superlatively and surpassing its defects. In Philo's treatment of the Jewish Sabbath, as an institution and an idea, he presents it in a way clearly designed to show that it surpasses the Platonic-Aristotelian idea of leisure (*scholē*) and the inherent social alienation it necessarily and willingly entails. In this treatment we begin to see how the Jewish idea of the Sabbath is a fundamentally different way of constituting the relationship with God, with other humans, and with the nonhuman environment. It suggests a different role for technology in theologically constituting full human personhood.

No doubt in opposition to the idea Plato and Aristotle presented, which was, in fact, a conceptualization of the social reality of their own culture, Philo writes as follows about the Sabbath:

> Furthermore when He forbids bodily labour on the seventh day, He permits the exercise of the highest activities, namely, those employed in the study of virtue's lore. . . . But since we consist of body and soul, he [Moses] assigned to the body its proper tasks [*ta oikeia erga*] and similarly to the soul what falls to its share, and his earnest desire was, that the two should be waiting to

relieve each other. Thus while the body is working, the soul enjoys a respite, but when the body takes its rest, the soul resumes its work, and thus the best forms of life [*hoi aristoi tōn biōn*], the theoretical and the practical, take their turn [*ameibōsin*] in replacing each other.[58]

Although he is using vocabulary formulated by Aristotle (*energeia, theōretikōs, praktikōs*), Philo is constituting their interrelations in a Jewish way. The highest actions (*tas ameinous praxeis*) are connected with the study and the teaching of the Torah. Moreover, like Josephus, Philo emphasizes the weekly reading and exposition of the Torah in the synagogue as a communal act involving the entire community.[59] He especially mentions servants, both male and female, as participants in the activities of the Sabbath, that is, both the positive involvement in Torah learning and the negative restraint from ordinary weekday labor. In fact, he even mentions that because the servants are not serving their masters on the Sabbath, the masters themselves have to do more menial tasks for themselves on that day than on weekdays.[60] And in his most specific rejection of Plato and Aristotle, he justifies this mutuality in the entire community—including slaves—because "no human [*anthrōpos*] is a slave from nature [*ek physeōs doulos oudeis*]."[61] Finally, he places both the active life and the theoretical life ultimately on the same level, that is, they are both constituents in a revolving cycle, neither being superior to the other. Thus the Sabbath limits the dominance of each one by the other because it is lived by all.

In a much latter rabbinic text, this concept of the Sabbath being a mixture of the theoretical and the bodily and the resultant blending of socioeconomic differences in the community, comes out in an even more vivid way. There we find a dispute between two of the Rabbis as to whether the Sabbath was given for pleasure (*ta'anog*) or for the study of the Torah.[62] The subsequent discussion resolves the dispute by concluding that the Sabbath was given for pleasure (and there is no doubt that "pleasure" here means sexual pleasure) to the scholars who "weary themselves" in the study of the Torah all week long, and that it was given for the study of the Torah to the laborers who, "being engaged in their labor," can engage in Torah study only on the Sabbath. So the Sabbath is no less "physical" than it is "spiritual," but it regularly overcomes these distinctions and the socioeconomic forms of dominance they entail.[63] The basic social activity eliminated on the Sabbath is economic production and interchange, where human intercourse is determined by things.[64] This is most explicitly typified in the prohibition of making fire on the Sabbath.[65] Finally, concerning the relationship between men and women (of which there is so much discussion these days, especially in religious communities), the Rabbis saw the "thou" (*attah*) addressed in the Decalogue to remember and keep the Sabbath, as being both male and female. In the rabbinic specification of Sabbath activity, not only are women freed from the usual "womanly" chores like cooking, sewing, and washing but they are also entitled to be full participants in the very act of sanctification (*qiddush*), whereby the holiness of the day is initially proclaimed.[66]

The overcoming of socioeconomic dominance on a regular cyclical basis through the Sabbath involves not just members of the covenanted community per se. Thus not only was one not to have a slave who was a member of the covenanted community (that is, one who had been circumcised and immersed and who was responsible for many of the commandments of the Torah) do his or her labor but one was to extend this privilege even to an uncircumcised slave.[67] In other words, even a nonparticipant in the covenant was not to be used for the sake of someone else in his or her observance and enjoyment of the Sabbath. For the same reason, gentiles, whether formally part of the Jewish polity (*ger toshav*) or not (*nokhri*), were also protected from exploitation by Jews on the Sabbath.[68] In rabbinic law one is not allowed to so much as suggest to a gentile to do any work on the Sabbath for a Jew, nor may a Jew force Sabbath observance on a gentile in the gentile's domain.[69] The gentile, then, is forced neither *to be for Judaism* nor *to be part of Judaism*. There is neither the dominance of the egoistic conqueror nor the dominance of the altruistic missionary.[70]

Coming closer to the question of the environment, the technological-ecological problem with which we have been concerned, already in the Decalogue one is prohibited from using animals on the Sabbath. In rabbinic law this extends to riding on them, not just "working" them in the strict agricultural sense.[71] Animals are also not to be slaughtered for food on this day.[72] Nevertheless, because a Jew is responsible for the well-being of his or her animals, they are to be fed on the Sabbath and, in the case of milking animals, they are to be milked on the Sabbath lest they suffer pain. To indicate that this is for their sake and not our own, the milk taken from them is not to be used by us.[73]

In terms of the nonsentient realm, there is to be no planting or reaping or any of the attendant activities on the Sabbath.[74] There is also not to be any hoarding or similar preparation on the Sabbath for any other day.[75] The prohibition of both production and commerce on the Sabbath is the final extension of Sabbath limitations from our relationship with the natural environment to our relationship with the technical environment of our own making. The Rabbis extended this prohibition to even touching things that may not be used on the Sabbath or serve no aesthetically pleasing function for the Sabbath (*muqtseh*).[76] The Sabbath is, then, a limit on our construction of the purposes whereby we technically order both time and space. It is not difficult to understand, therefore, why the imperial Romans, for whom ordering was an end in itself (and not just a means to an end as it was for the more intellectual Greeks), found the Sabbath so odious and were particularly contemptuous of the attraction it had for some of their own people.[77] *Pax Romana* and *Shabbat Shalom* are clearly and fundamentally different.

The Sabbath of Creation

The great bulk of the legal treatment of the Sabbath in the Halakhah concerns prohibitions as, indeed, the majority (365) of the 613 commandments of the Torah are negative precepts.[78] Concerning this, my late revered teacher Professor Abraham Joshua Heschel wrote: "Indeed, the splendor of the day is expressed in terms of abstentions, just as the mystery of God is more adequately conceived *via negationis*, in the categories of negative theology which claims that we can never say what He is, we can only say what He is not."[79]

Nevertheless, even negative theology does not end up with *nothing*, but is a dialectic that begins with distinctions in order to reach some hardly-won affirmations.[80] Returning to the Sabbath, what we have seen so far in terms of the Sabbath prohibitions is the outer gate of a palace, an outer gate designed to protect the treasures within.[81] One must begin with Halakhah because it is the most evident manifestation of Judaism. One does not end there, however. The inner treasures are expressed in Aggadah, which might be designated as Judaism's theological imagination.[82] Let us now look at some of the Aggadah of the Sabbath, in terms of the relationship between God and the human person, for it is this relationship that grounds the subsequent interhuman relationship and the relationship between humans and their environment, both technical and natural. Here we will find some even more profound thoughts that speak to our technological-nuclear crisis.

It has been noted by some perceptive observers that there is no idea of nature in the classical scriptural and rabbinic texts.[83] Now, this is an overstatement if nature is understood as a formal order immanent within creation itself. In both Scripture and rabbinic literature, there is clearly an idea of a formal order within creation, which even God has promised to maintain and respect.[84] Indeed, it is often invoked as a demonstration of God's constancy and consistency, namely, he has given "righteous" commandments to his human creatures and, by analogy, righteous directions to nature itself.[85] Nevertheless, if nature is understood, conversely, as an eternal realm, *always there*, to which both God and creation are answerable because they are both contained within it, then Judaism clearly places a much higher value on both divine creativity and human creativity, and sees them directly related without any such *tertium quid* as nature *coming-in-between*.[86] In rabbinic conceptuality an entity is either "made by divine hands" or "by human hands."[87] Human creativity is, then, an imitation of God.

Unfortunately, too many readers of the book of Genesis have assumed that the creative *imitatio Dei* is as follows: "In the beginning God created heaven and earth" (Genesis 1:1), then, "And God blessed them . . . fill the earth and conquer it [*ve-khivshuha*[88]] and dominate [*u-redu*] the fish of the sea, the birds of the heavens and all living things which swarm on the earth" (1:28). Just as God conquers and dominates his universe (the macrocosm), so man "created in his image" (*be-tsalmo*) conquers and dominates the earth and its environment (the microcosm). Creativity on both levels is thus essentially characterized as conquest and dominance. There is a hierarchy of power that entails a parallel hierarch of authority.

Nevertheless, Scripture itself in the next chapter presents a different view of the world in which the human person is placed by God. Here we find that the microcosm is a garden whose human occupants are "to tend it [*l'ovdah*] and to guard it [*le-shomrah*]" (Genesis 2:15). In this version of creation, the human person is uniquely human in being the subject of both a commandment (about eating from the tree of knowledge of Good and Evil) and a warning about the future ("You shall surely die" [2:17]). Here both a task and a destiny are presented. The human person is clearly limited. And in this version of creation, man is portrayed as being united with woman, with whom alone he shares the reciprocal intimacy of flesh and word (2:23–24).[89]

Most students of Scripture have noted the disparity between these two respective anthropologies. The critical question of separate biblical sources aside, because postbiblical Judaism's adherents experience Scripture—certainly the Pentateuch—as a unitary document and doctrine, the question arises: Which version of creation is theologically primary and which secondary to it, and thus to be interpreted through it? Furthermore, in which version do we see the essential relationship between God and the human person affirmed by subsequent Jewish tradition?[90]

In the Decalogue the following analogy is made between divine creativity and human creativity: "Remember the Sabbath day to hallow it. . . . For the Lord made the heavens and the earth, the sea and everything in it and he rested on the seventh day; therefore, he blessed the Sabbath day and hallowed it [*va-viqadeshehu*]" (Exodus 20:8, 11).

The human person's creaturely uniqueness is to be directly related to God, not as creator but in transcendence of creation. Both man and God on the Sabbath transcend their respective *technē*, for what the Sabbath does for creation, both divine and human, is to provide a limiting purpose—a *telos*—for both of them simultaneously.[91]

The mistake of many is to assume that the human person per se is the *telos* of creation, an "end-in-itself," to use Kant's reconstituted anthropocentric teleology.[92] But modern natural science has taught us how the ever-expanding and ever-complex universe shows less and less evidence of much anthropocentrism being true, and also that to celebrate "creative man" as the purpose of creation is to celebrate *homo faber* as the essence of humanness. Yet, have we not seen that *homo faber*, like Cain, finds his "responsibility [*avoni*] too great to bear" (Genesis 4:13)? Both scientific knowledge and moral experience reject such an arrogant conclusion.[93] Indeed, the Talmud notes that one of the reasons that the human person was created on the eve of the Sabbath, *after* everything else, is that if humans become arrogant, exalting themselves *over and above* the rest of creation, even the mosquito can always remind them, "You were created last."[94]

The climax of creation is not the human person but the Sabbath, and the Sabbath is the intimate symbol of the covenant, "an everlasting covenant [*brit olam*] between Me and the children of Israel, an everlasting symbol [*ot hi l'olam*]" (Exodus 31:16–17).[95] Creation is not complete on the sixth day when the human person is created but only on the hallowed seventh day. In other words, God created the universe in order to have a relationship with human beings, and human beings create their own microcosmic environment in order to have a relationship with God. That relationship is epitomized by the Sabbath.[96] The covenant is that relational reality. Unlike a conqueror and a tyrant whose power is its own justification, the Sabbath is to be observed by a tender and a guardian of a garden, one who is in need for that for which he or she labors. And this is in imitation of God, who tends and guards the universe.[97]

The role of the Sabbath as the *telos* of creation is brought out in this aggadic text: "Genivah said that it is like a king who made a bridal chamber [*huppah*]: plastering it, tiling it, painting it. But, what was the bridal chamber still lacking? — a bride to enter it. So, what was the world lacking? — the Sabbath."[98] This is a common *leitmotif* in rabbinic theology, namely, the Torah is the purpose of creation, that without it the world would revert to primordial chaos.[99] Because the Sabbath is considered the equivalent of all the commandments of the Torah, no doubt because it alone out of all of them is presented in the creation narrative, profanation of the Sabbath is considered to be a denial of God the creator.[100] And just as the Torah is the content of a mutual relationship so that God Himself is portrayed as keeping it, so is God himself portrayed as keeping the Sabbath.[101]

Just as divine making is ordered and limited for the sake of the Sabbath, so is human making. That is why the building of the Sanctuary, which symbolizes the cosmos itself, does not override the Sabbath.[102] The building of the Sanctuary stopped in time for the Sabbath. Indeed, the building of the Sanctuary is considered to be the height of intelligent human work (*mel'ekhet mahshevet*), and the thirty-nine types of work it entailed are the same thirty-nine specifications of the prohibition of work on the Sabbath.[103] If the height of human creative work is prohibited on the Sabbath, all the more so is ordinary human labor prohibited.

In terms of work as preparation for the Sabbath, note the following:

> They said about Shammai the Elder that all his days he ate in honor of the Sabbath. If he found a fair animal, he would say, "This is for the Sabbath." If he found one which was fairer, he would set aside the second animal and eat the first. . . . The School of Shammai says that on the first day of the week one should already start thinking about the coming Sabbath [*me-had shavyekha le-shabbteykha*].[104]

The Talmud contrasts this with the view of Hillel the Elder, that one should take each day as it comes and trust that God will provide for the Sabbath ahead. Although in strictly legal disputes the law follows the Hillelites,[105] it is worth noting that this dispute is not seen as strictly legal by later authorities; indeed, a number of them follow the moral example of Shammai and his school.[106] Along these lines, an earlier rabbinic text admonishes one to regard all of one's work as if all of it had been completed (*ke'ilu . . . asuyah*)[107] by each and every Sabbath. Hence, the Rabbis forbade any talk or even thought of business on the Sabbath.[108]

It should be emphasized, however, that all of this teleology is intelligible only in a covenantal context. It can be seen only in the context of the relationship *between* God and the human person. Nevertheless, as the author of Job especially pointed out, God's relationship with creation is not limited to the relationship with his human creation.[109] It is not a symbiosis. In terms of the relationship with the natural order per se, creation is an ongoing process — a point also made by contemporary cosmological physics in its view of an ever-expanding universe.[110] This comes out in the following dispute between the Hillelites and the Shammaites concerning the precise wording of the benediction said when fire is kindled to demarcate the end of the Sabbath and the beginning of the ordinary week (*havdalah*). The Shammaites say that one is to praise God who "has created [*she-bara*] the light of fire." For the Hillelites, on the other hand, the wording is "who creates [*borē*] the lights of fire."[111] The Talmud sees the theology behind this legal dispute as follows: "Rava said that no one disputes that God has created [*de-bara mashma*] it; what is disputed is future creation [*d'atid le-mivra*] implied in the term 'who creates [*borē*].' The Shammaites deny future creation; the Hillelites affirm it."[112] The Talmud then brings a number of scriptural citations that refute the concept of creation's being a *fait accompli*. And Rashi points out that the Hillelite affirmation of future creation means that creation is perpetual (*borē tamid*).[113] This is also reflected in the liturgy. Even on the Sabbath, as on weekdays, one praises God for being he "who in his goodness reneweth creation every day continually" (*be-khol yom tamid*).[114]

What emerges from this is that the essentially covenantal character of the Sabbath is not an anthropomorphic projection of a human experience onto the cosmos per se. Indeed, any physical evidence for the Sabbath's being different from weekdays — like the cessation of the falling of the manna during the Israelite sojourn in the Wilderness — was considered miraculous and not repeatable.[115] So the holiness of the Sabbath is known only when one is *before* God *with* the world, not *through* the world *unto* God. Time and space, the ways we experience and initially order the world, are constituted differently by the Sabbath.[116] Hence, Sabbath space-time is of a different world than ordinary space-time.

On the human side of the Sabbath, we also see a similar approach. It will be recalled that the world as macrocosm is the making of God and the world as microcosm is the making of man. Just as the macrocosm has a life of its own outside the covenant, so does the microcosm. This comes out in another dispute between the Hillelites and the Shammaites. The dispute concerns whether or not one's vessels — that is, manufactured things, including machines — must cease operating on the Sabbath (*shevitat kelim*). The Shammaites say yes; the Hillelites say no.[117] Their respective reasoning is explained as follows: the Shammaites hold that the prohibition of labor extends from the producer of a thing to the thing itself; the Hillelites hold that the prohibition is limited to the producer himself or herself.[118] Automatic technology need not be stopped for the Sabbath as long as it does not require human attention on the Sabbath. In other words, as long as it permits its makers and even its attendants to transcend it.[119] It will be recalled that the law is according to the opinion of the Hillelites.[120]

From this we can see that Judaism not only does not demand the renunciation of technology per se but also does not require that technology rest with us on the Sabbath. What it does require is that it serve humans on the Sabbath and not disturb their rest by requiring their attention. Limiting technology does not mean crippling it. For us today, the Sabbath does not mean an impossible Utopianism.

Indeed, *techne*, epitomized by the human person making fire, is considered a result of the Sabbath. A rabbinic legend indicates that the first human was terrified when the first Sabbath ended and the light of the sun was being taken away, terrified that he would be overcome by the unknown darkness of nature. At that point, God provides him with two stones with which to make fire. Thereupon he praised God for the fire. The text concludes that this is the reason that God is praised for fire and its light at the conclusion of every Sabbath.[121] Fire is thus not stolen from God; it is given by God. Adam is not Prometheus. Also, the last act of work before the onset of the Sabbath is to kindle lights for the Sabbath, lights whose illumination is to be enjoyed aesthetically but not used in any technical way.[122] The very transcendence of the Sabbath limits *techne*, but it limits nature too and teaches humans that they are not simply subject to nature and its darkness but they can clear a dwelling out of nature and light their own portion in the darkness. *Homo faber* qua *homo faber* too is sanctified when the fire warms and illuminates rather than when it burns and destroys. This can happen only when *techne* is preceded and succeeded by the peace of the Sabbath.

The Sabbath and Eschatology

Because the Sabbath so radically changes the human relationship with the environment, basically altering the uses of time and space, early in the history of Judaism it was seen as an eschatological symbol. As early as the noncanonical Hellenistic work *Life of Adam and Eve*, it is stated that "the seventh day is the sign of the resurrection and the world-to-come."[123] This motif has regularly been repeated. In fact, it is so commonplace that the grace after meals, to be recited regularly by every Jew, has the following petition to be recited after each of the three Sabbath meals: "May the All-Merciful let us inherit the day which shall be wholly a Sabbath and rest in the life everlasting."[124]

If the Sabbath is an eschatological symbol — or better, *the* eschatological symbol — then we have an example for the well-known theory of Mircea Eliade, a theory that asserts that the innovation of the Hebrew Bible was to present a linear idea of time as opposed to the idea of time as "eternal return," that sacred time is experienced in ever-recurring cycles.[125] In the linear idea of time, conversely, time is understood as having an ultimate climax when God and humankind will finally and irrevocably be reconciled. In this idea, the *telos* qua purpose and the *eschaton* qua temporal terminus become one and the same. As an eschatological symbol, the cyclical character of the Sabbath is removed from its essence and confined to its preeschatological manifestation. However, if this is the case, then the essence of the Sabbath pertains to the end of time but not to the time here and now that we are trying so desperately to save from being destroyed by the works of our hands. If this is the case, then the Sabbath—even affirming all its holiness, to be sure—does not in truth speak to the nuclear dilemma directly facing us in the present world. Our concern now is with life before death much more than life after death.

But there is another way of looking at the symbolism of the Sabbath.[126] At the very end of his presentation of all the laws of the Sabbath, Maimonides writes:

> Whoever keeps the Sabbath according to its law and honors it and makes it delightful [*u-me'angah*] to the best of his ability, it has already been explicated in prophetic tradition [*be-qabbalah*] that his reward in this world is greater than the reward stored up in the world-to-come. It is written, "Then you will delight [*tit'anag*] with the Lord, and He will make you ride on the high-places of the earth, and He will feed you from the heritage of Jacob your father, for the mouth of the Lord has spoken it" [Isaiah 58:14].[127]

Maimonides was probably the greatest critic of eschatology in the history of Judaism.[128] For him, the world-to-come is not the future *eschaton* of history, but it is a transcendent dimension, parallel to history and open to participation by those here and now capable and prepared to apprehend its reality.[129] For this reason, he radically disconnected the Messianic Age from any identification with this transcendent realm. For him, the Messianic Age will be a political realm within ordinary human history.[130] Even though this transcendent realm is timeless per se, the full human experience of it comes only after death, after the separation of the soul from the body. Here Maimonides' debt to Plato and the whole Platonic tradition is obvious. Nevertheless, when it comes to the Sabbath, he just as obviously departed from his Platonism and was stressing a more uniquely Jewish idea. And, it seems to me, that the idea is that the Sabbath, finite in time and kept and experienced by mortals, better intends our relationship with the transcendent God than does an image of our own eternity.[131]

Finally, if the Sabbath is essentially an eschatological symbol, a symbol of a spiritual age subsequent to our own time, then it ought clearly to take precedence over bodily human existence. No threat to bodily life, if this theory is true and carried to its logical conclusion, could possibly justify profaning the Sabbath in any way. Yet in the Halakhah—which no subsequent theology can contradict—"the Sabbath is made for man, not man for the Sabbath."[132] The Sabbath must be profaned when human life is threatened. This stance, no doubt, arose when the entire Jewish nation, which had remained faithful to the covenant, was threatened with extermination by the Seleucid forces of Antiochus Epiphanes during the Maccabean revolution. If the Jews would not defend themselves on the Sabbath, the enemy would slaughter all of them.[133] This could not be allowed to happen because the Sabbath as the epitome of the covenant requires human life as much as it requires divine life. And human life, unlike divine life, requires external actions to maintain its duration on earth. The covenant, then, through the Sabbath protects the human person from being destroyed by *homo faber*; through the six days of mandated labor it protects the human person from being the helpless victim of the forces of nature; and through the affirmation of the covenantal relationship between God and the human person it protects the human person from being subordinate to the Sabbath rather than to the God who gave it.[134]

In his great work on the Sabbath and its meaning for moderns, my late revered teacher Professor Abraham Joshua Heschel wrote over thirty years ago:

> To set aside one day a week for freedom, a day on which we would not use the instruments which have been so easily turned into weapons of destruction . . . a day on which we stop worshipping the idols of technical civilization . . . a day of armistice in the economic struggle with our fellow men and the forces of nature—is there any institution that holds out a greater hope for man's progress than the Sabbath?[135]

Surely, "man's progress" includes progress in overcoming the nuclear threat. Heretofore we have assumed that human progress is measured by what we have made.[136] But now the works of our hands have taken our souls away from us. Henceforth we can experience progress only in the return of our souls.[137] According to ancient Jewish lore, the epitome of that homecoming is the Sabbath and all that it brings with it.[138]

NOTES

1. *High Holyday Prayerbook*, ed. P. Birnbaum (New York, 1960), 541.

2. See R. Mosheh Margolis, *Penay Mosheh* on Y. Yoma 5.3/42c.

3. M. Yoma 5.1. See Maimonides, *Commentary on the Mishnah, ad locum* re Lev. 16:2; T. Kippurim 2.13; Y. Yoma 5.3/42c; B. Yoma 53b.

4. Y. Yoma, 5.3/42c.

5. For rabbinic disapproval of this concentration of political and ecclesiastical authority in one person during the Second Temple period, see B. Kiddushin 66a; Y. Horayot 3.2/47c.

6. See Karl Jaspers, *The Future of Mankind*, trans. E. B. Ashton (Chicago, 1961), 6.

7. See Hans-Georg Gadamer, *Truth and Method*, trans. G. Burden and J. Cumming (New York, 1982), 275ff.

8. Even some prominent contemporary theologians have made this charge. Note Gordon D. Kaufman, *Theology for a Nuclear Age* (Manchester and Philadelphia, 1985), 31: "In all of this our western religious symbolism has been more a hindrance than a help for our ecological blindness, and it too easily lends itself to the enforcement of legitimation of our parochial political objectives." Cf. J. Cohen, "The Bible, Man, and Nature in the History of Western Thought: A Call for Reassessment," *Journal of Religion* 65 (1985):155ff.

9. *Nicomachean Ethics*, 1094a1. Greek text from Loeb Classical Library ed. (Cambridge, Mass., 1926). My translation.

10. See ibid., 1040a10–20.

11. *Phänomenologie des Geistes*, ed. Hoffmeister (Hamburg, 1952), 286 (my translation). For Hegel's admiration of Aristotelian teleology, see ibid., 22.

12. Ibid., 291 (my translation). See A. Kojève, *Introduction to the Reading of Hegel*, trans. J. H. Nichols, Jr. (Ithaca, N.Y., 1980), 25; also Louis Dupré, *The Philosophical Foundations of Marxism*, (New York, 1966), 25ff.

13. See *Karl Marx: On Society and Social Change*, ed. N. J. Smelser (Chicago, 1973), 3ff., 86ff.

14. See "Economic and Philosophic Manuscripts" (1844) in *Writings of the Young Marx*, trans. L. D. Easton and K. H. Gaddat (Garden City, N.Y., 1967), 294–295. See also A. Schaff, *Marxism and the Human Individual*, trans. O. Wojtasiewicz (Garden City, N.Y., 1959), 77.

15. *Physics*, 194b25. Greek text from Loeb Classical Library ed. (Cambridge, Mass., 1929). Thus, in human practice, the ends are primordial; only the changeable means are under human control. Clearly, the former qua *physis* are superior to the latter qua *technē*. See *Nicomachean Ethics*, 1112a20ff.

16. *Phänomonolgie*, 291.

17. See *Physics*, 192a30.

18. Ibid., 194b25.

19. For Marx, "Death seems to be a harsh victory of the species over the particular individual and to contradict the species' unity, but the particular individual is only a particular generic being and as such mortal." ("Economic and Philosophic Manuscripts," *Writings of the Young Marx*, 307.) Cf. Franz Rosenzweig, *The Star of Redemption*, trans. W. W. Hallo (New York, 1970), 3–5.

20. *The Human Condition* (Garden City, N.Y., 1959), 137.

21. The vagueness of Kant's position was severely criticized by Hegel. See *Grundlinien der Philosophie des Rechts*, sec. 150; also A. Donagan, *The Theory of Morality* (Chicago, 1977), 9–14.

22. See "The Question Concerning Technology," trans. W. Lovitt in *Heidegger: Basic Writings*, ed. D. F. Krell (New York, 1977), 288–289.

23. See Jacques Ellul, *The Technological System*, trans. J. Neugroschel (New York, 1980), 129, 256–257.

24. See *Nicomachean Ethics*, 1100a10ff.; also Martin Heidegger, *An Introduction to Metaphysics*, trans. R. Manheim (Garden City, N.Y., 1961), 49–50.

25. "Death in the Nuclear Age" in *Jewish Reflections on Death*, ed. J. Riemer (New York, 1974), 41, 44. See my review of this anthology, with particular attention to Morgenthau's essay, *Judaism* 24 (1975):503–504.

26. There is much in Jewish tradition to support the view that the duration of the universe is by no means necessary. See, e.g., Gen. 9:11–17; Isa. 40:6–8, 54:9, 65:16ff; Ezek. 37:1–14; R. Saadyah Gaon, *Emunot Ve-De'ot*, 6.3; also David Novak, *Halakhah in a Theological Dimension* (Chico, Calif., 1985), 103ff. Thus Ecclesiastes' philosophical assumption of the earth's inherent permanence, which is the ontological basis of his general pessimism about the ultimate significance of any human action (1:2, 12:8), is one of the reasons that the very religious character of this book was questioned in Jewish tradition. See *Vayiqra Rabbah* 28.1, and R. Gordis, *Kohelet: The Man and His World* (New York, 1951), 39–42.

27. See his *The Phenomenon of Man*, trans. B. Wall (New York, 1959), 77f.

28. See *supra*, 73.

29. See H.L.A. Hart, *The Concept of Law* (Oxford, 1961), 188–189; John Rawls, *A Theory of Justice* (Cambridge, Mass., 1971), passim. Cf. Leo Strauss, *Natural Right and History* (Chicago, 1953), 166ff. For the difference between a ground (*archē*) and

a limit (*peras*), see Aristotle, *Metaphysics*, 1022a10. For the most extreme rejection of any kind of natural limit, see Jean-Paul Sartre, *Being and Nothingness*, trans. H. Barnes (New York, 1956), esp. 617ff.

30. Although Thomas Aquinas speaks of the *inclinatio naturalis* of self-preservation (*Summa Theologiae*, 2-2, q. 64, a. 5), it is the weakest moral ground and must be combined with grounds theologically and metaphysically constituted. See David Novak, *Suicide and Morality* (New York, 1975), 44ff.

31. See *Suicide*, trans. J. A. Spaulding and G. Simpson (Glencoe, Ill., 1951), chaps. 3, 5. For a critique of the constitution of society as transcendent (as God is transcendent), see David Novak, *Law and Theology in Judaism*, 2 vols. (New York, 1976), 2:19–20.

32. For a theological version of this widely held point of view, see Kaufman, *Theology for a Nuclear Age*, 44ff. This book is heavily influenced by the vastly popular book by Jonathan Schell, *The Fate of the Earth* (New York, 1982). Perhaps the most vivid expression of this point of view is still to be found in the fiction of D. H. Lawrence, esp. *The Rainbow* (New York, 1916), 2. For ancient precedents, see David Novak, *The Image of the Non-Jew in Judaism: An Historical and Constructive Study of the Noahide Laws* (New York and Toronto, 1983), 244ff.

33. See, e.g., W. G. Sumner, "The Challenge of Facts" in *The People Shall Judge*, 2 vols. (Chicago, 1949), 2:83–85.

34. *Republic*, 439Bff., 523Bff. For a naturist attempt to counter the view of Plato et al., see Mary Midgely, *Beast and Man: The Roots of Human Nature* (Ithaca, N.Y., 1978), 75–82.

35. See Lewis S. Ford, *The Lure of God: A Biblical Basis for Process Theism* (Philadelphia, 1978), 1–44.

36. See Spinoza, *Ethics*, pt. 2, props. 1, 5; Aristotle, *Metaphysics*, 1073a25ff.

37. *Process and Reality* (New York, 1929), 288–289. See ibid., 131, 263.

38. See G. E. Moore, *Principia Ethica* (Cambridge, 1903), 44–45.

39. See B. Sanhedrin 56b and 58b–59a; also Novak, *The Image of the Non-Jew in Judaism*, chaps. 2–8.

40. Cf. Plato, *Timaeus*, 29E–30C. Re the whole question of nature, see *supra*, 71ff.

41. *Metaphysics*, 1074b35. Greek text from Loeb Classical Library ed. (Cambridge, Mass., 1935).

42. *Moreh Nevukhim*, 2.5. For Maimonides' view of nature, see Novak, *The Image of the Non-Jew in Judaism*, 292–294.

43. See Aristotle, *Physics*, 215a1; also *De Caelo*, 269a1ff. See Midgely, *Beast and Man*, 199–200, as an example of the error of mixing the metaphors of heavenly nature and earthly nature.

44. See *Nicomachean Ethics*, 1177a10–15. That the ultimate purpose of practical reason (*phronēsis*) is to prepare one for *theōria*, see *Eudemian Ethics*, 1249^b 15–20.

45. See *Discoveries and Opinions of Galileo*, trans. S. Drake (Garden City, N.Y., 1957), 262–263; also R. G. Collingwood, *The Idea of Nature* (New York, 1960), 102–103.

46. Intelligence and intelligibility become located in the human observer/orderer. See Kant, *Critique of Pure Reason*, Bxiii; also Martin Heidegger, "Modern Science, Metaphysics and Mathematics," in *Heidegger: Basic Writings*, 265ff.; L. Gilkey, *Maker of Heaven and Earth* (Garden City, N.Y., 1959), 123ff.

47. See S. Toulmin, "Nature and Nature's God," *Journal of Religious Ethics* 13 (1985):44ff. Cf. Aristotle, *Physics*, 198b10ff.

48. *Natural Right and History*, 8. See also Jürgen Habermas, *Communication and*

the Evolution of Society, trans. T. McCarthy (Boston, 1979), 201; Alasdair MacIntyre, *After Virtue* (Notre Dame, 1981), 152.

49. See Kant, *Groundwork of the Metaphysic of Morals*, trans. H. J. Paton (New York, 1964), 95ff.; also Novak, *Suicide and Morality*, 94–97; *supra*, 73ff.

50. *Nicomachean Ethics*, 1177b1. See Plato, *Republic*, 370C, 374E; *Theaetetus*, 175E. In modern capitalism and socialism the relation is exactly inverted; as Max Weber noted, "One does not work to live; one lives to work" (quoted in Josef Pieper, *Leisure the Basis of Culture*, trans. A. Dru [New York, 1952], 20). Pieper rightly shows that for Plato and Aristotle, and for Aquinas following after them, *scholē* is essentially different from *decidia* (sloth) (ibid., 40.).

51. See *Politics*, 1278a1, 1325a25, 1328b35–1329a5. In assuming the indispensability of slavery, Aristotle follows Plato. See *Republic*, 469B–C. For the dispensability of slavery in Classical Judaism, conversely, see Novak, *Law and Theology in Judaism*, 2: 87ff. Furthermore, the Torah scholar (*talmid hakham*) is to live off his own labor and not be supported by the labor of others because he is a scholar. See Bekhorot 29a re Deut. 4:5 (cf. Tos., s.v. "mah") and Maimonides, *Hilkhot Talmud Torah*, 1.7, 9; also B. Shabbat 118a and parallels. Cf. R. Simon ben Zemah Duran, *Responsa Tashbats* (Lemberg, 1891), nos. 142–148; R. Obadiah Bertinoro, *Commentary on the Mishnah*: Avot 4.5; *Beresheet Rabbah* 72.5, 98.12.

52. Cf. Plato, *Republic*, 386Bff.

53. *Politics*, 1254a15. For some qualification, see *Nicomachean Ethics*, 1161b5–10.

54. *Phänomenologie*, 147. See Pliny, *Naturalis Historia*, 29.19.

55. *Politics*, 1254b5–10. In this passage *psychē* and *nous* are synonyms.

56. See *Meditations*, 6; also Spinoza, *Ethics*, prop. 12ff.; Locke, *Second Treatise of Government*, 5. Cf. Maurice Merleau-Ponty, *Phenomenology of Perception*, trans. C. Smith (London, 1962), 148ff.

57. See Heidegger, "The Question Concerning Technology," 296ff.

58. *De Specialibus Legibus*, 2.61, 64, trans. F. H. Colson, *Philo*, 9 vols. (Cambridge, Mass., 1937), 7:344–347. Philo characterizes this study (*hai dia logon kai dogmaton ton kat' aretēn*) as *philosophein* prescribed by the Torah. See also *De Decalogo*, 97–101. The Roman Catholic philosopher Josef Pieper attempts to synthesize the idea of the Sabbath and *scholē*. See *Leisure the Basis of Culture* (New York, 1952), 42–43. However, his attempt is questionable because the unity of the community of the faithful he sees in Sunday (his Sabbath) worship is based on all of them being related to the transcendent God in a communal activity ordained by revelation. (See ibid., 51–52 and esp. 54 for his critique of Proudhon's failure to see the sacred foundation of the equality he noticed in the Christian celebration of Sunday; also, 56–57, 60.) *Scholē*, on the other hand, is based on the immanent intellectual excellence of a few being permanently supported by the unceasing labor of many. Finally, his limitation of the Sabbath to the Christian celebration of Sunday (ibid., 63) is myopic. For the essential difference between the Jewish Sabbath and the Christian Sunday, see Hermann Cohen, *Religion of Reason out of the Sources of Judaism*, trans. S. Kaplan (New York, 1972), 367. Earlier, however, Cohen saw no harm in changing the Jewish observance of the Sabbath from Saturday to Sunday. See his "Der Sabbat in seiner kultur-geschichtlichen Bedeutung—Nachwort" in *Jüdische Schriften*, 3 vols., ed. B. Strauss (Berlin, 1924), 2:71–72; also E. G. Hirsch in *Jewish Encyclopedia*, 10:604–605.

59. *De Specialibus Legibus*, 2.62. See Josephus, *Contra Apionem*, 2.175, and *Antiquities*, 16.43.

60. *De Specialibus Legibus*, 2.66–68. See B. Shabbat 119a, and Maimonides, *Hilkhot Sabbat*, 30.6.

61. *De Specialibus Legibus*, 2.69. See *Quod Omnis*, 79; cf. *De Specialibus Legibus*, 2.123. For a reiteration of this social significance of the Sabbath, see Cohen, *Religion of Reason out of the Sources of Judaism*, 155ff.

62. *Pesiqta Rabbati: Decalogue*, 3, ed. Friedmann, 121a. See B. Ketubot 62a–b. Cf. B. Shabbat 119a–b re Isa. 58:13 and Rashi, s.v. "mehader."

63. For the community-creating character of the Sabbath, see, e.g., Y. Eruvin 3.2/20d and M. Buber, *Moses* (New York, 1958), 83–85.

64. See Isa. 58:13; Jer. 17:27; Neh. 10:32.

65. See B. Shabbat 70a re Exod. 35:3.

66. B. Berakhot 20b re Exod. 20:8 and Deut. 5:12; also ibid., 51b re T. Ber. 5.25.

67. See *Mekhilta*: Yitro re Ex 20:8–10, ed. Horovitz-Rabin, 230; also see 331. For the obligation of a circumcised slave to keep the Sabbath as well as many other commandments, see B. Hagigah 4a and parallels.

68. See B. Avodah Zarah 64b; Y. Yevamot 8.1/8d.

69. See M. Shabbat 16.6, 8; B. Shabbat 150a; Maimonides, *Hilkhot Shabbat*, 6.1. As for non-Jews observing the Sabbath, this is forbidden by the second-century C.E. Palestinian authority R. Simon ben Laqish (B. Sanhedrin 58b re Gen. 8:22; see *Devarim Rabbah* 1.8). Maimonides (*Hilkhot Melakhim*, 10.9) sees this prohibition as being directed against religious syncretism (cf. prohibitions against "judaizing" by the Church fathers, e.g., Ignatius, *To the Magnesians*, chap. 10). Nevertheless, later European authorities permitted it, undoubtedly because of their experience with Christian sabbatarian sects. See Novak, *The Image of the Non-Jew in Judaism*, 27–28, 48, 357, 366.

70. See, e.g., B. Yevamot 47a.

71. M. Betsah 5.2 and B. Betsah 36b.

72. M. Shabbat 7.1.

73. For the usual prohibition, see B. Shabbat 95a; Maimonides, *Hilkhot Shabbat*, 8.7; *Maharam Me-Rothenburg: Responsa*, nos. 82–83, ed. Kahana, 93–94. For permission to milk when the animal's pain is involved, see *R'osh*: Shabbat, 18.3 (re B. Shabbat 128b and 140b) and R. Yehiel M. Epstein, *Arokh Ha-Shulhan*: Orah Hayyim, 305.20.

74. M. Shabbat 7.1.

75. Exod. 16:27; B. Pesahim 46b; also *Encyclopedia Talmudit*, 9:116ff.

76. B. Pesahim 47b re Exod. 16:5.

77. See, e.g., Tacitus, *Historiae*, 4.3; Juvenal, *Satires*, 14.105–106; Augustine, *De Civitate Dei*, 6.11; also *Greek and Latin Authors on Jews and Judaism*, vols. 1–2, ed. M. Stern (Jerusalem, 1974–1980), passim. See the Roman-type argument of the apostate rabbi Elisha ben Abuyah on Y. Hagigah 2.1/77b (cf. Philo, *De Specialibus Legibus*, 2.60). For Jewish recognition of the attraction of the Sabbath to non-Jews, see Josephus, *Contra Apionem*, 2.282.

78. For detailed treatment of the Sabbath laws, see I. Grunfeld, *The Sabbath: A Guide to Understanding and Observance* (New York, 1959).

79. *The Sabbath: Its Meaning for Modern Man*, 2d. abb. ed. (New York, 1963), 15.

80. Re *via negativa* (*negationis*), see Novak, *Law and Theology in Judaism*, 2:36–37.

81. See Maimonides, *Moreh Nevukhim*, 3.51.

82. See A. J. Heschel, *God in Search of Man* (New York, 1955), 324ff.; also David Novak, *Law and Theology in Judaism*, 2 vols. (New York, 1974), 1:1ff.; D. Tracy, *The Analogical Imagination* (New York, 1981), 128, 149 n. 96.

83. See Strauss *Natural Right and History*, 81, and José Faur, "Understanding the Covenant," *Tradition* 9 (1968):41.

84. See, e.g., Jer. 8:7; Amos 3:3ff,; Job 28:23–28, 38:1ff.; M. Gittin 4.4 and B. Yevamot 61b; also *supra*, 30f.

85. See, e.g., Deut. 4:6–8; Ps. 104:1ff. Re the analogy between God's macrocosmic responsibility and the human soul's microcosmic responsibility, see B. Berakhot 10a.

86. See Martin Buber, *I and Thou*, trans. W. Kaufmann (New York, 1970), 64–65.

87. See, e.g., M. Kelim 17.12; M. Nega'im 11.3; Hullin 55b; Maimonides, *Hilkhot Hovel U-Maziq*, 6.4 re B. Makkot 7b; also Heschel, *The Sabbath*, 110–111. Both divine and human making (*ma'aseh*) are the result of conscious intention (*kavvanah*). See, e.g., B. Berakhot 61a re Gen. 9:6 and M. Kelim 25.9.

88. See B. Yevamot 65b; also *Sifre: Devarim*, no. 268 re Deut. 24:1, ed. Finkelstein, 287. These texts and their parallels deal with dominance (*kevishah/be'ilah*), as in the male penetration of the female in sexual intercourse. It is important to note, however, that in the second creation account, the woman is *brought* to the man (2:22) and that the man *cleaves* (2:24) to her. "Cleaving" (*ve-davaq*) means to be dependent. See Deut. 4:4; also *Beresheet Rabbah* 17.8; *supra*, n. 8.

89. See B. Yevamot 63a.

90. For a profound response to the two creation accounts in Genesis, based on this traditional assumption, see Joseph B. Soloveitchik, "The Lonely Man of Faith," *Tradition* 7 (1965):2ff. For an example of primary (literal) versus secondary (figurative) exegesis, based on theological-philosophical criteria, see Maimonides, *Hilkhot Yesoday Ha-Torah*, 1.8–9.

91. For *telos* as limit (*peras*), see Aristotle, *Metaphysics*, 994b15. See *supra*, 81, n. 15.

92. See *Critique of Judgment*, sec. 84.

93. For a sustained critique of this anthropocentrism in modern theology, see James M. Gustafson, *Ethics from a Theocentric Perspective*, 2 vols. (Chicago, 1981), 1:88ff.

94. B. Sanhedrin 38a.

95. For the concept of the Sabbath as intimacy between God and his people, see B. Betsah 16a re Exod. 31:17. For the concept of the Sabbath as mutuality between God and the human person, see B. Shabbat 119b re Gen. 2:1; also, Nahmanides, *Commentary on the Torah*: Deut. 5:15.

96. See R. Obadiah Sforno, *Commentary on the Torah*: Exod. 31:17. Furthermore, the Talmud states that "the human person [*adam*] was created on the eve of the Sabbath . . . that he might enter the realm of God's commandments [*mitsvah*] immediately" (B. Sanhedrin 38a). And the statement in the Mishnah with which this statement is associated, viz., that God's creation of each human individual *sui generis* requires each one of them to say, "The world was created for my sake" (M. Sanhedrin 4.5), was interpreted to mean that each person must regard his or her sin as having cosmic significance (see Rashi on B. Sanhedrin 37a, s.v. "bi-shevili"; also T. Kiddushin 1.13–14 and B. Kiddushin 40b re Eccl. 9:18). All of this, then, emphasizes that the human person is to be obedient to God and caring for the rest of creation.

97. See, esp., Ps. 104:1ff.

98. *Beresheet Rabbah*, 10.9, ed. Theodor-Albeck, 85. Cf. B. Sanhedrin 38a re Prov. 9:1–3.

99. See B. Pesahim 68b re Jer. 33:25 and *Rashba* and *Ran* thereon; also R. Jacob ibn Habib, *Ayn Ya'aqov*, intro., s.v. "shiv'ah."

100. Re the Sabbath as the equivalent of the whole Torah, see *Shemot Rabbah* 25.16. Re the Sabbath as primordial, see *Sofrim* 13.14 (cf. B. Rosh Hashanah 22a re Exod. 12:2). Re denial of the Sabbath as denial of divine creation, see *Mekhilta*: Yitro, ed. Horovitz-Rabin, 234 re Isa. 43:12.

101. See *Tanhuma*: Ki Tissa, no. 33, printed ed. Re divine observance of the Torah in general, see Y. Rosh Hashanah 1.3/57b re Lev. 22:9; Novak, *Halakhah in a Theological Dimension*, 122ff.

102. B. Shabbat 97b re Exod. 35:1; Y. Shabbat 7.2/9b; *Mekhilta*: Va-yaqehel, ed. Horovitz-Rabin, 345. See Jon D. Levenson, "The Temple and the World," *Journal of Religion* 64 (1984):282ff.

103. M. Shabbat 7.2; B. Shabbat 49b; B. Hagigah 10b and Rashi, s.v. "mel'ekhet mahshevet"; also R. David ibn Abi Zimra, *Responsa Radbaz* (Warsaw, 1882), 5, no. 1522 re B. Shabbat 41b and parallels; Maimonides, *Hilkhot Shabbat*, 1.5.

104. B. Betsah 16a. See *Mekhilta*: Yitro, ed. Horovitz-Rabin, 229.

105. B. Eruvin 13b.

106. See *Pesiqta Rabbati*: Decalogue, 3, ed. Friedmann, 115b.

107. *Mekhilta*: Yitro, ed. Horovitz-Rabin, 230.

108. B. Shabbat 150a re Is. 58:13; Maimonides, *Hilkhot Shabbat*, 24.1ff. For the difference between the norm and the ordinary practice, however, cf. the note of R. Moses Isserles (Rema) on *Shulhan Arukh*: Orah Hayyim, 128.44.

109. See Job 38:1ff.

110. See Steven Weinberg, *The First Three Minutes: A Modern View of the Origin of the Universe* (New York, 1977), 11–43.

111. M. Berakhot 8.5. See 9.2.

112. B. Berakhot 52b. See Heschel, *The Sabbath*, 134 n. 9.

113. B. Berakhot 52b, s.v. "de-bara mashma."

114. *The Authorized Daily Prayer Book*, ed. S. Singer (London, 1962), 180.

115. See *Shemot Rabbah* 25.15. The account of the river "Sabbation," which did not flow on the Sabbath, is clearly folklore. See B. Sanhedrin 65b; Josephus, *Bellum Judaicum*, 7.79–99; Pliny, *Naturalis Historia*, 31.24.

116. For this reason the Sabbath is considered to be the transcendent source of the other days of the week. See *Zohar*: Noah, 1:75a–b. Cf. Plato, *Timaeus*, 37D.

117. M. Shabbat 1.8; B. Shabbat 18a and Tos., s.v. "ve-layma." See Maimonides, *Hilkhot Shabbat*, 3.1. The founder of the Karaites, Anan ben David, in his *Book of Precepts*, extends the reasoning behind the Shammaite ban of *shevitat kelim* on the Sabbath to the enjoyment of a fire, even if kindled before the Sabbath and continuing to burn by itself on the Sabbath—something even the Shammaites themselves did not forbid—based on an analogy between Exod. 35:3 and 20:10. See *Karaite Anthology*, ed. and trans. L. Nemoy (New Haven, 1952), 17–18.

118. T. Shabbat 1.21 and Y. Shabbat 1.5/3d re Exod. 20:9.

119. See B. Eruvin 104a and Maimonides, *Hilkhot Shabbat*, 23.4.

120. Cf. *Mekhilta*: Mishpatim, ed. Horovitz-Rabin, 332.

121. *Midrash Tehillim*, sec. 92, ed. Buber, 202b–203a. See Y. Berakhot 8.6/12b; A. J. Heschel, *Who Is Man?* (Stanford, 1965), 83.

122. See B. Shabbat 23b and 25b re Lam. 3:17 and Tos., s.v. "hadlaqat ner."

123. *Vita Adae et Evae*, 41.1 in *Apochrypha and Pseudepigrapha of the Old Testament*, ed. R. H. Charles (Oxford, 1913), 2:151. See M. Tamid 7.4 and *Mekhilta*: Ki Tissa, ed. Horovitz-Rabin, 343.

124. *The Authorized Daily Prayer Book*, 383. See *Midrash Tehillim*, sec. 92, p. 201a. Also see Gershom Scholem, *On the Kabbalah and Its Symbolism*, trans. R. Manehim (New York, 1969), 145–146. The statement that "the Sabbath is one sixtieth of the world-to-come" (B. Berakhot 57b) indicates the gap between the earthly Sabbath and the heavenly Sabbath. For the Rabbis, one-sixtieth was a negligible quantity. See

Hullin 97b and B. Nedarim 39b. For the Sabbath in Christian eschatology, see Augustine, *De Civitate Dei*, 22.30.

125. See *The Myth of the Eternal Return* (New York, 1954), 102ff; *The Sacred and the Profane* (New York, 1961), 106–107, 110–111. Cf. Rosenzweig, *The Star of Redemption*, 310–315.

126. Re symbolism, see Paul Tillich, *Systematic Theology*, 3 vols. (Chicago, 1951), 1:239; also Novak, *The Image of the Non-Jew in Judaism*, 128–130.

127. *Hilkhot Shabbat*, 30.15.

128. See David Novak, "Maimonides' Concept of the Messiah," *Journal of Religious Studies* 9 (1982):42ff.; Novak, "Does Maimonides Have a Philosophy of History?" in *Studies in Jewish Philosophy: Collected Essays of the Academy of Jewish Philosophy, 1980-1985*, ed. N. M. Samuelson (Lanham, Md., 1987), 409ff.

129. See *Hilkhot Teshuvah*, 8.8. Note the critique of R. Abraham ben David of Posquières (Rabad) *ad locum* re B. Sanhedrin 97a interpreting Isa. 2:11.

130. See *Hilkhot Melakhim*, 11.1ff.

131. See *Qohelet Rabbah* 1.3 re Zeph. 1:3.

132. See B. Yoma 85b and parallels. Cf. Mark 2:27 and parallels.

133. See I Macc. 2:32–42; Josephus, *Contra Apionem*, 2.2 and *Antiquities*, 12.6. Cf. Jubilees 50:12 and Louis Finkelstein, "The Book of Jubilees and the Rabbinic Halaka," *Harvard Theological Review* 16 (1923):51.

134. See B. Yevamot 6a–b re Lev. 19:3; also, *Midrash Tehillim*, sec. 92, ed. Buber, 202b; Maimonides, *Hilkhot Shehitah*, 14.16.

135. *The Sabbath*, 28. See Maimonides, *Moreh Nevukhim*, 2.31/end.

136. For a Jewish critique of the modern idea of progress, see Leo Strauss, "Progress or Return? — The Contemporary Crisis in Western Civilization," *Modern Judaism* 1 (1981):29.

137. See Ps. 19:8. For loss of soul as the state of being under the control of *alien* forces, see Lam. 1:11, 16, 19.

138. See B. Betsah 16a re Exod. 31:17 and parallels; also Louis Ginzberg, *Legends of the Jews*, 7 vols. (Philadelphia, 1925), 5:112–113, n. 104.

8

Violence in Our Society:
Some Jewish Insights

Practical Continuity and Discontinuity

The increasing level of violent crime in our society is a sad fact that has affected almost all Americans. If someone has not yet been the victim of a violent crime, he or she probably knows someone who has. Violence and the fear of violence have had a profoundly negative effect on the fabric of our social life. Our homes have become fortresses; we are afraid to be alone on the street; security has become our obsession — all with good reason. Americans regard this worsening situation as intolerable and are looking for insights to show how our society, and especially our legal system, can become more effective in protecting people from violent crime.

Judaism has a long and varied tradition in reflecting on the causes of violent crime and in developing strategies to deal with this grave problem. Therefore, it should be of interest to those searching for insights and guidance from the various moral and legal systems that have contributed to Western civilization.[1]

The contemporary search for insights and guidance has an ultimately practical goal. In the end we want to know what is to be done here and now. But it is no easy matter to apply Jewish sources to the contemporary crime problem. In certain areas Judaism is practically up-to-date, that is, it has a body of rules and precedents that are evidently and immediately relevant to the situation at hand. Real life poses practical questions, and Judaism, in its legal manifestation as Halakhah, is a ready-made source for working out normative answers. One need think only of the ease with which questions about new situations are answerable in Jewish ritual law. Thus, for example, the revolution in food chemistry of the past several decades has been met by contemporary halakhists with considerable ingenuity. They have been able to decide quickly which new products are *kosher* and which are not.[2] This practical relevance is due to the historical continuity in both the body of the law itself and the community whose law it is. In our example of the dietary laws, the law has never stopped dealing with questions of what is *kosher* and what is not, and there has always been a community of Jews whose diet has been ruled by that law.

In the case of Jewish criminal law there has been no such practical continuity because Jews lacked the necessary political independence that it presupposes. For centuries there has been little if any development of Jewish criminal law, and even the most law-abiding Jews have had to look to the law of the non-Jewish state for criminal justice.[3] Even in the State of Israel today Jews have not had political independence long enough, and have lacked sufficient ideological consensus, to develop a thoroughly modern Jewish criminal code. Israeli law in this area is still eclectic, and is likely to remain so for the foreseeable future, drawing upon a number of sources, of which traditional Jewish law is only one.[4] Therefore, one cannot simply cite the sources of Jewish criminal law and expect them to be relevant to the situation at hand, for there is a historical gap between the law and the community who would be bound by it, and there is also a historical gap between the law and the current situation to which it is being applied.

Also, unlike Jewish ritual law, Jewish criminal law, even when it was immediately practical (*halakhah le-ma'aseh*), dealt with situations whose meaning was not specifically Jewish. Only Jews need be concerned whether or not a certain food product is *kosher*, but all persons, being essentially social beings, need to be concerned about how murderers and thieves are to be dealt with. Therefore, even in a totally traditional Jewish society questions of criminal justice must at some point be discussed within a broader human context.[5]

For these reasons this chapter will employ as its criterion of selection the stipulation that only the sources that deal with human society per se, as distinct from the Jewish people as a uniquely covenanted community, will be discussed. Inasmuch as these sources are not immediately and specifically practical, for the reasons I have just noted, they will be presented for their relevance to theoretical reasoning about general approaches to the social problem of crime. In other words, their relevance is more for the philosophy of the law than for the law itself. Hence, the method of reasoning will be more speculative than the type of immediately practical deduction from sources, which is possible only when the development of the law has kept pace with the development of history. Furthermore, non-Jewish thinkers, who in their own way expressed thoughts similar to those of Judaism, will be freely quoted.[6]

The Sources of Violence

Before we examine Halakhah — Jewish legal tradition — on the treatment of crime and criminals, we must consult Aggadah, that is, a tradition of Jewish speculation about human relationships both with God and man.[7] This tradition has many important insights about the causes and meaning of human violence, insights that are especially important in our age, when we are threatened with the ultimate nuclear violence, for which there are no obvious legal analogies. Here are two such insights that go to the very heart of the matter.

The first act of human violence recorded in Scripture was the murder of Abel by his brother Cain. The Rabbis speculated about what caused Cain to do this violent act.

> "And Cain said to Abel his brother" (Genesis 4:8). And about what were they speaking contentiously? They said, "Come let us divide up the world." One took land and the other took movable property. The one said, "The land upon which you stand is mine," and the other said, "What you are wearing is mine." . . . Judah son of Rabbi said that they were contending over the first woman.[8]

Both interpretations are complementary. We react violently when we feel deprived of what should be ours, whether it is love or possessions. Indeed, as the Talmud notes, often our possessions mean more to us than even our lives, and certainly the lives of others.[9] However, in truth, we own nothing.[10] "Do not fear when one becomes rich . . . for when he dies he takes nothing; his glory will not descend with him" (Psalms 49:17–19). The type of possessiveness that results in denying the space of our neighbor itself results from a denial of God's ownership of the universe.

Violence also results when our quest for individual, familial, or political security takes priority over the needs of others. This is aptly expressed in a Talmudic teaching. According to the Torah, manslaughterers were to be exiled to "cities of refuge" (Numbers 32:11). Although manslaughter is not as heinous as premeditated murder, it is still the result of unacceptable carelessness and disregard for the sanctity of human life. The Torah also states that although nine and a half of the Israelite tribes lived west of Jordan, and only two and a half on the east bank, each side of the Jordan had three cities of refuge. In other words, bloodshed was at least three times as frequent on the east side of the Jordan (Gilead) than it was on the west side. "Abaye stated that murderers are prevalent in Gilead, as Scripture says, 'Gilead is a city of doers of iniquity; it is covered with bloody footprints.'" (Hosea 6:8).[11] Why was this so? After all, the twelve tribes were equally Jewish. The Rabbis recall that the two and a half tribes who lived on the east side of the Jordan had asked Moses for the privilege, arguing, "We will build sheep pens for our possessions here and cities for our children" (Numbers 32:16). Noting that when Moses finally acceded to their request, he answered them in reverse order, namely, "Build for yourselves cities for your children and pens for your flocks" (Numbers 32:24), a late midrash states:

> They made what is primary [iqqar] secondary [tafel] and what is secondary primary. Why? Because they loved their possessions more than their own bodies. . . . Moses said to them, "Do not do this; do what is primary first;

build cities for your children." . . . God said to them that "because you loved money more than your lives, surely there will be no blessing for you."[12]

Violence was so widespread there because of pervasive materialism.

The midrash quoted above concludes with the Mishnah's famous dictum "Who is rich? He who is happy with his portion [*be-helqo*]."[13] And considering that in truth we own nothing, what is that portion? "My portion is the Lord, I say, therefore I wait for him" (Lamentations 3:24). "Whom do I have in heaven? With you I desire nothing on earth. Even when my body and my heart are destroyed, God is my everlasting portion" (Psalms 73:25–26).

Ultimately, then, violence arises out of the terror we experience when God is absent. "For the wicked are like the troubled sea when it cannot rest, throwing up dirt and refuse. 'There is no peace for the wicked,' says my God" (Isaiah 57:20–21). The violence we fear, which stalks around us, which even dwells in our own hearts, and the far greater nuclear violence that hangs so darkly on the horizon of humankind will never be overcome until the people of the earth allow their Creator to be their King and Redeemer.

Theological Foundations of Criminal Justice

If our approach to violence is to emerge out of a Jewish perspective, then Jewish approaches to criminal justice must be seen in the broader context of Jewish ideas about the relation between divine and human justice, human equality, and the ethical imperative of treating others as we ourselves wish to be treated.

The immediate purpose of law, for Judaism, is to increase justice in this world. Thus Scripture states, "Judges and officials you shall appoint for yourself in all your cities . . . and they shall judge the people with just ruling [*mishpat tsedeq*]. . . . Justice justice shall you pursue" (Deuteronomy 16:18, 20). Moreover, the pursuit of justice in this world is considered ultimately to be a participation in the divine justice that rules the entire universe. Thus Scripture portrays God explaining his consultation with Abraham about his judgment of the evil cities of Sodom and Gomorrah as follows: "For I know that he will command his children and his household after him to keep the way of the Lord to do righteousness and judgment [*tsedaqah u-mishpat*]" (Genesis 18:19). This fundamental idea, that human justice is a participation in divine justice, leads to four important corollaries.

One, human justice is a *conscious* participation in divine justice. Thus divine justice, although not fully intelligible to human beings ("your ways are not my ways" [Isaiah 55:8]), must be at least partially intelligible to them. Human beings can, therefore, interpret even divine law in ways that do not violate what is evidently just to them.[14] Thus immediately after God announces the possibility of Abraham's participation in his justice, Abraham confronts God with the challenge "It is obscene [*halilah*] for you that the innocent be treated like the guilty! Shall the judge [*ha-shofet*] of the whole world not do justice [*mishpat*]?!" (Genesis 18:25). Hence, the destruction of Sodom and Gomorrah by God must be based on the elementary principle of *human* justice that the innocent be treated differently from the guilty. By emphasizing that human justice is this conscious participation in universal divine justice, we reinforce the intuition that our pursuit of justice is not merely a human convention but is in concert with the very order of the universe itself.[15]

Two, human justice is *only* a participation in divine justice. Finite human beings are not expected to effect perfect and complete justice in this world. The Rabbis described it as follows:

> Scripture states, "You shall not be afraid of any man for the judgement is God's" [Deuteronomy 1:17]. R. Hanin said that you should not inhibit [*lo takhnees*] your words in the presence of man. Let the witnesses know about whom they are testifying and before whom they are testifying and who in the future will punish them. And so the judges. . . . Indeed about Jehoshaphat it is said, "He said to the judges: see what you do, for you do not judge for man but for God" [II Chronicles 19:6]. Perhaps the judge will say, "What do I need this trouble for?" Scripture there states, "He is with you in the matter of judgement." The judge can rule only on what his eyes see.[16]

This means a number of things. First, it means that the administration of human justice requires not only the reason of the mind but, just as important, the courage of the heart. The awareness that our justice is a participation in divine justice, which alone is ultimately victorious, enables us to fight against the injustice of those who by human standards seem to be victorious now.[17] Second, it means that even more than we are judging, we are being judged. If this is so, human justice is not our own project that we can stop and start at will, expand or limit as we see fit. It is but part of our overall response to God, a response we cannot avoid, hard as we often try.[18] Therefore, an injustice to a fellow human creature is an injustice to the Creator. "He who ridicules those in misery reviles their Maker" (Proverbs 17:5). Third, it means that we are required to do only what is humanly possible in this world. Human fallibility will, of course, lead to partial, even inaccurate, justice at times. However, as a famous passage in the Mishnah puts it, "Because you cannot finish the job does not release you from its obligation." And this can be asked of us because, as the passage concludes, "And the Master of your labor is faithful to recompense your effort; and know that the righteous receive their reward in the future world."[19] All of this saves us from the despair that inevitably comes when justice is pursued on grounds of human idealism alone, for idealism frequently turns into cynicism, which is born of despair from the failure of our best efforts in an unredeemed world. As the Talmud notes, "There is no [full] reward in this world."[20] Only recognition of the finite character of human existence and human society, coupled with faith in a transcendent Judge, whose everlasting reign extends far beyond this world of ours, can sustain the type of courage and persistence that the pursuit of human justice requires. On human grounds alone, the pursuit of justice is a *hope-less* paradox.[21] We will not experience full justice until the Messiah comes, upon whom will descend "the spirit of the Lord" and who will thus "judge not by what is seen by his eyes nor by what is heard by his ears" (Isaiah 11:2-3).

Three, human justice is the concern with the *sanctity* of human life and activity whose subject is the human person created "in the image of God."[22] This means that the purpose of society is not the enhancement and protection of its own institutions but, rather, the enhancement of human life and community, and the products of that activity we call "property."[23] Society's task in the area of criminal justice is to protect the persons and their world, whose sanctity has been tangibly denied by other persons, and to express its strongest possible outrage.

The sanctity of human persons as the image of God is the foundation of human equality, which is, in turn, the basic ethical norm. It means that all humans are sacred entities requiring respect and protection. Judaism demands that we treat every person as the image of God even if that person is incapable of ever responding that way to us. This would include the unborn, the infant, the psychotic, the retarded, the senile, the comatose, and the mortally ill. In other words, over and above strict reciprocal justice (*tsedeq*) it demands the transcendence of charity (*tsedaqah*).[24] It also means that all people possessing normal mental and emotional powers are considered responsible beings, morally answerable for their deeds.

Ontological equality as the foundation for the equal treatment of persons comes out in a well-known old midrash: "'You shall love your neighbor as yourself' [Leviticus 19:18]. R. Akibah said that this is *the* great principle in the Torah. Ben Azzai said that 'this is the book of the generations of man' [Genesis 5:1] expresses an even greater principle."[25] "Greater" means *more comprehensive* and *more fundamental.*[26] What Ben Azzai was saying to R. Akibah is that the ethical norm prescribing love of one's fellow human being as oneself is based upon the idea of equality of human persons as stated in the passage he cites, which continues, "On the day God created man [*adam*] in the image of God he created him. Male and female he created them and blessed them . . ." (5:2). The same foundation of ethics is embodied in another well-known text from Mishnah: "Therefore was man [*adam*] created singly to teach you that whoever destroys one human life is accounted by Scripture as if he destroyed an entire world . . . and for the sake of peace among human beings [*shlom ha-beriyot*] so that no one can say to another, 'My father is greater than your father.'"[27]

Four, human justice is practiced when the *common human situation* becomes the fundamental ethical norm. Thus, in one of the most famous passages in the Talmud, the following dialogue is recorded:

A certain gentile came before Shammai and said, "Convert me on the condition that you teach me the entire Torah while I stand on one foot." He pushed him away. . . . Hillel converted him saying to him: "What is hateful to you, do not do to another. This is the entire Torah and the rest is commentary. Go and learn!"[28]

This does not mean that Judaism is simply reducible to a general ethical norm, one that is by no means unique to Judaism.[29] What it does mean is that the most *evident* ethical teaching of Judaism is that people have enough in common to be able to project their own basic human situation onto each other. Society as a communion of persons can establish common norms because of the capacity of most of these persons to participate fully in this communion.

The participation has both an active and a passive aspect. The very dictum of Hillel brings this out, namely, "What is hateful to you" (what you do not want *done* to you) "do not do to another" (do not *cause to be done* to somebody else.[30] In other words, common experience becomes the formal criterion of conduct. Ethics considers what humans *are* in common as more important than what divides them. Furthermore, it insists that we regard the consequences of our acts *as if* they happened to us. This has important meaning for not only how society judges human acts *before* they are performed but also how society judges those acts *after* they are performed. Judgment before the act is society's duty to exhort us to "resist evil and do good" (Psalms 37:27). Judgment after the act is society's duty to "destroy evil from your midst" (Deuteronomy 21:21).[31]

Overreaction to Crime

Despite the justified concern about lawlessness in our society, twentieth-century governments, with their deliberate violations of human rights, have, on the whole, acted far more criminally than individual criminals or bands of criminals. It is therefore quite justifiable to be suspicious when criminal prosecution and punishment are proposed on the utilitarian grounds of being "good for society." We have seen far too much of the evil results of justifying cruelty to individuals in the name of some higher collective good, which is the rationale of the concentration camp. Indeed, as an influential contemporary legal philosopher has wisely noted: "The government will not re-establish respect for law without giving the law some claim to respect. It cannot do that if it neglects the one feature that distinguishes law from ordered brutality. If the government does not take rights seriously, then it does not take law seriously either."[32]

Moreover, as Immanuel Kant emphasized:

> Juridical punishment can never be administered merely as a means for promoting another good, either with regard to the criminal himself or to civil society. . . . For one man ought never to be dealt with as a means subservient to the purpose of another. . . . Against such treatment his inborn personality has a right to protect him . . . and woe to him who creeps through the serpent-windings of utilitarianism to discover some advantage that may discharge him from the justice of punishment, or even from the due measure of it, according to the pharisaic maxim: "It is better that one man should die than that the whole people should perish."[33]

Kant opposes the sacrifice of individual right for collective good and assumes, erroneously, that what he opposes is Jewish ("pharisaic") teaching. His quotation is from the New Testament where the priests and Pharisees are described as justifying turning Jesus over to the Roman authorities, not only because of what they conceived to be his actual sin against God's law but because "if we thus release him, all will believe in him and, then, the Romans will come and destroy us and this place and the nation. . . . You do not understand that it is beneficial for us that one man should die for the sake of the people and the whole nation should not perish."[34]

This is a caricature of Judaism by the most anti-Jewish of the Gospels, the Gospel of John.[35] Ironically enough, the so-called pharisaic approach has been behind efforts throughout history to deny rights to minorities, especially Jews, and to persecute them because of the consequentialist argument that they pose a potential danger to society. Pharaoh used this same logic when he unjustly enslaved the children of Israel. "And he said to his people, 'Behold the Israelite people is greater and stronger than we are. Let us be prudent [*havah nithakemah*] with it lest it increase and also add to our enemies and fight against us . . . '" (Exodus 1:9-10). (Much the same logic was used by the United States during World War II to imprison Japanese Americans unjustly and illegally.) We Jews have been history's prime victims of the social paranoia that arises from overreaction to crime and the threat of crime; we should surely be repelled by it the most. Actually, this type of injustice is repudiated by normative (pharisaic!) Judaism, as shown by this influential rabbinic text:

> A caravan of persons walking down a road are accosted by gentiles, who say to them, "Give us one from among you that we may kill him, and if not, then we will kill all of you." Let all of them be killed rather than a Jewish life be handed over to them. But if they designated a particular person, for example, Sheba ben Bichri, then let him be given to them and all of them not be killed.[36]

As pointed out by the Palestinian Talmud, this rule applies "only if he is deserving of death as Sheba ben Bichri."[37] In other words, only an already convicted criminal may be so handed over, and even this was disputed by other sources.[38] However, none of the sources permits the sacrifice of an innocent life merely to assuage the threat of disaster to the community. Jewish tradition has opposed the sort of consequentialist collectivism that justifies the sacrifice of individual rights for some perceived social benefit.[39]

The rejection of this type of punishment also comes out in the overall rabbinic treatment of the juvenile delinquent. The Torah states:

> And when a man has a wayward and rebellious son, who listens neither to the voice of his father nor his mother, and they discipline him but he still does not listen to them, his father and his mother may seize him and bring him to the elders of his city . . . and all the men of his city shall stone him to death, and you shall destroy the evil from your midst and all Israel shall hear and fear [Deuteronomy 21:18-19, 21].

The Mishnah reasons about this law as follows: "The wayward and rebellious son is judged by the probable way he will end up [*needon al shem sofo*]. Let him die innocent rather than guilty. For the death of the wicked is beneficial [*hana'ah*] to them and to the world."[40]

In the parallel text in the *Sifre*, this view is brought in the name of R. Yose, who stated, "The Torah reaches to the end of the matter."[41] The Talmud later elaborates on this view, based on the parents' complaint that their son is "a glutton and a drunkard" (Deuteronomy 21:20):

> R. Yose the Galilean says that because he ate a large quantity of meat and drank a large quantity of Italian wine the Torah states that he is to be stoned?! However, the Torah reaches to the end of the matter with the wayward and rebellious son. For in the end he will deplete his father's resources and not finding what he is used to, he will go out in public and rob people.[42]

The parallel text in the Palestinian Talmud says that he will "kill people" (*ve-horeg et ha-nefashot*).[43] Finally, a midrashic text reasons, "The Torah states that let one life be lost rather than many lives."[44] Putting all these interpretations together we seem to have an exact expression of utilitarian/consequentialist reasoning.

Nevertheless, the full rabbinic treatment of this legal institution so qualifies it that it become virtually impossible to put it into practice.[45] In fact, this whole institution was declared by one opinion (although it is disputed) to be one "which never was and never will be operative. Why was it written? That one might explain it and receive reward [*darosh ve-qabbel sekhar*]."[46] In other words, it is purely theoretical. Indeed, it lent itself to fruitful speculation about the pathology of bad family situations.[47] It also seems that the Rabbis felt uncomfortable with a statute that seemed to resemble closely the Roman *patria potestas*, that is, the legal power of the father to kill his children because they are his chattel.[48] Furthermore, the logic that allows the loss of one life for the sake of others goes against the rabbinic teaching that "one who destroys one life is as if he destroyed an entire world."[49] It is also at odds with the ruling that "one life is not destroyed for the sake of another."[50]

But in the very passage in the Mishnah following the text about the juvenile delinquent, the principle of "he is judged by the probable way he will end up" is applied *in practice* to cases of breaking and entering.[51] The Rabbis use this formula to give the would-be victim the benefit of a doubt over the criminal about to attack him or her. The would-be victim must kill without waiting to be killed. This is consequentialist logic, to be sure, but it differs from that pertaining to the juvenile delinquent because of the element of self-defense. Thus *only* when the danger is imminent and obvious can preemptive measures be taken, based on prediction of the inevitable result if the measure is not taken. Clearly, at this point "your life takes precedence over that of another."[52]

Another argument for not sacrificing lives merely to benefit the social unit is that the strict maintenance of the distinction between true guilt and true innocence is itself a social good.

To destroy the verifiable distinction between known criminals and ordinary citizens, which is the result of the suppression of the individual's right to the due process of law, actually encourages the crime it is supposed to discourage. For if every citizen is regarded as a criminal or potential criminal, there is no incentive not to be one because everyone's fate is likely to be the same. Reasonable concern with the rights of those accused of crimes, if aware that justice and true social order are complementary, actually contributes to the common good. Only a jurisprudence that is neither overly protective of individual rights nor is in effect a "police state" contributes to true justice and social order. The error of these two extremes is that one treats virtually every criminal as if he were a law-abiding citizen, while the other treats virtually every law-abiding citizen as if he were a criminal.[53]

There is nothing wrong with emphasizing social utility as long as it is understood that human society is not a collection of individuals to be conditioned for the sake of a greater whole but a communion of persons ordered toward a *common good*.[54] The common good consists of whatever enables them to preserve the inherent sanctity of their lives and activity and fulfill themselves. The good is *common* because it applies to all equally, and because human sanctity is best expressed and developed in the common life of human society.[55] Society must protect its members from crime that inhibits this common good, but society must not itself become criminal in the process.[56]

Retributive Justice: *Lex Talionis*

Criminal justice in Judaism has been characterized both by Jews and non-Jews by the norm, "an eye for an eye, a tooth for a tooth, a hand for a hand, a foot for a foot, a burning for a burning, a wound for a wound, a bruise for a bruise" (Exodus 21:24–25). One can see this norm concerning punishment as following, logically, from the basic norm about the equality of treatment of human persons, for when we say, "What is hateful to you, do not do to another," we could infer that "when you do what is hateful to you to another, another will be permitted to do so to you in return." In other words, an equal standard of action leads to an equal standard of retribution.

Although the seeming harshness of the "eye-for-an-eye" law has made it a pejorative slogan for many critics of Judaism, it nevertheless impressed no less a philosopher than Kant. Note how he in effect paraphrased it:

> But what is the mode and measure of punishment which public justice takes as its principle and standard? It is just the principle of equality. . . . It may be rendered by saying that the undeserved evil which anyone commits on another, is to be regarded as perpetrated on himself. Hence it may be said: "If you steal from another, you steal from yourself; if you strike another, you strike yourself. . . ." This is the right of retaliation (*jus talionis*); and properly understood it is the only principle which in regulating a public court . . . can definitely assign both the quality and the quantity of a just penalty.[57]

What the principle of retribution states is that the consequences of an act determine a reaction proportionate to it. This accomplishes two things. One, it declares in advance that society will hold its members fully responsible for the consequences of their own acts. To use the Mishnah's phrase, citizens are warned to "calculate the loss against the gain."[58] Second, by making the punishment proportionate to the act, it prevents society from overreacting to crime,[59] for if the criminal has sinned by denying the equal rights of his victim through the excessive extension of his own rights, society can rectify this injustice only by restricting the criminal's rights proportionately. To do more than this would be to commit, in essence, the same excess it judged to be criminal in an individual.[60]

One could, perhaps, see equal retribution as personal vengeance taken out of the hands of the victim (or the victim's family) and made into a legal institution, one that can be administered more objectively and more fairly by society.[61] But its origins in the desire for vengeance cannot be totally overcome, for a careful phenomenology of our personal interest in justice begins in our desire for vengeance: that the harm done *me* be done *similarly* to the *one* who did it. Vengeance can only be sublimated; to do more than that actually destroys criminal justice.

Attempts totally to overcome vengeance quickly lose the sense of strict equality that makes criminal justice *just* because they eliminate the personal element in it. What replaces this personal element is a therapeutic model of criminal justice, one first put forth philosophically by Plato.[62] According to this view, persons are parts of society, as limbs are parts of the body. Just as limbs that are even potentially dangerous to the survival of the body (cancerous limbs, for example) are to be amputated for the good of the whole organism, so persons who are even potentially dangerous to society are to be removed for the good of the whole organism. But following this model, no two limbs are ever equal in value for the whole organism. Thus in systems of law influenced by this philosophical view of society, persons have no integrity per se, but only *value* or disvalue for society. That value or disvalue is to be determined by the rulers of society *ad hoc*. There are no standards that apply to everyone's action and that can be known *ab initio*.[63] Accordingly, no person's right (that is, his or her personal claim on society) is necessarily equal to anyone else's right. Actually, here persons have no claims on society per se; society has claims on them. Surely, the contemporary experience with totalitarianism offers many vivid examples.

Despite the fact that in early postbiblical Jewish tradition there were those who interpreted "an eye for an eye" literally, eventually the Pharisaic view prevailed, that "an eye for an eye" means monetary compensation to the victim of violence.[64] Thus the Mishnah states:

> A person who injures another is liable for five things: the damage, the pain, the medical expense, the loss of income, and the disgrace. How is payment for damage determined? If one blinded someone's eye, cut off his hand, or broke his foot, we then look upon him as if he were a slave to be sold in the

market and estimate the difference in value before and after the injury. How is payment for pain determined? It is as if one were burned by a spit or nail, even on his fingernail, that is, in a place where there is no bruise, and we then estimate how much a similar type of person would be willing to be paid to bear such pain. . . . How is loss of income determined? It is as if he were a watchman in an onion patch [and now could not work at even this job], because he has already been paid the value of his hand or his foot. How is payment for disgrace determined? This all depends on who was disgracing and who was disgraced.[65]

Here we see a dramatic shift from an emphasis on retribution in personal injury cases to an emphasis on restitution. We are to be more concerned with some restoration of the injured person's economic status—the only thing we can restore—than in making the criminal suffer similar injury and all that it entails. The needs of the victim of crime become our primary concern. Nevertheless, this does not ignore the standard of equality we saw in the basic ethical norm enunciated by Hillel. For we can now, based on the Pharisaic and rabbinic understanding of "an eye for an eye," see the following corollary: "If you do what is hateful to you to another, we see to it that what the victim lost will be restored to him or her as much as possible by you." Inasmuch as the lost eye or limb cannot be restored, the best we can do is virtually to eliminate the economic disadvantage that the victim's mutilated state entails.[66]

This concern with the needs of the victim is based on two considerations. First, we are more concerned with rectification than punishment. In other words, rather than making the criminal suffer physical pain and mutilation similar to the victim's, a procedure that neither helps the victim nor reforms the criminal, we make the criminal compensate the victim as he would have to compensate himself if he had harmed himself. Second, true equality is in practice impossible through a procedure as brutal as reciprocal mutilation. This comes out in three of the arguments the Talmud presents to show that "an eye for an eye" is to be taken symbolically rather than literally. The first two arguments follow:

R. Dostai ben Judah says that "an eye for an eye" means monetary compensation. You say monetary compensation, but could not one say it means an eye literally? What is the eye of one party was large and the eye of the other was small? . . . R. Simon bar Johai says, . . . "what if a man blind in one eye [*suma*] blinded the eye of another. . . . How could I uphold 'an eye for an eye'?" And Scripture states, "There shall be one procedure [*mishpat ehad*] for you" (Leviticus 24:22)—one equal [*ha-shaveh*] for all of you.[67]

Some later Rabbis point out that even according to this logic, monetary payment should perhaps be limited to those cases where physical retribution could not be exactly equivalent; where equivalence is possible, physical retribution should be carried out.[68] However, this misses the full force of the interpretation of "one procedure" as *one equal procedure*, which mandates an absolute standard of equality without exception. Such absolute equality does not exist in the real world; equality is originally a mathematical concept we postulate symbolically rather than actual state of affairs we experience. Money is something whose value is symbolic, something whose value is postulated.[69] Therefore, only monetary compensation could cover all possible cases *equally*.[70]

A third argument in favor of monetary compensation is the following: "It was taught in the School of Hezekiah 'an eye for an eye . . . a life for a life' [Exodus 21:23], but not a life and an eye for an eye. For if you think this is to be taken literally, there are times you will find . . . that blinding someone will kill him."[71] This interpretation, familiar to us as Portia's argument in Shakespeare's *Merchant of Venice*, makes an important point.[72] In performing physical retribution, we may endanger the very life of the criminal, and society itself must not commit a worse crime in the name of justice than did the criminal in the name of injustice.

Here the example cited is not exceptional but, rather, is paradigmatic of the general principle of equality in judgment.[73] Physical mutilation of any kind violates the principle of equality because it can never be equal in reality. The body parts of one person in and of themselves are incommensurate with the body parts of another person. As such, the actual words "an eye for an eye" are to be interpreted figuratively.[74] As Maimonides puts it, "The assailant deserves to lose the limb; therefore, he pays for the damage."[75] In other words, the assailant could be physically punished only if we were able to inflict the mutilation with absolute equality—which, of course, we cannot do.

Monetary compensation is the best we can do under these imperfect circumstances. Money is the *tertium quid* that introduces a standard whereby a just commensurate relation can be stipulated between the assailant and the assaulted. To attempt to practice literal equality by physical means in cases of physical injury would result in real inequality in the end. As the examples brought in the Talmud indicate, that would result in a legal assault as serious as the original assault on the victim.

The classical example of rabbinic exegesis on behalf of the traditional *lex talionis* is the midrash that distinguishes between atonement money being mandated for personal injury but prohibited for homicide.[76] Although Maimonides did not find this distinction legally convincing,[77] he nevertheless alludes to it in the *Guide of the Perplexed* in his discussion of the reasons for the scriptural commandments. There he alludes to it as a concept rather than as an actual interpretation of Scripture. He writes:

> The punishment meted out to anyone who has done wrong to somebody else consists in general in his being given exactly the same treatment that he has given somebody else. . . . For necessarily there must be a soul for a soul— the young and the old, the slaves and the free, the men of knowledge and the ignorant, being considered equal.[78]

Maimonides distinguishes between "necessary equality" on the one hand, and "general equality" on the other hand.[79] Human lives are subject to necessary equality, whereas human body parts are subject to general equality. What is the basis of this essential difference? Maimonides himself simply states it, but like so many of his simple statements in the *Guide*, it invites our rational speculation.

Perhaps one can reason as follows. In the case of personal injury, the value of body parts of different persons is directly incommensurate because the value of A's eye in relation to his or her whole life is always going to be different from the value of B's eye in relation to his or her whole life. Therefore, we have to introduce the third factor, money, in relation to which the value of an eye of the assaulted can be estimated and then the commensurate value in money can be extracted from the assailant. Here we have indirect commensurability, what Aristotle called "proportional" equality as opposed to the more direct "arithmetic" equality.[80] This it seems is what Maimonides meant by "general equality." In the case of homicide, however, we are not dealing with a part of a larger whole; rather, we are dealing with a whole itself. Only if human life is considered to be a part of a larger whole, for example, the clan or the state, could Maimonides' principle of general equality apply. Clearly, though, in Judaism human life is not evaluated in terms of its being part of a larger whole. This is what, it seems, Maimonides meant by "necessary equality." Or as the same point is made earlier in the Talmud, "Why do you think your blood is redder than the other person's; perhaps the other person's blood is redder than yours?!"[81]

We have seen that Jewish law is concerned with the needs of the victim of violent crime and yet that the criminal has the right to be spared "cruel and unusual punishment" disproportionate to the crime. Both of these points are rooted in an overriding concern with equality.

Furthermore, because equality is best served by monetary restitution, Jewish law tended to make virtually all crime, with the exception of murder, a civil tort rather than a strictly criminal matter. Thus thieves were required to repay what they had stolen plus additional charges based upon the loss of income their victims suffered because of the theft.[82] If a thief was unable to repay the victim, the court sold the offender as a bondman to another Jew for a six-year minimal period. The purchaser paid the full price to the victim of the theft at the outset of this period of indentured servitude, thereby immediately compensating for the principal the victim lost.[83] Additional charges were given the status of a claim against the thief; to be paid later.[84] Furthermore, the thief was placed, in effect, in a supervised work rehabilitation program. Instead of languishing in a prison, as is the case today when thieves serve sentences that cannot be in proportion to what they actually did in their crimes, the thief was allowed to become an economically participating member of society (albeit closely supervised) immediately following conviction. In this way the needs of three parties were satisfied. The victim was compensated for loss. The criminal was on the road to resocialization rather than being made more antisocial by confinement in prison with worse criminals. And society had a better chance to have a contributing member rather than one more criminal outcast.[85] Society harms itself by doing anything to create conditions for the maintenance of a sustained criminal population. Thus the Mishnah notes that as soon as a person has been punished for his crime, he is once again "like our brother."[86]

Retributive Justice: Capital Punishment as Social Outrage

Though we have seen that where a victim of crime can be compensated and where the criminal can be resocialized, retribution is replaced by restitution, in cases of murder, capital punishment is mandated. Here equal retribution is the only concern, for the victim cannot be compensated and the criminal does not deserve to return to society. "Whosoever sheds human blood, by humans shall his blood be shed" (Genesis 9:6). "You shall take no ransom for the life of a murderer who is convicted to die, for he shall surely be put to death" (Numbers 35:31). Here again Kant well expressed the difference between murder and other crimes.

> But whoever has committed murder, must die. There is in this case, no juridical substitute or surrogate, that can be given or taken for the satisfaction of justice. There is no *likeness* or proportion between life, however painful, and death; and therefore there is no equality between the crime of murder and the retaliation of it but what is judicially accomplished by the execution of the criminal.[87]

Beginning in the postbiblical period, capital punishment has been a subject of profound and constant debate within Judaism. The debate's *locus classicus* is the following Mishnah:

> A Sanhedrin which executed once in seven years is called "murderous" (*hovlaneet*). R. Eleazar ben Azaryah says once in seventy years. R. Tarfon and R. Akibah say that "if we had been in the Sanhedrin, no one would have ever been executed." Rabban Simon ben Gamliel says that even they are increasing shedders of blood in Israel.[88]

The Mishnah is presenting the following opinions:

R. Eleazar ben Azaryah and the anonymous authority whose statement is recorded just before his accept capital punishment with reluctance and believe it should be administered cautiously and infrequently.

R. Tarfon and R. Akibah, on the other hand, oppose capital punishment. We have other evidence for this. In another passage R. Akibah stated, "Whoever sheds blood diminishes the image of God."[89] Furthermore, R. Akibah's close disciple, R. Meir, interpreted the verse describing an executed criminal as "an affront to God" (Deuteronomy 21:23), as follows: "It is like identical twin brothers. One is the king of the whole universe and the other a criminal. After a while the criminal was crucified. Everyone who passed by stopped and said, 'it looks like the king is crucified.'"[90] Finally, it was R. Akibah who ruled that when the Sanhedrin did condemn someone to die, its members were to fast that same day.[91] No doubt many Rabbis were shocked by the ease with which the Romans executed persons, based as it was on the absence of a doctrine of the sanctity of human life.[92] R. Akibah himself was the most celebrated victim of Roman capital punishment among the Rabbis.[93]

Later sages were embarrassed by what seemed to be an outright general rejection of the Torah's prescriptions to execute certain criminals, especially murderers. Therefore, they explained that R. Tarfon and R. Akibah would interpret the laws of evidence so strictly that it would be practically impossible to sentence anyone to die.[94] This interpretation of R. Tarfon and R. Akibah made capital punishment a "law on the books," a matter of warning that was not carried out. As the one Rabbi noted in the case of the juvenile delinquent that we discussed earlier, "It never was and never will be."[95] Rabban Simon ben Gamliel, though, at the end of our Mishnah, criticizes their approach as virtually tolerating crime and criminals.

Despite the impressive stature of R. Tarfon and especially R. Akibah, and despite the cogency of their theology, what was interpreted as their view of the laws of evidence in capital cases was not accepted by the later Rabbis.[96] To be sure, Maimonides cites the anonymous Mishnaic statement that one execution in seven years makes a court "murderous," but he obviously sees this as an ideal only, for he continues, "and even so, if it turns out that every day there is a criminal worthy of death, they execute him."[97] Apparently, it is the view of Rabban Simon ben Gamliel that prevails.

Jewish acceptance of the death penalty can be understood in two ways. First, it may uphold capital punishment as a deterrent to further murders. Alternatively, it may explain capital punishment as society's expression of ultimate outrage at the blood shed in its midst. The question of whether or not capital punishment is in fact a deterrent is the subject of unending debate, especially today when we have the long-term prison sentence as an alternative. It is unlikely that either side will ever convince the other because, though fear of punishment would seem to deter most people from committing crimes, it is unclear whether the punishment must be as harsh as death to have this deterrent effect.[98]

One could make a much better case for capital punishment as society's expression of ultimate outrage and its attempt to perform a tangible act of expiation, and this is exactly the approach taken by Maimonides. In conceptualizing the law of capital punishment, Maimonides stresses that premeditated murder violates the very foundation of society. This alone is sufficient reason for the death penalty even if there will be no deterrent effect, as in a so-called crime of passion that will probably not be repeated.

> Even though there are sins worse than bloodshed, none of them involves the destruction of the social order [*yishuvo shel olam*] like bloodshed, not even idolatry. . . . It is forbidden for a court to have mercy on a murderer. They should not say that the victim has already been killed, so what benefit [*to'elet*]

is there in killing someone else, for they will be derelict, therefore, in his execution.[99]

This social necessity to expiate the sin of bloodshed is at the heart of the symbolic biblical rite of atonement in cases of murder where the culprit has not yet been apprehended. A calf's neck is broken in a stream, and the elders of the nearest community say: "Our hands did not shed this blood and our eyes did not see it. Atone O Lord for your people Israel whom you have redeemed and do not let innocent blood be shed in the midst of your people Israel" (Deuteronomy 21:8).

The Mishnah asks, "Do we think that the judges are murderers?!"[100] It then answers this rhetorical question by stating, "It means that when the victim came to us we did not send him away without food, nor did we let him go without protection." This picturesque language indicates that the judges, as society's representatives, can exonerate themselves only if they have been diligent in their primary function of criminal justice, that is, the protection of the people.

The point is sharpened in the Palestinian Talmud's discussion of this Mishnah. Is it for neglect of the needs of the victim, or is it for neglect of the need to deal effectively with criminals, that expiation is being made?

> The Palestinian rabbis interpreted it as pertaining to the criminal and the Babylonian rabbis interpreted it as pertaining to the victim. The Palestinian rabbis interpreted it as pertaining to the criminal, namely, it was not that we freed him; that we did not execute him; that we did ignore him; that we released him and procrastinated in his trial.[101]

A question arises: If the judges do not know who the murderer is, then how can they exonerate themselves from having legally enabled him to commit another crime? The answer is that they are not speaking about a particular criminal but, rather, they are speaking about their judicial treatment of murderers in general. In other words, they are exonerating themselves from neglect of their primary public duty to protect society from crime. Less than full diligence in this task means that justice has not been pursued. Therefore, the Mishnah adds that "when murderers increased this rite of atonement was abolished."[102] When law and order break down, the judicial system and its authorities must take their share of the blame, and public expiation is impossible.

The moral outrage that capital punishment is to express can be seen in the following law in the Mishnah, "Whoever is convicted of a capital offense [ha-mithyayyev be-nafsho] does not pay monetary damages; as Scripture states, 'If there is no fatality [lo . . . ason], then damages shall be assessed'" (Exodus 21:22).[103] The scriptural proof-text concerns a case where someone, because of gross negligence, caused a pregnant woman to abort her unborn child. The loss of the fetus is considered a tort with damages payable to the father of the unborn child. If also, however, the pregnant woman herself died, then the case is a criminal matter and removed from the area of torts. The Talmud emphasizes that causing loss of life (*ibud neshamah*) wipes out liability for a simultaneous tort to another person.[104]

The rationale behind this law seems to be that in cases of damages less than murder, payment serves to restore the loss to the victim and restore the criminal to normal society, that is, to renew relationships of trust with him. When murder has occurred, however, such restoration is impossible, for the victim can never return to receive restitution and the criminal can never expiate his crime in this world. Therefore, if the guilty party were to pay for monetary damages he caused, and then be executed for murder, he would have reestablished his normal social relationship through the payment before his death, even though *all* Israel is bidden to "destroy the evil from your midst and . . . hear and fear" (Deuteronomy 21:21). The law here teaches us, in the words of the medieval glosses on the Talmud, the Tosafot, that "capital cases involve what is bad for everyone [*ra la-kol*], but in civil cases it is good for one party and bad for another . . . and no one should profit [*marviah*] from someone's death at all."[105]) The death of an innocent victim is a loss to the whole society as a communion of persons, and the execution of the murderer is something that must involve the equal outrage of every member of the society, transcending private interest of any kind.

In addition to society's need for expiation, there is also the criminal's need to be relieved of guilt, which is a heavy burden that cannot be carried indefinitely. When God gave Cain, the first murderer, an indefinite sentence, Cain cried, "My guilt [*avonee*] is too great to bear!" (Genesis 4:13). If guilt can be nullified through restitution, well and good: as we have seen, the victim's right is restored, and the criminal receives atonement and remains within the community. The Talmud brings this out vividly:

> And so it says about David, "And David did justice [*mishpat*] and charity (*tsedaqah*)" (II Samuel 8:15). However, is it not so that anywhere there is justice there is no charity, and anywhere there is charity there is no justice? . . . Yet this is justice and charity: justice for this one in that his property is returned to him; charity for that one in the stolen item is removed from him.[106]

However, when a life has been deliberately taken, the death of the murderer is the only means of atonement for him as well as for society. Thus the Mishnah prescribes the following procedure immediately prior to execution: "They say to him, 'Confess, for such is the way of those convicted to die to confess, and whoever confesses has a portion in the world-to-come. . . . ' And if he does not know what to confess, they say to him, 'Say: "may my death be atonement for all my sins."'"[107] In other words, by performing justice in this world, we also provide the convicted criminal with the opportunity to be worthy of divine mercy in the other world. In this spirit, it seems, English judges, when pronouncing the death sentence, used to conclude with these words to the convicted criminal, "May God have mercy on your soul." Interestingly, this Mishnah links up the atonement of a repentant criminal about to be executed with atonement for society as a whole. In describing the criminal's confession, the Mishnah relies on the scriptural account of the crime and punishment of one Achan ben Zerach by Joshua and the elders of Israel. There the spiritual health of the whole community was endangered by the crime committed in its midst, and until expiation was performed, "the anger of the Lord was directed against the people of Israel" (Joshua 7:1).

If one opposes capital punishment, what are the alternatives? In our society few murderers serve even life sentences in prison. After twenty-five years, often less, a murderer is set free. In essence, society tolerates murder by allowing the murderer to return to society after a finite period of time whereas the victim never returns. The deterrence issue aside, a community's toleration of murderers manifests the low value it gives to human life. Furthermore, even if a life sentence really meant *life*, is not prison still part of our society? The inmate still has social contact with other prisoners, visitors, prison personnel. Finally, is there any more festering sore on the American body politic than our prison system? Prisons do not rehabilitate. By creating a long-term prison population we have generated a criminal subculture in which antisocial elements reinforce one another's criminality.

It follows that the ancient prescription of capital punishment for murderers is the only rational punishment society can exercise. It provides opportunity for expiation (*kapparah*) both for society and the criminal himself. Society's wound is healed and the communion of persons is restored when the one responsible for murder is removed.[108] A prison term does not accomplish these goals and does more harm than good.

The Benefit of the Doubt for the Victim

Many citizens today believe that the criminal receives more of the benefit of a doubt than the victim or the would-be-victim. The multiplication of technicalities, they say, encourages the criminal to calculate that there is little possibility ever of punishment.

The Jewish legal tradition stands in sharp contrast. To be sure, we have seen that the rights of the criminal are respected in that we are not to demand more than proportionately equal retribution, and that society is not to be brutally dehumanized by administering cruel punishment. Nevertheless, Judaism gives the rights of the innocent victims and would-be victims clear precedence in cases of doubt. This is evident from rabbinic interpretation of the following biblical verse: "If a thief be found breaking and entering and he is struck and he dies, it is not homicide. If the sun is shining upon him, it is homicide . . ." (Exodus 22:1). This seems to mean that in a daylight break-in, with the greater likelihood of there being witnesses, the thief would be less likely to commit murder. To kill him, then, might well be overreaction, that is, unjustifiable homicide. At nighttime, however, because there is less likelihood of witnesses being able to identify the culprit, he might very well commit murder if confronted by his victim. In this case preemptive killing is in effect self-defense and, hence, justifiable homicide.[109]

However, the ancient Rabbis interpret the phrase "if the sun is shining" as a simile:

> R. Ishamel says, "Could this mean that the sun was shining on him alone? Is it not shining on the whole world? Hence the phrase means that just as the sun is the sign of peace in the world, so also, if it is known that the thief's intentions were not homicidal, then to kill him is homicide."[110]

Examples are then brought to show that there are other such similes used in Scriptural law.[111] The Talmud further develops this distinction:

> Our Rabbis teach . . . if it is clear to you as the sun that his intentions are homicidal toward you, kill him; if not, do not kill him. But another source teaches . . . if it is clear to you as the sun that his intentions toward you are not homicidal, do not kill him; if not, kill him.[112]

The Talmud sees a contradiction between the two sources. The first seems to give the benefit of the doubt to the thief; unless he is unquestionably going to murder you, assume he will not and do not kill him. The second source gives the benefit of the doubt to the victim; unless the thief is unquestionably not going to murder you, assume he will and do whatever is necessary for protection, including killing him if nothing else will suffice. The Talmud concludes that the second source states the rule and the first source states the exception, namely, the nonhomicidal burglar is assumed to be the rare exception as in the improbable case of a father burglarizing the home of his own son.[113] Therefore, if a victim of a burglary defends himself or herself and even kills the burglar in the process, the burden of proof is to show that this burglar was obviously an exception to the general rule that burglars will murder rather than be stopped or apprehended.

But why do we assume that all burglars are ready to kill? Philo of Alexandria, the most important thinker in Hellenistic Judaism, suggested that this is so because all burglars are armed, and, in addition, will use their tools for murder as well as burglary.[114] The Talmud, though, provides a subtler psychological basis for the law:

> Rava argued that the reason Scripture stated "breaking-in" is because everyone assumes that a person will not stand by while his possessions are being stolen. Thus the thief will reason: "If I go in, the owner will stand up to me and not let me go; hence I will kill him." For this reason Scripture in effect says: "If he comes to kill you, you may preemptively kill him."[115]

The point is that without the benefit of the doubt being given to the victim, the criminal will assume that the benefit of the doubt is in his favor. Such an assumption contributes to the incentive to commit a crime. Removing this assumption from the realm of probability reduces that incentive. In short, the legal system must not provide any further incentive for crime than that which the criminal has already provided himself.

Jewish law not only gives the victim the benefit of the doubt but also mandates that others may act on behalf of the victim with whatever means are necessary.

> Our Rabbis taught that Scripture's use of the phrase "and he (the thief) is struck" (Exodus 22:1) means that this can be done by anyone; and the use of the phrase "and he dies" means by whatever means necessary. This had to be explicitly stated because one might have otherwise thought that only the owner of the threatened property, and not someone else, would take the risk of defending it, therefore only he could kill the burglar. Therefore Scripture lets us know that since the owner is considered to be mortally pursued, anyone else may rescue him.[116]

This discussion clearly indicates that all citizens, and especially the police, who are empowered to act on behalf of the citizenry, may defend the victims of crime by any means necessary.

An Afterword

This chapter has attempted to deal with the question of violence in our society from the perspective of Jewish criminal law and some more general Jewish reflections on human violence. Although it has not offered specific prescriptions, inasmuch as Jewish criminal law is nowhere operative in the world today, it has offered some overall insights from the tradition that should play a role in influencing current opinion.

A number of the conclusions I have drawn from the Jewish sources are controversial, going against tendencies in current American jurisprudence. I hope that nonetheless these findings will contribute toward the ongoing debate over the future direction of the criminal justice system.[117]

NOTES

1. See David Novak, *Halakhah in a Theological Dimension* (Chico, Calif., 1985), 82ff.

2. See Isaac Klein, *Responsa and Halakhic Studies* (New York, 1975), 44ff.; Klein, *A Guide to Jewish Religious Practice* (New York, 1979), 301ff.

3. See S. Shilo, *Dina De-Malkhuta Dina* (Jerusalem, 1974), for the fullest discussion of the whole question. Still the best book in English on Jewish criminal law is S. Mendelssohn, *The Criminal Jurisprudence of the Ancient Hebrews* (Baltimore, 1891).

4. See M. Elon, *Ha-Mishpat Ha'Ivri*, 2d ed. 2 vols. (Jerusalem, 1978), 2:94ff. But see *infra*, 187f.

5. See A. Donagan, *The Theory of Morality* (Chicago, 1977), chap. 1.

6. As Maimonides noted, "Accept the truth from whoever said it." *Shemonah Peraqim*, introduced, ed. J. Kafih (Jerusalem, 1965), 247a.

7. See my late revered teacher Abraham Joshua Heschel, *God in Search of Man* (New York, 1955), 336ff.

8. *Beresheet Rabbah* 22.7, ed. J. Theodor-C. Albeck (Jerusalem, 3 vols. 1965), 1: 213; see note, *ad locum*.

9. B. Berakhot 61b re Deut. 6:5.

10. See Gabriel Marcel, *Being and Having*, trans. K. Farrer (New York, 1965), 131–132, 154ff.

11. B. Makkot 9b–10a and T. Makkot 3.1. Even premeditated murderers first went to a city of refuge until they were tried and convicted. Thus these cities contained more than just manslaughterers. See M. Makkot 2.6.

12. *Tanhuma*: Mattot, end, printed ed.

13. M. Avot 4.1 re Ps. 128:2. See *supra*, 147. This should not be interpreted as a theological foundation for socialism. The error of all socialism*s*, from Plato to Marx and until this very day, is that they confuse the problem of *possessiveness* with the having of *possessions*. However, even when possessions are socialized, human possessiveness merely changes its object. Status and position replace things. In fact, things are in essence symbols of social status and power. See Ruth Benedict, *Patterns of Culture* (New York, 1946), 160ff. The power of both communist and capitalist bureaucracies is the contemporary example of this. Furthermore, the possessiveness of the individual is simply transferred to society. See *infra*, 210ff. For the naivete of Plato, see *Republic*, 462Bff. For the naivete of Marx, see *Karl Marx: The Essential Writings*, ed. F. L. Bender (New York, 1972), 86ff.

14. See Novak, *Halakhah in a Theological Dimension*, 29ff.; *supra*, 30f.

15. See Aristotle, *Nicomachean Ethics*, 1134b20; Maimonides, *Moreh Nevukhim*, 2.40; Thomas Aquinas, *Summa Theologiae*, 1–2, q. 91, a. 1 and a. 2.

16. T. Sanhedrin 1.8–9, ed. Zuckermandl, 415–416; B. Sanhedrin 6b. See B. Rosh Hashanah 21b and B. Kiddushin 49b. See *supra*, 113.

17. Note: "When the wicked sprout like grass and the workers of evil spring forth, it is that they be permanently destroyed. But you are above [*marom*] forever O' Lord" (Ps. 92:8–9).

18. On the unavoidability of God's law, see B. Shabbat 88a re Exod. 19:17 and B. Avodah Zarah 2b–3a.

19. M. Avot 2.16.

20. B. Kiddushin 39b. For discussion of whether or not there is *any* reward in this world, see Tos., *ad locum*, s.v. "matnitin."

21. See Isa. 40:27–29, 31; Ps. 58:12. For the rabbinic notion of divine punishment of evil even when human justice is inoperative, see, e.g., B. Sanhedrin 37b and B. Ketubot 30a–b; B. Baba Metsia 83^b.

22. See Abraham Joshua Heschel, *Man's Quest for God* (New York, 1954), 124–127.

23. See Jacques Maritain, *Man and the State* (Chicago, 1951), 12ff.

24. See David Novak, *Law and Theology in Judaism*, 2 vols. (New York, 1976), 2: 108ff.; Novak, *Suicide and Morality* (New York, 1975), 60ff. For the notion of charity as a nonreciprocal act (*hesed shel emet*), see *Beresheet Rabbah* 91.5 re Gen. 47:29. For the sanctity of the life of the unborn, see B. Sanhedrin 72b; the infant, M. Niddah 5.3 and B. Yevamot 80a–b; the psychotic, retarded, and senile, M. Baba Kama 8.4; the comatose and mortally ill, M. Shabbat 23.5 and B. Shabbat 151b.

25. *Sifra*: Qedoshim, ed. Weiss, 89b. See *infra*, 211.

26. See M. Kadushin, *Worship and Ethics* (Evanston, Ill., 1964), 31.

27. M. Sanhedrin 4.5. In the printed text of the Babylonian Talmud the reading is "a Jewish life" (*nefesh ahat me-yisrael*). See R. Rabinovicz, *Diqduqay Sofrim, ad locum*, and Maimonides, *Hilkhot Sanhedrin*, 12.3. From the context of the passage in the Mishnah, however, it is clear that the whole passage is concerned with humankind in general. See R. Samuel David Luzzatto (Shadal), *Commentary on the Torah*: Gen. 9:6, ed. P. Schlesinger (Tel Aviv, 1965), 50; R. Israel Lifschütz, *Tiferet Yisrael* on M. Avot 3.14; L. Roth, "Moralization and Demoralization in Jewish Ethics," *Judaism* 11 (1962):289ff. Cf., however, B. Yevamot 61a and Tos., s.v. "kivray."

28. B. Shabbat 31a.

29. See Franz Rosenzweig, *Kleinere Schriften* (Berlin, 1937), 109. For some non-Jewish expressions of this maxim, independent of any Jewish influence, see Herodotus, *Persian Wars*, 3:142.3; Aristotle, *Nicomachean Ethics*, 1132b21 and 1166a1; *Politics*, 1253a15. Also see Tobit 4:16; Philo, *Hypothetica*, 7.6; I. Heinemann, *Ta'amay Ha-Mitsvot Be-Sifrut Yisrael*, 2 vols. (Jerusalem, 1962), 1:46.

30. In a number of rabbinic texts Hillel's maxim is seen as a paraphrase of "You shall love your neighbor as yourself" (Lev. 19:18). See *Targum Pseudo-Jonathan* on Lev. 19:18 and 19:33; *Avot de-Rabbi Nathan* B, chap. 28, ed. Schechter, 27a (where the maxim is quoted in the name of R. Akibah, the authority who declared Lev. 19:18 to be "*the* great principle in the Torah" [see *supra*, n. 25]); B. Sanhedrin 84b, Rashi, s.v. "ve'ahavta"; R. Bahyah ibn Pakudah, *Hovot Ha-Levavot*, 8.3.22; R. Moses of Coucy, *Sefer Mitsvot Gedolot*, pos. no. 9; *Sefer Hasidim*, ed. Bologna, no. 470; R. Hasdai Crescas, *Or Ha-Shem*, 2.6.1; R. Obadiah Sforno, *Commentary on the Torah*: Lev. 19:18 (quoting M. Avot 2.4). See also Thomas Aquinas, *Summa Theologiae*, 1–2, q. 99, a. 1 and a. 3; Hermann Cohen, *Jüdische Schriften*, 3 vols., ed. B. Strauss (Berlin, 1924), 1:194. However, there were important Jewish thinkers who emphasized that love of neighbor is a higher (covenantal) norm than Hillel's (natural) norm. See Y. Nedarim 9.4/41c and R. David Fraenkel, *Qorban Ha'Edah*, s.v. "haven"; Maimonides, *Sefer Ha-Mitsvot*, pos. no. 206 and *Hilkhot De'ot*, 6.3 and *Hilkhot Evel*, 14.1; *Sefer Ha-Hinukh*, no. 243; Franz Rosenzweig, *The Star of Redemption*, trans. W. W. Hallo (New York, 1970), 239. Also see Jacques Maritain, *On the Use of Philosophy* (New York, 1965), 36–37. The Jewish thinker Ahad Ha'Am (d. 1927) attempted to show that the negative formulation of this maxim distinguishes Jewish ethics from Christian ethics. See *Philosophica Judaica: Ahad Ha-Am*, ed. and trans. L. Simon (Oxford, 1956), 132. However, in the earliest Christian text following the New Testament, the negative form of this maxim appears too. See *Didache*, 1.2.

31. Exhortation (*azharah* must always precede punishment (*onesh*). See B. Sanhedrin 54a.

32. Ronald Dworkin, *Taking Rights Seriously* (Cambridge, Mass., 1978), 205.

33. *The Philosophy of Right*, pt. 2, quoted in *Philosophical Perspectives on Punishment*, ed. G. Ezorsky (Albany, N.Y., 1972), 103–104. Kant's notion of "man as an end in himself" is the second formulation of the categorical imperative. See *Groundwork of the Metaphysic of Morals*, trans. H. J. Paton (New York, 1964), chap. 2; also, Novak, *Suicide and Morality*, 89ff.

34. John 11:48, 50.

35. See M. Hay, *Thy Brother's Blood: The Roots of Christian Anti-Semitism* (New York, 1975), 309.

36. T. Terumot 7.20, ed. Lieberman, 148–149.

37. Y. Terumot 8.10/46b. The Talmuds (B. Sanhedrin 46a; Y. Hagigah 2.2/78a) describe two instances where persons who committed relatively minor crimes were executed by the court on the grounds that "the hour required such" and one must

"make a fence around the Torah" (M. Avot 1.1). Maimonides sees it as a reaction to a breakdown in public morality (*Hilkhot Sanhedrin*, 24.4 and *Hilkhot Rotseah*, 2.4.; see *Tur*: Hoshen Mishpat, 425). Does, then, the court have the right to execute a minor offender as an *example* for others, a procedure that can be justified only by consequentialist reasoning? Nevertheless, all of these offenders acted contrary to Jewish law, knowing in advance that their acts were grossly provocative (see, e.g., Exod. 32:26ff.; Lev. 24:10ff.; Num. 25:1ff.) and they might very well be executed (see B. Sanhedrin 78b). However, no one could be executed simply as an example of the right of the state to take a life as it pleased (see I Kings 22:21; B. Sanhedrin 46a, Rashi, s.v. "ve-lo"; also B. Kiddushin 43a re II Sam. 12:9; R. Isaac Abrabanel, *Commentary on the Former Prophets*: II Sam. 12:9; B. Sanhedrin 19a-b). For an attempt to deal with these texts in light of modern politics, see S. Federbush, *Mishpat Ha-Melukhah Be-Yisrael* (Jerusalem, 1973), 75–76. The fact that certain traditional Jewish texts lend themselves to consequentialist reading is undeniable, but modern Jewish experience with tyranny should influence us to read them in other ways.

38. See Y. Terumot 8.10/46b and *Beresheet Rabbah* 94.9, ed. Theodor-Albeck, 3: 1184–1185 and notes, *ad locum*; also *Vayiqra Rabbah* 19.6, 3 vols., ed. Margulies, 2: 432 re M. Ohalot 7.6. For an excellent study of all these texts, see E. J. Schochet, *A Responsum of Surrender* (Los Angeles, 1973).

39. Also see my teacher Germain Grisez, "Against Consequentialism," *American Journal of Jurisprudence* 23 (1978):21ff. for a similar emphasis by a distinguished Roman Catholic ethicist.

40. M. Sanhedrin 8.5.

41. *Sifre*: Devarim, no. 220, ed. Finkelstein, 253.

42. B. Sanhedrin 72a.

43. Y. Sanhedrin 8.7/26b.

44. *Midrash Tannayim* re Deut. 21:21, ed. Hoffmann, 131.

45. See M. Sanhedrin 8.1–4 and Bavli and Yerushalmi, *ad locum*; also *Encyclopedia Talmudit*, 3:362ff.

46. T. Sanhedrin 11.6 and B. Sanhedrin 71a.

47. See *Tanhuma*: Ki Tetse, beg., printed ed.

48. See David Novak, *Law and Theology in Judaism*, 2 vols. (New York, 1976), 2: 56–58.

49. M. Sanhedrin 4.5. See *supra*, n. 27.

50. M. Ohalot 7.6; B. Sanhedrin 72b; Y. Shabbat 14.4/14d. See David Novak, *Law and Theology in Judaism*, 1:118, 132–134.

51. M. Sanhedrin 8.6. See Novak, *Law and Theology*, 1:130ff.

52. *Sifra*: Behar, ed. Weiss, 109c and B. Baba Metsia 62a re Lev. 25:36. Cf. T. Baba Kama 10.28 and B. Pesahim 25a.

53. H. A. Posner and D. Novak, "Exclusionary Rule: Analysis of American and Jewish Traditions," *New York Law Journal* 188, no. 71 (October 12, 1982):17.

54. See D. Daiches, *Moral Judgment*, quoted in *Philosophical Perspectives on Punishment*, ed. G. Ezorsky (Albany, N.Y., 1972), 142. Re the idea of common good in halakhic parlance, see *supra*, 98, n. 1.

55. See John Finnis, *Natural Law and Natural Rights* (Oxford, 1980), 154–156.

56. For the rejection of the notion that immoral means may accomplish moral results, see LXX on Deut. 16:20; B. Sukkah 29b–30a; Y. Hallah 1.5/58a.

57. *The Philosophy of Law*, pt. 2, quoted in *Philosophical Perspectives on Punishment*, ed. G. Ezorsky (Albany, N.Y., 1972), 104.

58. M. Avot 2.1.

59. See B. Sanhedrin 90a.

60. See, e.g., Num. 35:26 and Maimonides, *Hilkhot Rotseah*, 5.11.

61. Thus although personal vengeance (*neqamah*) is proscribed (Lev. 19:18), vengeance is taken by society on behalf of the victim (see Exod. 21:21 and B. Sanhedrin 52b; Num. 35:16–34). Vengeance in the strictest sense can be taken only by God, presumably because only God can execute it exactly (see Deut. 32:35; Ps. 94:1–2).

62. See *Republic*, 410A. For the notion of the inherent evil of vengeance, see *Crito*, 49D. Cf. *Laws*, 735E. My friend L. E. Goodman sees a much closer affinity between the Torah and Plato on this point than I do, however. Cf. his *On Justice: An Essay in Jewish Philosophy* (New Haven, 1991), 44ff.

63. See Plato, *Republic*, 427A. Cf. Karl R. Popper, *The Open Society and Its Enemies: Plato*, 5th ed. rev., 2 vols. (Princeton, 1966), 1:138–139 and passim.

64. Cf. Judges 1:6–7; Josephus, *Antiquities*, 4.280; Philo, *De Specialibus Legibus*, 3.181–182; Matthew 5:38–39; *Mekhilta*: Mishpatim, ed. Horovitz-Rabin, 277 and B. Baba Kama 84a (the opinion of R. Eliezer ben Hyrkanus); Louis Finkelstein, *The Pharisees*, 2 vols. (Philadelphia, 1938), 2:641; R. Samuel David Luzzatto, *Commentary on the Torah*: Exod. 21:23 (cf. intro., 19–20); Haim H. Cohn, *Jewish Law in Ancient and Modern Israel* (New York, 1976), 78.

65. M. Baba Kama 8.1. R. Akibah also tried to make the charges for public humiliation equal for all Jews on the basis of their common patrimony, irrespective of social and economic distinctions between them (ibid., 8.4). The law, however, is not according to him. See Maimonides, *Hilkhot Hovel U-Maziq*, 3.11.

66. See R. Judah Halevi, *Kuzari*, 3.46–47; also Giorgio del Vecchio, "The Struggle Against Crime," trans. A. H. Campbell, in *The Philosophy of Punishment*, ed. H. B. Acton (New York, 1969), 200–201; Emil Brunner, *Justice and the Social Order*, trans. M. Hottinger (New York, 1945), 221–224.

67. B. Baba Kama 83b. See B. Ketubot 32b and Tos., s.v. "ela."

68. Because of these various possible exceptions, a number of commentators emphasized the traditional as well as the rational foundation of *lex talionis*. See Ibn Ezra, *Commentary on the Torah*: Exod. 21:24 in the name of R. Saadyah Gaon; Maimonides, *Hilkhot Hovel U-Maziq*, 1.2; Nahmanides, *Commentary on the Torah*: Exod. 21:24.

69. See Aristotle, *Nicomachean Ethics*, 1133a30.

70. For other examples of the principle of general equality in rabbinic penology, see B. Yevamot 110a and parallels; B. Gittin 40a–b; Baba Metsia 101b; Makkot 2a; Y. Baba Kama 8.1/6b re Deut. 19:19.

71. B. Baba Kama 84a. Also some commentators have emphasized the notion of the inexactness of human physical suffering. See Ibn Ezra, *Commentary on the Torah*: Exod. 21:24 and Lev. 24:17. On the other hand, the Rabbis emphasize the exactness of divine measuring as opposed to human measuring (which would be required for physical *lex talionis* to be just). See, e.g., *Beresheet Rabbah* 10.9; *Vayiqra Rabbah* 6.5 re Exod. 24:6; also Philo, *Quis Rerum*, 28.141–143 and 38.182.

72.   Therefore prepare thee to cut off the flesh.
                     Shed thou no blood, nor cut less nor more
                     But just a pound of flesh. If thou tak'st more
                     Or less than a just pound — be it but so much
                     As makes it light or heavy in the substance
                     Or the division of the twentieth part
                     Of one poor scruple; nay, if the scale do turn
                     But in the estimation of a hair —
                     Thou diest, and all thy goods are confiscate.

Shakespeare, *The Merchant of Venice*, act 4, scene 1.

73. For the equality of women and men in Jewish civil and criminal law, see B. Baba Kama 15a.

74. For other examples of figurative interpretation in halakhic midrash, see *Mekhilta*: Mishpatim, ed. Horovitz-Rabin, 293; *Sifre*: Devarim, no. 237, ed. Finkelstein, 269–270 and no. 243, p. 273.

75. *Hilkhot Hovel U-Maziq*, 1.3.

76. *Sifra*: Emor, ed. Weiss, 104d–105a.

77. *Hilkhot Hovel U-Maziq*, 1.3.

78. *Guide of the Perplexed*, 3.41, trans. S. Pines (Chicago, 1963), 558. Also see R. Joseph Albo, *Iqqarim*, 4.36, and David Novak," The Idea of Natural Law in the Thought of Rabbi Joseph Albo" (Heb.), *Hadoar* 82 (November 13, 1982):46–47.

79. In rabbinic terminology the word for "equal"—*shaveh*—is used in the sense of necessary equality. See, e.g., M. Baba Kama 1.3; Y. Ketubot 10.2/33d.

80. This equality is called either "proportional" (*to analogon*) or "geometrical" (see *Nicomachean Ethics*, 131a30ff.). In proportional/geometric equality there are four terms, whereas in arithmetic equality there are only two terms. Thus in the case of *lex talionis* there are (1) the eye of the victim, (2) the victim, (3) the eye of the culprit, and (4) the culprit. The equality here is not liberally between the terms (a = c), but in the ratio a : b = c : d.

81. B. Pesahim 25b.

82. Exod. 21:37; *Mekhilta*: Mishpatim, ed. Horovitz-Rabin, 291–292.

83. Ibid., 247 re Exod. 21:2.

84. B. Kiddushin 18a re Exod. 22:2; Maimonides, *Hilkhot Gezelah*, 2.12.

85. The bondman who wanted to remain with his master longer than the specified time of indenture was to have his ear bored (Exod. 21:5-6). According to Rabban Yohanan ben Zakkai, this was considered a punishment for choosing a human master over God (T. Baba Kama 7.5; B. Kiddushin 22b re Lev. 25:55). In other words, the desire not to return to the equality of normal social life under the Covenant is considered sinful.

86. M. Makkot 3.15 re Deut. 25:3. See *Sifre*: Devarim, no. 286, ed. Finkelstein, 304.

87. *The Philosophy of Law*, pt. 2, quoted in *Philosophical Perspectives on Punishment*, 105.

88. M. Makkot 1.10. See Josephus, *Antiquities*, 13.294. It should be noted that this debate is academic in that the Romans removed the right of capital punishment from Palestinian Jews at least half a century earlier than the time of these Rabbis. See Y. Sanhedrin 1.1/18a and 7.2/24b; B. Sanhedrin 41a; B. Avodah Zarah 8b; John 18: 31. Also see A. N. Sherwin-White, *Roman Society and Roman Law in the New Testament* (Oxford, 1963); Haim H. Cohn, *The Trial and Death of Jesus* (New York, 1977), 31–32, 346–350 n. 43. Cf. T. Sanhedrin 9.11; B. Sanhedrin 52b; B. Ketubot 30a-b.

89. T. Yevamot 8.7 re Gen. 9:6, ed. Lieberman, 26; B. Yevamot 63a; *Beresheet Rabbah* 34.6.

90. T. Sanhedrin 9.7, ed. Zuckermandl, 429. See B. Sanhedrin 46b. It seems that R. Meir believed the execution itself is an affront to God. The Mishnah (M. Sanhedrin 6.4) and the *Sifre*: Devarim (no. 221), on the other hand, interpret "an affront to God" to refer to the crime itself, in this case, blasphemy.

91. *Sifra*: Qedoshim, ed. Weiss, 90a; B. Sanhedrin 63a re Lev. 19:26.

92. See, e.g., T. Yevamot 14.7; B. Yevamot 25b (cf. T. Yevamot 2.11/4b); B. Gittin 28b; B. Baba Kama 114a.

93. See B. Berakhot 61b; Louis Finkelstein, *Akiba: Scholar, Saint and Martyr* (Philadelphia, 1962), 272ff.

94. B. Makkot 7a.

95. T. Sanhedrin 11.6 and B. Sanhedrin 71a.

96. See *Alfasi*: 5 Makkot, end chap. 1 (ed. Vilna, 3a), and *Rabbenu Asher* (R'osh): Makkot 1.15. See also M. Sanhedrin 9.5 and B. Sanhedrin 81b.

97. *Hilkhot Sanhedrin*, 14.10. Also see his *Commentary on the Mishnah*: Makkot 1.10.

98. For a seeming deterrence theory of capital punishment, however, see Maimonides, *Hilkhot Rotseah*, 2.5–6 re B. Sanhedrin 46a; R. Solomon ibn Adret, *Responsa Rashba*, 3.393 and 4.311; R. Joseph Karo, *Bet Yosef* on *Tur*: Hoshen Mishpat, 2, beg.; Y. Baer, *A History of the Jews in Christian Spain*, 2 vols., trans. L. Schoffman (Philadelphia, 1978), 1:232–233. Re deterrence reasoning, see J. Andenaes, "Does Punishment Deter Crime?" in *Philosophical Perspectives on Punishment*, 324ff.

99. *Hilkhot Rotseah*, 4.9 and *Hilkhot Sanhedrin*, 20.4.

100. M. Sotah 9.6.

101. Y. Sotah 9.6/23d.

102. M. Sotah 9.9. For the guilt of social inertia in the face of public crime, see Maimonides, *Hilkhot Melakhim*, 9.14 re Gen. 34.

103. M. Ketubot 3.2.

104. B. Ketubot 37a. See B. Baba Kama 22a–b; Y. Makkot 1.1/31a.

105. B. Sanhedrin 3b, Tos., s.v. "mokee."

106. B. Sanhedrin 6b. Cf. M. Sanhedrin 4.5.

107. M. Sanhedrin 6.2. For the absence of physical cruelty in Jewish capital punishment, see B. Sanhedrin 43a re Prov. 31:6 and 52a re Lev. 19:18.

108. The law of the Torah that prescribes the execution of an animal that killed a human (Exod. 21:28) does so, undoubtedly, because it is abhorrent to have in our midst an animal that destroyed a human life (see M. Eduyot 6.1 and B. Berakhot 27a; *Sefer Ha-Hinukh*, no. 52; cf. M. Sanhedrin 7.4). How much more abhorrent is it to know that those who willingly murdered a fellow human being did so with impunity!

109. See Ibn Ezra, *Commentary on the Torah* and Rashbam, *Commentary on the Torah, ad locum.*

110. *Mekhilta*: Mishpatim, ed. Horovitz-Rabin, 293.

111. E.g., Exod. 21:19; Deut. 22:17 and 22:26.

112. B. Sanhedrin 72a.

113. Ibid., 72b.

114. *De Specialibus Legibus*, 4.7. The Talmud distinguishes between armed and unarmed criminals. See, e.g., B. Baba Kama 57a.

115. B. Sanhedrin 72a.

116. B. Sanhedrin 72b. For the notion of taking the law into one's own hands, see B. Baba Kama 27b. For reservations about vigilante action, however, see B. Sanhedrin 82a.

117. For how Judaism can be such an influence in a democratic, pluralistic society, see *infra*, 237ff.

9

Non-Jews in a Jewish Polity: Subject or Sovereign?

Scholarship and Normativeness

It is only during the past forty years or so, since establishment of the State of Israel, that the status of non-Jews in a Jewish polity could be more than a merely theoretical question. Theretofore, the question was a subject of only historical research or theological reflection. From the time of the final Roman takeover of the Hasmonean kingdom in 37 B.C.E. until 1948, no group of non-Jews lived until the control of a Jewish polity. (The status of *individual* non-Jewish slaves living under the rule of *individual* Jewish slaveowners, in earlier periods of Jewish history, is an altogether different issue and need not concern us here.)[1] The normative question, in a Jewish sense, has always been one concerning the status of Jews in a non-Jewish polity—at least until 1948. Indeed, for the majority of world Jewry, who do not live in the State of Israel, that is still the religious question, namely, the justification and application of the principle "the law of the non-Jewish state [*dina de-malkhuta*] is binding on Jews [*dina*]."[2] (The question of Jewish rights in a non-Jewish polity, which has concerned Jews since the Emancipation, is an altogether different question, one decided by non-Jewish criteria.) However, for the growing number of Jews who now live in the State of Israel, the presence there of a population of non-Jews (mostly Arab, either Muslim or Christian) requires a careful examination of the sources of Jewish tradition concerning the status of non-Jews in a Jewish polity for purposes that are now more practical (*halakhah le-ma'aseh*) than just theoretical (*talmud*).[3] And the question is now more practical too—although less directly to be sure—for the majority of Jews who live outside the State of Israel because, for most of them, the State of Israel is the *Jewish* state, not just the *Israeli* state. (Whether or not most Israelis share that view is debatable.)

For the more familiar religious question of the status of Jews in a non-Jewish polity, legal precedent is extremely important. If one consults S. Shilo's comprehensive study of this complex subject,[4] it becomes evident that the responsa literature here is vast and detailed. Hence, even new specific questions can and must be placed at the cutting edge of an uninterrupted practical sequence.

For our question of non-Jews in a Jewish polity, however, legal precedent — and by "legal precedent" I mean case law (*ma'aseh she-hayah*) as opposed to codified law (*halakhah pesuqah*) — is irrelevant because it does not exist. Indeed, there are no such precedents even in the rabbinic sources, much less in the responsa literature, simply because there has been no Jewish experience in this area for at least two thousand years.[5] Whatever has been written in this area in the past century — such as the brief discussions by R. Yehiel Michal Epstein (the author of the popular halakhic work *Arokh Ha-Shulhan*), or by the religious Zionist theoretician, Dr. Simon Federbush, or by the late Ashkenazic chief rabbi of the State of Israel, R. Isaac Halevi Herzog[6] — all of these discussions have had to leap over two millennia of specifically normative silence back into the more general classical scriptural and rabbinic sources on this overall topic.

If all we have for the new task at hand, then, is historical research or theological reflection, which one is primary and which secondary for our methodological purposes? Clearly, beginning with historical research and making it the determining factor in our method of inquiry will lead us to a normative dead-end. For historical research qua objective science can tell us, somewhat convincingly, only what *has happened* and, much less convincingly, what *might happen*. It cannot, however, by its own "value-free" criteria, tell us what *is-to-be*, which is the normative form any moral answer must take.[7] Modern philosophers, since Hume, have for the most part taken as axiomatic that one can never derive an "ought" from an "is," a prescription from a description. And although I would dispute that axiom on the metaphysical level,[8] it is difficult to dispute when one looks at the more empirical "is" with which modern historians deal, as Yosef Yerushalmi has recently reminded us in his seminal book, *Zakhor*.[9] I mention this obvious point simply because modern Jewish scholarship has such a heavy investment in the whole historical enterprise that it is easy to lose sight of the fact that the study of history is itself not *Torah*. Even in the type of historical research we find in the process of determining halakhic precedent, the enterprise is not essentially "historical" in the modern sense, for the normative sources and the normative content of these precedents are always considered by those who accept their authority to be superhistorical. Historical research, then, can be only a "handmaid" to the Torah itself.[10] And for our question at hand, only Torah will suffice.

What we are left with in our normative quest, is theological reflection, that is, reflection on the various scriptural and rabbinic discussions of the status of non-Jews in a Jewish polity. Unlike historical research per se, this theological reflection is not that of an uncommitted spectator but, rather, of a committed participant in a normative reality.[11] Accordingly, one can suggest "oughts" because of its vision of the overall "to-be" of Torah. Nevertheless, it is not Halakhah in the specific sense of an actual ruling (*pesaq din*) because it does not deal with particular cases. It is concerned with more general moral principles than with more specific moral rules.[12] It is, rather, an exegesis of primary sources (both Halakhah and Aggadah) and a philosophical concern with their fundamental truth. And what is especially exciting about such reflection here and now is that it can suggest practical norms.[13] Indeed, the move from theory to practice is imminent. Thus our reflection is more than academic.

I consider the clearest and most suggestive paradigm for such theological reflection in this area to be the dispute between Maimonides and Nahmanides on whether non-Jews in a Jewish polity are subject or sovereign.

Maimonides' Theory of Non-Jews in a Jewish Polity

Maimonides' theory of the status of non-Jews in a Jewish polity is largely presented in a theological-political treatise, "The Laws of Kings and Their Wars" (*Hilkhot Melakhim u-Milhamotayhem*), which is the last section of *The Book of Judges* (*Sefer Shoftim*), the last division of his encyclopedia of Jewish law and theology, *Mishneh Torah*. This treatise is theological-political rather than strictly legal (and thus by including it and other such treatises in *Mishneh Torah*, Maimonides surely meant *Mishneh Torah* not to be a "legal code" in the same sense that *Tur* and *Shulhan Arukh* are legal codes).[14]

Maimonides' treatise is theological-political for two reasons: (1) it did not involve any possible contemporary cases and was thus inapplicable in Maimonides' time; and (2) it has not been subject to subsequent legal review in the way other areas of the Law, whose operation has been uninterrupted, have been subject to such review. Therefore, it is, in essence, an exercise in philosophical exegesis for the sake of a political theology. Hence, one cannot cite Maimonides' rulings here as being immediately practical in the same way many rulings of the *Shulhan Arukh* are immediately practical.[15] This is quite important to bear in mind because Nahmanides takes issue with Maimonides in the context of an exegetical work, his *Commentary on the Torah*, rather than in a strictly legal work.

The classical term for a non-Jewish participant in a Jewish polity is a *ger toshav*, which is a rabbinic term combining two scriptural terms, *ger* and *toshav*, to designate what we would call a "resident-alien."[16] For Maimonides, one becomes a *ger toshav* in one of two ways: either at one's own individual initiative, or as the result of being part of a non-Jewish society conquered by a Jewish polity in war.

The first way, that is, by individual initiative, is essentially Maimonides' restatement of two Talmudic sources.

> Who is a *ger toshav*? He is a gentile who accepts upon himself not to engage
> in idolatrous worship, along with acceptance of the rest of the commandments
> commanded to the Noahides, and who has not been either circumcised or
> immersed. Such a person is to be accepted and he is one of the pious of the
> nations of the world [*me-hasiday ummot ha'olam*]. Why is he called *ger
> toshav* [literally, "alien-dweller"]? It is because it is permitted for us to have
> him dwell among us in the Land of Israel. . . . We accept a *ger toshav* only
> at a time when the Jubilee is in effect, but at this time, even if he accepted
> upon himself all the Torah in its entirety except for one detail, we do not
> accept him.[17]

As Maimonides points out in a closely related text, voluntary membership in a
Jewish polity (or any Jewish community now) must be full conversion to
Judaism or nothing at all.[18] For the institution of the *ger toshav* to be operative, we are required not only to have a Jewish polity in the land of Israel but
to have a Jewish polity in the land of Israel with all twelve tribes in residence,
which is the prerequisite for the Jubilee system to be operative. That is why
Maimonides would eliminate the possibility of a *ger toshav* even in a Jewish
polity such as we now have in the State of Israel, and even if that Jewish
polity were governed by the Torah.

However, when it comes to the institution of the *ger toshav* as the result of
being part of a non-Jewish society conquered by a Jewish polity in war,
Maimonides seems to construct a more probable political scenario. And here
he goes far beyond the scriptural and rabbinic sources.

> And so it is with a non-Jewish city that has made peace with us, a covenant
> [*berit*] is not to be made with them until they renounce idolatry and destroy
> all its shrines and accept the rest of the commandments commanded to the
> Noahides. For any nation that has not accepted the commandments com-
> manded to the Noahides is to be killed if under our power. . . . And so did
> Moses our Master command by word from God [*mi-pi ha-Gevurah*] to force
> [*la-kof*] all the inhabitants of the world to accept the commandments com-
> manded to the Noahides. And whoever does not accept them is to be killed.
> The one who accepts them is called a *ger toshav* wherever [*be-khol maqom*],
> and he must accept them upon himself in the presence of three rabbinic judges
> [*haverim*].[19]

This scenario is more probable because Maimonides does not make the prior
applicability of the Jubilee system a *conditio sine qua non* for this type of *ger
toshav*. And, as is well known, Maimonides regarded the reestablishment of a
Jewish state in the land of Israel to be without religious impediment.[20] Thus
we have before us the assumption of a universal moral law, one to be enforced
by Jews wherever they have political power over non-Jews.

Furthermore, enforcement of this universal moral law is to be in tandem
with the Jewish subjugation of a captured people.

> War is not to be conducted with anyone in the world until peace has been
> offered to them, whether in a permitted offensive war [*milhemet reshut*] or in

a mandated war [*mllhemet mitsvah*]. If they made peace and accepted the seven commandments commanded to the Noahides, not even one life is to be killed. . . . If they accepted the payment of tribute [*mas*] but not servitude [*he'avdut*] or vice versa, they are not to be heard until they accept both. The servitude that they are to accept is that they will be despised [*nivzim*] and be at the lowest level of society and will not be able to lift their heads in Israel but will be subjugated [*kevushim*] under them. They are not to be appointed to any offices where they have authority [*ve-lo yitmanu*] over Jews for any reason whatsoever. The tribute to be received from them is that they are to be ready for the service of the king with their bodies and with their property, such as the building of walls and the strengthening of fortifications.[21]

Non-Jewish subjects of Jewish rulers seem to have the same status as Jewish and Christian subjects have under Muslim rulers, that is, they have the status of *dhimmis*.[22] They are a tolerated group of second-class aliens subject to a constitutionally structured authority over them. Indeed, Maimonides emphasizes how that authority is to be lawful and equitable, not capricious and deceitful. "It is forbidden to be deceitful in the covenant with them and to lie to them because [*ahar*] they have made peace and accepted the Noahide laws."[23]

Maimonides has here achieved a major *tour de force* in reworking the scriptural and rabbinic sources on this issue. The question that remains, however, is whether acceptance of the Noahide laws is for the sake of subjugation, or whether subjugation is for the sake of acceptance of the Noahide laws. In other words, the question is the perennial question facing all political theory: whether might makes right, or right makes might — the question of whether political power needs to be rationally justified.[24]

In the scriptural sources, there seem to be two kinds of war against gentiles: one with the seven Canaanite nations and the Amalekites; the other with all other enemies of the people of Israel. Both kinds of war are presented as offensive enterprises.[25] In the first case, absolute annihilation seems to be the only mandated course of action, with no compromise of any kind possible. In this case, that is, with the Canaanites and the Amalekites, the reason for this uncompromising imperative seems to be the inherent moral wickedness of these peoples, not just their animosity to the people of Israel. Thus the Amalekites are considered those who "do not fear God" (Deuteronomy 25:18), in the sense of not fearing divine retribution for their immorality toward and with other human beings.[26] The Canaanites are to be totally dispossessed from the land of Israel because of "all these abominations [*to'evot*] they have done" (Leviticus 18:27), such as incest and child sacrifice. Nevertheless, what exact body of law they violated, and whether they knew in advance that what they were doing was evil and subject to divine punishment are not spelled out in these early sources. Also, the option of their rectifying their past sins does not seem to be presented as a possibility leading to their being treated by less harsh means than annihilation.

In the second case, that is, non-Canaanite/Amalekite societies conquered by a Jewish polity, compromise is possible, but that compromise seems to be based on the purely external political consideration of subjugation, not on the internal morality of the subjugated people itself. It seems to be an issue of *might*, not *right*. Thus, in the text from the Palestinian Talmud, which Maimonides cites, the two cases are essentially conflated, but that conflation is based on political not moral criteria.

> Before entering the land, Joshua sent three letters. In the first one he sent to them, he offered the option of flight to whoever wanted to flee. The second option he then offered was that whoever wanted to make peace could make peace. The last option he then offered them was that whoever wanted to wage war, war would be waged with them.[27]

This seems to be based on the earlier qualification of the *Sifre* concerning the mandate to annihilate the Canaanite nations based on the scriptural reason, namely, "in order [*lema'an*] that they not teach you to practice all their abominations which they practiced for their gods and, thus, you will sin against the Lord your God" (Deuteronomy 20:18). The *Sifre* sees this as a condition antecedent so that "if they repented [*asu teshuvah*], they are not to be killed."[28] Whether that "repentance" is for the general *moral* violation of the Noahide laws, or particular resistance to Israel's *political* power, is still unclear.[29]

Maimonides' great innovation is to make Jewish subjugation of non-Jewish captive peoples a matter of morality: a morality as binding on the conqueror as it is on the conquered. Both the power of the conqueror and the powerlessness of the conquered are now subject to the rule of law: the former being restrained; the latter being protected, for any Jewish subjugation of non-Jews as the result of military victory is justified only by joint adherence to the seven Noahide laws. These laws, for Maimonides, are the maximal moral standard for all non-Jews (*benay Noah*), and they are the minimal moral standard for Jews, the Mosaic Torah being their full actualization.[30]

The insistence upon a moral justification for Jewish subjugation of a non-Jewish society highlights a seeming contradiction between two related passages in *Hilkhot Melakhim u-Milhamotayhem* concerning the initial justification of a war with a gentile society—what in Western political theory is called *jus ad bellum*.[31] This is important for us to analyze here because, it will be recalled, for Maimonides, the only way one can become a *ger toshav* in a non-Jubilee-observing Jewish polity is when that person or group of persons came under Jewish rule as the result of a Jewish victory in war.

In the rabbinic sources, there are three kinds of war: (1) *milhemet hovah*, that is, a mandated offensive war against the Canaanites and the Amalekites;[32] (2) *milhemet mitsvah*, that is, a defensive war, minimally conditioned by a threat to the security of the Jewish state (an example would be the Israeli preemptive strike against the Egyptian forces in the Sinai poised for attack in June 1967);[33] and (3) *milhemet reshut*, that is, a permitted war, seemingly authorized by pure self-interest, namely, the expansion of military power for political or even economic ends.[34]

Maimonides reduces the kinds of war from three to two: *milhemet mitsvah* (mandated war) and *milhemet reshut* (permitted war). This can be understood if one recalls that, for Maimonides, the type of mandate designated by the rabbinic term *hovah* is a totally unconditional imperative.[35] However, if the repentance of even the Canaanite/Amalekites is always possible, acceptable, and even encouraged, then there can be no *milhemet hovah* in this unconditional sense.

Now in the case of a mandated war, there is moral justification: either self-defense or the refusal of the Canaanites/Amalekites to abide by the Noahide laws. However, in the case of permitted war, Maimonides here simply repeats the Talmudic justification, which seems to be based on pure self-interest:

> The king's first duty is to fight a mandated war [*milhemet mitsvah*]. What is a "mandated war"? It is the war against the seven Canaanite nations and the war against the Amalekites and the aid of the Jewish people from the hand of an enemy who has come upon them. Thereafter, he may fight a permitted war [*milhemet reshut*] with the rest of the nations, in order [*keday*] to enlarge the border of Israel and to increase his power [*gedulato*] and fame [*ve-shom'o*].[36]

However, it seems, as we saw earlier when examining a related passage from this very treatise, that the *only* justification for a Jewish war of subjugation of a non-Jewish society is "to force all the inhabitants of the world to accept the commandments that were commanded to the Noahides."[37]

Nevertheless, there is a possible solution to this seeming contradiction within this treatise on kingship and war. For, Maimonides, also following the Talmud, indicates that the head of a Jewish state[38] must have the parliamentary approval of the Sanhedrin before he can legally declare a permitted, offensive war.

> In a mandated war [*milhemet mitsvah*] he need not receive the permission [*reshut*] of the court, but he may go out on his own initiative at any time and force the people to go out. But, in the case of a permitted war, he cannot bring the people out except with the consent of the court of seventy-one.[39]

Now the question is: What sort of objections could a Sanhedrin (that is, the Great Court of seventy-one)[40] raise against the proposal by the head of state to declare a permitted war? Obviously, pragmatic political objections could be raised, such as the nonfeasibility of victory, too great a cost in lives and materials, negative diplomatic results, and so on and so forth. However, Maimonides himself, just before setting down this principle, states that the only acceptable reason for the head of state to engage in any offensive military enterprise is a moral one:

> And in all these things the king's law [*dino*] is law. In all of them his deeds should be for the sake of God, and his purpose [*magamato*] and thought are

to be to elevate the status [*le-harim*] of the true faith [*dat ha'emet*] and to fill the world with what is right [*tsedeq*], and to break the power of the wicked, and to fight the wars of the Lord. For a king is not made king initially except to implement justice [*la'asot mishpat*] and conduct wars.[41]

Therefore, it seems a Sanhedrin member could raise moral objections to a royal proposal of war, such objections as: Is the proposed war's moral justification a true reason or a rationalization? What will be the proposed war's moral effect on the Jews engaging in it? Will it provide too great a diversion from such prior Jewish needs as Torah study or the rectification of injustices within Jewish society? Will it needlessly brutalize the recruits called up to fight?[42]

The burden of proof is clearly on the head of state, for he is making a claim on the lives, property, and integrity of his own people.[43] This being so, a careful reading of all of Maimonides' statements on the subject of war and the subjugation of the non-Jews defeated therein seems to indicate that the *only* justification for *any* war and, therefore, the *only* justification for *any* act of subjugation of non-Jews, is a moral one. The ramifications of this conclusion from Maimonides' political theology are considerable.

Despite the fact that the law applies both to the Jewish conquerors and the non-Jews conquered in a Jewish polity, the administration of the law always lies in the hands of the Jewish authorities or those non-Jews they designate as subordinate authorities.

> The Jewish court is obligated [*hayyavim*] to appoint judges for these resident-aliens [*ha-gerim ha-toshavim*] to judge them according to these laws so that civilized society [*ha'olam*] not be destroyed. If the court sees fit [*ra'u*] to appoint non-Jewish judges from the non-Jews, it may do so. But, if it sees fit to appoint for the non-Jews Jewish judges, it may do so.[44]

This is a point that Maimonides emphasizes a bit earlier in this treatise, namely, the obligation of the Jewish authorities to interfere in the quasi-judicial independence of their non-Jewish subjects, if need be.

> How are the non-Jews commanded concerning adjudication [*ha-dinin*]? They are obligated to place various kinds of judges [*dayyanin ve-shoftim*] in every district to adjudicate according to these six commandments and to admonish the people concerning them. And a Noahide who violated any one of these seven commandments is to be executed by decapitation [*yehareg be-sayyaf*]. Because of this, all of the citizens [*ba'alay*] of Shechem deserved [*nitehayyavu*] to be executed for Shechem [their prince] robbed [Dinah] and they saw it, they knew about it, but they did not judge him.[45]

This obligation, then, is morally justified, not just politically rationalized, for the justification of the execution of the Shechemites by Simeon and Levi, the brothers of Dinah, is not because of the Shechemites' tacit approval of what Shechem did to *their* sister, but because of the tacit approval of his rape of *any* woman.[46]

It is because of the assumption of this type of moral culpability on the part of non-Jews, a moral culpability that itself requires Jewishly administered punishment whenever possible, that non-Jewish subjects have legal status in a Jewish polity. They have such status because it is assumed that they have moral personality. The moral personality comprises freedom of choice and responsibility for adherence to an objective body of law fairly applied. Nevertheless, this legal status entails neither political equality nor political independence. Furthermore, Maimonides constitutes neither a right nor a duty of the Jewish authorities to allow their non-Jewish subjects to be their political equals in the same polity, or even to be their politically independent neighbors in a separate state of their own. Ordered subjugation seems to be the only acceptable course of action when Jews have political power over non-Jews, in the view of Maimonides.[47] That subjugation, however, may never be arbitrary. It may never dispense with the due process of law.

Nahmanides' Critique of Maimonides' Political Theology

It can be said, with considerable justice I believe, that Nahmanides was Maimonides' most profound critic,[48] for his critique was not only the most extensive of all but resulted from a carefully thought out theological system. Thus he countered many of Maimonides' theories from a unified theological perspective of his own.

Because Nahmanides' most comprehensive work was his *Commentary on the Torah*, he usually began his critique of Maimonides' theology at the exegetical point of difference between them. In our case at hand, he begins his critique of Maimonides' view of the obligation of Jewish interference in the political life of subject peoples as follows, questioning his interpretation of the execution of the citizens of Shechem by Simeon and Levi. After indicating that many have questioned the moral propriety of what Simeon and Levi did, Nahmanides accurately states Maimonides' view and then begins his critique of it:

> And these points are not correct, as far as I am concerned. For if the matter were so, Jacob our Father would have himself been obligated to have the merit of being the first [*qodem ve-zokheh*] to kill them. And, if he was afraid of them, then why was he angry with his sons and cursed their wrath such a long time later, and he punished them by separating and dispersing them? Did they not [according to Maimonides' theory] meritoriously fulfill a commandment, and did they not trust their God, who saved them?[49]

Nahmanides then continues with his own view of the role Jews should play or not play in the political morality of a non-Jewish society subject to their power:

> In my opinion, the obligation of adjudication [*ha-dinin*] that was assigned to the Noahides in their seven commandments required that they place judges in every district, but He commanded them concerning such matters as stealing

and cheating, . . . etc., just like the obligation of adjudication for which Jews were commanded.[50]

Moreover, even if the citizens of Shechem were indeed guilty of violations of the seven Noahide laws, including tacit approval or passive indifference to a crime committed in their midst, Nahmanides concludes his thought on this subject by most emphatically stating that "the matter is not assigned [*masur*] to Jacob and his sons to exercise legal judgment against them [*la'asot bahem ha-din*]."[51] In other words, Jewish political powers will inevitably invite political disaster when they attempt to exercise moral authority over a society of non-Jews. Thus he makes a far sharper distinction between moral law and political authority than Maimonides does. Non-Jews, even non-Jews over whom Jews have power (as was the case with the Shechemites), are definitely bound by a moral law, but the task of its political enforcement belongs to them not to the Jews. For Nahmanides seems to be implying, at least, that when Jews do enforce that law, political considerations of self-interest, imperialism if you will, inevitably outweigh the moral zeal that originally was invoked in the justification of the subjugating policy. The assumption of the moral personality of non-Jews seems to imply that their political sovereignty is preferable to their subjugation by even Jewish rulers.

The Basic Theological Issue in the Dispute

The difference we have seen between Maimonides and Nahmanides on this point is more than an exegetical dispute about the propriety or impropriety of the killing of the Shechemites by Simeon and Levi. It is, rather, a theological dispute about the relation of Jewish normativeness and non-Jewish normativeness, or the relation between the more general universal law and the more singular law of the Torah. The question at issue is: Does the true normativeness of non-Jews require their being subject to Torah-constituted Jewish rule whenever possible, or does their true normativeness entail only their political sovereignty?

This theological dispute can be seen as rooted in the differing views of Maimonides and Nahmanides on the Jewish criterion of non-Jewish normativeness: the seven Noahide laws. The precedent for their difference seems to be found in the *locus classicus* of the Noahide laws in the Babylonian Talmud.

What is the scriptural basis of these commandments? R. Yohanan said that Scripture states, "And the Lord God commanded the human being [*ha'adam*], saying that from every tree in the garden you may surely eat" [Genesis 2:16]. "He commanded" [*va-yitsav*]; this refers to the commandment of adjudication [*ha-dinin*]. And so Scripture also states, "For I know him that he will command [*yitsaveh*] his children, etc." (Genesis 18:19) . . . "God" [*Elohim*]; this refers to the prohibition of idolatry. And so Scripture also states, "You shall have no other gods" [Exodus 20:3]. . . . But some taught it differently. "He commanded"; this refers to the prohibition of idolatry. "God"; this refers to the commandment of adjudication . . . as it is written, "and the householder shall approach the judges [*elohim*]" [Exodus 22:7]. But, if "He commanded" refers to the prohibition of idolatry, how does Scripture let us know this [*m'ay mashma*]? R. Hisda and R. Isaac bar Avdimi [spoke on this point], one of them saying that it comes from this verse "They quickly turned away from the path I commanded them [*tsivitim*], they made for themselves [a molten calf], etc." [Exodus 32:8]; the other one saying that it comes from this verse, "Ephraim is persecuted, deprived of just redress, because he has followed after nought [*tsav*]" [Hosea 5:11].[52]

That the dispute between these rabbinic authorities is more than a strictly exegetical difference about the meaning of two words in a scriptural verse is brought out by the sixteenth-century scholar R. Moses Isserles:

It is clear as the noonday sun that R. Yohanan . . . thinks that a Noahide is commanded only to observe the judicial procedure of society [*ha-minhag ha-medini*] and to adjudicate between persons equitably [*mishpat ha-yosher*], but not in the way of the Jewish laws that Moses gave us from Sinai, but only by the rule of law (*hoq nimusi*). . . . Jewish law is one thing and Noahide law is something else.[53]

The view of R. Isaac, on the other hand, assumes something else:

Noahide laws are the same as the laws the Jews were commanded at Sinai and, therefore, he derives them from a verse [Exodus 22:7] said at Sinai . . . except where there is direct evidence of a difference.[54]

For R. Yohanan, non-Jewish normativeness is essentially independent; for R. Isaac, it is essentially dependent on Jewish interpretation and, ideally, on Jewish enforcement.

Now it is clear that Maimonides builds his view of Noahide law upon the view of R. Isaac.

The first human being was commanded concerning six things: (1) concerning idolatry . . . (6) and concerning adjudication. Even though all of them are ours because of a tradition [*qabbalah*] from Moses our master and reason inclines [*ve-ha-da'at noteh*] toward them, it can be generally inferred from the words of Scripture that he was commanded conceding these things.[55]

Although, as is his frequent procedure, Maimonides eliminates the actual exegesis of Genesis 2:16 found in the Talmud, he nevertheless agrees with R. Isaac that the foundation of the Noahide law is the prohibition of idolatry. And that prohibition, along with its corresponding positive commandment to affirm God's existence, is something of which Judaism has the clearest monotheistic vision—even though these two commandments per se are considered by Maimonides to be rationally evident to human reason and thus not dependent on revelation to Israel.[56]

This can be seen in Maimonides' famous statement in this treatise about
the metaphysical status of the Noahide laws.

> Whoever accepts the seven commandments and is careful to practice them,
> such a person is one of the saints of the nations of the world, and he has a
> portion in the world-to-come. But, he is one who accepts them because the
> Holy-One-blessed-be-He commanded them in the Torah and made them
> known through Moses our master that Noahides are commanded regarding
> them. If, on the other hand, he practiced them because of rational inclination
> [hekhrea ha-da'at], he is not a ger toshav, and he is not one of the saints of the
> nations of the world, but he is only one of their sages [ela me-hakhmayhem].[57]

A number of commentators, both medieval and modern, have misunderstood this passage and have concluded that, for Maimonides, all morality
can be derived only from specific revelation. However, if this were the case,
Maimonides would not have spoken of the possibility of discerning the Noahide laws by what might be termed *ordinary human reason*. Clearly, such
discernment is possible, although it is not wholly sufficient to fulfill the ultimate end of human existence, which is the direct knowledge of God in a realm
transcending ordinary human existence on earth.[58] Furthermore, as I have
argued in my extensive treatment of the Noahide laws, for Maimonides, revelation is not essentially distinct from human reason, but it is its final realization.[59] Therefore, when Jews, who have the truest revelation (even if most of
them do not properly understand its metaphysical truths), also have political
power over non-Jews, these non-Jews should not be left to their own moral
devices, for their own moral devices are based on either insufficient human
reasoning in the strictly moral sense, or incomplete revelation in the metaphysical sense. (This can be seen in Maimonides' interest in Jewish proselytizing of
both Muslims and Christians.)[60] In the case of both Jews and non-Jews, the
improvement of the body (tiqqun ha-guf) — including the body politic — is always for the sake of the improvement of the soul (tiqqun ha-nefesh).[61] Accordingly, we can see that being the great systematic theologian he was, Maimonides' view of the political, moral, and metaphysical status of non-Jews is
consistently correlated.

Conversely, for Nahmanides, the realms of morality and revelation are
much more separate. In terms of revelation, this separation is for the sake of
laying greater emphasis on the essential difference between the natural and
the supernatural. Nahmanides' emphasis of a greater independent role for
nature (teva) — which is the whole realm of ordinary human experience (min-
hago shel olam), including political-moral experience — is for the sake of his
emphasis of the realm of the supernatural (nissim) by contrast.[62] Nevertheless,
what emerges from this emphasis is a very different view of the moral relationship between Jews and non-Jews.

This view of a more independent natural/rational morality comes out in
Nahmanides' treatment of the paradigmatic non-Jewish sin, the violence (ha-
mas) that brought about the punishment of the Flood.

Violence is robbery and oppression. And He gave the reason [*ha-ta'am*] to Noah as being violence, but he did not mention sexual perversion [*hash'hatat ha-derekh*], because violence is the sin that is known and evident [*ha-yadua ve-hameforsam*]. And our Rabbis said that because of it their doom was sealed. The reason for this is that its prohibition is a rational commandment [*mitsvah muskelet*], one for which they had no need of a prophet to admonish them. Furthermore, it is evil against God and humanity.[63]

Maimonides, too, emphasized in the section of *Mishneh Torah* concerning murder that the prohibition of violence and bloodshed is something immediately evident to any rational person.[64] One need not be skilled in metaphysics to appreciate the evident reason for its prohibition. Nevertheless, Maimonides rejects the notion of rational commandments (*mitsvot sikhliyot*) as defined by Saadyah and those who follow him (and Nahmanides by anticipation) precisely because it assumes that nonmetaphysically grounded morality is sufficient as well as evident.[65] For Nahmanides, it is sufficient, at least within its own context, even though revelation is needed to constitute the human relationship with God. But, for Nahmanides, revelation is not the culmination of a rational continuum, as it is for Maimonides.[66] Hence, in the ordinary realm of human political experience, basic norms do not need revelation in the same way non-Jews do not need Jews for their moral well-being. Ultimately, the differing views of Maimonides and Nahmanides about the moral independence of non-Jews stem from their differing views of the essence of revelation. For both, however, theology and politics are most definitely correlated.

Subjugation or Sovereignty?

It would be less than candid of me if I did not state that my own preference is for the approach of Nahmanides on this whole question, and this is for theological, philosophical, and political reasons. It seems to provide a basis for rethinking the whole enterprise of Zionism as a truly religious program for the Jewish people at this point in our history. Moreover, its credibility is enhanced by the fact that in Nahmanides' system, the settlement of the land of Israel (*yishuv Erets Yisrael*) is one of the 613 commandments of the Written Torah, one binding on all Jews at all times.[67] It is not so in Maimonides' system. And this is consistent with the far greater role that the sanctity of the land of Israel plays in Nahmanides' theology than it does in Maimonides' theology.[68] Hence, we have a model of how greater Zionist commitment can indeed be developed in tandem with a rejection of the subjugation of any other people, even on moral grounds.

Leaving the matter at this point seems to offer two divergent opinions, neither having any greater *prima facie* claim than the other. However, in traditional rabbinic style, I am going to conclude by attempting to demonstrate that Maimonides' whole approach might not be supportive after all of the position of those who would attempt to justify religiously a policy of Jews subjugating a non-Jewish people.

It will be recalled that for Maimonides any subjugation is justified only on moral, not political, grounds. So might can be exercised only when it is right. The rightness of any such exercise is dependent on the proper intention of the head of state proposing it. "And in all wars, his deeds should be for the sake of God, and his purpose and thought are to be to elevate the status of the true faith and to fill the world with what is right."[69] In another passage, from his "Laws Concerning the Sanhedrin," where Maimonides presents the legal power of a court to suspend individual privileges in case of a grave emergency, he similarly warns:

> All of these things are to be done according to what the judge will see as proper [ra'uy] under the circumstances and what the hour requires. And in all of them, let his deeds be for the sake of God; let not the dignity of human beings be light in his eyes . . . but let him act only to add to the honor of God.[70]

Therefore, if the intention of the head of state is doubtful, then it is also doubtful whether any subjugation is morally justifiable.

For this type of suspension of authorized right, there is specific rabbinic foundation. Thus in the case of the right of a brother to take his deceased brother's wife if they had been childless together (yibum), the Talmud notes:

> In earlier times, when their intention [mitkavvnin] was for the sake of the commandment, the commandment of the levirate took precedence over the commandment of release [halitsah]. But now that their intention is not for the sake of the commandment, the Rabbis said that the commandment of release takes precedence over the commandment of the levirate. . . . As it was taught: Abba Saul said that one who marries [ha-kones] his dead brother's childless widow [yevimto] for the sake of her beauty, or for the sake of marriage per se, or for the sake of anything else, it is as if he had relations with someone prohibited to him [k'ilu pogea b'ervah].[71]

Even though Maimonides does not accept the reasoning here, other important medieval halakhic authorities do accept it.[72] He obviously did not regard proper intention as determinate in this specific matter. Nevertheless, he himself seemed to be using the same type of qualifying reasoning presented here in this Talmudic text in his treatment of the limits of political, judicial, and military power. That is why I have quoted it in this context. Indeed, there are other examples in the Talmud where our moral inadequacy disqualifies us from exercising certain powers initially granted to us by the Torah.[73]

The problem of the exercise of political power over non-Jews is a relatively new problem for Jews. We are much more experienced in suffering Jewish powerlessness. In the half century or so between the 1930s to the 1990s, we have run the full gamut from powerlessness to considerable power. Yet we, more than any other people on earth, know in our very flesh how easily the most vicious abuse of power in all of human history was so easily rationalized by religious rhetoric. Although we do not derive norms from history directly, as I argued at the beginning of this chapter, surely historical experience can vividly illustrate what we already know from the Torah to be true. Moreover, even by Maimonidean standards, are we so sure of our own moral purity that we can now embark on a program of subjugation of any other people without fear for our souls? Are we not afraid of seeming to resemble ever so much the moral refuse of our age, they who have shed and are shedding so much human blood? Has not our tradition added restrictions to our lives when the old leniencies might make us morally odious in the eyes of the world?[74] Is not the Torah's command to pursue peace immensely comprehensive?[75]

The Torah requires neither our suicide nor our brutalization, for at a time in our history, one far more dangerous for our survival than this time, when the Roman legions were preparing to destroy the Temple and disperse our people, Rabban Yohanan ben Zakkai, in direct defiance of the zealots and militarists of that day, made his realpolitik the proposition "Let us go forth and make peace with them" (*nayfoq ve-na'avayd shelama be-hadyyhu*).[76] By that policy he was able to secure "Yavneh and her sages," an achievement that saved both the Jewish body and the Jewish soul. His policy at that time bespoke the true tendency of the Torah, what some today call *da'at Torah* in a somewhat loose sense of that term.[77] I believe that it still bespeaks the true tendency of the Torah now.

NOTES

1. See David Novak, *Law and Theology in Judaism*, 2 vols. (New York, 1976), 2: 87ff.

2. See B. Baba Batra 54b and parallels.

3. See B. Baba Batra 130b; Y. Hagigah 1.8/76d; Y. Sukkah 1.1/52a. See *supra*, 160f.

4. *Dina De-Malkhuta Dina* (Jerusalem, 1974), passim.

5. See David Novak, *The Image of the Non-Jew in Judaism: An Historical and Constructive Study of the Noahide Laws* (New York and Toronto, 1983), 11ff.

6. See R. Yehiel Michal Epstein, *Arokh Ha-Shulhan He'Atid* (Jerusalem, 1973), 89ff.; S. Federbush, *Mishpat Ha-Melukhah Be-Yisrael*, 2d ed. (Jerusalem, 1973), 56ff.; I. H. Herzog, "The Rights of Minorities According to Jewish Law" (Heb.), *Techumim* 2 (1981):169ff. See also B. Wein, *Hiqray Halakhah* (Jerusalem, 1976), 9ff.

7. See Thomas Aquinas, *Summa Theologiae*, 1–2, q. 94, a. 2; also Leo Strauss, *Natural Right and History* (Chicago, 1953), 9ff.

8. See *supra*, 50ff.

9. *Zakhor: Jewish History and Jewish Memory* (Seattle, 1982), esp. 87ff.; also David Novak, "The Role of Dogma in Judaism," *Theology Today* 45 (1988):52ff.

10. For the notion of any secular discipline functioning as *ancilla theologiae*, see H. A. Wolfson, *Philo*, 2 vols. (Cambridge, Mass., 1947), 1:144ff.

11. See H. G. Gadamer, *Truth and Method*, Eng. trans. (New York, 1982), 274ff.

12. On this distinction, see John Finnis, *Natural Law and Natural Rights* (Oxford, 1980), 63–64.

13. See B. Kiddushin 40b and parallels; also R. Isaiah Halevi Horowitz, *Shenay Luhot Ha-Berit*, Torah She-bi-Khtav: R'eh (Amsterdam, 1948), pt. 2, 82b–83a.

14. See I. Twersky, *Introduction to the Code of Maimonides* (New Haven, 1980), 188ff.; also I. Klein, *The Code of Maimonides VII: The Book of Agriculture* (New Haven, 1979), intro., xxiii–xxv.

15. Therefore, R. Joseph Karo, e.g., who certainly considered himself to be a follower of Maimonides on most halakhic issues, states about Maimonides' view of the beatitude reserved for Noahides who observed Noahide law as divine law (*Hilkhot Melakhim*, 8.11) that it seems to him to be Maimonides' "own opinion" (*me-sevara de-nafshayh*), i.e., his taking sides in an earlier rabbinic dispute (*Kesef Mishneh* thereon re T. Sanhedrin 13.2 and B. Sanhedrin 105a)—even though Karo himself agrees with this opinion of Maimonides. In more practically relevant decisions of Maimonides, however, Karo argued for Maimonides' conclusions in much more legally compelling language. See, e.g., *Hilkhot Tefillah*, 11.1 and *Kesef Mishneh, ad locum*.

16. For the still separate designation of *ger* and *toshav* in a Tannaitic source, see *Sifra*: Behar, ed. Weiss, 110a re Lev. 25:47. For *ger toshav* as one designation, see *Encyclopedia Talmudit*, 6:289ff.

17. *Hilkhot Isuray Bi'ah*, 14.7–8 re B. Avodah Zarah 64b and Arakhin 29a. (This latter text stipulates the Jubilee requirement.)

18. *Hilkhot Avodah Zarah*, 10.6.

19. *Hilkhot Melakhim*, 8.9–10.

20. See ibid., 11.1. Also, Maimonides (ibid., 6.1) does not require the presence of the *Urim Ve-Tumin* oracle for the king to declare a permitted war (*milhemet reshut*), as was mentioned in the Talmud re King David (B. Berakhot 3b–4a and B. Sanhedrin 16a–b). He requires only king and Sanhedrin (*Commentary on the Mishnah*: Sanhedrin 2.4), both institutions having no present religious impediment to prevent their being reinstituted whenever it becomes politically feasible. Cf. *Sefer Ha-Mitsvot*, shoresh 14 (end), where he also mentions the requirement of the high priest. However, even here he does not mention the specific requirement of the *Urim Ve-Tumim*. Indeed, it was not necessarily the high priest who used it (see B. Yoma 73a). For Nahmanides, on the other hand, the *Urim Ve-Tumim* is essential. See *Sefer Ha-Mitsvot*: "Negative Commandments According to Nahmanides," no. 17 re B. Shevu'ot 16a.

21. *Hilkhot Melakhim*, 6.1. Cf. *Sifre*: Devarim, no. 199, ed. Finkelstein, 237 re Deut. 20:10 (see Rashi, *ad locum*). See R. Abraham de Boten, *Lehem Mishneh* on Maimonides, *Hilkhot Melakhim*, 6.1 re Nahmanides' *Commentary on the Torah*: Deut. 20:10, who interprets the verse as does Maimonides.

22. See S. W. Baron, *A Social and Religious History of the Jews*, 2d rev. ed., 17 vols. (New York, 1957), 3:120ff.

23. *Hilkhot Melakhim*, 6.3.

24. See Plato, *Republic*, 336Bff.; also *supra*, 22ff.

25. See Deut. 20:1; 25:19.

26. See Gen. 20:11.

27. *Hilkhot Melakhim*, 6.5 re Y. Shevi'it 6.1/36c; also *Devarim Rabbah*, 5.13.

28. *Sifre*: Devarim, no. 204, ed. Finkelstein, 238. Rashi (B. Sotah 35b, s.v. "ve-katvah"), however, takes this condition to apply only to Canaanites (and all gentiles) *outside* the land of Israel, but not to those inside the land of Israel because their repentence would always be suspect (see Est. 8:17 and B. Yevamot 24b). This interpretation is rejected by Nahmanides in his *Commentary on the Torah*: Deut. 20:10.

29. For the modern distinction employed here between "morality" and "politics,"

see Strauss, *Natural Right and History*, 177–180 re Machiavelli. What moderns call "politics" in the amoral sense, the ancients called "tyranny." See Strauss, *On Tyranny*, rev. ed. (Ithaca, N.Y., 1968), 22–24.

30. See *Hilkhot Melakhim*, 9.1.

31. See John Langan, S.J., "The Elements of St. Augustine's Just War Theory," *Journal of Religious Ethics* 12 (1984):25ff.

32. M. Sotah 8.7; B. Sotah 44b. See Maimonides, *Sefer Ha-Mitsvot*, pos. no. 187, for why this commandment is perpetual (*noheg le-dorot*) even though there are no more "Canaanites" left in the world (re M. Yadayim 4.4). However, he seems to imply that the Amalekites are still extant (see ibid., no. 188).

33. B. Sotah 44b; Y. Sotah 8.10/23a.

34. See B. Berakhot 3b–4a and B. Sanhedrin 16a–b.

35. *Hilkhot Berakhot*, 11.2. This seems to answer the surprise expressed by R. Joseph Karo in *Kesef Mishneh* on *Hilkhot Melakhim*, 5.1.

36. *Hilkhot Melakhim*, 5.1. Nevertheless, that the king not act for personal aggrandizement, see ibid., 3.6. Re "breaking the power of the wicked," see ibid., 3.10. For a thorough presentation and analysis of these sources, see G. Blidstein, *Eqronot Mediniyyim Be-Mishnat Ha-Rambam* (B'er Sheva, 1983), 98ff.

37. *Hilkhot Melakhim*, 8.10.

38. Re whether or not the president of the State of Israel has the status of a king, at least in certain aspects, see R. Ovadia Yosef, *Responsa Yehaveh Da'at* (Jerusalem, 1978), 2 vols. 2:106–109 (no. 28).

39. *Hilkhot Melakhim*, 5.2.

40. See *Hilkhot Sanhedrin*, 1.3; also *Hilkhot Mamrim*, 1.1.

41. *Hilkhot Melakhim*, 4.10. See ibid., 7.15. Re *da'at emet*, see *Hilkhot Hagigah*, 3.1, 6. Re *da'at emet* as universal monotheism, see ibid., 7.15 and *Sefer Ha-Mitsvot*, pos. no. 191; also Blidstein, *Eqronot Mediniyyim Be-Mishnat Ha-Rambam*, 217ff.

42. See, esp., Nahmanides, *Commentary on the Torah*: Deut. 23:10.

43. See B. Baba Kama 46a.

44. *Hilkhot Melakhim*, 10.11.

45. Ibid., 9.14.

46. See *Beresheet Rabbah* 80.6 re Gen. 34:7. Cf. Gen. 29:26.

47. Therefore, the Jewish philosopher Hermann Cohen was incorrect when he asserted that the *ben Noah/ger toshav* implies citizenship in the modern sense, viz., equality based on secular criteria. See his "Nächstenliebe im Talmud," *Jüdische Schriften*, 3 vols., ed. B. Strauss (Berlin, 1924), 1:159ff. See *infra*, 231f.

48. See David Novak, *The Theology of Nahmanides: Systematically Presented* (forthcoming).

49. *Commentary on the Torah*: Gen. 34:13, 2 vols., ed. Chavel (Jerusalem, 1959), 1:191. For rabbinic embarrassment with the act of Simeon and Levi, see B. Megillah 9a re Gen. 49:6 (in the name of LXX; cf. LXX, ed. Rahlfs, *ad locum*) and Y. Megillah 1.9/71d; also *Mekhilta*: Bo, ed. Horovitz-Rabin, 50–51; *Beresheet Rabbah* 98.6, ed. Theodor-Albeck, 1256 and n. 6 thereon.

50. *Commentary on the Torah*, 1:192.

51. Ibid.

52. B. Sanhedrin 56b.

53. *Responsa Rema*, ed. Ziv (Jerusalem, 1970), 45–46 (no. 10).

54. Ibid.

55. *Hilkhot Melakhim*, 9.1. For the origin of the phrase, see Hullin 90b, where it is contrasted with *da'at Torah*.

56. See *Sefer Ha-Mitsvot*, pos. no. 1 and neg. no. 1; *Moreh Nevukhim*, 2.33 re B. Makkot 23b.

57. *Hilkhot Melakhim*, 8.11. For a full discussion of this text, see Novak, *The Image of the Non-Jew in Judaism*, 276ff.

58. See *Hilkhot Teshuvah*, 8.3ff.

59. Novak, *The Image of the Non-Jew in Judaism*, 280ff.

60. See *Sefer Ha-Mitsvot*, pos. nos. 3, 9; *Teshuvot Ha-Rambam*, 3 vols., ed. Blau (Jerusalem, 1960), 1:282–285 (nos. 148–149), 2:726 (no. 148); also David Novak, *Jewish Christian Dialogue: A Jewish Justification* (New York, 1989), chap. 3.

61. *Moreh Nevukhim*, 3.27. See ibid., 2.40.

62. See, e.g., *Commentary on the Torah*: Lev. 26:11; also D. Berger, "Miracles and the Natural Order" in *Rabbi Moses Nahmanides (Ramban): Explorations in His Religious and Literary Virtuosity*, ed. I. Twersky (Cambridge, Mass., 1983), 107ff.

63. *Commentary on the Torah*: Gen. 6:13, ed. Chavel, 2:52. See also ibid.: Gen. 6:2.

64. *Hilkhot Rotseah*, 4.9.

65. See *Shemonah Peraqim*, chap. 6.

66. This can be seen in Nahmanides' refusal to count belief in God as one of the 613 commandments of the Written Torah, even the first in the series, as did Maimonides. See note on Maimonides, *Sefer Ha-Mitsvot*, pos. no. 1, and *Commentary on the Torah*: Exod. 20:2; also Novak, *The Theology of Nahmanides* (forthcoming). For Nahmanides, revelation itself is the only real "proof" of God's existence. For Maimonides, on the other hand, God's existence can be inferred from the existence and/or order of the universe. See *Moreh Nevukhim*, 2, intro. ff.

67. See *Notes on Maimonides' Sefer Ha-Mitsvot*: Addenda, pos. no. 4; *Commentary on the Torah*: Num. 33:53 (cf. Rashi, *ad locum*).

68. E.g., see *Commentary on the Torah*: Deut. 6:10 re Hullin 17a; Novak, *The Theology of Nahmanides*, chap. 6 (forthcoming). Cf. Maimonides, *Hilkhot Melakhim*, 8.1 and note of Radbaz, *ad locum*.

69. *Hilkhot Melakhim*, 4.10.

70. *Hilkhot Sanhedrin*, 24.10. Re moral constraint of judicial authority, see B. Baba Batra 12a and Tos., s.v. "metsar"; 100a and Meiri, *Bet Ha-Behirah*: Baba Batra, ed. Menat (Jerusalem, 1971), 321; R. Solomon ibn Adret, *Responsa Rashba* (Vilna, 1884), 5, no. 178. Cf. B. Yevamot 89b re Ez. 10:8.

71. B. Yevamot 39b re T. Yevamot 6.9; see Y. Yevamot 1.1/2d.

72. See Maimonides, *Hilkhot Yibum Ve-Halitsah*, 1.2. Cf. B. Yevamot 39b, Tos., s.v. "Amar Rav"; *Rabbenu Asher* (Rosh): Yevamot, chap. 4, no. 17.

73. See, e.g., M. Sotah 9.9, T. Sotah 14.1 and B. Sotah 47b re Num. 5:31 and Hos. 4:14; B. Kiddushin 12b re Deut. 24:1 (see Tos., s.v. "mishum"; *Sifre*: Devarim, no. 268; Y. Yevamot 5.2/6d; B. Ketubot 8b); B. Baba Kama 8a re Deut. 24:11; B. Baba Metsia 47b and parallels, B. Eruvin 81b (and Rashi, s.v. "devar Torah") re Lev. 27:19 (see B. Shabbat 128a, Tos., s.v. "ve-natan"); also M. Berakhot 2.5 and *Tur*: Orah Hayyim, 70.

74. See e.g., B. Baba Kama 38a and Novak, *The Image of the Non-Jew in Judaism*, 60ff.; B. Baba Kama 113a–b; Y. Baba Metsia 2.5/8c; Maimonides, *Hilkhot Gezelah V'Avedah*, 11.3 and Karo, *Kesef Mishneh, ad locum*; R. Moses Isserles, *Rema* on *Shulhan Arukh*: Orah Hayyim, 334.26 and I. Jakobovits, "A Modern Blood-Libel— L'Affaire Shahak," *Tradition* 8 (1966):58–65.

75. See *Sifre*: Devarim, no. 199, ed. Finkelstein, 237 (and note, *ad locum*) in the very context of the obligation of "and you shall offer peace terms to her" (Deut. 20:10).

76. B. Gittin 56a. This text is invoked by Dr. Mordecai Breuer in his "Notes on the Issue of Returning the Territories of the Land of Israel and the Saving of Human Life" (Heb.) published in a pamphlet, *Af She-'Al: Mitsvah min Ha-Torah?* by the religious peace movement in Israel, Oz Ve-Shalom (Jerusalem, 1978), 15–16. In other words, one can see the action of Rabban Yohanan ben Zakkai as being normative. For historical analysis of this crucial episode in the life and career of Rabban Yohanan ben Zakkai, see J. Neusner, *A Life of Yohanan ben Zakkai*, 2d rev. ed. (Leiden, 1970), 145ff. Along the lines of rabbinic personal precedent being normative, see, e.g., B. Mo'ed Qatan 27b.

77. For the original meaning of this term, see Hullin 90b.

10

Economics and Justice:
A Jewish Example

Economics: Production, Distribution, Rectification

When one speaks of economics and justice, three distinct areas should be delineated at the outset: (1) the just economics of production; (2) the just economics of distribution; (3) the just economics of rectification.[1] This delineation, however, should not be taken as final in any sense; rather, it should be only the identification of three closely connected spheres of the moral ordering of one overall activity essential for human society. None of these respective spheres can be adequately understood without close consideration of its relation to the others.

Society's distribution of the things necessary for the bodily needs of its members cannot be conducted on the basis of a strictly arithmetic equality and still be considered just by any rational criterion. Thus if society has, let us say for purposes of simple illustration, one hundred members, the things possessed by that society cannot be justly divided into one hundred equal parts. Such a literal egalitarian distribution corresponds neither to need nor to desert. At the level of the distribution of food, to take the most elementary example, this type of distribution would undersatisfy a farm worker, giving him too little for his bodily needs, and it would oversatisfy a child, giving her too much for her bodily needs. Such egalitarian distribution would amount to a quick liquidation of that society's things, a process appropriate only when a business closes, where there is no real concern for the actual needs of the present, much less any projection toward the future.

Such arithmetic equality is appropriate only in the sphere of rectification, namely, the literal restoration of private property misappropriated in one way or another. Here a person's claim on a portion of society's things is based on past distribution alone. The question of present need (or desert) is irrelevant because rectification is the *re*distribution of things by the criterion of the *status quo ante*. Rectification, unlike distribution, is concerned only with things as possessions, what one already has or should have. It follows from this that societies that do not permit their members the private possession of at least some things cannot practice true rectifying justice.[2]

At the level of present need, the mode of distribution must be proportional if the distribution is to be just and accomplish its intended purpose. To return to our example of the distribution of food, a farm worker requiring twenty parts of the food supply of one hundred parts *in relation* to his need for those twenty parts is equal to a child requiring five parts of the food supply *in relation* to her need for those five parts $(A : C = B : D)$. The equality lies in the relation, not in any of the entities so related.[3]

Nevertheless, if the respective needs of the members of a society were the only criterion of distribution, such a distribution would still amount to a liquidation of that society's things. That liquidation would just be a little slower than the one mentioned above. For the present satisfaction of the needs of the members of a society in no way provides for the future replenishment of the things now distributed proportionally. Distribution according to need alone could be sustained into the future only if the source of necessary things were infinite and always at hand. If this were true, then there would be no requirement to distinguish between the needs of someone who produces more of society's things and someone who produces less. As individuals, both might exert the same amount of energy and have the same needs. But because a society must be concerned with continuing into the future, and because the source of necessary things is finite and usually not at hand, criteria of distribution are also based on desert. Those who produce more of what is needed by the members of society should be given more than those who produce less. These rewards, even more than being recompense for past productivity, are incentives for future productivity. It seems that anyone who does not at least partially correlate the economics of distribution and the economics of production is operating under an illusion of infinite supply and immediate availability. Such an illusion is often the indulgence of those who have never had to work for a living.

Just distribution, in any society, seems to require a balance between need, on the one hand, and desert on the other. Distribution based on need alone, in effect, leads to the eventual liquidation of the things necessary for human life, with no real thought of how they are to be replenished. Abjuring any division of labor, it is too inclusive to be adequate for the social need for structure and continuity. Conversely, distribution based on desert alone is too exclusive. It eliminates any just claim on society for necessary things on the part of those who are not productive, those who cannot supply anything that the members of society need. The needs of these people, if one strictly follows the logic of distribution by desert alone, can be met only by the subjective largesse of the more productive members of society. However, such largesse is not based on any objective social norms and is, therefore, not bound by any criteria of justice.

Such a narrow criterion of justice would, indeed, destroy what most humans consider the most basic social reality: the family. Even though the production of material necessities is an important part of family life, it is surely not its primary activity. The family is much more than an economic unit. Rather, the primary family activity is the most intimate interpersonal contact possible. By transcending, but not eliminating, issues of productivity, family life essentially includes members who are not productive by any measurable standard: the very young, the very old, the infirm, the handicapped — even the unborn. Their needs far outstrip their economic deserts. Because all of us are never totally assured of our own productivity, we desire family life, so it seems, because the family is where we are accepted for what we are rather than for what we make. Society, in any fully human sense, must be a balancing between the needs of the hearth and the deserts of the marketplace, between being and making.[4]

Biblical Economics

A theologian rooted in the Hebrew Bible will have difficulty in formulating a theory of human productivity and justice because the Hebrew Bible seems to be concerned only with the just human distribution and redistribution (rectification) of necessary things. It is God who is presented as the true and faithful producer and provider of the things we basically need, and God's production and provision of these things are presented as matters of grace, not justice. Thus the experience of the people of Israel being fed manna for forty years in the Wilderness by the grace of God alone is taken to be the paradigm of the covenant through which the Lord is still related to his people.

> And he afflicted you and made you hungry and fed the manna, which you had not known and your fathers had not known, so as to let you know that humans [ha'adam] do not live by bread alone, but rather on everything that proceeds out of the mouth of the Lord do humans live. (Deuteronomy 8:3)

Moreover, shortly thereafter humans are warned about taking pride in their productive accomplishments, all wealth coming from God for his own covenantal purposes.

> And if you say: "My strength and the power of my hand have produced all this wealth [hayil] for me," then you shall remember the Lord your God, that it is he who gives you strength to produce wealth in order to uphold his covenant. (Deuteronomy 8:17–18)

To be sure, this does not mean that humans do not have to produce anything for themselves and that God simply supplies their needs without any effort on their part. Even in the Garden of Eden, the first humans were required to "work" (*l'ovdah*) the garden from which they were to eat (Genesis 2:15).[5] In the verse from Deuteronomy quoted above, *bread* is the prime example of that which humans can eat only "by the sweat of your brow" (Genesis 3:19). The fact that humans do not live by bread *alone* does not mean that they can live without it either. Nevertheless, the Lord is seen to be like a loving father whose assignment of activities to his children is not meant to make himself indispensable but, rather, to enable them to participate in his overall care of the family, living together upon the ancestral estate. Making bread is one such necessary activity within that overall context. Living "by bread alone" is when humans think their productive powers are fully sufficient for their needs, bodily let alone spiritual.[6]

The covenant between God and his people involves a set of responsibilities on the part of the people chosen by God to participate in it upon the land he has given them to be their home. These responsibilities can be seen in the following Biblical passage:

> . . . when you come to the land which I give you, the land shall rest as a Sabbath for the Lord. Six years you shall plant your field . . . and you shall gather in its produce. And in the seventh year it shall be a complete Sabbath for the land, . . . your field you shall not plant. . . . The Sabbath of the land shall be for you [plural]: for your [singular] food and for that of . . . your hirelings and tenants. . . . (Leviticus 25:2–4, 6)

The prime responsibility, of course, is *to* God: the land is his and the people are there only as "sojourners and tenants along with Me" (*immadi*, Leviticus 25:23). Hence, they can never regard the land or its produce as their possession in any final sense.

The prime responsibility includes three subresponsibilities: responsibility *for* the land; responsibility *with* one another; and responsibility *toward* one's own future. The responsibility *for* the land is to allow it to refresh itself every seventh year, to allow it a measure of freedom *from* human control in the same sense that one's servant is never truly one's "slave" because he or she must be allowed the freedom of Sabbath rest as much as is allowed to his or her "master" (Exodus 20:10).[7] As in Eden, the land is to be both "worked and kept" (*le-shomrah*, Genesis 2:15). The human guardians are prior in God's concern to the land itself. They are certainly not equals. But that priority does not entail any real human lordship.[8]

The responsibility *with* one another means that the produce of the land is to be shared. All are to share the land's produce during not only the seventh year but even before the seventh year; neighbors are seen as participants in the same family-type community in which the strong help the weak for the sake of the well-being of the whole. "And when your brother becomes impoverished and his means decrease when he is with you, you shall strengthen him as a sojourner and a tenant; and your brother shall live with you" (*imakh*, Leviticus 25:35). The reason given for all of this mutual help is covenantal.

"For the children of Israel are servants of mine; my servants they are whom I took out of the land of Egypt; I am the Lord your God" (Leviticus 25:55).[9]

Only at the level of responsibility *toward* one's own future is there any indication of an imperative to be productive. Even here, though, the imperative is not direct but only by implication. Thus when the promise of God's providing during the fallow seventh year is presented, it is presented as a divine assurance in the face of the understandable human anxiety: "What will we eat during the seventh year; indeed, we will not be planting or harvesting our produce" (*tevu'atenu*, Leviticus 25:20). The implication here is that during the other six years of this cycle we should be planting and harvesting, and that the results of this labor will be *ours*. This is implied in the same sense that the Israelite is not only commanded to cease from his or her labor on the seventh day but therewith commanded to "do all your labor" on the other six days (Exodus 20:9).[10] The projection of one's individual efforts toward one's own private future wealth is not toward an unlimited future, though, as in the case of modern capitalism, or toward an unlimited collective future as in the case of modern socialism, but toward a future limited by a seven-year cycle. In the case of the possession of land outside one's own ancestral portion, that cycle is extended sevenfold—to the forty-nine-year cycle of the Jubilee (Leviticus 25:8–13).

The maldistribution of wealth—some getting too much and others too little—is considered to be an intolerable imbalance in the covenantal reality. It requires rectification. Rectification is a matter calling for both divine grace and human justice. Those who suffer from maldistribution of the material necessities of life are encouraged to cry unto the Lord, who assures them that "I shall hear because I am gracious" (Exodus 22:26). After all, God is the ultimate source of all the things humans (and the rest of creation) need (Psalms 104:13–15). Nevertheless, the more fortunate members of the community are not to stand idly by while their less fortunate brethren simply wait for God's mercy. They themselves are required to be the immediate providers of those material needs, and they are subject to severe divine punishment if they do not act justly with those in need of them (Exodus 22:22–23).

The preferred way of providing this just, intercovenantal aid seems to be the lending of necessities, or money for necessities, by the more fortunate to the less fortunate members of the community (Exodus 22:24–26; Leviticus 25:35–37; Deuteronomy 15:7–10). A loan, by definition, is given in order subsequently to be repaid. Maimonides, in his comprehensive treatment of the entire biblical and rabbinic system of aid for the less fortunate members of the community, eloquently emphasizes that the purpose of all such aid is to create conditions whereby the recipient will "not have to ask other human beings for aid."[11]

The wider implications of the primacy of the loan can best be seen when contrasted with two other means for the redistribution of wealth: charity and state welfare. The most obvious alternative to the loan is simple charity: giving necessities or money for necessities with no strings attached—a gift pure and simple. In fact, such magnanimousness seems to be an act of true *imitatio*

Dei—imitation of God, whose grace cannot, of course, ever be repaid by its recipients. However, such an analogy is faulty in terms of the very logic of the covenant, for God is our superior, whereas we are all supposed to be essentially equal *before* him. The maldistribution of wealth, whatever the cause might be, is a threat to the covenant because it entails too great a disparity between the rich and the poor members of the community. The disparity is ineffectively relieved by human charity inasmuch as the recipients of that charity thereby become the dependents of those giving it to them. And even though their bodily needs might be temporarily satisfied by the charity they have received, the subsequent result more often than not is that they become more passive, thereby losing as much if not more of their covenantal dignity through their being the objects of charity than through their being the subjects of poverty. This does not mean that there are not times when charity is mandated; however, it is not meant to be the primary means for the proper redistribution of wealth in the context of the covenant.[12]

The second alternative to the loan is one with which we moderns are quite familiar. The state bypasses the interpersonal mutuality of the loan and simply redistributes wealth from a centralized base: state welfare. Why depend on the unpredictable goodwill required for loans when redistribution of wealth can be programmed by the state? Here an example from the career of Joseph is illuminating. It will be recalled that after the seven years of plenty, predicted by Pharaoh's dreams, which Joseph so astutely interpreted, the Egyptian people do not have enough food stored up to sustain themselves during the next seven years of famine. In desperation they beg Joseph, as the Pharaoh's prime minister: "Buy us and our land with food, and we and our land will be Pharaoh's slaves" (Genesis 47:19). Now in this act of mass surrender one can see a process of equalization (what a modern tyranny called *Gleichshaltung*). And, after all, is not Pharaoh only the personification of the state? Hence, will not being his slaves subsequently redound to the benefit of them all?

In theory this sounds right, but in true practice "personifications" do not act, only real *persons* do. The creation of state ownership of all wealth, then, can lead only to the tyranny of the few who actually run the state over the many who now serve the state. Such a state quickly develops a bureaucracy with a life and interests of its own. Such a political/economic system is inconsistent with the covenantal sovereignty of God alone and the mutual *personal* interdependence of his people.

The fear that this would easily happen in Israel, as it indeed had happened in its neighboring societies — societies not part of the covenant with the Lord — lies at the heart of the antimonarchical argument presented repeatedly in the Bible. Thus when warning the people of Israel of the results of their unqualified desire for a strong centralized monarchy, the prophet Samuel emphasizes:

> This will be the way of the king [*mishpat ha-melekh*] who will rule over you:
> He will take your sons and use them for his own cavalry. . . . [H]e will take
> your best fields and vineyards and olive groves and give them to his servants.
> . . . [A]nd you will be his servants.[13] (I Samuel 8:11, 14, 17)

Note that the prophet says that wealth will be redistributed, but not at all equally. Rather, those who prove to be more useful to the power of the state will be more greatly rewarded irrespective of the true needs of all the people.[14] Some servants will get much more than others.

From all of this we see that the just redistribution of wealth, that which is most integral to the principles of the covenant, is best accomplished by an economic atmosphere in which the medium of redistribution is the loan. This is in contrast to an atmosphere of charity, which exacerbates the class divisions between the rich and the poor. And this is in contrast to an atmosphere of centralized state redistribution of wealth, a system that quickly makes the state and its operators ends in themselves, creating a new type of inequality, one even more difficult to dislodge because it is backed by political tyranny along with its inevitable military might.[15]

The Sabbatical Year and the Cancellation of Loans

The Sabbatical Year was prescribed to be a time when the people of Israel were to refrain from making claims on the land of Israel. The land was to lie fallow. And it was a time when they were to refrain from making claims on one another. All loans during that year were to be canceled. Moreover, anticipation of the cancellation of loans during the seventh year was not allowed to be a factor that could in nay way justify not making loans altogether.

> When there will be among you one of your brothers who is needy (*evyon*) . . . do not make your heart stubborn and remove your aid. . . . Beware, lest there be something base [*beli'al*] in your heart saying: "The seventh year, the year of release is nearing." And you will become stingy with your needy brother and you will not give to him. Then he will call unto the Lord about you and you will be guilty. . . . For those in need will not totally cease from the midst of the land. . . .[16] (Deuteronomy 15:7–9, 11)

What we see from this is that the more fortunate members of the covenanted community must always be aware of the possibility that their fulfillment of the commandment to lend material necessities or money for them to their less fortunate brethren could, in effect, turn out to be the fulfillment of an obligation to give them charity per se.

It is plausible to assume that the normal situation at that time, with which the biblical legislation is concerned, was as follows: Those borrowing from others were likely to be people whose harvests from their own land had been too meager to provide them and their families with the bare necessities of life. Borrowing from a more fortunate neighbor probably meant taking a loan until the next harvest when, it was hoped, the produce would be sufficient to provide the material things needed by the borrower and enough of a surplus to repay the debt, or at least part of the debt, the remainder to be repaid from the surplus of the next harvest or harvests. However, if this could not be done, and the borrower had already used up any reserve upon which to draw (like the hapless people of Egypt during the time of Joseph), then by the time of the Sabbatical Year, when there would be no harvest for anyone, the only alternative to cancellation of the debt would be for the poor brother to indenture himself to the rich one.[17] Here, it seems, the overall need for covenantal mutuality during the Sabbatical year (like the Sabbath, upon which it was explicitly modeled) took precedence over the exercise of private property privileges.

Apparently this system worked on the whole until the time of Hillel the Elder, who led the Jewish people in Palestine during the latter part of the first century B.C.E. During that time the Mishnah specifically mentions that this great and influential sage invented a legal fiction called *prosbul*, designed to enable the repayment of loans during the Sabbatical Year without literal violation of the scriptural law. Without this measure the system of the rich lending to the poor was in danger of coming to a halt.[18]

The Mishnah describes *prosbul* as consisting of the following formula uttered by a lender before a court and then written down and attested in a formal legal document afterward: "I herewith turn myself over to you judges X and Y in such and such a place, that any debt owed me I may collect at any time I want."[19] In other words, the legal fiction here is that a political institution, the court, is seen as being exempt from the personal commandment to cancel debts during the Sabbatical Year. The political institution has the power to reassign property as it sees fit, or, as in the case of *prosbul*, to reassign in its own name the power to a lender to demand repayment of a loan from a borrower even during the Sabbatical Year. Of course, some later Rabbis were concerned with what seemed to be a radical departure from the spirit of the law by a forced interpretation of its letter. One of them, the third-century Babylonian sage and jurist Samuel of Nehardea, proclaimed that if he had the power, he would remove this institution altogether. He saw it as a means that gave too much power to the human court. He termed it "the arrogance [*ulbana*] of the judges."[20] Nevertheless, despite such protest, the Talmud makes it quite clear that the dispensation of *prosbul* was too deeply embedded in the Jewish legal system and the economic life of the Jewish community to be repealed.[21]

The Mishnah designates *prosbul* as one of the enactments (*taqqanot*) of Hillel designed for "the repair of the world" (*tiqqun ha'olam*), which is a rabbinic concept similar to that of *bonum commune*, namely, where the good of society as a whole requires the adjustment of private legal rights.[22]

The historical question, of course, is why did the people during the time of Hillel refrain from lending because of the imminent approach of the Sabbatical Year? Why was the possibility about which the Torah had long before warned realized only in the time of Hillel?

In the most comprehensive critical monograph written to date on the *prosbul*, the Hungarian Jewish scholar Ludwig Blau argued over sixty years ago that the *prosbul* was necessary when the Jewish people in Palestine had ceased being primarily an agricultural community and had become, in response to new economic circumstances in the larger world around them, a community of craftsmen and traders. Hence, there was such a fundamental shift in the economic *Sitz im Leben* that only a legal fiction like *prosbul* could save even the letter of the law of the Sabbatical Year cancellation of debts. Blau saw this as a basic conflict between religious morality and economic reality, one calling for a compromise of sorts.[23]

The fundamental shift was that loans were now no longer a response to *past* misfortune, closely akin to charity as we have seen. Rather, in the new commercial economic climate, loans were now for the sake of *future* gain; they were now a means of investment. Loans were extended to enable a craftsman or trader to purchase equipment or stock for the sake of future profit. Furthermore, it seems that loans were now more important and more prevalent than they had been theretofore. In the past, with the exception of years of unusual drought or other natural calamity, borrowers were more probably the unfortunate few whose agricultural harvest had been an exception to a general situation of sufficiency, if not plenty. Thus a situation in which "you will not have to borrow" (Deuteronomy 28:12) was considered a blessing; and in which you have to borrow, a curse (v. 44). In the more commercial climate, however, loans would now become more the rule than the exception. Furthermore, because commerce was not limited by the seven-year cycle of the Sabbatical Year system, and because commercial profit is far less predictable than annual harvest, it seems that loans had also become more long term than they had been in the past.

Earlier than Blau, the nineteenth-century Austrian Jewish scholar Isaac Hirsch Weiss had pointed out the moral dilemma that Hillel faced and ultimately resolved by his *prosbul* enactment. The dilemma was not so much the conflict between old religious law and new economic opportunities but, rather, between two norms of religious law itself. On the one hand, there was the more specific norm requiring cancellation of loans during the Sabbatical Year. On the other hand, there was the more general norm mandating (but not humanly forcing) the rich to lend to the poor. In the scriptural context in which these two norms are juxtaposed and related to each other, it is clear that the Sabbatical Year is the primary concern and lending to the poor the secondary concern. The reason for this can best be explained by the fact that the Sabbatical Year was the definite reality for all, whereas the need for loans was the reality for only the poverty-stricken few. During the period of Hillel, however, there seems to have been a fundamental economic shift so that the need for loans became more usual. Also, as we shall soon see, the Sabbatical Year itself was not the same institution during the period of the First Temple (before 586 B.C.E.) that it was during the period of the Second Temple. Thus, for Weiss, the moral requirement of the covenant was to strengthen the institution of lending so that the poor would be able to survive in the new commercial economy. Hence, lending now became primary and the specifics of the Sabbatical Year secondary.[24] In fact, long after Hillel's enactment had been in force, a Babylonian sage offered a philologically forced but conceptually insightful etymology of the word *prosbul*. (Although the word is no doubt originally Greek – indeed, Blau showed its origin in a Hellenistic legal institution – the etymology supplied in the Babylonian Talmud is Aramaic, the *lingua franca* of the Babylonian Jews.) *Prosbul* was interpreted as being that which is beneficial to both rich and poor. The rich do not lose their money through loans never repaid; the poor do not find that the opportunity to borrow money is "closed in their faces."[25]

The late German and then Israeli Jewish scholar Chanoch Albeck and the American Jewish scholar David Weiss Halivni have argued that although *prosbul* was an innovation, it was not without precedent in rabbinic jurisprudence that preceded Hillel.[26] Looking at these precedents enables us better to see more specifically how an ethic of production/distribution emerged out of the reinterpretation of older sources concerned primarily with an ethic of rectification/distribution.

The Sabbatical Year and the Jubilee

From the primary biblical sources dealing with the institution of the Sabbatical Year, we see that the system of letting the land lie fallow and the cancellation of loans every seven years is part of a larger economic system, that of the Jubilee. The Jubilee system is based on the following premise: Every native-born Israelite has an ancestral portion of land within the patrimony of his own particular tribe, an inviolable allotment from the time of the conquest of Canaan under Joshua. If one needs money more than the ancestral portion, one is allowed to lease the portion, the lease price being prorated according to number of years before the Jubilee Year, which comes every fiftieth year. During the Jubilee Year, "You shall declare liberty [*deror*] in the land to all its inhabitants; it shall be a jubilee for you, then a man shall return to his ancestral portion [*ahuzato*], then shall you return, each man, to his family" (Leviticus 25:10).[27]

From this we see that all wealth is ultimately inherited landed wealth. Furthermore, landed wealth is part of a complete system whereby the entire land of Israel is under the total control of all twelve original tribes of Israel. The system is an economically closed one. The people of Israel are seen as being totally dependent on God's grace and the justice they are to practice with one another among themselves. If, on the other hand, the entire land of Israel is not under the control of all twelve original tribes of Israel, the Rabbis recognized that the Jubilee system could not possibly work. They saw its very operation as being legally contingent on the reality of the closed system mentioned above. Historically, this meant for them that the Jubilee system had ceased during the time before the destruction of the First Temple in 586 B.C.E., when the ten northern tribes went into Assyrian exile, never again to return to their ancestral land.[28] Thus with the absence of the real assurance that one would return to one's ancestral portion of the land within one's lifetime, or certainly one's children during their lifetimes, and with the Jewish control of the entire land of Israel being now partial at best, there was no longer the ancient assurance that made the whole economy subordinate to landed patrimony. One no longer had the ancient assurance that one would get back within a predictable time span what had been temporarily lost. The economic system under which the Jewish people were now living in postexilic Palestine and the Diaspora was not under their control. They were now subject to larger political forces and to the larger economic forces of an international market oblivious to the laws of the Jews. Economic survival and productive growth called for reinterpretation of the revealed law. But, as we have seen, economic survival and productivity are not good in and of themselves. They are good only because without them the differences between the haves and the have nots become exacerbated and the social mutuality required by the covenant is severely curtailed.

Rabbinic interpretation also saw the biblically mandated system of the Sabbatical-Year cancellation of loans as being contingent on the operation of the Jubilee.[29] However, even though there was no longer a strictly biblical requirement for either institution, the Rabbis, by their own biblically warranted authority, relegislated the law of the Sabbatical-Year release as "a memorial of the Sabbatical Year," that it not be totally forgotten in practice.[30] This is not the only such example of rabbinic relegislation of a biblical institution no longer required by scriptural law itself.[31] Nevertheless, even though such practices might appear the same, whether based on biblical revelation or rabbinic legislation, their structure was now essentially changed. The essential change concerns the teleology of the legal institution.

Based on the theological principle "My thoughts are not your thoughts" (Isaiah 55:8), it was always assumed that whatever reasons for God's commandments could be inferred from the formulae of their promulgation, the basic fact that they are God's revealed will always takes precedence.[32] Thus even if one could infer the reason/*telos* of a commandment, and even if one could judge that the commandment no longer served its original purpose, such a judgment was deemed invalid and the commandment could not be repealed based on such a judgment.[33] The assumption is that God's revealed will has absolute authority because it is wholly sufficient. Human reasoning, conversely, has only relative authority because it is never wholly sufficient. Human reason is never foundational but only confirmational at best when interpreting divine law. Hearing God's voice takes precedence over reading God's mind, even when that seems possible.

With rabbinic legislation, however, the assumption is that humans can fully understand why other humans have legislated as they have.[34] To be sure, it was not at all easy for later Rabbis to repeal the legislation of earlier Rabbis, even when the original reason for the original legislation called for such repeal.[35] Rabbinic law is based on precedent, but precedent never has the absolute authority of revelation. Even without formal repeal per se, later rabbinic reinterpretation of earlier rabbinic legislation could be far more explicitly radical than reinterpretation of any biblical norm.

The relegislation of the norms of the Sabbatical Year by the Rabbis (probably going back to the time of Ezra and the constitution of the Second Jewish Commonwealth) seems to have been for the sake of the covenantal mutuality the original biblical revelation was thought to have intended.[36] The difference between the original biblical revelation and the subsequently reconstituted human institution is, however, as follows: Whereas in the case of the former essential intent is only inferred, in the case of the latter essential intent is now assumed. Whereas in the case of the former the inference of essential intent could have only a hermeneutical function, one that at best could influence only certain details of practical application, in the case of the latter the assumption of essential intent directly determines the full range of practical application or nonapplication.[37] In our case of the Sabbatical Year, a medieval gloss on the Talmud questions why the Rabbis did not reconstitute the scriptural institution of the Jubilee as they had reconstituted the scriptural institution of the Sabbatical Year. The answer given is that this would not be in the best economic interests of the community inasmuch as the land would have to lie fallow for two consecutive years: the forty-ninth year, the Sabbatical Year and the fiftieth year, the Jubilee Year.[38] Here we clearly see that an economic concern is assumed to have been essentially part of the original rabbinic intent in reconstructing the Sabbatical Year and, similarly, not reconstructing the Jubilee Year. But even though concern for Jewish economic interests was seen as being entailed by some biblical law, one could not approach that law and so radically transform it, or even suggest that others had so radically transformed it, based on such an inference.[39]

We have seen how the recognition that God himself is no longer the immediate provider of Jewish economic well-being, as he had been when all twelve tribes of Israel were in full domicile in the land of Israel, led to a greater emphasis on human means of productivity. However, it should also be noted that this transition was not taken to be a cause for celebration. Lest we read modern notions of historical progress into this whole transition, let it be emphasized that this whole transition was seen to be the result of divinely mandated exile as the punishment for sins committed when the people of Israel were in full domicile upon the land of Israel (Leviticus 26:33–34). The great hope for full redemption is that God will fully restore Israel to its pristine state of dependence upon his direct providence in its promised land.[40]

The current situation of greater self-reliance, including greater economic self-reliance, cannot be taken as indicating what Adam Smith called "an invisible hand [promoting] an end which was no part of his [the human economic actor's] intention."[41] Rather, it indicates the absence of the invisible divine hand, at least as far as we can experience it now as we could before the exile. Nevertheless, it also means that this sad fact of our temporary self-reliance must be accepted as our historical reality and that any attempt to ignore our current need for economic productivity can be regarded only as pseudomessianic.[42] Such pseudomessianism can be seen in the attempts to model an ethics of economic distribution primarily upon rectifying justice, that is, to see economic justice as primarily recompense for past injustices or misfortunes.

Direct Precedents of *Prosbul*

The changed economic situation that led Hillel to institute the legal fiction of *prosbul* can also be seen as the reason for two earlier norms pertaining to the cancellation of loans during the Sabbatical Year.

The Mishnah teaches that "whoever lends money for which a deposit has been taken, and whoever turns his notes over to the court: these debts are not subject to the cancellation of the Sabbatical Year."[43] The Talmud explains this exception on the basis of the wording of the biblical text: "What will be [*asher yihyeh*] for you with your brother" (Deuteronomy 15:3), which implies that the law of release does not pertain to "something of your brother's already under your hand."[44] This can be understood if one is aware of the diminished economic importance of land and the increased economic importance of moveable things.[45] In a situation where the land is the chief source of livelihood, the poor who would need loans in the event of a bad harvest would also be the people whose few possessions are directly needed for their bare subsistence. Their future would be seen in the immediate productivity of the land, not in the future value of things apart from the land.[46] It seems that this is why biblical law does not permit the lender to hold on extended deposit any collateral that the poor could possibly offer for a loan. Any such extended deposit would only exacerbate, not alleviate, their poverty (Exodus 22:25–26; Deuteronomy 24:12–13).[47]

It seems that in a more commercial economy, moveable things not only would be the immediate life necessities of food, shelter, and clothing but would be more and more articles used in extended trade and investment. Therefore, the very fact that the Mishnah sees the deposit as being something that the lender keeps throughout the Sabbatical Year indicates that such things are not life necessities in any immediate sense, that the borrower can surely live without them. In other words, the loan is not given because the borrower has only the shirt on his back, so to speak. Rather, the loan is now more probably for the sake of investment into the future, a risk taken by both lender and borrower based on the hope that the future will yield a better income than the present. In this case, the need for the Sabbatical-Year release from indebtedness, which in the agricultural context would be akin to charity for the sake of literal livelihood, would no longer be required. Redistribution determined by considerations of future productivity is fundamentally different from redistribution as a form of rectification of past misfortune. A deposit in the former case is, then, fundamentally different from a deposit in the latter case.

As for the ruling that one who turned his notes over to the court is not subject to the cancellation of debts by the Sabbatical Year, the Talmud interprets the scriptural words "and what will be for you with your brother [*et ahikha*] shall you release your hand" (Deuteronomy 15:3) to preclude someone who already delegated the power to collect his debts to a public institution, the court, as opposed to directly dealing with a private party, "your [singular] brother."[48] Some rabbinic sources see this ruling as being the legal basis for Hillel's enactment of *prosbul*.[49] So we might speculate upon this connection and ask how this ruling paved the way for *prosbul*.

It seems that the ruling about the lender personally turning his notes over to the court for collection during the Sabbatical Year refers to a provision for individual dispensation from a general legal requirement. We might envision this in the following scenario: A lent B money before the Sabbatical Year. According to biblical law, B's debt to A is cancelled if he could not pay it before the Sabbatical Year. The assumption here seems to be that B's poverty, which had caused him to borrow from A in the first place, had not been alleviated by the time the Sabbatical Year came around. Hence, what began as a loan from A should now be a form of charity for one *in extremis*. However, what if the tables were turned, that is, B's poverty had indeed been alleviated by the time the Sabbatical Year came around, but A now found himself in similarly desperate circumstances? Rather than having A become the direct recipient of charity, it seems that the law made a provision for him to plead hardship to the court and have the judges, in effect, dispense him from the biblical requirement to cancel all debts owed him during the Sabbatical Year.

Prosbul built upon this by eliminating the requirement that the lender make a personal request of the court to collect each of his debts for him. What *prosbul* enabled the lender to do — and here we see quite clearly the *fictio juris* involved — is to act *as if* his debts had *already* been collected by the court and he simply completed the process of collection.[50] In other words, he no longer had to turn his notes over to the court personally but only prepare a standardized statement in advance that, in effect, gave him blanket authority to collect the debts himself during the Sabbatical Year. The essential difference between the earlier individualized procedure and the later standardized procedure is the requirement for the lender to make a personal appearance before the court, in the case of the former, and specify the content of each of his notes. It seems that such a personal appearance with its specific request probably entailed a personal plea of poverty in order to facilitate what was actually a dispensation from a general legal requirement. But as we have also seen, loans in a commercial context are fundamentally different from loans in an agricultural context. In the new commercial situation, loans are for the sake of investment into the future, not for the sake of rectifying past misfortune. The element of poverty no longer seems to be the motivating factor in most cases. Therefore, the requirement that one make a personal appearance before the court and plead poverty in order to be able to collect debts is one that would, in effect, make liars out of the great majority of those who lent money to borrowers for commercial purposes. Furthermore, because loans became much more prevalent in the new commercial context, the old requirement that one make a personal appearance before the court would create a burdensome overload on the time and the energy of the judges. *Prosbul* facilitated the whole process of lending money by eliminating what had become needless bother for both lenders and judges.

Covenantal Interdependence

As has been emphasized throughout this chapter, the covenantal reality of mutual interdependence of the community before God constantly informed the theoretical interpretation and the practical application of the specifics of the Law, in our case under discussion, the specifics of the law of the Sabbatical Year. Concern with economic productivity became part of the covenantal reality as long as it could be justified as a means for improving the lot of the community as a whole. It is in opposition to that covenantal reality, however, when it is seen as an end in itself, thereby justifying differences between the rich and the poor, the powerful and the powerless. The legal institution of *prosbul*, and its subsequent alternatives, allowed the new productivity caused by commerce to be affirmed for the sake of the covenant. By emphasizing the covenantal necessity of human mutuality before God, Jewish tradition affirmed the value of individual incentive without the glorification of individual human selfishness, and it affirmed the value of communal restraints without the glorification of collective human power. It saw both as tentative human *modi vivendi* until the time when "the kingdom is the Lord's" (Obadiah 1:21) and the present system of checks and balances will no longer be needed. But at the present time they are needed, and any attempt to jump over the present requirements and to institute the kingdom of God by political means must be explicitly rejected as dangerous pseudomessianism.[51] Therefore, whatever current political/economic system most closely approximates the covenantal reality should have the support of those committed to Jewish tradition. All the premessianic systems of human politics and economics are flawed, but some are clearly more flawed than others. The least flawed system deserves the most support as long as one is ever cognizant of the real difference between that which "will endure forever" (Isaiah 40:8) and that which like all other human systems will surely pass away too.

NOTES

1. The delineation between distributive and rectifying justice is, of course, based on Aristotle, *Nicomachean Ethics*, 1130b30ff. However, one does not find in Aristotle, here or in the *Politics*, criteria of justice pertaining to production. Production seems to have been for slaves, hence beneath the criteria of true political justice (1134a25). Moneymaking, like slavery, was seen to be something done "under constraint" (*biaios*, 1096a5), hence lacking in the leisure needed for a life of practical, let alone intellectual, excellence. See 1171b1; also *Politics*, 1278a1, 1325a25, 1328b35ff.; *Eudemian Ethics*, 1215ᵃ 27–32; M. I. Finley, "Aristotle and Economic Analysis," in *Articles on Aristotle*

2: *Ethics and Politics*, ed. J. Barnes, M. Schofield, and P. Sorabji (New York, 1977), 148ff. See also *supra*, 136. Cf. Michael Novak, "Productivity and Social Justice," in *Will Capitalism Survive?* ed. E. W. Lefever (Washington, 1979), 34–35.

2. See Karl Marx, *The Essential Writings*, ed. and trans. F. L. Bender (New York, 1972), 86ff.

3. See Aristotle, *Nicomachean Ethics*, 1131a6.

4. See Gabriel Marcel, *Being and Having*, trans. K. Farrer (New York, 1965), 132. Max Weber argued that the separation of the workplace from the home is an important precondition for the emergence of capitalism. See *The Protestant Ethic and the Spirit of Capitalism*, trans. T. Parsons (New York, 1958), 21–22.

5. See M. Avot 1.10 and *Avot de-Rabbi Nathan*, ed. Schechter (New York, 1945), version A, chap. 11.

6. That is why before any benefit from worldly things may be enjoyed, God must first be praised to emphasize that "the earth is the Lord's" (Ps. 24:1). See Y. Berakhot 6.1/9d.

7. See Philo, *De Specialibus Legibus*, 2.62; also Josephus, *Contra Apionem*, 2.175; *Antiquities*, 16.43.

8. See *supra*, 143ff.

9. And as the Rabbis note in explaining why Scripture stigmatizes the man who voluntarily extends his indentured servitude beyond six years (Exod. 21:6): "removing from himself the yoke of God and causing the yoke of flesh and blood to rule over him." T. Baba Kama 7.5; also B. Kiddushin 22b.

10. See *Avot de-Rabbi Nathan*, version A, chap. 11; also M. Ketubot 5.5.

11. *Hilkhot Mattnot Aniyyim*, 10.7 re Lev. 25:35; see also B. Shabbat 118a.

12. Thus, for example, in fulfilling the commandment to honor one's parents, which includes caring for their bodily needs, that care is to be administered out of their *own* funds. Only if they are destitute are they to become the objects of charity like anyone else in interminable poverty. See B. Kiddushin 32a and Tos., s.v. "oru" re B. Ketubot 49b and Y. Kiddushin 1.7/61c.

13. See B. Sanhedrin 20b.

14. Re general rabbinic suspicion of those in political power, see, e.g., M. Avot 1.10, 2.3.

15. See Friedrich A. Hayek, *The Road to Serfdom* (Chicago, 1954), 140ff.

16. For discussion of the various biblical terms for poverty and their meanings, see *Vayiqra Rabbah* 34.6.

17. See *Sifra*: Behar re Lev. 25:39, ed. Weiss, 109c; Maimonides, *Hilkhot Avadim*, 1.1.

18. M. Shevi'it 10.3.

19. M. Shevi'it 10.4. See B. Gittin 36a.

20. B. Gittin 36b. For Samuel's solution to the problem of the Sabbatical Year and loans, one involving prior negotiation between borrower and lender without intervening court action, see B. Makkot 3b; also *Responsa Ha-R'osh*, ed. Venice (1552), 77.2. For earlier nonlegal approaches to the same problem, see M. Shevi'it 10.8–9.

21. B. Gittin, 36b.

22. M. Gittin 4.3. See *supra*, 000 n. 1;

23. "Prosbul im Lichte der Griechischen Papyri und der Rechtsgeschichte," in *Festschrift zum 50jährigen Bestehen der Franz-Josef-Landesrabbinerschule in Budapest*, ed. L. Blau (Budapest, 1927), 96ff. See Louis Ginzberg, "The Significance of the Halachah for Jewish History," trans. A. Hertzberg, in *On Jewish Law and Lore* (Philadelphia, 1955), 79ff.

24. *Dor Dor Ve-Dorshav*, 5 vols. (Jerusalem and Tel Aviv, n.d.), 1:163. See also Karo, *Kesef Mishneh* on Maimonides, *Hilkhot Mamrim*, 2.2; *Maharam Schiff* on B. Gittin 36a.

25. B. Gittin 36b–37a. See Blau, *Festschrift*, 112ff.

26. Albeck, *Commentary on the Mishnah*: Zera'im (Jerusalem, 1957) addenda, 383; Halivni, *Meqorot U-Mesorot*: Nashim (Tel Aviv, 1968), 539 n. 1.

27. Even long after the Jubilee had ceased to be in operation, sale of an ancestral portion of land was considered morally reprehensible. See Y. Ketubot 2.10/26d and Y. Kiddushin 1.5/60c.

28. See Arakhin 32b re Lev. 25:10.

29. B. Gittin 36a–b; Y. Gittin 4.3/45c–d. See B. Kiddushin 38b and Tos., s.v. "hashmattat kesafim."

30. B. Gittin 36b.

31. See, e.g., B. Pesahim 116b; also *Responsa Ha-Ritba*, no. 97, ed. J. Kafih (Jerusalem, 1959), 114–115.

32. See B. Berakhot 19b re Prov. 21:30; Y. Ta'anit 2.4/65d.

33. See B. Sanhedrin 21b re Deut. 17:16–17; *Bemidbar Rabbah* 19.1. See *supra*, 37f.

34. See B. Gittin 14a and parallels.

35. See M. Eduyot 1.5.

36. For the human reconstitution of the original covenant in the postexilic Second Jewish Commonwealth, see Neh. 10:1ff.; Y. Shevi'it 6.1/36^b.

37. See, e.g., B. Avodah Zarah 36b; Maimonides, *Hilkhot Mamrim*, 2.1ff.

38. B. Gittin 36b, Tos., s.v. "ve-tiqqun rabbanan." Also rabbinic sources indicate that the additional taxes imposed by the Roman occupiers of Palestine made observance of the Sabbatical Year much more difficult. See *Vayiqra Rabbah* 1.1 re Ps. 103: 20, ed. Margulies, 1:4–5.

39. See M. Nega'im 12.5 re Lev. 14:36; *Sifra*: Metzora, ed. Weiss, 73a; also T. Arakhin 4.24.

40. See Y. Berakhot 6.1/10a; B. Ketubot 111b re Ps. 72:16; *Beresheet Rabbah* 15.7 re Job 28:5, ed. Theodor-Albeck, 1:139.

41. *The Wealth of Nations*, pt. 4, chap. 2 (New York, 1937), 423.

42. See B. Yoma 69b.

43. M. Shevi'it 10.2.

44. Y. Shevi'it 10.2/39c. See T. Shevi'it 8.6 and Saul Lieberman, *Tosefta Kifshuta*: Zera'im (New York, 1955), 587.

45. See B. Shevu'ot 47b and *Rabbenu Asher* (R'osh): Gittin, 4.17. Cf. Maimonides, *Hilkhot Shemittah Ve-Yovel*, 9.14 and Karo, *Kesef Mishneh ad locum*.

46. For the legal differences between real estate (*qarqa'ot*) and moveable things (*metaltalin*), and the ancient priority of the former over the latter, see M. Kiddushin 1.5; B. Kiddushin 26a–b; I. H. Herzog, *The Main Institutions of Jewish Law*, 2d ed., 2 vols. (London and New York, 1965), 1:99ff.

47. Of course, the high political/economic standards of the covenant were frequently violated in practice. See, e.g., II Kings 4:1; Jer. 34:8ff; Amos 2:8; Job 22:6. However, such violation does not prove the thesis of Max Weber (following earlier Bible critics) that the Torah's legislation in these areas is only "utopian." Cf. *Ancient Judaism*, ed. and trans. H. H. Gerth and D. Martindale (Glencoe, Ill., 1952), 68.

48. Y. Shevi'it 10.2/39c; also, *Sifre*: Devarim, no. 113, ed. Finkelstein, 173.

49. Y. Shevi'it 10.2/39c; *Sifre*: Devarim, no. 113. See Maimonides, *Hilkhot Shemittah Ve-Yovel*, 9.15–16. The Babylonian sources, on the other hand, do not make

this connection. See B. Makkot 3b, Tos., s.v. "ha-moser." That is why the Babylonian sources have the tendency to see the *prosbul* as far more radical than the Palestinian sources do. See B. Gittin 36b re Ezra 10:8; Halivni, *op. cit.* (see *supra*, n. 26).

50. *Rabbenu Nissim Gerondi* (Ran) on *Alfasi*: Gittin, chap. 4, ed. Vilna, 18b–19a; Meiri, *Bet Ha-Behirah*: Gittin, ed. Schulsinger (Jerusalem, 1972), 155. Re the important function of legal fiction, note: "When a new juridical form arises it is joined directly on to an old and existing institution and in this way the certainty and development of the old is procured for the new. This is the notion of Fiction, which was of the greatest importance in the development of Roman Law and which has often been laughably misunderstood by moderns. . . ." Karl Friedrich von Savigny, *Vom Beruf unserer Zeit für Gesetzgebung und Rechtswissenschaft* (2d ed., 1828), 32, trans. and quoted by Lon L. Fuller, *Legal Fictions* (Stanford, 1967), 59.

51. See Maimonides, *Hilkhot Melakhim*, 11.1ff., who emphasized that even in the time of the Messiah, the Law will remain binding in all its specifics; *a fortiori* before the Messiah comes!

Endnote: With the rise of an economy increasingly dependent on extended commercial credit, beginning in the late Middle Ages, the biblical prohibition of Jews' taking interest from other Jews and paying it to them (Lev. 25:35–38; Deut. 23:20–21; M. Baba Metsia 5.1ff.) became a problem similar to that of the cancellation of debts in the Sabbatical Year in earlier times. In this case, it was becoming more attractive for Jews to do business with non-Jews, to whom the biblical prohibition of interest does not apply (B. Baba Metsia 70b). Although there were strong and wide-ranging rabbinic qualifications of the original biblical permission of paying interest to non-Jews and taking it from them because it was feared that such Jewish involvement with them would lead to assimilation (ibid., 71a), already in the twelfth century the prohibitions no longer applied. By that time, the institution of interest was seen as a matter of ordinary commerce that Jews could scarcely avoid due to their economic integration in the society at large (ibid., 70b–71a, Tos., s.v. "tashikh"; *Tur*: Yoreh De'ah, 159). Gradually, just as the rabbinic qualification of the biblical permission of taking interest from non-Jews and paying it to them was recontextualized, so was the biblical prohibition of taking interest from Jews and paying interest to them recontextualized—but being a recontextualization of a biblical law, it required a much more formally elaborate *fictio juris*.

Based upon the distinction between lending money and partnership (*shuttfut*), the Talmud permits a situation in which one partner is paid for putting up capital for another partner to invest (*isqa*—B. Baba Metsia 68b, 104b–105a). This is, of course, functionally quite similar to taking interest. This original *fictio juris* was further extended into a device called *heter isqa*, whereby the "investing partner" (*ba'al ha-ma'ot*) was, in effect, guaranteed a profit on his or her investment from the "working partner" (*ha-mit'aseq*—see Maimonides, *Hilkhot Shlukhin Ve-Shuttfin*, 6.1ff.). In a functional, if not a strictly legal, sense, of course, this is the equivalent of interest. Like *prosbul*, the *heter isqa* became a standardized procedure (*shtar isqa*) as early as the sixteenth century. For the most thorough study of this complex legal institution, see Y. Y. Blau, *Sefer Berit Yehudah*, 2d rev. ed. (Jerusalem, 1979), 624ff.

What is important to recognize is that the ultimate justification for this *fictio juris* is covenantal: "in order to provide livelihood to the members of the covenant" (*benay berit*, Blau, *Sefer Berit Yehudah*, 624 n. 1, quoting R. Joshua Falk, *Sefer Me'irat Aynayyim*: Quntres Ha-Ribbit, ext. no. 22). Accordingly, following this reasoning, when loans were for immediate personal needs rather than for commercial projects, many halakhists could see no justification for the *fictio juris* of the *heter isqa* and urged compliance with the spirit as well as the letter of the scriptural prohibition of interest (see Blau, *Sefer Berit Yehudah*, 601ff., n. 18). In these cases loans are more akin to charity and less akin to investments. Needless to say, in an environment with an evergrowing presence of commercialism, it is often quite difficult to make this distinction with full consistency.

For a classic study of the interaction of Halakhah and new economic realities, see Jacob Katz, *The "Shabbes Goy": A Study in Halakhic Flexibility*, trans. Y. Lerner (Philadelphia and New York, 1989), 3–132. For similar problems with the prohibition of interest in Christian moral theory, and solutions proposed roughly contemporary with the Jewish solutions, see John T. Noonan, *The Scholastic Analysis of Usury* (Cambridge, Mass., 1957), esp. 199ff.; B. Nelson, *The Idea of Usury*, 2d ed. (Chicago, 1969), 73ff.

11

American Jews and
the United States:
The Mission of Israel Revisited

Four Types of American Jews

An American Jew can see his or her relationship to the United States in one of four ways, and which of these four ways is assigned prime importance ultimately reveals how that Jew is related to Judaism itself.

1. Some American Jews see their relationship to the United States in essentially juridical terms—that is, they see themselves as anonymous legal persons who are subjects of the law of this democracy. Many of these Jews have served as leaders of other Americans who resist any emphasis on the interests of subgroups (what not so long ago were known as "hyphenated Americans") in public life. For them, the United States is still the "melting pot" that is supposed to create one enduring public realm, devoid of "special interests." For all such Americans, this public realm is the primary source of human values.

These Jews never think of Judaism as more than a denomination of like-minded individuals, and many of them have eliminated it from their lives altogether. Those who have not eliminated Judaism from their lives have relegated it to a very private and esoteric place. Needless to say, this means that they have at most a rather tenuous relationship with Judaism itself, which, in the words of the Talmud, does not approve of "being placed in a corner, only to be studied by whoever wants to do so."[1] And in so restricting the role of religion in their lives, they have, as the studies of Richard John Neuhaus and others make abundantly clear, also departed from the vision of this country shared by a large majority of Americans, now or ever.[2] In some significant ways these Jews have become what might be called "constitutional fundamentalists." Like religious fundamentalists (with whom many of these Jews would be horrified to find themselves in the same logical company), they read "sacred texts" (for them, the Constitution of the United States) outside the context of history—either the history of the American people or the history of the Jewish people. All of this makes their position (at least outside U.S. courtrooms) rather difficult to advocate. In a significant way, these Jews are the most doctrinaire of American secularists.[3]

2. Some American Jews see their relationship to the United States in essentially political terms—that is, they see themselves as members of a special interest group in the overall fabric of the nation's power politics. As a special interest group, Jews have a distinct political agenda of concerns: the military and economic security of the State of Israel, the emigration of Jews from countries where they are being persecuted, the elimination of restrictive quotas. Like any successful special interest group in the United States—and it has been said by friend and foe alike that the Jews might very well be *the* most successful special interest group today—Jews have had to argue that their *special* interests in fact coincide with the *general* national interest or, even better, they have argued that they actually promote the general interest. Thus, for example, the valid portrayal of the State of Israel as "the only democracy in the Middle East" not only establishes an affinity between Americans and Israelis but is presented actually as part of the even more forceful argument that Israel is the only stable and reliable ally of the United States in a most unstable region of the world.[4]

Usually, these Jews are less reluctant to remove their Judaism from their public life. They are more visibly Jewish than most of the previous group. Nevertheless, to a large extent their Jewish self-definition is determined by reaction to external threats: Arab threats to the security of the State of Israel, anti-Semitic threats to Jewish cultural and even physical survival in various countries, and the threats to Jewish opportunity in the United States by various, often more covert, types of American anti-Semitism. To a certain extent, they confirm the famous thesis of Jean-Paul Sartre that it is anti-Semitism that in fact determines who and what is a Jew.[5] Moreover, by being so externally oriented, many of these same Jews have not had sufficient concern for the internal aspects of Jewish survival, for what might be called the "cultural" aspects of Jewish life—such matters as Jewish education (especially as intensely pursued in yeshivas and day schools), the threat of intermarriage and cultural assimilation, and the deteriorating quality of Jewish family life. This "political" Judaism not only elevates a part of Judaism (and certainly not the most important part) to a level of almost total concern and thereby causes more thoughtful and learned Jews to question its ultimate Jewish authenticity, but also creates problems in dealing with a large segment of Americans— mostly Christian Americans—who do not see political affiliation and activism as the most fundamentally characterizing factor of a community. These Jews are often embarrassingly unprepared for what pro-Jewish gentiles now expect from them.

3. Some American Jews see their relationship to the United States in essentially cultural terms—that is, they see the nation as a "pluralistic" society in which Jewish cultural identity is to be maintained without a loss of political power or legal rights. For these Jews—and they are certainly not alone in this age of emphasis on ethnicity (most forcefully spearheaded by the whole "black is beautiful" phenomenon)—the United States is a loose network of ethnic and religious communities having a sort of tacit contract with the polity as a whole, namely, that the various communities will affirm the polity's political and legal primacy in return not merely for the passive tolerance but for the active encouragement of ethnic particularity.[6] Not so long ago, being "American" in the cultural sense entailed behaving like a white Anglo-Saxon Protestant (even if not actually joining the Episcopal Church); now WASPs are no longer role models but just one more ethnic group along with the rest of the immigrants and their children (and not even *primus inter pares*).

This cultural Judaism has led to an even more visible and more internally lived "Jewishness" than that of the "political" Jews. To cite a personal example, I still marvel at the ease my children feel in being practicing Jews in the United States today compared with the self-consciousness practicing Jews of my generation felt when we were their age (and there are more of "us" now than before).[7]

Nevertheless, one could see this as wanting in terms of the theory of Jewishness more Jews ascribe to than any other (even though fewer actually understand it): Zionism, for, if the Jews are essentially a cultural group, as Zionism asserts, then their chances for cultural survival and growth are far greater in a society in which they constitute the clear majority, in a land filled with their own historical associations than in a land where they are a small minority of relative newcomers. Jews who place this sort of emphasis on culture are the most vulnerable to the Zionist doctrine of *shelilat ha-golah* (the negation of the Diaspora), which asserts that Jewish culture outside Israel is inevitably doomed, especially when the Jewish state exists and is developing a Jewish culture.[8]

Furthermore, although many of these "cultural" Jews would see their culture as inextricable from their religion, their self-definition is rarely based on the classical Jewish doctrine of the covenant: the divine election of Israel and Israel's ongoing response to it. This not only makes their connection with Classical Judaism tenuous but also fails to enable them to respond to the sincere beseeching of the Americans who feel the greatest affinity with the Jewish people (including the State of Israel): Christians who have cleansed themselves of anti-Semitism, which *they* now regard as anti-Christian. These *friends* look to Jews to speak as the covenanted people of God; they ask Jews to speak the language of the Torah. When Christians asked (often demanded) that we Jews speak in a language *they* assigned us (a language rejecting our own vocabulary from intelligibility), then we were correct to suspect the Jews who were willing to respond in such terms. However, this objection hardly applies when we are now being asked by many Christians in this country to "instruct us," as Scripture puts it, "from His ways" (Micah 4:2).[9]

4. Finally, a fourth group of Jews, which has always been quite small but which has included some of the most important religious thinkers in the American Jewish community, see their relationship to the United States in essentially religious terms. Now there is a good deal of overlapping between these "religious" Jews and the "cultural" Jews, especially when "*cultural*" is not a synonym for "*antireligious*," as it has been for those who saw culture as a sufficient substitute for religion (as was the case with many advocates of "Hebrew culture" or "Yiddish culture"). Certainly, those whose Judaism is essentially religious are committed to Jewish culture—the Hebrew language, a recognizable and authentic Jewish way of life, the State of Israel—for all of these cultural factors have religious origins and meanings. In fact, this could be said about all historical culture. Thus the error of the antireligious Jewish "culturalists" was based as much on their ignorance or distortion of culture (the term *culture* comes from the Latin *cultus*) as on their reduction of Judaism to "Jewishness."[10]

The Mission of Israel

What distinguishes "religious" Jews from merely "cultural" Jews is their relationship with non-Jews, which in the United States primarily means their relationship with Christians. (Although religious Jews would agree with even the "juridical" Jews and the "political" Jews that we cannot accept the notion of "Christian America," they do recognize to a greater extent than these other types of Jews that Americans are indeed more Christian than anything else.) It is beyond dispute that Classical Judaism in both its scriptural and rabbinic developments has been concerned with what God requires of the gentiles as well as what God requires of the Jews, albeit not equally.[11] Our relationship with American Christians concerns what God requires here and now of our respective communities, and how and why these demands do indeed coincide on crucial public issues more often than not.

Heretofore, this essentially religious approach to Jewish life in the United States has taken one of two forms: the first that of Liberal Judaism; the second (and, interestingly enough, the newer phenomenon) that of Traditional Judaism. (I avoid using the denominational labels Orthodox, Conservative, and Reform because they do not apply precisely enough to the intellectual typology I am employing here.)

Liberal Judaism, first in the thought of its German progenitors and later in the thought of their American disciples and successors, in response to the new relationship with the gentiles that came with the Emancipation, developed the idea of the "Mission of Israel." This was the idea that Judaism not only is not a particularistic ethnic "fossil" (to use Arnold Toynbee's infamous characterization) to be overcome in the progress of history but is the true vanguard of the universal culture that the modern world proclaimed (*Weltgeschichte* in Hegel's terminology).[12] This was seen as being due to Judaism's unique "ethical monotheism." The theory of ethical monotheism is based on the assumption that the essence of Judaism is its ethical teaching. Following Kant, unquestionably the philosopher who made the greatest impression on Liberal and even Traditional Jews, the essence of this ethical teaching is characterized by its *universalizability*.[13] Because this ideal "ethical culture" has not yet been historically realized, and because Judaism and the Jewish people understand and maintain its pristine purity better than all others, Jews are therefore required to preserve their unique cultural and religious identity in the interest of this not-yet-achieved "Messianic" climax of universal history. The aspects of Jewish tradition that seemed to be not only particularistic but antiuniversal were deemed unworthy of the ethical essence of Judaism and hence stood in need of "reform." In Germany this "reformation" was theorized rather conservatively by such theologians as Hermann Cohen (d. 1918) and Leo Baeck (d. 1956).[14] In the United States it was more radically theorized by such theologians as Kaufmann Kohler (d. 1926) and Emil G. Hirsch (d. 1923)[15] — both sons-in-law of the radical Reform theologian David Einhorn (d. 1879), who had a smaller impact on American Jewish life and thought than they did primarily because he immigrated earlier than they, and his speech and writing was almost exclusively in German. The more radical character of American Reform thinking was further bolstered by the more open religious atmosphere here in the nineteenth century, which stood in such stark contrast to the more circumscribed one that obtained in Europe, especially in Central Europe after the abortive revolutions of the 1840s.[16]

As the corollary of ethical monotheism or "Prophetic Judaism," the idea of the "Mission of Israel" gained additional impetus in the United States from arriving at the same time as, and possibly from being influenced by, the Social Gospel school of thought advocated by Walter Rauschenbusch and other Protestant thinkers. All of this was an attempt to see religion as providing the true ethical impetus for a culture and a society that were becoming more and more secular in both theory and practice. For Jews especially this was a rather audacious attempt to relate Classical Judaism to contemporary American life without abandoning Judaism altogether, as had the former rabbi Felix Adler (d. 1933), the founder of the Ethical Culture movement.[17] One need not be a Liberal Jew in any sense of that term to admire the project as the first real attempt to define a Jewish religious participation in American life, existentially concerned with both Judaism and the United States as a society in which Jews need no longer abandon Judaism in order to be true participants.

Nevertheless, we rarely hear the slogan "Mission of Israel" any longer, let alone find the idea articulated even by Liberal Jews. I think this is because it did not find a conceptualization or an expression that truly spoke to the needs of either the Jews or the United States. First, the Liberal Jews who advocated this idea were almost all anti-Zionists (perhaps the great exception being Stephen S. Wise [d. 1949]). Zionism, as a nationalistic project for a sovereign Jewish state in the land of Israel, was anathema to the Jews who saw Judaism's "mission" as being the dissemination of its universal ethical teaching and providing leadership for an essentially nonsectarian United States. However, most Jews (even most Reform Jews after the 1937 repudiation of the overtly antinationalistic pronouncements of 1885) have been too committed to what Mordecai M. Kaplan (d. 1983) called "Jewish peoplehood" to define Judaism in what seemed to be Protestant denominational terms.[18] The Holocaust and the establishment of the State of Israel in the 1940s made this historical persistence an absolute political necessity. In the end, the Mission of Israel seemed to be inauthentically Jewish on both cultural-religious and political grounds.

Second, the social and political program of the advocates of the Mission of Israel was always rather vague on specific issues. When push came to shove, they almost always came out in favor of the liberal political programs of those whose basic outlook was secular. Always in the background one could hear the ghost of Felix Adler, well-trained in philosophy as he was, cutting away at this theology with Occam's razor, asking what was uniquely Jewish or should be uniquely Jewish about this approach.[19] (Merely to identify its ancient origins in Judaism — which is rather doubtful anyway in this liberalized version — is to commit the congenital fallacy.) If it was not uniquely Jewish, then continuing to call it the Mission *of Israel* could smack only of chauvinism. One suspects, therefore, that the enthusiasm for the Mission of Israel expressed from so many pulpits earlier in this century was more for the sake of showing Judaism to be *au courant* intellectually and socially than for the sake of actually attempting to redirect this nation in a more Jewishly approved way. Perhaps the greater ease that third-, fourth-, and even fifth-generation American Jews now feel in American culture and society makes these apologetic exercises anachronistic.

However, something akin to the Mission of Israel (although the term itself is not used) has emerged in the most unexpected quarters, among some of the most Traditional Jewish thinkers in the United States, who are usually characterized by even their fellow Jews as xenophobic in their approach to the general society and culture. To cite a most important example, in 1963, during one of the periods of intense public debate over the perennial issue of prayer in the public schools, Rabbi Moses Feinstein (d. 1986), without a doubt the most influential halakhic authority in the United States — an East European-born and -educated rabbi who wrote and spoke only in Hebrew or Yiddish — was asked what the Jewish approach to this issue should be. The further irony was that this non-English-speaking (at least in public) authority was being asked by a colleague in a community of American Jews where all children are educated in intensely religious parochial schools. (In fact, in this ultra-Traditional milieu, sending one's children to a public primary or secondary school — for some even to a college — would result in instant and severe ostracism.) Why, then, was this question asked and why did Rabbi Feinstein write a pointed response to it, a response widely read by Traditional Jews learned enough to understand its contents and implications? The answer to this question reveals much about Classical Judaism and the new, more confident position of Traditional Jews in American culture and society.

Rabbi Feinstein's response draws upon the classical Jewish doctrine of the Noahide laws.[20] This doctrine states that whereas the Jews are obligated to observe the 613 commandments in the Pentateuch (along with rabbinic interpretations and additions), the gentiles are obligated to observe the seven commandments the Rabbis determined were commanded by God to Adam and then to Noah and his descendents—that is, to humankind.[21] Two of the foremost of these commandments are the twin prohibitions of blasphemy and idolatry. Based on the logical axiom that the negative presupposes the positive, Rabbi Feinstein quite cogently argued that these prohibitions presuppose an actual relationship with God, the type of relationship that would certainly include regular prayer. Because Judaism by its affirmation of the doctrine of the Noahide laws obviously approves of this relationship and should therefore advocate it, Rabbi Feinstein concluded that Normative Judaism can express approval of prayer in the public schools.

Rabbi Feinstein's response indicates that, contrary to popular prejudice, Traditional Jews are in fact concerned with the moral and spiritual life of the general society at large (although he was not entirely comfortable with taking a public stand on this issue). It is only that this has not been a concern to which the tradition assigns a top priority in comparison with more internal Jewish concerns. The *raison d'être* of Judaism is not to teach the gentiles but to obey God's Torah, whether the gentiles are interested in it or not. (The theological weakness of the Mission of Israel idea is that it seems to be a good deal more interested in the approval of the gentiles than in the approval of God.) If, however, the gentiles do see light in Israel (Isaiah 42:6), then, as an ancient rabbinic text puts it, they should "send their representatives and take the Torah for themselves."[22] Nevertheless, Rabbi Feinstein's seriousness in dealing with this topic at all indicates two important sociological facts: (1) Traditional Jews are now enough a part of American culture and society that they must have an opinion on such questions of public debate; and (2) Traditional Jews are concerned that the United States develop along ethical and religious lines that are not antithetical to Judaism's *theocentric* worldview.[23] This theocentric worldview might be characterized as one that insists that the law of God is to be the basic norm for every society and for every human person. This is for the sake of the survival of both Judaism and civilization itself.

For both existential and intellectual reasons, I am in basic sympathy with this approach, which is certainly in the spirit of Classical Judaism (that is, the Judaism that is grounded in Scripture and the rabbinic writings). But it has to be developed further in order that it might speak more directly to the great debate over moral principles we are now living through in American democracy.

The problem with this approach, at least as heretofore articulated by its Traditional Jewish advocates, is that it is "theocratic," which is to say that it deduces legal prescriptions from religious texts. This seems to run counter to the tendency of our democracy from its founding up until the present. Indeed, Maimonides, one of the greatest formulators of Classical Judaism, spoke about *forcing* the gentiles to follow the Noahide laws—if, of course, Jews ever have the power to do so.[24] The difficulty with applying theocratic norms in a democracy that if not secularist is certainly secular *de facto* and *de jure* has also been faced by Roman Catholic traditionalists as well. And, indeed, we Traditional Jews can learn much from the Jesuit theologian John Courtney Murray (d. 1967), who made such strides in presenting Roman Catholic ethical teaching in a way that it could be defended against charges that it was "theocratic" *ipso facto* and hence "un-American."[25]

Law and Morality: Jewish and American

Many assume that there is an insuperable dichotomy between religious doctrine and democracy in our society, but I would like to argue that a closer look at how theology functions in the history of Judaism and how religious doctrine functions in the history of this country might well show that the dichotomy is not insuperable after all.

Let me begin with two personal recollections, the type of oral reports of the words of teachers in which the discourse of the Talmud abounds.

In the autumn of 1957 I entered the college of the University of Chicago. One of the courses I was required to take that first year was Social Sciences I, which dealt with the history of American political thought. At the same time, I was involved in the intense study of the Talmud, particularly in a tractate (*Baba Kama*) that deals with Jewish civil law. It was the custom at that time for distinguished professors in fields related to our course of study to be invited periodically to lecture to the combined sections of the course. Two of these lectures made a lasting impression on my thinking and I still remember them quite well.

In the first lecture, William Thomas Hutchinson (d. 1976), an expert on American constitutional history, presented the thesis that the reason the U.S. Constitution of 1789 was far more enduring than the constitution promulgated in France at the same time after the French Revolution is that the former was the result of almost two hundred years of colonial experience, whereas the latter was the result of purely philosophical speculation. What Hutchinson was presenting, it seems in retrospect, was a common law view of this country's history, contending that theory is enunciated only after sufficient precedent has been accumulated for a deliberate judgment to be made.[26]

The second lecture I remember that year was by Avery Craven (d. 1980), a historian whose specialty was the period around the Civil War. Craven presented the thesis that the real preamble to the Constitution of the United States is not what is formally called the preamble but, rather, the Declaration of Independence. He illustrated his point by analyzing the institution of slavery. On strictly constitutional grounds, slavery was permitted and slaves had the status of chattel. That point was made with legal cogency by Chief Justice Roger B. Taney in the famous Dred Scott decision of 1857. However, the Declaration of Independence, despite the fact that it was written by Virginia slaveholder Thomas Jefferson, declared that "all men are created equal" (a theological statement if there ever was one, despite the fact that it was made by a nonchurchgoing Deist, Jefferson). According to Craven, the Civil War and the resulting Thirteenth Amendment to the Constitution outlawing slavery affirmed the priority of the philosophical foundation of the Constitution over specific legal reasoning in a matter of crucial importance in the life of this democracy. In fact, as I recall, Craven went so far as to say that had the events that made the Thirteenth Amendment possible not taken place, it is doubtful whether our constitutional form of government would have endured.[27]

Now, on the surface, the theses of Hutchinson and Craven seem to contradict each other. Hutchinson emphasized the priority of precedent over theory, whereas Craven emphasized the priority of theory over precedent. However, deeper examination tells us they are in truth complementary in the sense that they both draw on a dialectic between precedent and theory.

Precedent by definition is historically prior, but precedent does lead to theory, which then begins to serve as a guide specifying which precedents ought subsequently to be emphasized and which ought to be deemphasized. Once there is enough precedent behind a theory, that theory becomes regulative, a *conditio sine qua non* for the further development of the *system* of precedent. When precedents are invoked that ignore the tendency of the system's development, then theory must *inform* the process of selection. It functions as a criterion of judgment. The relation is dialectical in that neither the theoretical pole nor the practical pole can be reduced to the other. Thus the theory is more than an inductive generalization from the precedents, and the precedents are not simply deduced from the theory. Like an electrical current, the full sociopolitical reality lies between the two poles.[28]

Even in those earlier days of my education, it seemed to me that something similar was also taking place in Normative Judaism. Later on, when I began to write about Jewish thought, I systematically examined the relation of theology and law in Jewish tradition.[29] Now in Normative Judaism ethical rules (*mitsvot*) are codified in law (*Halakhah*), and the ethical/legal structure is theological in the sense that its origin is seen in God's will and its purpose is seen as being the highest good, that being the nearness of God (Psalms 73:28). Any attempt, therefore, to remove Jewish ethics from its overall theological context is ultimately incredible. However, this does not mean that law is deduced from theology (*Aggadah*). The law in its immediate manifestation often has an independent life of its own, developing along lines of precedent and the human assessment of human situations; as the Talmud puts it, "the human judge can judge only what his human eyes see."[30] This is important because it enables the law to draw upon a wealth of human experience, and it encourages creative human judgment to operate. This mitigates, to a great extent, the type of dogmatism that attempts to force all experience into a Procrustean bed, the type of dogmatism that too readily has the answer before the question itself has been adequately experienced and formulated.[31]

Nevertheless, in the great issues that the law has faced—issues dealing with fundamental questions of the definition of human personhood, the sanctity of human sexuality, the nature of human sociality, the vocation of the Jewish people—in these great issues the system of precedent alone is insufficient in and of itself because it is usually ambiguous, presenting prima facie conflicting options for judgment. It is ambiguous precisely because the authorities of the past could not solve all the problems in advance; they could not be substitutes for the living authorities of the present and the future.[32]

At these crucial points, the great authorities invoked theological principles developed on the nonlegal side of Classical Judaism. But, let it be emphasized, they invoked these principles when and only when there was at least some purely legal precedent for them to choose. When the great issues (what contemporary legal theorists call "hard cases") arose, the system of precedent was indeed not sufficient in and of itself, but nonetheless it was still necessary. Thus, for example, when the whole theology of Kabbalah began to be fully explicated in the late Middle Ages, there was a tendency in some circles to see its main document, the *Zohar*, as having achieved a normative status equal to and even surpassing that of the Talmud. On the other hand, there were authorities who regarded it as antinomian and therefore having no normative status at all. Finally, in the early sixteenth century, the Egyptian authority R. David ibn Abi Zimra ruled that in and of itself the law in the Talmud takes normative precedence over the theology of the *Zohar*. However, when the law in the Talmud is itself unclear (as it frequently is, thankfully), then the theology of the *Zohar* might be invoked to decide what is actually to be done here and now.[33]

Law and Theology

The application of all this to the great debate over moral principles in the United States today can be the new agenda of the Mission of Israel, an agenda far more authentically Jewish and socially critical than that of the earlier Liberal proponents of this idea.

Let us take the most persistent and intense issue of social debate in this country for over a decade — abortion — an issue that shows no signs whatsoever of being any less controversial during the foreseeable future. It is the focus of so much attention because it deals with the most fundamental moral issue possible: the status of human personhood and society's relation to it. Because it is patently clear that this sort of moral question cannot be reduced to a matter of merely legal precedent, the 1973 *Roe versus Wade* decision of the United States Supreme Court by no means settled the issue; if anything, it exacerbated it. Here we have a clear conflict of moral principles, a *Kulturkampf* with monumental ramifications.

The legal system is ambiguous enough to call for extralegal factors in making a judgment. The Fourteenth Amendment to the Constitution speaks of the right of every "person" to "equal protection of the laws." However, nowhere does it define personhood. A human fetus, whose personhood is by no means immediately evident, may or may not be entitled to the *equal* protection the Constitution mandates for *persons* and only for persons. Here is where the legal system must look to some other system to supply such definitions. In situations such as this we see that what is *good* (the subject of ethics) must be determined before determining what is *lawful* (the subject of law). It is ethics that gives law the basic principle that it is good to benefit human persons and evil to harm them. But even ethical systems do not determine a definition of personhood; rather, they presuppose one. Questions of personhood are ontological before they are ethical, let alone before they are legal. In other words, what is *true* about the *being* of human persons must be determined before it is determined what human persons are to do (the good) and before it is determined what human persons may demand of others in society (the lawful). The debate over abortion, then, is ultimately nothing less than a clash between opposing ontologies. That is why the debate is so profound and so prolonged. The theological view that the fetus is essentially a human person from conception is part of one such ontology.[34]

Nevertheless, even though the issue of abortion is ultimately ontological, ethics and law cannot simply be deduced from one's ontology/theology, as many on both sides of the abortion debate seem to think. Thus accepting the broadest definition of human personhood does not solve questions of mortal conflict *between* persons, for example, such as the question of whether the fetus can in some cases be regarded as an unwarranted intruder (*rodef*) in the womb of another person — as in rape. These questions have been intensely debated in Jewish tradition, and there is considerable literature on the subject even in English.[35] It has been generally assumed that no one in the normative (that is, halakhic) tradition of Judaism can cogently assign the fetus the status of a nonperson on the level of a thing, having no rights at all. Conversely, no one can cogently maintain that the life of the fetus takes precedence over that of his or her mother. The real question — involving hard cases — is how widely or narrowly we are to interpret situations of "threatening intrusion."

In the context of the Jewish normative tradition no one can simply say, "Based on my theological principles, this is the only ethical course of action." When legal precedent already exists, one can use his or her theological principles only to exercise judgment and attempt to persuade others. This is also the case in the American tradition — *mutatis mutandis*. Those who say that religion may not determine the law in our constitutional democracy, that religion may not *impose* its principles on society as a whole, are technically correct. The First Amendment to the Constitution not only protects us from being subject to the rule of any religious community but protects the nonreligious minority (and let it be emphasized that they are the *minority* in the United States) from being subject to the rule of a consensus of all or most of the religious communities (an extremely remote possibility at present and in the foreseeable future). However, it is totally unwarranted to infer from this social fact that the absence of religion in the process of *specific* legal reasoning requires its elimination from the *general* realm of social discourse and persuasion (as opposed to political coercion). Such an inference is an example of the fallacy of generalization, for if this inference is made, then we are indeed left with what Richard John Neuhaus calls "the naked public square."[36] If "naked" is synonymous with "vacuous," then history as well as nature (to paraphrase

Aristotle) is abhors a vacuum. In the situation at hand, the vacuum is inevitably filled with the type of secularism that makes the elimination of religion from the public realm its own dogma.

It seems to me that the intention of our American doctrine of the separation of church and state is to deny the legitimacy of deducing politically acceptable action from dogma—anyone's dogma. But aside from that type of dogmatic deduction (so obvious among those who engage in one-issue politics), one's dogmas and doctrines should be brought into the public square, especially when it can be shown that they have strong affinities with the dogmas and doctrines (more generally, the ideas) that have *inspired* American democracy in the first place and that have sustained it at times of great crisis in its history.

The point made so tellingly by the late German-American Protestant theologian Paul Tillich, that no one really acts without an "ultimate concern," is especially germane,[37] for it means that no area of human discourse and action is "value-free." And it is better for one's values to be publicly visible ("up front" as the colloquial expression goes) and thus socially responsible and responsive than to keep one's values (or, better, one's ontological/ethical principles) a purely private matter and thereby run the risk of becoming socially irresponsible and unresponsive (that is, "dogmatic" in the pejorative sense of that term). Here too the American Protestant theologian Reinhold Niebuhr still has much to teach all of us about how biblical theism can be seen as the most adequate foundation for democracy without making it "theocratic" (which literally means "the rule of God," but usually means "the rule of the church").[38]

Jews and Judaism in the United States Today

The concluding question to be addressed is one my grandfather used to ask: "So, is all of this good or bad for the Jews?" Well, I believe that this is good for the Jews—very good—because I believe that Judaism has some very important points to make in the moral and legal discourse of our society. There is a mission of Israel, and the exercise of that "missionary" project is wholly consistent with the cultural, political, and even juridical interests of Jews in American society.

If we Jews regard ourselves as having a mission in the United States today, then we obviously cannot accept the Zionist doctrine of the "negation of the Diaspora" (*shelilat ha-golah*).[39] This does not mean, however, that we can or should return to the anti-Zionism of the earlier Liberal Jewish proponents of this idea. We Jews are a community constituted by the Torah, and that alone makes us quite different from a "denomination" in the American Protestant sense of that term. Our Torah-constituted community must be concerned with the land of Israel and the State of Israel, nonobservant—even atheistic—Jews, the Hebrew language, and other "ethnic" matters. (The Greek *ethnos* means "people"; and because Jews are *Am Yisrael*—"the people who strive with God"

[Genesis 32:29], refusing to journey in this world without God [Exodus 33: 15] — I resist any secularist interpretation of Jewish "peoplehood.")

The fact that we affirm that the Lord God of Israel is also the Creator of heaven and earth, and the fact that we are bound by the law and teaching of the Torah *wherever* we happen to live, indicates on religious grounds the validity of any Jewish community to exist anywhere the Torah can be studied and the commandments kept.[40] Furthermore, we are morally bound to support in every way a society that allows us the freedom to live as authentic Jews and that itself is bound by a law we consider grounded in the law of God — and that many non-Jewish Americans also consider grounded in the law of God.

All of this simply means that we American Jews can cogently argue on precise Jewish religious grounds that the United States has value for us and that we have value for it. I emphasize this because I believe that the religious and intellectual life of American Jewry has been impoverished by the assumption — consciously maintained by some, unconsciously by others — that Jewish life here is at best transient, that this country is a *trayfeh medinah* (literally, a "nonkosher society," a charge made at the turn of the century by some East European rabbis who attempted — on the whole with little success — to dissuade their flocks from joining the mass migration), and that Jewish life on this soil is ultimately doomed. There is little in Jewish tradition and little in American Jewish experience (as recent studies have now shown) to validate this view.[41] (It is to be hoped that it will become a topic of more and more dialogue between Israeli and American Jews.)

Nevertheless, my Jewish enthusiasm for the United States does not mean that I am oblivious to the charge that such enthusiasm too closely resembles the naive enthusiasm of pre-Hitler German Jews for Germany, an enthusiasm so ghastly refuted by history. To those who have charged me with such naiveté, I answer as follows: (1) Unlike certain German Jewish thinkers, I do not assign any messianic status to my native country; it is simply a *good* place for Jews — spiritually as well as materially; it is not necessarily the *best* place for Jews. My enthusiasm is thus more empirical and less idealistic. (2) Like most German Jews who lost all their enthusiasm for Germany once it became a bad place for Jews — spiritually as well as materially — I too *would* lose all my enthusiasm for the United States *if* it ever (God forbid!) became a bad place for Jews.[42] In a radically unredeemed world my enthusiasm for any human society is very much qualified. Without such qualification my enthusiasm would be pseudomessianism.[43] (3) My enthusiasm for the United States in no way rejects the unique Jewish opportunities afforded by living in the land of Israel and being a citizen of the Jewish state there.[44]

There are moral insights about which Judaism and American Jews can beneficially *inform* American social and political life. Because Jews and Judaism have suffered so, especially in this century of incomparable horrors, perhaps it is best to express them as a series of negations or quasi-prophetic warnings.

One, Judaism and American Jews have a good deal to warn the United States about concerning the danger of depersonalization in our society. The most important aspect for society of the Jewish doctrine of the human person as the image of God is that it gives the widest definition of human personhood possible without eliminating the equally important distinction between the human and the nonhuman.[45] The tendency in the twentieth century has been the exact opposite—namely, to limit personhood based on arbitrary factors such as physical condition, race, age, and so on. This has been done by the state in the person of those who have the political power to do so. Here is where Judaism and the experience of the Jews once again coalesce: the Jews have been the most agonized victims of the denial of this doctrine of Judaism. The Jews who are intent that Americans (let alone Europeans, who are closer to the scene of the crime) "never forget" the Holocaust and all that led up to it and made it possible must eschew arbitrary definitions of human personhood so contrary to both Torah and Jewish experience.

Two, Judaism and American Jews have a good deal to warn this country about concerning the danger of deculturalization in our society. Judaism not only encourages Jews to live according to our own traditions and culture but also encourages non-Jews to do the same. This can best be illustrated by a hasidic story my late revered teacher Professor Abraham Joshua Heschel once told me about the Baal Shem Tov, the founder of Hasidism in eighteenth-century Poland. It seems that the Baal Shem Tov had a Catholic coachman. One day when out riding, they passed the shrine of a saint, the type that dotted the Polish countryside. The coachman did not make the sign of the cross when they passed by it. The Baal Shem Tov immediately ordered a close disciple who was with him to fire the man. He reasoned that if this man's own tradition was no longer sacred to him, he certainly would not respect a tradition sacred to others. The story is typical of very sound and persistent Jewish doctrine.

The modern industrial process of deculturalization, turning everyone into a copy of his or her neighbor, thereby imitating the mass production of our machines, creates a dangerous cultural and emotional vacuum. It denies an overall purpose to human life and simultaneously destroys our link with the past that once did reveal such purposes to us.[46] In so doing, it makes modern societies vulnerable to the likes of Hitler, whose simplistic appeals to fears and fantasies no longer had to face, in any strong sense, the mediating safeguards of subtle and multifaceted tradition. The Jews who delight in being in the forefront of all that is irreverently avant-garde should ponder whether similar Jewish contributions to the traditionless culture of Weimar Germany may not have destroyed those aspects of German historical culture that might have served as better bases of resistance to Hitler had they not been so discredited already.[47] Here again, we see how Torah enlightens Jewish experience and how Jewish experience illustrates Torah.

Three, Judaism and American Jews can also teach the United States about the dialectic between faith and history. The problem with so much of Christian moral teaching in this country, especially *traditional* Christian moral teaching (Catholic, Orthodox, or Evangelical), is its fundamentalism. Now, *fundamentalism* means many things, but it seems to be generally characterized by a conviction that "all the answers are right here in the Book," and that it is only obstinacy or ignorance that prevents God's plan from being implemented to heal immediately all our social (and personal) ills. (In this sense, fundamentalism is certainly not exclusively Christian—or Islamic; most of the Traditionalist Jewish community is just as fundamentalistic.) According to this view, history, as the accumulated experience of highly fallible humans, has no value; indeed, it constitutes a threat to the Truth. Here is where the Jewish obsession with the Law—so often denigrated by Christians who misread Paul—is germane,[48] for, as we have seen, the Law is not a divine oracle that lights up whenever we approach it with a question.[49] The Law is, rather, a divinely grounded *and* historically developing system that subjects the most cogently argued theory to the collective precedents of the centuries-old community. That is its covenantal character.[50] But fundamentalism is impatient with this slow, often bumbling process, and this is precisely why, in our century especially, it has often been so easily manipulated by all sorts of political fanatics who offer instant and easy solutions to complex social problems. The Law saves us from this type of utopian pseudomessianism, just as it saves us from the relativistic vacuum wherein all norms are taken simply as matters of taste and therefore outside the range of rational discourse.

For all these reasons, I believe that the United States today provides an important religious challenge to Judaism and American Jews. It seems that at long last we are being taken seriously by some of the most thoughtful elements in American society, and we are being taken seriously as "Jewish Jews." How seriously we will take ourselves will largely depend on the piety, learning, and insight of those whom we make the leaders and spokespersons of our community. Heretofore, we American Jews, contrary to the tendency of almost all previous Jewish history—let alone the mandate for the Torah[51]— have hardly looked for piety, learning, or insight into Judaism in our leaders. But the times have changed radically. We must be up to them, demanding that those who speak about us and for us be capable, spiritually and intellectually, of articulating and implementing our special role in the life of American society and culture.[52]

NOTES

1. B. Kiddushin 66a.
2. See Neuhaus's *The Naked Public Square* (Grand Rapids, Mich., 1984).
3. See Leo Pfeffer, *Creeds in Competition* (New York, 1958), 46ff.
4. See Joseph Churba, *The Politics of Defeat: America's Decline in the Middle East* (New York, 1977), esp. 166ff.
5. See his *Anti-Semite and Jew*, trans. C. J. Becker (New York, 1948), 67ff.
6. The greatest and most significant proponent of this idea was Horace M. Kallen (d. 1974); see his *Cultural Pluralism and the American Idea* (Philadelphia, 1956), esp. 85ff.
7. See Charles E. Silberman, *A Certain People: American Jews and Their Lives*

Today (New York, 1985), 254ff., and Chaim I. Waxman, *American Jews in Transition* (Philadelphia, 1983), 124ff.

8. This doctrine was promulgated at the very beginnings of Zionism. See Ahad Ha'Am's 1909 essay, "The Negation of the Diaspora," trans. L. Simon, in *The Zionist Idea: A Historical Analysis and Reader*, ed. Arthur Hertzberg (Philadelphia, 1959), 270–277. For a critique of this doctrine along cultural lines, see Mordecai M. Kaplan's 1948 essay, "The Negation of Jewish Life in the Diaspora," ibid., 539–542.

9. See David Novak, *Jewish-Christian Dialogue: A Jewish Justification* (New York, 1989), intro.

10. See Peter L. Berger, *The Sacred Canopy* (Garden City, N.Y., 1969), 41.

11. See David Novak, *The Image of the Non-Jew in Judaism: An Historical and Constructive Study of the Noahide Laws* (New York and Toronto, 1983), esp. chap. 4.

12. See Emil L. Fackenheim, *The Religious Dimension in Hegel's Thought* (Chicago, 1967), 231–233.

13. See Kant's *Groundwork of the Metaphysic of Morals*, trans. H. J. Paton (New York, 1964), 88ff.

14. See Cohen's *Religion of Reason out of the Sources of Judaism*, trans. S. Kaplan (New York, 1972), 283ff., and Baeck's *The Essence of Judaism*, trans. V. Grubenwieser and L. Pearl (New York, 1948), 68ff.

15. See Kohler's *Jewish Theology—Systematically and Historically Considered* (New York, 1918), 325ff., and Hirsch's *My Religion*, ed. G. B. Levi (New York, 1925), 259–262, 288ff.

16. See Michael A. Meyer, *Response to Modernity: A History of the Reform Movement in Judaism* (New York, 1988), 181ff.

17. For a sharp reaction to Adler's agnosticism by Liberal Jewish thinkers who were most threatened by it, see Benny Kraut, *From Reform Judaism to Ethical Culture: The Religious Evolution of Felix Adler* (Cincinnati, 1976), 135ff.

18. See Kaplan's *Judaism as a Civilization: Toward a Reconstruction of American-Jewish Life* (New York, 1934), 227ff. See also the earlier critique of Ahad Ha'Am, "Slavery in Freedom," in *Selected Essays*, trans. L. Simon (Philadelphia, 1912), 184ff. Interestingly enough, Ahad Ha'Am's critique is specifically directed against the Traditionalist French rabbi S. Munk. The idea was usually, but not exclusively, advocated by Liberal Jewish thinkers.

19. See Kraut, *From Reform Judaism to Ethical Culture*, 169ff.

20. See his *Igrot Mosheh*: Orah Hayyim, 4 vols. (New York, 1963), 2:196–198, no. 25. Interestingly, in 1939, in celebration of the 150th anniversary of the Constitution of the United States, Rabbi Feinstein advocated a stricter separation of religion and the state. See *Darash Mosheh*, no. 10 (B'nai B'rak, 1988), 415–416. (I thank my friend Professor Chaim I. Waxman for this reference.)

21. See *supra*, n. 11.

22. T. Sotah 8.6. For the ancient rabbinic recognition of the universal human need for both laudatory and petitionary prayer, see B. Berakhot 20b; B. Sotah 10a–b and 35b.

23. What I have called Judaism's "theocentricity" was first named "theocracy" by Josephus, *Contra Apionem*, 2.164–167: ". . . some peoples have entrusted the supreme political power (*tēn exousian*) to monarchies, others to oligarchies, yet others to the masses. Our lawgiver, however, was attracted by none of these forms of polity, but gave to his constitution the form of what—if a forced expression be permitted—may be termed a 'theocracy,' placing all sovereignty and authority (*tēn archē kai to kratos*)

in the hands of God." Trans. H. St. John Thackeray, *Josephus*, 9 vols. (Cambridge, Mass., 1926), 1:358–359.

24. *Hilkhot Melakhim*, 8.10. See Novak, *The Image of the Non-Jew in Judaism*, 53–56.

25. See *supra*, 68f. For ancient Jewish suspicions of the combination of ecclesiastical and secular power, see B. Kiddushin 66a and Y. Horayot 3.2/47c.

26. Along these lines note the following exchange from Robert Bolt's play, *A Man for All Seasons* (New York, 1962), act I, pp. 65–66.

> ROPER: Then you set man's law above God's!
>
> MORE: No, far below, but let *me* draw your attention to a fact, I'm *not* God. The currents and eddies of right and wrong, which you find such plain sailing, I can't navigate. I'm no voyager. . . . This country's planted thick with laws from coast to coast — man's laws, not God's — and if you cut them down . . . d'you think you could stand upright in the winds that would blow then?

See also M. Avot 3.2; B. Sanhedrin 39b re Ezek. 5:7 and 11:12; Plato, *Crito*, 50Aff.

27. See Craven's *Civil War in the Making* (Baton Rouge, 1959), 64ff.; also Carl Becker, *The Declaration of Independence* (New York, 1922), 6.

28. Thus in Talmudic discourse, when there is a debate over practice, the question is often asked: "How do they differ in theory [*be-m'ay qa-mipalgay*]?" (See, e.g., B. Kiddushin 47a–b.) And when there is a debate over theory, the question is often asked: "How do they differ in practice [*m'ay baynyyhu*]?" (See, e.g., B. Baba Metsia 15b–16a.)

29. See David Novak, *Law and Theology in Judaism*, 2 vols. (New York, 1974–1976), 1:1ff. and 2:xiiiff.; Novak, *Halakhah in a Theological Dimension* (Chico, Calif., 1985), 11ff., 61ff.

30. B. Sanhedrin 6b. Although the Law if *from Heaven* (M. Sanhedrin 10.1), and is *for the sake of Heaven* (M. Avot 2.12), it is nevertheless *not in Heaven* (B. Baba Metsia 59b re Deut. 30:12). "Heaven" (*Shamayim*) is a frequent synonym for "God" in rabbinic literature.

31. See Z. W. Falk, *Law and Religion: The Jewish Experience* (Jerusalem, 1981), 66–74.

32. See B. Rosh Hashanah 25a–b re Deut. 17:9 and Menahot 29b.

33. See *Responsa Radbaz* (Warsaw, 1882), no. 1,111; also Louis Jacobs, *Theology in the Responsa* (London, 1975), 122–123.

34. See Novak, *Law and Theology in Judaism*, 1:114ff. Re ethics presupposing ontology, see *supra*, 16f.

35. See, e.g., D. M. Feldman, *Birth Control in Jewish Law* (New York, 1968), 251ff.; J. D. Bleich, *Contemporary Halakhic Problems*, 2 vols. (New York, 1977), 1: 325ff.

36. Charles E. Silberman in his widely discussed book, *A Certain People*, criticizes Neuhaus — inaccurately and unfairly, I think — for advocating "an explicitly Christian society" (p. 357). Yet, read in context, Neuhaus (*The Naked Public Square*, pp. 80ff.) is *describing* the true state of affairs about the source of moral authority of most Americans. He is not prescribing a "Christian America" in the "theocratic" sense, which would exclude Jews and other Americans whose sources of moral authority do not come from Christianity. See ibid., 127 and especially the following on 261: "For a revival of religion to help in leading us out of the dark night of cultural contradictions

there must be a profound security about the relationship between Christians and Jews. . . . We must ponder anew the divine mystery of living Judaism. . . . For good reasons, Jews and others who are uneasy about the idea of 'Christian America' will continue to prefer the naked square until it is manifest that Christians have internalized — as a matter of doctrine, even of dogma — reverence for democratic dissent."

37. See Tillich's *Dynamics of Faith* (New York, 1957), 1ff.; *supra*, 48ff.

38. See *supra*, n. 23. For a still-astute appreciation of Niebuhr on this point, see Arthur Schlesinger, Jr., "Reinhold Niebuhr's Role in American Political Thought and Life," in *Reinhold Niebuhr: His Religious, Social and Political Thought*, ed. C. W. Kegley and R. W. Bretall (New York, 1956), 126ff. And note T. S. Eliot's 1939 statement that "the term 'democracy' as I have used it again and again, does not contain enough positive content to stand alone against the forces that you dislike — it can easily be transformed by them. If you will not have God (and He is a jealous God), you should pay your respects to Hitler or Stalin." *The Idea of a Christian Society*, 2d ed. (London, 1982), 82. It might seem odd that I would quote, of all people, T. S. Eliot, who, it is assumed, was an anti-Semite. That he was so in his early writing is incontrovertible (see, e.g., his 1920 poem, "Burbank With A Baedeker: Bleistein With A Cigar," in *The Complete Poems and Plays: 1909-1950* [New York, 1971], 24) — that is, before his conversion to Anglican Christianity in 1927. After that, he underwent a moral conversion as well. One should read, e.g., his moving 1941 appeal on behalf of the Jews of France (*The Idea of a Christian Society* 2d ed. [London, 1982], 138).

39. See *supra*, n. 8.

40. See M. Kiddushin 1.9 and B. Kiddushin 37a.

41. See *supra*, n. 7.

42. Cf. Hermann Cohen, who in 1915 wrote, "So fühlen wir uns als Deutsche Juden in dem Bewusstsein einer zentralen Kulturkraft, welche die Völker im Sinne der messianischen Menschheit zu verbinden berufen ist. . . ." "Deutschtum und Judentum," *Jüdische Schriften*, 3 vols., ed. B. Strauss (Berlin, 1924), 2:277-278. I make no such claims for the United States, claims that in even in their own time were excessive, let alone in retrospect after Germany's descent into the Nazi horror that led to Cohen's widow Martha's death in the Theresienstadt concentration camp. See Gershom Scholem, "Jews and Germans," *Commentary* 42, no. 5 (1966):31-38.

43. See David Novak, "Judaism, Zionism and Messianism — Telling Them Apart," *First Things* 10 (1991):22-25.

44. See the critique of Edward Alexander of the earlier version of this essay (*Jews in Unsecular America*, ed. Richard John Neuhaus [Grand Rapids, Mich., 1987], 41-60), in "Where Is Zion?" *Commentary* 86, no. 3 (1988):50, and my response to it, ibid. 87, no. 1 (1989):10.

45. See Novak, *Halakhah in a Theological Dimension*, 96ff.

46. See Michael Novak, *The Rise of the Unmeltable Ethnics* (New York, 1973), esp. xxxiiiff.

47. See George L. Mosse, *German Jews Beyond Judaism* (Bloomington, Ind., 1985), chap. 2.

48. See E. P. Sanders, *Paul and Palestinian Judaism* (Philadelphia, 1977), 550-551.

49. See Novak, *Law and Theology in Judaism*, 1:80-82.

50. See *supra*, 33ff. Also note: "What brought pauper and prince, foolish and wise, poor and rich, slave and master together? What was the magic spell that chased away all distinction? It was the Law. Nobody could live outside it or above it. . . . It

was the Law that spared Judaism the gruesome inhumanities of religious madness." S. Goldman, *The Jew and the Universe* (New York, 1936), 179.

51. See, e.g., Y. Hagigah 1.7/76c re Ps. 127:1.

52. Along these lines note: "What is required now is the critique of culture in the light of Jewish teaching . . . [to] offer the Jewish community periodic reports that would document the assertion of the tradition (its 'supernatural' dimension) regarding the immediate social and political concerns the Jewish community faces." Arthur A. Cohen, "Embarrassed by Principle," *Present Tense* 12 (1985):41.

Index

Abaye, 124
Abba Saul, 200
Abel, 41, 87, 135, 162
Abortion, 105, 234–35
Abrabanel, R. Isaac, 43, 126–27, 131, 183
Abraham, 31, 53, 101, 163
R. Abraham ben David of Posquières (Rabad), 101, 159
R. Abraham de Boten (*Lehem Mishneh*), 202
R. Abraham ibn Ezra, 123–24, 126, 130, 131, 184, 186
Absolutism, medical, 117
Achan ben Zerach, 178
Ada, 93
Adam, 87, 91, 94–95, 150, 231
Adler, Felix, 229–30, 240
Agape, 49, 52–53, 64
Aggadah, 27, 29, 85–87, 89–90, 92, 94, 118, 129, 130, 146, 161–62, 189, 233. *See also* Theology
Agunah, 85
R. Aha bar Hanina, 17
R. Aha bar Jacob, 28
Ahad Ha'Am, 182, 240
Ahasuerus, 28
AIDS, 4, 104–17
R. Akibah, 86, 165, 174–75, 182, 184
Albeck, Chanoch, 215, 222
Albo, R. Joseph, 25, 40, 99, 185
Alêtheia, 49. *See also* Truth
Alexander, Edward, 242
Altruism, 127
Amalek, 14, 191, 193, 203

Anan ben David, 158
Ancilla theologiae, 201
Andenaes, J., 186
Anscombe, G.E.M., 63
Anselm, 55
Anthropocentricity, 122, 157
Anthropology, 147
Anthropology, philosophical, 54
Anthropomorphism, 149
Antiochus Epiphanes, 151
Anti-semitism, 11, 226–27, 242
Aphrodite, 98
Aptowitzer, Viktor, 116
Arabs, 187
Arendt, Hannah, 42, 137
Aristotle, 20, 30, 40, 41, 44, 52, 54, 56, 62, 63, 64, 65, 67, 71–74, 81, 82, 99, 100, 135–38, 140–43, 153, 154, 155, 157, 173, 181, 182, 184, 220, 236
Arndt, W. F., 42
(Rabbenu) Asher (R'osh), 116, 156, 186, 204, 221
Ashkenazim, 133
Asmakhta, 119
Astrophysics, 71, 73. *See also* Physics; *Physis*
Atheism, 126
Athens, 43
Atlas, S., 102
Augustine, 49, 54–56, 63, 64, 66, 99, 156, 159
Authority, 3, 5, 22–24, 33, 35, 39, 46–48, 107, 111, 116, 117, 152, 204, 234
Authorization (*reshut*), 113, 116
Autonomy, 8, 15, 17, 37, 41, 45–48, 52–54, 55, 58, 60, 63, 137
R. Avdimi bar Hama bar Hasa, 28
R. Avin, 87
R. Azariah, 94

Baal Shem Tov, 238
Baeck, Leo, 229, 240
Baer, Y., 186

245